Springer Books on Professional Computing

Springer Books on Professional Computing

Computer Confidence: A Human Approach to Computers
Bruce D. Sanders. viii, 90 pages. 23 figures. 1984. ISBN 0-387-90917-6

The American Pascal Standard: With Annotations
Henry Ledgard. vii, 97 pages. 1984. ISBN 0-387-91248-7

Modula-2 for Pascal Programmers
Richard Gleaves. x, 145 pages. 18 figures. 1984 ISBN 0-387-96051-1

Ada in Practice
Christine N. Ausnit, Norman H. Cohen, John B. Goodenough,
R. Sterling Eanes.

The World of Programming Languages
Michael Marcotty, Henry Ledgard. xvi, 360 pages. 30 figures. 1986.
ISBN 0-387-96440-1

Taming the Tiger: Software Engineering and Software Economics
Leon S. Levy. viii, 248 pages. 9 figures. 1987. ISBN 0-387-96468-1

The Unix System Guidebook, Second Edition
Peter P. Silvester. xiv, 334 pages. 16 figures. 1988. ISBN 0-387-96489-4

C: A Software Engineering Approach
Peter A. Darnell, Philip E. Margolis. xx, 624 pages. 62 figures. 1991.
ISBN 0-387-97389-3

Peter A. Darnell   Philip E. Margolis

C: A Software Engineering Approach

With 62 Illustrations

Springer-Verlag
New York Berlin Heidelberg London Paris
Tokyo Hong Kong Barcelona Budapest

Peter A. Darnell
Visual Solutions
Westford, MA 01886
USA

Philip E. Margolis
New York, NY 10023
USA

Original cover art by Bernard Bonhomme, Incandescent Ink, Inc.

Material in this revised edition was previously published under the title *Software Engineering in C*,
©1988 Springer-Verlag New York, Inc.

Darnell, Peter A.
   C, a software engineering approach / by Peter A. Darnell, Philip E. Margolis.
   — 2nd ed.
      p.   cm. — (Springer books on professional computing)
   Rev. ed. of: Software engineering in C. c 1988.
   Includes index.
   1. Software engineering. 2. C (Computer program language)
   I. Margolis, Philip E.   II. Darnell, Peter A. Software Engineering
in C.   III. Title.   IV. Series.
   QA76.758.D37   1990
   005.26'2—dc20   90-31417

Printed on acid-free paper.

Photocomposed copy prepared from the authors' Interleaf file.
Printed and bound by R.R. Donnelley & Sons, Harrisonburg, VA.
Printed in the United States of America.

9 8 7 6 5 4

ISBN 0-387-97389-3 Springer-Verlag New York Berlin Heidelberg
ISBN 3-540-97389-3 Springer-Verlag Berlin Heidelberg New York

In memory of Roo Darnell, friend and brother, and one of the most promising young software engineers we have ever known.

Preface

This book describes the C programming language and software engineering principles of program construction. The book is intended primarily as a textbook for beginning and intermediate C programmers. It does not assume previous knowledge of C, nor of any high-level language, though it does assume that the reader has some familiarity with computers. While not essential, knowledge of another programming language will certainly help in mastering C.

Although the subject matter of this book is the C language, the emphasis is on software engineering—making programs readable, maintainable, portable, and efficient. One of our main goals is to impress upon readers that there is a huge difference between programs that merely work, and programs that are well engineered, just as there is a huge difference between a log thrown over a river and a well-engineered bridge.

The book is organized linearly so that each chapter builds on information provided in the previous chapters. Consequently, the book will be most effective if chapters are read sequentially. Readers with some experience in C, however, may find it more useful to consult the table of contents and index to find sections of particular interest.

Each chapter is autonomous inasmuch as it covers a single, well-defined area of the C language, such as scalar data types or control flow. Moreover, the chapters themselves are organized linearly, so that each section uses information provided in earlier sections. Again, experienced C programmers may want to skim introductory sections.

Although this book covers all C features, it makes no claim to being a reference manual. The organization and pace are designed for those learning the language rather than those who already know the language. If you plan to do extensive programming in C, we recommend that you supplement our book with *C: A Reference Manual*, by Harbison and Steele.

This book describes all features of the C language defined by Kernighan and Ritchie (known as the K&R standard), as well as all features defined in the C Standard proposed by the American National Standards Institute (ANSI). Where the two versions differ, we highlight the difference either by explicitly describing each version in the text or by describing the ANSI feature in a shaded box. A list of differences between the two standards appears in Appendix E. For more information about the ANSI Standard, you should read the official specification, which you can obtain by writing to:

> American National Standards Institute
> 1430 Broadway
> New York, NY 10018

In addition to using shaded boxes to describe ANSI extensions, we also use boxes to highlight common errors made by C programmers. These "Bug Alerts" are intended as buoys to mark places where we and others have run aground.

The examples in this book have all been tested on three machines: A PC-compatible Zenith Z-151 running the Microsoft Version 3.0 C compiler, an Apollo DN3000 running the DOMAIN C compiler (Version 4.78), and a Sun Microsystems 3/50 computer running Version 3.1 of the Sun compiler. Whenever possible, we have tried to use realistic examples gleaned from our own experiences. Occasionally we refer to "our machine," which means any of these three computers. The most significant aspect of "our machine" is that it allocates four bytes for **int**s.

Appendix A describes all of the runtime library functions defined in the ANSI standard. Many of these functions are derived from UNIX functions and are present in current C runtime libraries. Be careful, though, because some ANSI functions behave differently from identically-named functions in older libraries.

Appendix B shows the syntax of the ANSI C language in the form of "railroad diagrams." Each rectangular box in a diagram represents another diagram defined elsewhere. Items that appear in ovals are C keywords and predefined names that must appear exactly as they are written. Circles are used to represent punctuation tokens. Unless stated otherwise, it is always legal to insert spaces and newlines between one item and another.

Appendix C lists all names reserved by the ANSI standard. This includes keywords, library function names, and type definitions used by the library. You should avoid declaring variables that conflict with these names.

Appendix D lists certain ranges that an ANSI-conforming compiler must support. This includes, for example, the range of values that must be representable in a floating-point number.

Appendix E lists the major differences between the ANSI Standard and the K&R standard. Each entry in this list contains a reference to the section in the book where the difference is described. Note that this list is not exhaustive.

Appendix F contains the source listings for a C interpreter. In Chapter 12, we refer to this program as an example of using good engineering techniques to produce a large software product.

Acknowledgments

First and foremost, we wish to acknowledge our debt to the authors of the two most influential books about C: Samuel Harbison, Brian Kernighan, Dennis Ritchie, and Guy Steele.

In addition to the books by these authors, we also leaned heavily on the Draft Proposed ANSI Standard, and we thank all of the members of the ANSI X3J11 Subcommittee for their efforts in creating this document.

Many people reviewed various parts of this book at various stages. We are indebted to all of them, particularly David Boundy, David Boyce, Gary Bray, Clem Cole, Karen Darnell, Norman Garfinkle, John Humphrys, Ben Kingsbury, Diane Margolis, Doug McGlathery, Beth O'Connell, John Peyton, Bill Plauger, Barry Rosenberg, Jim Van Sciver, Kincade Webb, Bob Weir, and John Weiss. We are also indebted to the software development team at Dynatech Data Systems, especially Elizabeth Stark and Jonathan Edney. Special thanks go to Chuck Connell, Sam Harbison, and Tom Pennello, who read the manuscript in its entirety and offered numerous invaluable suggestions. We would also like to thank Kathy Ford for her assistance in preparing the artwork, and Andrea Morris for her expert editorial advice. Naturally, we accept responsibility for any flaws that remain.

Finally we would like to thank Apollo Computer Inc. and Stellar Computer Inc. for providing the working environments in which to produce this book. The entire book was formatted using the Interleaf Version 3.0 electronic publishing system running on an Apollo DN3000 workstation.

Suggested Reading

We have found the following books extremely helpful in mastering C and in absorbing general software engineering principles.

Aho, Alfred V., and Jeffrey P. Ullman. *Principles of Compiler Design*. Addison-Wesley, 1972.

Brooks, Frederick P., Jr. *The Mythical Man Month: Essays on Software Engineering*. Addison-Wesley, 1974.

Date, C. J. *An Introduction to Database Systems*. 4th ed. Addison-Wesley, 1986.

Foley, J. D., and A. Van Dam. *Fundamentals of Computer Graphics*. Addison-Wesley, 1980.

Harbison, Samuel P., and Guy L. Steele Jr. *C: A Reference Manual*. 2d ed. Prentice Hall, 1984.

Kernighan, Brian W., and P. J. Plauger. *Software Tools*. Addison-Wesley, 1976.

Kernighan, Brian W., and P. J. Plauger. *Elements of Programming Style*. McGraw-Hill, 1978.

Kernighan, Brian W., and Dennis M. Ritchie. *The C Programming Language*. Prentice-Hall, 1978.

Knuth, Donald E. *The Art of Computer Programming*. Addison-Wesley, 1973.

Shore, John. *The Sacher Torte Algorithm*. Penguin Books, 1986.

Contents

Chapter 7

Chapter 8

Chapter 9

List of Figures

List of Tables

List of Boxes

Chapter 1

Introduction to Programming

You cannot endow even the best machine with initiative. — Walter Lippmann, <u>A Preface to Politics</u>

Although computers are capable of performing complex and difficult operations, they are inherently simple-minded and docile machines. They must be told exactly what to do, and they must be instructed in a precise and limited language that they can comprehend. These instructions are known as *software*. The machinery that actually executes the instructions is known as *hardware*.

At the hardware level, computers understand only simple commands, such as "copy this number," "add these two numbers," and "compare these two numbers." These modest commands constitute the computer's *instruction set* and programs written using these instructions are said to be written in the computer's *machine language*.

One of the surprising aspects of computer science is the rich array of useful operations that can be performed by combining these simple instructions. Unfortunately, it is extremely tiresome to write programs in machine language because even the simplest tasks require many instructions. Moreover, in most machine languages, everything—instructions, data, variables—is represented by *binary numbers*. Binary numbers are composed entirely of zeroes and ones (each digit is called a *bit*, short for "binary digit"). These programs, consisting of a jumble of zeroes and ones, are difficult to write, read, and maintain.

In the 1940s and 1950s, all programs were written in machine language, or its close cousin, *assembly language*. Assembly language is a major improvement over machine language, although it is only once removed from the computer's instruction set. In assembly language, each instruction is identified by a short name rather than a number, and variables can be identified by names rather than numbers. Programs written in assembly language require a special program, called an *assembler*, to translate assembly language instructions into machine instructions. Today, programs are written in assembly language only when execution speed is a high priority.

The vast majority of programs written today are written in languages called *high-level languages* that were first developed in the 1950s and 1960s. High-level languages allow programmers to write programs in a language more natural to them than the computer's restrictive language.

One can view programming languages as lying along a spectrum with machine languages at one end and human languages, such as French and English, at the other end (see Figure 1-1). High-level programming languages fall somewhere in between these extremes, usually closer to the machine language. High-level languages allow programmers to deal with complex objects without worrying about details of the particular computer on which the program is running. Of course programming languages differ from human languages since they are designed solely to manipulate information. They are much more limited and precise than human languages.

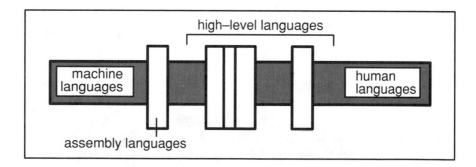

Figure 1–1. Language Spectrum. Computer languages lie along a spectrum with machine languages at one end and human languages at the other end.

1.1 High-Level Programming Languages

Every high-level language requires a *compiler* or *interpreter* to translate instructions in the high-level programming language into low-level instructions that the computer can execute. The remainder of this section applies only to compilers. We describe interpreters in Chapter 12.

A compiler is similar to an assembler, but much more complex. There is a one-to-one correspondence between assembly language instructions and machine instructions. In contrast, a single instruction in a high-level language can produce many machine instructions.

The farther a programming language is from a machine language, the more difficult it is for the compiler to perform its task. But languages that are far removed from the computer architecture offer two main advantages:

- High-level languages remove the programmer from the idiosyncracies of each computer architecture.

- Programs written in high-level languages are easier to read and maintain.

Once a programmer has learned a high-level language, he or she need not be preoccupied with how the compiler translates programs into a machine language. As a result, programs written for one computer can be executed on another computer merely by recompiling them. This feature is known as software *portability*. In Figure 1-2, for instance, a single program written in a high-level language is translated into three machine language programs by three separate compilers.

Another advantage of high-level languages is *readability*. Their relative closeness to human languages makes programs not only easier to write, but easier to read as well. The operation of a well-written program in a high-level language can be readily apparent to a reader because the symbols and instructions resemble human symbols and instructions rather than the computer's internal symbols and instructions. In contrast, even the best written assembly language programs must be closely analyzed to construe their operation. For example, consider the simple C statement

```
a = b+c-2;
```

which assigns the value "b plus c minus 2" to *a*, where *a*, *b*, and *c* are variables.

In assembly language, this could be written

```
LOAD  b,  %r0
LOAD  c,  %r1
ADD  %r0,  %r1
SUB  &2,  %r1
STORE  %r1,  a
```

Obviously, the C version is easier to read and understand.

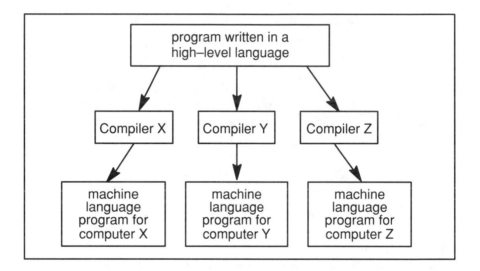

Figure 1–2. Different Compilers for Different Machines. The same program written in a high-level language can be compiled into different machine language programs to run on different computers.

Closely related to readability is *maintainability*. Because they are more readable, programs written in high-level languages are much easier to modify and debug.

Despite these advantages, there are prices to pay when using high-level languages. The most important price that must be paid is reduced *efficiency*. When a compiler translates programs into machine language, it may not translate them into the most efficient machine code. Just as it is possible to use different words to say the same thing, it is also possible to use different machine instructions to write functionally equivalent programs. Some combinations of instructions execute faster than others. By writing directly in the machine language, it is usually possible to select the fastest version. Writing in a high-level language, the programmer has little control over how a compiler translates code. The result, especially when an unsophisticated compiler is used, can be inefficient code.

Nevertheless, high-level languages are superior to machine and assembly languages in most instances. For one thing, sophisticated compilers can perform tricks to gain efficiency that most assembly language programmers would never dream of. The main reason for the superiority of high-level languages, however, is that most of the cost of software development lies in maintenance, where readability and portability are crucial.

The issues raised—portability, efficiency, and readability—are central concepts that we will revisit throughout this book. Many of the assumed advantages of high-level languages, such as portability and readability, are only realized through careful programming. Likewise, the disadvantages, such as reduced efficiency, can be mitigated once the language is well understood.

1.2 History of C

The C language was first developed in 1972 by Dennis M. Ritchie at AT&T Bell Labs as a *systems programming language*—that is, a language to write *operating systems* and system utilities. Operating systems are the programs that manage the computer's resources. Well-known examples of operating systems include MS/DOS and OS/2 for IBM PC-compatible computers, VMS for VAXes, and UNIX, which runs on a variety of computers.

Ritchie's intent in designing C was to give programmers a convenient means of accessing a machine's instruction set. This meant creating a language that was high-level enough to make programs readable and portable, but simple enough to map easily onto the underlying machine.

C was so flexible, and enabled compilers to produce such efficient machine code, that in 1973, Ritchie and Ken Thompson rewrote most of the UNIX operating system in C. Traditionally, operating systems were written in assembly language because execution speed was critical and because only assembly languages gave programmers the full control they needed to access special memory locations. The coding of UNIX in C demonstrated C's value as a systems programming language.

The main advantages of writing an operating system in a high-level language are speed of implementation and maintainability. A fortuitous side-effect, however, is that the operating system can be moved to other computers by recompiling it on the target machines. This process is called *porting*. UNIX was originally written for a DEC PDP-7 in a language called B (C's predecessor). Later, UNIX was ported to a PDP-11 and recoded in C. Before long, UNIX was ported to other types of computers. Every port required a new C compiler so the fortunes of C and UNIX were tightly bound. For C, this was both good and bad. On the one hand, the language spread more quickly than it might have on its own. On the other hand, C was, in many people's minds, strictly a UNIX systems language. It is only in recent years that C has come to be viewed as a more general-purpose programming language.

Throughout most of its history, the only formal specification for the C language was a document written by Ritchie entitled *The C Reference Manual*. In 1977, Ritchie and Brian Kernighan expanded this document into a full-length book called *The C Programming Language* (often referred to as the *K&R standard*). Though a useful reference guide for programmers, it was unsatisfactory for compiler builders because too many details were omitted. Despite its shortcomings, it remained for years the only C text and acquired the status of a *de facto* standard.

In the early days of C, the language was used primarily on UNIX systems. Even though there were different versions of UNIX available, the versions of the C compiler maintained a large degree of uniformity. The version of C running under UNIX is known as PCC (Portable C Compiler). Like the K&R standard, PCC also became a *de facto* standard.

With the emergence of personal computers (PCs) and the growing popularity of C, however, the K&R and PCC standards were no longer satisfactory. Suddenly, C compilers were being written to run on new machines and under different operating systems. It became difficult or impossible to adhere to the original standards. Another problem was that C was such a small language that compiler developers felt a strong temptation to add their own favorite constructs. Before long, there were many variants of C, each differing in little ways.

One of C's original strengths had been its portability, but over the years it lost this advantage. Programs written for one compiler could not be guaranteed to compile correctly on another computer. Eventually, the American National Standards Institute (ANSI) formed a subcommittee to define an official version of the C language.

1.3 ANSI Standard

The American National Standards Institute is the foremost standards organization in the United States. ANSI is divided into a number of committees that have responsibility for approving standards that cover a particular technical area. The X3 Committee, chartered in 1961, is responsible for Computer and Information Processing Standards.

In February of 1983, James Brodie of Motorola Corporation applied to the X3 Committee to draft a C standard. ANSI approved the application, and in March the X3J11 Technical Committee of ANSI was formed. X3J11 is composed of representatives from all the major C compiler developers, as well as representatives from several companies that program their applications in C. In the summer of 1983, the committee met for the first time, and they have been meeting four times a year since then. The final version of the C Standard was ratified as an ANSI standard in 1989.

The ANSI Standard for the C language is specified in a document entitled *American National Standard for Information Systems — Programming Language C*. In addition to this specification, there is a Rationale Document, which clearly explains the goals of the X3J11 Committee:

> The Committee's overall goal was to develop a clear, consistent, and unambiguous Standard for the C programming language which codifies the common, existing definition of C and which promotes the portability of user programs across C language environments...
>
> The work of the Committee was in large part a balancing act. The Committee has tried to improve portability while retaining the definition of certain features of C as machine-dependent. It attempted to incorporate valuable new ideas without disrupting the basic structure and fabric of the language. It tried to develop a clear and consistent language without invalidating existing programs. All of the goals were important and each decision was weighed in the light of sometimes contradictory requirements in an attempt to reach a workable compromise.

Although the official standard was ratified only recently, it has been stable in draft form for several years. ANSI-conforming compilers, therefore, are already becoming commonplace.

To obtain copies of the ANSI Standard and Rationale Document, send your request to:

> American National Standards Institute
> 1430 Broadway
> New York, NY 10018

1.4 Nature of C

The C programming language has acquired the reputation (not entirely undeserved) for being a mysterious and messy language that promotes bad programming habits. Part of the problem is that C gives special meanings to many punctuation characters, such as asterisks, plus signs, braces, and angle brackets. Once a programmer has learned the C language, these symbols look quite commonplace, but there is no denying that a typical C program can be intimidating to the uninitiated.

The other, more serious, complaint concerns the relative dearth of rules. Other programming languages, such as Pascal, have very strict rules to protect programmers from making accidental blunders. It is assumed in Pascal, for instance, that if a programmer attempts to assign a *floating-point* number (same as a real number) to a variable that is supposed to hold an integer, it is a mistake, and the compiler issues an error message. In C, the compiler quietly converts the floating-point value to an integer.

The C language was designed for experienced programmers. The compiler, therefore, assumes little about what the programmer does or does not intend to do. This can be summed up in the C tenet:

> *Trust the programmer.*

As a result, C programmers have tremendous liberty to write unusual code. In many instances, this freedom allows programmers to write useful programs that would be difficult to write in other languages. However, the freedom can be, and is, abused by inexperienced programmers who delight in writing needlessly tricky code. C is a powerful language, but it requires self-restraint and discipline.

One of our main points made repeatedly throughout this book is that there is a huge difference between *good* programs and *working* programs. *A good program not only works, but is easy to read and maintain.* Despite what some people claim, it is very possible to write *good* programs in C. Unfortunately, many C programmers are content to write programs that merely work.

Chapter 2

C Essentials

> *"A little learning is a dangerous thing."* —
> Alexander Pope, <u>An Essay on Criticism</u>

One of the hardest parts about learning a programming language is that everything is interrelated. It often seems impossible to understand anything before you know everything. In this chapter, we describe the C essentials — what you need to know to write your first programs. To avoid getting bogged down in details, we gloss over some of the intricacies of the C language in this chapter. In later chapters, we provide a more thorough discussion of the topics introduced in this chapter.

2.1 Program Development

Program development consists of a number of steps, as shown in Figure 2-1. Some of the latter steps vary from one computing environment to another. In this chapter, we describe these latter development stages in general terms. (Box 2-1 describes how to develop a program in a UNIX environment.) You should read the system documentation for your computer to find out how to compile and link programs in your particular environment.

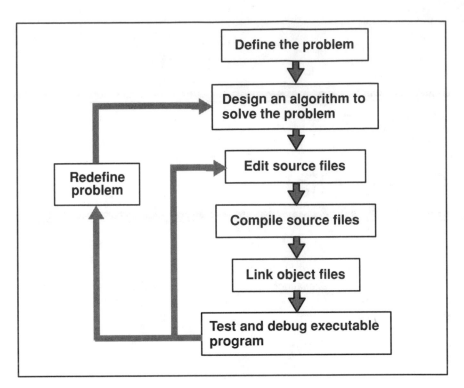

Figure 2-1. Stages of Program Development.

The first step in developing a program is to clearly define the problem and design an *algorithm* to solve it. An algorithm is a well-defined set of rules to solve a particular problem in a finite number of steps. The art of programming consists of designing or choosing algorithms and expressing them in a programming language. This stage of the development process is extremely important, though it is often given short shrift by beginners and experts alike. We'll have more to say about the design stage in later sections of the book. For now, we are concerned with the later stages of software development that occur after you have defined the problem and designed an algorithm.

As shown in Figure 2-2, there are three general steps:

1.   Edit each source file.

2.   Compile each source file to produce an object file.

3.   Link the object files together to produce an executable program.

Note that the source and object code can be spread out in multiple files, but the executable code for a program generally resides in a single file. Box 2-1 briefly describes how these steps appear in a UNIX environment.

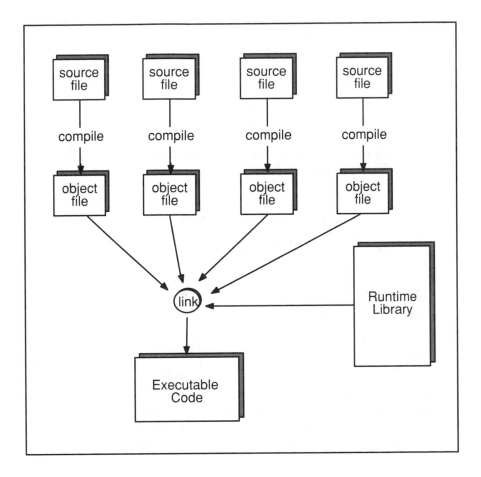

Figure 2-2. Compiling and Linking. Source files must be compiled to produce object files. The separate object files are then linked together to form the executable file.

2.1.1 Compiling Source Files

By the end of the design stage, you should have defined a set of routines, called *functions*, each of which solves a small piece of the larger programming problem. The next step is to actually write the code for each function. This is usually done by creating and editing C language text files. These files are called *source files*.

Box 2-1: Compiling and Linking in a UNIX Environment

In UNIX environments, you edit the source files with a text editor, such as *ed* or *vi*. To compile the program, you invoke the compiler with the *cc* command, followed by the name of the source file. For example,

```
$ cc test.c
```

The dollar sign is a *command prompt* that signifies that the operating system is waiting for user input. Different operating systems use different characters for the command prompt. Throughout this book, we shade characters emitted by the computer to differentiate them from characters that you enter from the keyboard.

UNIX requires the names of C source files to end with a **.c** extension. If your source file contains errors, the compiler prints out the error messages, but does not create an object file. If the program is error-free, the compiler produces an object file with the same name as the source file except that it has a **.o** extension instead of a **.c** extension. Under UNIX, the **cc** command also invokes the linker and produces an executable file called *a.out* by default. You can override this default filename by using the **–o** option. For example,

```
$ cc -o test test.c
```

forces the executable file to be named *test*. If the *cc* command contains only one source filename, then the object file is deleted. However, you can specify multiple source files in the same compilation command. The UNIX *cc* program compiles each one of them separately, creating an object file for each, and then it links all the object files together to create an executable file. For instance, the command

```
$ cc -o test module1.c module2.c module3.c
```

produces four files—three object files called *module1.o*, *module2.o*, and *module3.o*, and an executable file called *test*. To run the program, you enter the executable filename at the command prompt:

```
$ test
```

The loading stage is handled automatically when you execute a program.

The task of the compiler is to translate source code into machine code. How the compiler does this is beyond the scope of this book. Suffice it to say that the compiler is itself a program (or group of programs) that must be executed. The compiler's input is source code and its output is *object code*. Object code represents an intermediary step between the source code and the final *executable code*. The final steps are handled by two additional utilities called the *linker* (or *binder*) and the *loader*.

2.1.2 Linking Object Files

After creating object files by invoking the compiler, you would combine them into a single file by invoking the linker. In addition to combining object files, the linker also links in functions from the runtime library if necessary. The result of the linking stage is an *executable program*.

Although linking is handled automatically by some operating systems (e.g., UNIX), the linker is actually a separate program. In some environments it must be invoked separately.

2.1.3 Loading Executable Files

There is one additional step that is often ignored because it is usually handled automatically by the operating system. This is the loading stage, in which the executable program is loaded into the computer's memory. Most operating systems automatically load a program when you type the name of its executable file. A few operating systems, however, require you to explicitly run a loader program to get your program into memory.

2.1.4 The Runtime Library

One of the reasons C is such a small language is that it defers many operations to a large runtime library. The runtime library is a collection of object files. Each file contains the machine instructions for a function that performs one of a wide variety of services. The functions are divided into groups, such as I/O (Input and Output), memory management, mathematical operations, and string manipulation. For each group there is a source file, called a *header file*, that contains information you need to use these functions. By convention, the names for header files end with a *.h* extension. For example, the standard group of I/O functions has an associated header file called *stdio.h*.

To include a header file in a program, you must insert the following statement in your source file:

```
#include <filename>
```

For example, one of the I/O runtime routines, called *printf()*, enables you to display data on your terminal. Before you use this function, you should enter the following line in your source file:

```
#include <stdio.h>
```

Usually, this would be one of the first lines in your source file. We describe the **#include** directive and other preprocessor commands in more detail later in this chapter.

2.2 Functions

The most important concept underlying high-level languages is the notion of *functions*. In other languages, they may be called *subroutines* or *procedures*, but the idea is the same. *A C function is a collection of C language operations.* A function usually performs an operation that is more complex than any of the operations built into the C language. At the same time, a function should not be so complex that it is difficult to understand.

Typically, programs are developed with layers of functions. The lower-level functions perform the simplest operations, and higher-level functions are created by combining lower-level functions. The following, for instance, is a low-level function that calculates the square of a number. This is a simple function, yet it performs an operation that is not built into the C language.

```
int square( num )
int num;
{
   int answer;

   answer = num * num;
   return answer;
}
```

As shown in Figure 2-3, software engineering rests on the concept of hierarchies, building complex structures from simple components.

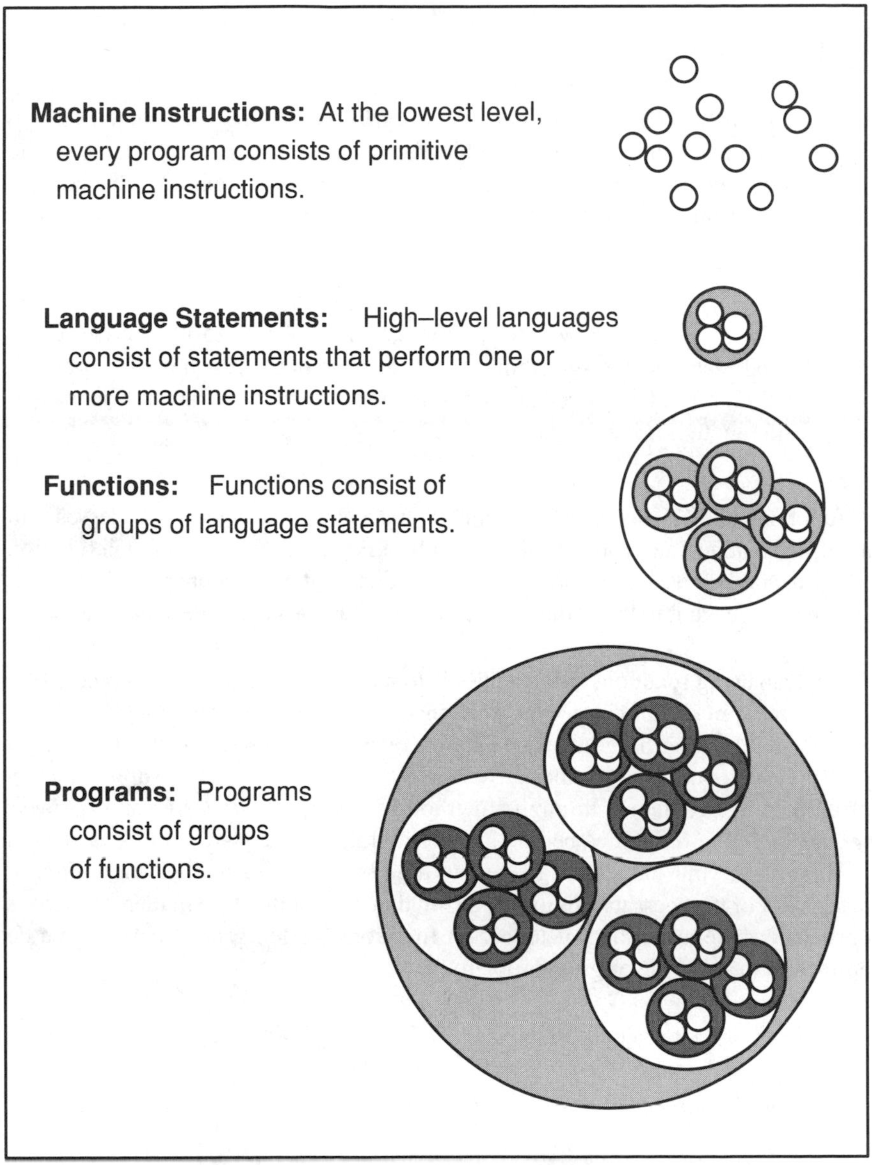

Machine Instructions: At the lowest level, every program consists of primitive machine instructions.

Language Statements: High–level languages consist of statements that perform one or more machine instructions.

Functions: Functions consist of groups of language statements.

Programs: Programs consist of groups of functions.

Figure 2-3. Software Hierarchy. Software engineering is based on a hierarchy of programming components.

You can think of function names as abbreviations for long, possibly complicated sets of commands. You need only define a function once, but you can *invoke* (or *call*) it any number of times. This means that any set of operations that occurs more than once is a candidate for becoming a function. Functions are more than just a shorthand, however. They enable you to *abstract* information. This means that a complex operation can be constructed out of simpler operations. This yields two benefits:

1. *Ease of change and enhanced reliability.* If you need to change program behavior, either to fix a problem or to adapt to new requirements, the change need only be made in one place because there is only one copy of each function. Remember, *needless redundancy is the hobgoblin of software engineers!*

2. *Better readability.* With the low-level details of an algorithm hidden away in functions, the algorithm is easier to read. In fact, even if a set of operations is used only once in a program, it is sometimes worthwhile to make it a function if it aids readability.

A function is like a specialized machine that accepts data as input, processes it in a defined manner, and hands back the results. For example, the *square()* function takes a number as input and returns the square of the number as the result. Whenever we want to know the square of a number, we "call" the square function.

The key to using functions successfully is to make them perform small pieces of a larger problem. Ideally, however, each piece should be general enough so that it can be used in other programs as well. For example, suppose you want to write a program that counts the number of words in a file. The best way to approach this programming problem is through a method called *top-down design* and *stepwise refinement.* The basic idea behind this methodology is to start with a description of the task in your natural language and then break it into smaller, more precise tasks. Then, if necessary, divide those smaller tasks into still smaller operations until you arrive at a group of low-level functions (called *primitives*) that can be employed to solve the original problem.

As an example, let's start with the task

   Count the number of words in a file

As the first step in the refinement process, we can divide this step into the following steps:

   open the file;
   while there are more words in the file
       read a word;
       increment the word count;
   print the word count;
   close the file.

Finally, we can refine the steps even further by expanding *read a word*:

open the file;
while there are more words in the file
  read characters until you get a non-space character;
  read characters until you get a space character;
  increment the word count;
print the word count;
close the file.

Before you actually write the code for a program, you should write down the steps as we have. This outline of the program is called *pseudocode* because the steps are written in a shorthand language that is somewhere between your natural language and the programming language. Once you've written the pseudocode, it is usually fairly easy to translate it into a high-level language.

Many of the steps shown in the pseudocode can be broken down even further. However, these steps are sufficiently low-level because there are runtime functions to perform them. For example, there is an *fopen( )* function that opens a file, an *fgetc( )* function that reads a character from a file, a *printf( )* function that prints text, and an *fclose( )* function that closes a file. Of course, you won't always be so lucky as to have all the routines available. Sometimes you'll need to write your own. However, the runtime library does contain a powerful set of primitives, so you should always check it before writing your own function. Appendix A describes the functions in the runtime library.

One point worth stressing is that functions should be small, yet general. The *fopen()* function, for example, is written so that you can pass it any filename and it will open the corresponding file. In fact, *fopen()* is even more general, allowing you to specify whether the file contains text or numeric data, and whether it is to be opened for read or write access. This is a good illustration of the principle that the best functions perform small autonomous tasks, but are written so that the tasks can be easily modified by changing the input.

As you develop a program, dividing it into functions, you are likely to learn more about the particular problem you're trying to solve. Don't be discouraged, therefore, if you find it hard to go from the original problem statement to the C language source code. Like everything, it gets easier with practice.

2.3 Anatomy of a C Function

Since functions are the building blocks of all C programs, they are a good place to start describing the C language. The general layout is shown in Figure 2-4, although some of the elements are optional. The required parts are the function name, the parentheses following the function name, and the left and right braces, which denote the beginning and the end of the *function body*. The other elements are optional.

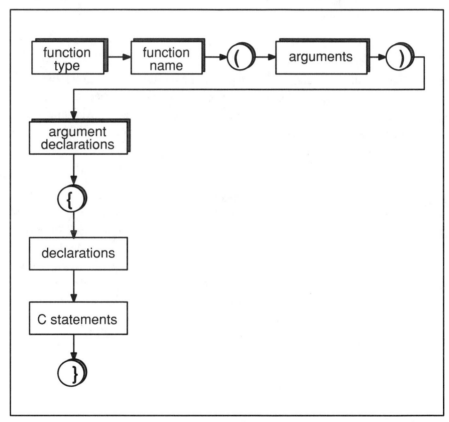

Figure 2-4. Elements of a Function. The shaded components are optional.

The function shown in Figure 2-5 is the *square()* function that we introduced earlier. The figure identifies all of the function's components.

We'll describe each line in turn. The first line has three parts. The first word, **int**, is a *reserved keyword* that stands for "integer." It signifies that the function is going to return an integer value. There are about thirty keywords in C, each of which has a language-defined meaning. Keywords are always written in lower-case letters and are reserved by the C language, which means that you may not use them as names for variables. (The complete list of keywords appears in Table 2-2.)

The second word, *square*, is the name of the function itself. This is what you use to call the function. We could have named the function anything, but it is best to use names that remind you of what the function actually does. The parentheses following the name of the function indicate that *square* is, in fact, a function and not some other type of variable. *num* is the name of the *argument*.

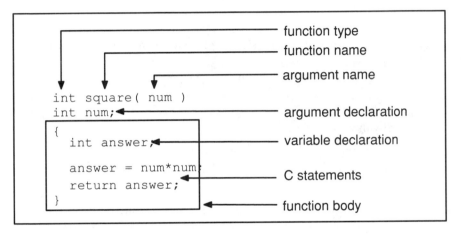

Figure 2-5. Anatomy of the square() *Function.*

Arguments represent data that are passed from the calling function to the function being called. On the calling side, they are known as *actual arguments*; on the called side, they are referred to as *formal arguments*. As with naming functions, we could give the argument any name we want, but *num* seems sufficiently descriptive.

Functions can take any number of arguments. For example, a function that computes *x* to the *y* power would take two arguments, separated by a comma (the spaces between the parentheses and the arguments are optional):

```
int power ( x, y )
```

The second line of the *square()* function is an argument declaration. Again, we use the keyword **int**, which signifies that the input is going to be an integer. The semicolon ending the line is a punctuation mark indicating the end of a statement or declaration.

The function body contains all of the executable statements. This is where calculations are actually performed. The function body must begin with a left brace and end with a right brace.

The line following the left brace is a declaration of the integer variable called *answer*. Program variables are names for data objects whose values can be used or changed. The declaration of *answer* follows the same format as the declaration of *num*, but it lies within the function body. This indicates that it is not an argument to the function. Rather, it is a variable that the function is going to use to hold a value temporarily. Once the function finishes, *answer* becomes inaccessible. All variables declared within a function body must be declared immediately after a left brace.

The next line is the first *executable statement*—that is, the first statement that actually performs a computation. It is called an *assignment statement* because it assigns the value on the right-hand side of the equal sign to the variable on the left-hand side. You would read it as: "Assign the value of *num* times *num* to *answer*." The symbol * is an *operator* that represents multiplication and "=" is an operator that represents *assignment*. Assignment is the process of storing the value of the expression on the right-hand side of the equal sign in the data object represented by the left-hand side of the equal sign.

The next statement is a **return** statement, which causes the function to return to its caller. The **return** statement may optionally return a value from the function, in this case *answer*.

Before proceeding, we need to take a closer look at some of these function components—particularly variables, variable names, constants, expressions, and assignment statements.

2.3.1 Variables and Constants

The statement

```
j = 5+10;
```

seems straightforward enough. It means "add the values 5 and 10 and assign the result to a variable called *j*." But there are actually a number of underlying assumptions that give this statement meaning. It seems intelligible to us only because we are accustomed to dealing with the symbols involved. We know that "5" and "10" are integer values, "+" and "=" are operators, ";" delimits the end of the statement, and *j* is a variable whose value can be changed. To the computer, however, all of these symbols are merely different combinations of on/off bits. To make sense out of the expression, a computer must be told at some point what each of these symbols means. This is one of the functions of the compiler.

The compiler knows that when it sees a combination of digits 0 through 9, it is looking at an integer value. If there is a period within the string of digits (i.e., 3.141), then it is looking at a floating-point number. These are just two out of a multitude of rules that the compiler uses to make sense out of a program. This stage of the compiler, where such rules are used to identify operators, delimiters, numbers, and names, is called *lexical analysis*. Later, a *parse* stage will examine these computer parts of speech to see if they have been combined legally.

Two important programming tokens are *constants* and *variables*. As their names imply, a constant is a value that never changes, whereas a variable can represent different values. Consider again the statement

```
j = 5+10;
```

The symbols "5" and "10" are constants because they have the same value no matter where they appear in a program. The symbol *j*, on the other hand, is the name of a variable that is able to represent different values. After this statement, *j* will have the value 15, but we could make another assignment later in the program that would give it a different value. A variable achieves its "variable-ness" by representing a location, or *address*, in computer memory.

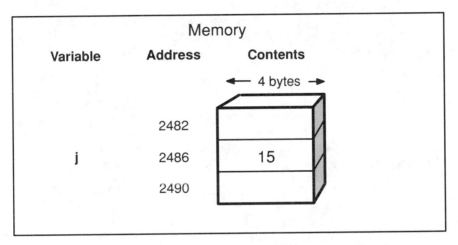

Figure 2-6. *Memory after* `j = 5 + 10`. *(We assume that j requires four bytes of storage, as shown by the addresses.)*

The variable *j* is located at some address, say 2486. So the assignment statement really means: "add the constants 5 and 10, and then store the result at memory address 2486" (see Figure 2-6).

The statement

```
j = j - 2;
```

says "fetch the contents of address 2486, subtract the constant 2 from it, and store the result at 2486." In this case the value of *j* is first read and then a new value is written. Box 2-2 describes a useful analogy for thinking about computer memory.

Box 2-2: The Mailbox Analogy

A good way to think about memory is as a series of mailboxes, where each box has a unique address. A thousand boxes would have addresses from 0 through 999 (in C, as in most computers, addressing begins at zero instead of one). Inside each box is a slip of paper with a number on it. To store the value 5 in box 200, you would open the box, erase whatever number is on the slip of paper, and write a 5 on it. To see what is in box 350, you would open the box and read the value on the slip of paper, and then return the slip unchanged. The only restrictions on the mailboxes are that each one can hold only one slip of paper, or value, at a time.

It is a small conceptual jump from the mailbox example to computer memory. The processes are identical with one small addition in the computer model. In a computer, it sometimes takes more than one mailbox to store a value. A large integer, for example, might require four bytes, or mailboxes. In this case, the compiler would store the value by opening four consecutive mailboxes and writing a portion of the number in each. To read the value, it would again need to open all four mailboxes.

A computer language lets you give a mailbox a name so that you need not remember its numeric address. Whenever you declare a variable, the compiler finds an unused mailbox and binds the address of the unused box to the variable name. Then when you use the variable name in an expression, the compiler knows what box to open.

2.3.2 Names

In the C language, you can name just about anything: variables, constants, functions, and even locations in a program. The rules for composing names are the same regardless of what you are naming. Names may contain letters, numbers, and the underscore character _, but must start with a letter or underscore. Names beginning with an underscore, however, are generally reserved for internal system variables.

The C language is *case sensitive,* which means that it differentiates between lowercase and uppercase letters. So the names

```
VaR
var
VAR
```

are all different. The advantage of case sensitivity is that you have more names to choose from, but it also means that you should follow strict naming conventions to ensure readability and maintainability.

A name cannot be the same as one of the *reserved keywords* (see Table 2-2). Also, you should avoid using names that are used by the runtime library unless you really want to create your own version of a runtime function. See Appendix C for a complete list of reserved names. Table 2-1 shows some legal and illegal names.

Legal Names

```
j
j5
__system_name
sesquipedalial_name
UpPeR_aNd_LoWeR_cAsE_nAmE
```

Illegal Names

`5j`	Names may not begin with a digit.
`$name`	Names may not contain a dollar sign.
`int`	**int** is a reserved keyword.
`bad%#*@name`	Names may not contain any special character except an underscore.

Table 2-1. Legal and Illegal Variable Names.

There is no C-defined limit to the length of a name, although each compiler sets its own limit. The ANSI Standard requires compilers to support names of at least 31 characters. Some older compilers impose an 8-character limit.

auto	double	int	struct
break	else	long	switch
case	enum	register	typedef
char	extern	return	union
const	float	short	unsigned
continue	for	signed	void
default	goto	sizeof	volatile
do	if	static	while

Table 2-2.   *Reserved C Keywords. You may not use these as variable names.*

There is some strategy involved in choosing names that make your program easier to understand. When, for instance, do you use uppercase, when do you use lowercase, and when do you use the underscore characters? Also, when is a single-letter name like *i* or *m* suitable and when should a name be longer and more meaningful? These are questions that we'll address as we proceed. As a general rule, you should use lowercase letters for variable names and uppercase for macro names. Another important and obvious rule—but one that is often overlooked—is to choose names that reflect their use. For instance, a variable that is used to store the fractional part of a floating-point value could be called *fractional_ part*.

2.3.3 Expressions

An expression is any combination of operators, numbers, and names that denotes the computation of a value. For example, all of the following are expressions:

```
5                    A constant
j                    A variable
5 + j                A constant plus a variable
5 * j + 6            A constant times a variable plus a
                     constant
f()                  A function call
f()/4                A function call, whose result is
                     divided by a constant
```

The building blocks of expressions include variables, constants, and function calls. There are additional building blocks, but these are enough to get started. The building blocks by themselves are expressions, but they can also be combined by *operators* to form more complex expressions. There are literally dozens of operators, but the following are some of the most basic ones:

+	Addition
–	Subtraction
*	Multiplication
/	Division

Chapter 5 describes operators and expressions in detail.

2.3.4 Assignment Statements

The *square()* function contains one example of an assignment statement:

```
answer = num * num;
```

The general format of an assignment statement is shown in Figure 2-7. The expression on the right-hand side of the assignment operator is sometimes called an *rvalue*. The left-hand side of an assignment statement, called an *lvalue*, must evaluate to a memory address that can hold a value. Originally, the term "lvalue" was coined to define the expression on the left-hand side of an assignment expression. However, this definition has been loosened over the years to mean any expression that represents a memory address—some lvalues refer to constants whose values cannot be changed. Still, the distinction between lvalues and rvalues is a useful one. For example, it wouldn't make any sense to turn the previous assignment statement around,

```
num * num = answer;
```

because the expression *num * num* is not an lvalue—it does not represent a memory location.

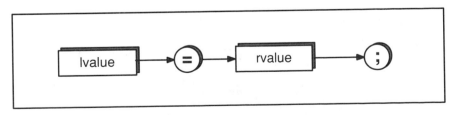

Figure 2-7. Syntax of an Assignment Statement.

2.4 Formatting Source Files

One aspect of C programming that can be confusing to beginners or ex-FOR-TRAN programmers is that *newline* characters in the source code are treated exactly like spaces (except when they appear in a character constant or string literal). A newline is a special character that causes subsequent characters to appear on the beginning of the next line. Whenever you press the RETURN key on your keyboard, a newline is generated. Because C ignores newlines, we could have written the *square()* function as

```
int square( num ) int num; { int answer;
answer = num*num; return answer; }
```

While this is equally readable to the computer, it is less readable to humans, and is therefore considered poor programming style. The compiler doesn't care how many spaces or newlines you insert between program components. For example, the following is also legal:

```
int
square( num )
int             num
{         int
 answer   ;
answer      =     num


*     num;
return answer; }
```

Again, this is an example of poor programming style. Note, in addition that, unlike FORTRAN, you *cannot* insert spaces within names or keywords.

Like other programming languages, the C language requires a conscious effort on the programmer's part to use consistent and readable conventions. Our own style, exhibited in the examples throughout the book, represents our personal preference, but is by no means the only good way to write programs. The main points to keep in mind are readability and consistency.

2.4.1 Comments

A comment is text that you include in a source file to explain what the code is doing. Comments are for human readers—the compiler ignores them. Commenting programs is an important, though often neglected, aspect of software engineering. The C language allows you to enter comments by inserting text between the symbols /* and */. In the following example, the asterisks that begin each line are included to aid readability—only the first and last ones are required.

```
/* square ()
 * Author: P. Margolis
 * Initial coding: 3/87
 * Purpose:
 * This function returns the square of its
 * argument.
 */

int square ( num )
int num;
{
   int answer;

   answer = num *num;/*Does not check for overflow*/
   return answer;
}
```

The compiler ignores whatever characters appear within the comment delimiters. Note that a comment can span multiple lines. Formatting comments so they are readable but do not interrupt the flow of the program is difficult in all languages, including C. One method is to devote entire lines to comments. Another is to put comments to the right of the code. You should use this second method only if the comment can fit on a single line. We use both formats in examples throughout the book. Nested comments are not allowed in C, as described in Box 2-3.

A more important issue is *what* to comment. In general, you should comment anything that is not obvious. This includes complex expressions, data structures, and the purpose of functions. In fact, all functions should contain a *header comment* that describes what the function does. It is also useful to comment changes to programs so that you can keep track of modifications. This is particularly important if you are working on a small piece of a larger project. However, comments without information content can make a program difficult to read. Do not comment the obvious. The following, for example, is poor commenting style:

```
j = j + 1;   /* increment i */
```

Also, lengthy comments cannot compensate for unreadable code. Commenting is largely a stylistic issue for which it is difficult to impose hard-and-fast rules. The best way to learn is by studying the examples in this book and other code written by experienced programmers.

Box 2-3: Bug Alert — No Nested Comments

You cannot place comments within comments to form nested comments.
For example,

```
/* This is an outer comment
 * /* This is an attempted inner comment */
 *
 *  This will be interpreted as code.
 */
```

C identifies the beginning of a comment by the character sequence /*. It then
strips all characters up to, and including, the end comment sequence */.
What's left gets passed to the compiler to be further processed. In the example above, therefore, the compiler will delete everything up to the first */
sequence, but pass the rest to the compiler. So the compiler will attempt to
process

```
 *
 *  This will be interpreted as code.
 */
```

Not recognizing these lines as valid C statements, the compiler will issue an
error message.

2.5 The *main()* Function

Having written and compiled the function *square( )*, we still can't quite execute it.
Every executable program must contain a special function called *main( )*, which is
where program execution begins. The *main( )* function can call other functions.
For example, to invoke *square( )*, you could write

```
main()
{
   extern int square();
   int solution;

   solution = square( 5 );
   exit( 0 );
}
```

This assigns the square of 5 to the variable named *solution*. The rules governing a
main( ) function are the same as the rules for other functions. Note, however, that
we don't identify the function's data type and we don't declare any arguments.
This is a convention that we adopt for now. *main( )* actually does return a value
and it takes two arguments. We defer a discussion of these aspects until Chapter
9.

The *exit()* function is a runtime library routine that causes a program to end, returning control to the operating system. If the argument to *exit()* is zero, it means that the program is ending normally without errors. Nonzero arguments indicate abnormal termination of the program. Calling *exit()* from a *main()* function is exactly the same as executing a **return** statement. That is,

```
exit ( 0 );
```

is the same as

```
return 0;
```

You should include either *exit()* or **return** in every *main()* function. (For ANSI-conforming compilers, you need to include the *stdlib.h* header file wherever you call the *exit()* function.)

We declare two names in *main()*. The first is the function *square()*, which we are going to call. The special keyword **extern** indicates that *square()* is defined elsewhere, possibly in another source file. The other variable, *solution*, is an integer that we use to store the value returned by *square()*.

The next statement is the one that actually invokes the *square()* function. Note that it is an assignment statement, with the right-hand side of the statement being the function invocation. The argument 5 is placed in parentheses to indicate that it is the value being passed as an actual argument to *square()*. You will recall that *square()*'s name for this passed argument is *num*. The *square()* function then computes the square of *num* and returns it. The return value gets assigned to *solution* in the *main()* function.

We now have a working program, but it is not particularly useful for a couple of reasons. One problem with this program is that there is no way to see the answer. In this simple case, it's obvious that the variable *solution* gets the value 25, but suppose we pass *square()* a larger value whose square we don't already know. We need to add a statement that prints out the value of *solution* so we can see it. There are a number of runtime routines that can display data on your terminal, but the most versatile is *printf()*. Adding *printf()* to our program gives us the program shown on the next page.

```
#include <stdio.h>    /* Header file of printf() */

main()
{
    extern int square();
    int solution;

    solution = square( 27 );
    printf( "The square of 27 is %d\n", solution );
    exit( 0 );
}
```

Note that we need to include the header file *stdio.h* because *printf()* is an I/O function. We describe the *printf()* function in more detail later in this chapter. For now, all you need to know is that **%d** is a special code that indicates to the *printf()* function that the argument to be printed is a **d**ecimal integer. The actual output will be the value stored in *solution*. The **\n** sequence is a special sequence that forces *printf()* to output a *newline character,* causing the cursor to move to the beginning of the next line.

Assuming *main()* is stored in a source file called *getsquare.c,* and *square()* is located in a file called *square.c,* you could compile and link this program with the following command (in a UNIX environment):

```
$ cc -o getsquare getsquare.c square.c
```

To run the program, type *getsquare* at the prompt:

```
$ getsquare
The square of 27 is 729
$
```

The *getsquare* program still isn't very useful, however, since it can only print the square of one number. To find out the squares of other numbers, we would have to edit the source file, change the argument to *square(),* and then recompile, relink, and reexecute the program. It would be better if we could dynamically specify which number we want to square while *getsquare* is running. To do this, we need to use another runtime routine called *scanf(). scanf()* is the mirror function to *printf().* Whereas *printf()* outputs the value of a variable, *scanf()* reads data entered from the keyboard and assigns them to variables.

Adding *scanf()* to our program, we get

```
#include <stdio.h>

main()
{
   extern int square();
   int solution;
   int input_val;

   printf( "Enter an integer value: " );
   scanf( "%d", &input_val );
   solution = square( input_val );
   printf( "The square of %d is %d\n", input_val,
           solution );
   exit( 0 );
}
```

Note that we declare another variable, *input_val*, to store the value entered from the keyboard. We then pass this value as the argument to *square()*. The expression,

```
   &input_val
```

means "the memory address of *input_val*." We pass the address of *input_val* so that *scanf()* can store a value at that address. The **&** symbol is an important C operator that we discuss in more detail in Chapter 3. A typical execution of *getsquare* would be:

```
 $  getsquare
 Enter an integer value: 8
 The square of 8 is 64
 $
```

We can execute this program any number of times, giving it different input with each execution.

2.6 The *printf()* Function

The *printf()* function can take any number of arguments. The first argument, however, is special. It is called the *format string* and it specifies how many data arguments are to follow and how they are to be formatted. The format string is enclosed in double quotes, and may contain text and *format specifiers*. A format specifier is a special character sequence that begins with a percent sign (%) and indicates how to write a single data item.

For example, in the statement

```
printf( "The value of num is %d", num );
```

there are two arguments. The first is the format string

```
"The value of num is %d"
```

The second is the data item, in this case a variable called *num*. The format string can be broken down further into two parts: a text string

```
The value of num is
```

and a format specifier

```
%d
```

The **%d** specifier indicates that the first data item, *num*, is a decimal integer. There are other specifiers for other types of data. Following is a partial list:

%c	Character data item
%f	Floating-point data item
%s	Null-terminated character array (string)
%o	Octal integer
%x	Hexadecimal integer

We describe these specifiers and others in later chapters. In addition to specifying the type of data to be printed, you can also specify such attributes as left justification, right justification, padding characters, and whether a plus sign should be printed for positive numbers. These details are described in Appendix A.

For now, the only additional thing you need to know about *printf( )* is that the format string can contain any number of format specifiers, but there must be a data argument for each one. For example,

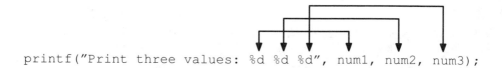

```
printf("Print three values: %d %d %d", num1, num2, num3);
```

Note that the first format specifier corresponds to the first data item, the second specifier to the second data item, and so on. We separate each specifier by a space so that a space will be printed before each number. Otherwise the numbers would be printed one after the other without any separation.

The data items can also be expressions, such as *num* ∗ *num*:

```
printf( "The square of %d is %d\n", num, num∗num );
```

The backslash (\) followed by *n* forms a special symbol called an *escape sequence*. When escape sequences are sent to an output device, such as a terminal, they are interpreted as signals that control the format of display. The **\n** escape sequence forces the system to output a newline. There are other escape sequences, which we describe in the next chapter.

2.6.1 Continuation Character

To span a quoted string over more than one line, you must use the *continuation character*, which is a backslash. For example, here's a program that uses the continuation character to print a long string:

```
main()
{
   printf( "This string is too long to fit on one \
line, so I need to use the continuation \
character." );
}
```

Prior to the ANSI Standard, the continuation character could only be used to continue character strings. The Standard extended this notion so that you can now stretch variable names over multiple lines. For the sake of readability, however, you should use the continuation character sparingly. (The ANSI Standard supports an alternative notation for extending strings across multiple lines. This feature is described in Chapter 6.)

2.7 The *scanf()* Function

The *scanf()* function is the mirror image of *printf()*. Instead of printing data on the terminal, it reads data entered from the keyboard. The format of *scanf()* is similar to *printf()*. Like *printf()*, *scanf()* can take any number of arguments, but the first argument is a format string. *scanf()* also uses many of the same format specifiers. The specifier %**d**, for example, indicates that the value to be read is an integer. The major difference between *scanf()* and *printf()* is that the data item arguments must be lvalues and they must be preceded by the *address of* operator **&**. For example,

```
scanf( "%d", &num );
```

directs the system to read integer input from your terminal and store the value in the variable called *num*. The ampersand is a special operator that finds the address of a variable. We discuss it in more detail in the next chapter.

The best way to learn how to use *printf( )* and *scanf( )* is to experiment with them. The exercises at the end of this chapter suggest some programs you can write. You can also look at the complete descriptions of *printf( )* and *scanf( )* in Appendix A.

2.8 The Preprocessor

You can think of the C preprocessor as a separate program that runs before the actual compiler. It is automatically executed when you compile a program, so you don't need to explicitly invoke it. The preprocessor has its own simple grammar and syntax that are only distantly related to the C language syntax. All preprocessor directives begin with a pound sign (#), which must be the first nonspace character on the line.

Unlike C statements, a preprocessor directive ends with a newline, not a semicolon.

We discuss the preprocessor in detail in Chapter 10. For now, we need only take a closer look at the **#include** facility, already mentioned in connection with header files, and a new preprocessor command called **#define**.

2.8.1 The Include Facility

The preprocessor **#include** directive causes the compiler to read source text from another file as well as the file it is currently compiling. In effect, this enables you to insert the contents of one file into another file before compilation begins, although the original file is not actually altered. This is especially useful when identical information is to be shared by more than one source file. Rather than duplicating the information in each file, you can place all the common information in a single file and then include that file wherever necessary. Not only does this reduce the amount of typing required, but it also makes program maintenance easier, since changes to the shared code need only be made in one place. The **#include** command has two forms:

```
#include <filename>
```

and

```
#include "filename"
```

If the filename is surrounded by angle brackets, the preprocessor looks in a special place designated by the operating system. This is where all system include files, such as the header files for the runtime library, are kept. If the filename is surrounded by double quotes, the preprocessor looks in the directory containing the source file. If it can't find the include file there, it searches for the file as if it had been enclosed in angle brackets. By convention, the names of include files usually end with an *.h* extension.

Consider what happens when the preprocessor encounters the command

```
#include <stdio.h>
```

The preprocessor searches in the system-defined directory for a file called *stdio.h*, and then replaces the **#include** command with the contents of the file. We won't show you the entire *stdio.h* file because it's long and complicated and varies from one compiler to another. But a typical section of the file looks like the following:

```
/*  Definitions of functions compiled separately
 *  that don't return int's.
 */

extern FILE *fopen(),*fdopen(),*freopen(), *popen(),
            *tmpfile();
extern long ftell();
extern char *gets(), *fgets(), *ctermid(),
            *cuserid(), *tempnam(), *tmpnam();
```

These are declarations of functions in the runtime library. As a simpler example of how the **#include** directive works, suppose you have a file called *global_decs.h*, which contains the following:

```
int global_counter;
char global_char;
```

Then in a source file you use the **#include** directive:

```
#include "global_decs.h"
main()
{
    .
    .
    .
}
```

When you compile the program, the preprocessor replaces the **#include** directive with the contents of the specified file, so the source file looks like

```
int global_counter;
char global_char;
main()
{
    .
    .
    .
}
```

2.8.2 The *#define* Directive

Just as it is possible to associate a name with a memory location by declaring a variable, it is also possible to associate a name with a constant. You do this by using a preprocessor directive called **#define**. For instance,

```
#define NOTHING 0
```

binds the name *NOTHING* to the constant zero. The two symbols *NOTHING* and *0* now mean the same thing to the compiler. The statements

```
j = 5 + 0;
j = 5 + NOTHING;
```

are exactly the same.

The rules for naming constants are the same as the rules for naming variables, but you must be careful not to confuse the two. For example, having defined *NOTHING* as zero, you cannot write

```
NOTHING = j + 5;
```

any more than you can write

```
0 = j + 5;
```

In both cases, the compiler should issue an error since you are attempting to change the value of a constant. To avoid confusion between constants and variables, it is a common practice to use all uppercase letters for constant names and lowercase letters for variable names.

Naming constants has two important benefits. First, it enables you to give a descriptive name to a nondescript number. For example,

```
#define MAX_PAGE_WIDTH 80
```

Now, in your program you can use *MAX_PAGE_WIDTH*, which means something, instead of "80," which doesn't tell you much. Creative naming of constants can make a program much easier to read.

The other advantage of constant names is that they make a program easier to change. For example, the maximum page width parameter might appear dozens of times in a large text formatting program. Suppose that you want to change the maximum width from 80 to 70. If, instead of using a constant name, you used the constant 80, you will need to change 80 to 70 wherever it appears and hope that you are changing the right 80's. If you use a constant name, you need only change the definition,

```
#define MAX_PAGE_WIDTH 70
```

and recompile.

Exercises

1. Write a *main()* routine that prints *Hello world.*

2. Write a function that returns the cube of its argument. The function and argument should be declared as **int**s:

   ```
   int cube ( num )
   int num;
   ```

3. Write a function called *fourth_pow()* that returns the fourth power of its argument. Use *square()* in your solution. Then write a *main()* function that calls *fourth_pow().*

4. Write a *main()* function that reads an integer from the terminal, finds its cube by calling *cube()*, and prints the cube.

5. Link *main()* and *cube()* together and run them.

6. In what ways does a computer program resemble a living organism? (See Douglas Hofstadter's *Godel, Escher, Bach* for an in-depth discussion of computer and biological hierarchies.)

7. Write pseudocode for a program that strips comments from a C source file.

8. Which of the following names cannot be used to name variables? Why are they illegal?

   ```
   var                 VAR                 INT
   int                 p.s                 p_s
   p$s                 p#s                 qqqqqqqqqq
   double              p?s_2               ggg_234_456
   double_var          struct              structure
   12fff               @f                  default
   ok                  not_ok              void
   VOID                Void                voId
   _12                 _bufp
   ```

9. The following function contains a number of bugs. Find the bugs and fix them.

   ```
   main( x )
   {
     scanf( "How many bugs are in this programs?,
            prob_count )
     printf( This program has %d problems\n,
            prob_count );
   ```

Chapter 3

Scalar Data Types

What's in a name? That which we call a rose
By any other name would smell as sweet. — Shakespeare,
<u>Romeo and Juliet</u>

The ability to divide data into different types is one of the most important features of modern programming languages. It enables you to work with relatively complex objects instead of the more mundane objects that the computer manipulates at its lowest level. You can deal with integers, characters, and floating-point numbers, all of which are familiar entities. At the bit and byte level, the computer may not understand these concepts. It is up to the compiler, therefore, to make sure that the computer handles bits and bytes in a way consistent with their data type. A *data type* is really just an interpretation applied to a string of bits.

The C language offers a small but useful set of data types. There are eight different types of integers and two types of floating-point objects (three with the ANSI Standard). In addition, integer constants can be written in decimal, octal, or hexadecimal notation. These types—integers and floating points—are called *arithmetic types*. Together with pointers and enumerated types, they are known as *scalar types* because all of the values lie along a linear *scale*. That is, any scalar value is either less than, equal to, or greater than any other scalar value.

In addition to scalar types, there are *aggregate types*, which are built by combining one or more scalar types. Aggregate types, which include arrays, structures, and unions, are useful for organizing logically related variables into physically adjacent groups. There is also one type—**void**—that is neither scalar nor aggregate. Figure 3-1 shows the logical hierarchy of C data types.

This chapter describes scalar variables and constants and the **void** type. Chapters 6 and 8 describe aggregate types.

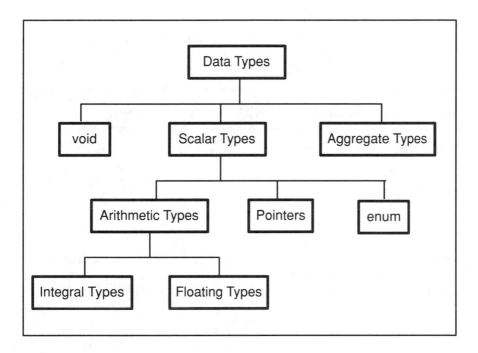

Figure 3-1. Hierarchy of C Data Types.

3.1 Declarations

Every variable must be declared before it is used. A declaration provides the compiler with information about how many bytes should be allocated and how those bytes should be interpreted. To declare *j* as an integer, you would write

```
int j;
```

The word **int** is a reserved word that specifies the integer data type. There are nine reserved words for scalar data types, as shown in Table 3-1.

char			
	double	short	signed
int			
	enum	long	unsigned
float			

Table 3-1. Scalar Type Keywords.

The first five—**char**, **int**, **float**, **double**, and **enum**—are basic types. The others—**long**, **short**, **signed**, and **unsigned**—are *qualifiers* that modify a basic type in some way. You can think of the basic types as nouns and the qualifiers as adjectives.

As a shorthand, you can declare variables that have the same type in a single declaration by separating the variable names with commas. You could declare *j* and *k* with

```
int j,k;
```

which is the same as

```
int j;
int k;
```

All the declarations in a block must appear before any executable statements. The order in which they are declared, however, usually makes no difference. For instance,

```
int j,k;
float x,y,z;
```

is functionally the same as

```
float x;
int k;
int j;
float z,y;
```

It is usually a good idea to group declarations of the same type together for easy reference.

All of our examples so far have used single-character variable names, which seems to contradict our earlier advice about using meaningful names. However, single-character names are acceptable in certain circumstances, particularly in short example programs and test programs. To make them a bit more meaningful, there is a convention borrowed from FORTRAN. The names i, j, k, m, and n are generally used for integer counters and temporary variables; x, y, and z are used for floating-point temporary variables; and c is used for temporary character variables. You should never use the single-character names *l* (el) or o (oh), since they are easily confused with the digits 1 (one) and 0 (zero).

3.1.1 Declaring the Return Type of a Function

Just as you can declare the data type of a variable, you can also declare the type of value returned by a function. The following declares *foo()* to be a function that returns a value of type **float**:

```
float foo( arg )
int arg;
{
    .
    .
    .
}
```

Unlike other variables, functions have a default return type (**int**) if you do not explicitly give them a return type. For example,

```
foo()
{
    .
    .
    .
}
```

declares a function *foo()* whose return type is **int**. Many programmers use this convention, although we recommend that you explicitly enter the **int** type to make the program more readable. Some programmers also omit the return type for functions that return no value. This was acceptable in older compilers that did not support another syntax for declaring such functions. More modern C compilers, however, support the **void** type, which allows you to explicitly declare that a function does not return a value. See Section 3.12 for more about **void**.

3.2 Different Types of Integers

Although **int** is the basic integer data type, it is also the least descriptive. On all machines, an **int** is treated as an integer in that it cannot hold fractional values, but it has different sizes on different machines. Some compilers allocate four bytes for an **int** while others allocate only two bytes. (Still others allocate three bytes or just one byte.) In addition, the size of a byte is not constant. On most machines, a byte is eight bits, but there are even exceptions to this rule.

The only requirements that the ANSI Standard makes is that a byte must be at least eight bits long, and that **int**s must be at least 16 bits long and must represent the "natural" size for the computer. By natural, they mean the number of bits that the CPU usually handles in a single instruction. In our examples throughout the book, we assume that a byte is eight bits and that an **int** is four bytes.

If you don't care how many bytes are allocated, you can use **int**. If the size matters, however, you should use one of the size qualifiers, **short** or **long**. On most machines, a **short int** is two bytes and a **long int** is four bytes. To declare *j* as a **short int** and *k* as a **long int**, you would write

```
short int j;
long int k;
```

The compiler would allocate at least two bytes for *j* and at least four for *k*. Note that since the number of bytes is different, the range of values is different, as shown in Table 3-2. If you need to store values less than –32,768 or greater than 32,767, you should obviously use a **long int**.

The compiler is smart enough to infer **int** even if you leave it out. You could write, for example,

```
short j;
long k;
```

In the interest of brevity, most C programmers use this shorthand.

The number of bits used to represent an integer type determines the range of values that can be stored in that type. Consider, for example, a 16-bit **short int**. Each bit has a value of 2 to the power of *n* where *n* represents the position of the bit:

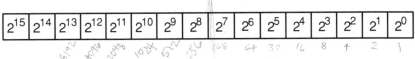

For instance, the decimal value 9 would be represented by setting bits 0 and 3:

```
0 0 0 0 0 0 0 0 0 0 0 0 1 0 0 1
                    2³  +   2⁰ =   8 + 1 = 9
```

To represent negative numbers, most computers use *two's complement notation*. In two's complement notation, the leftmost bit (called the *most significant bit* because it represents the largest value) is a *sign bit*. If it is set to one, the number is negative; if it's zero, the number is positive. To negate a binary number, you must first complement all the bits (change zeroes to ones, and ones to zeroes), and then add 1 to it. To get –9, for instance, you would first complement the bits, giving you

```
1 1 1 1 1 1 1 1 1 1 1 1 0 1 1 0
```

Then you would add one:

```
1 1 1 1 1 1 1 1 1 1 1 1 0 1 1 1
```

There is a less popular notation called *one's complement*, in which you simply complement the bits to negate a number, without adding one. While this notation may seem simpler, it has several drawbacks, one of which is that there are two representations for zero:

```
0 0 0 0 0 0 0 0 0 0 0 0 0 0 0 0
```

and

```
1 1 1 1 1 1 1 1 1 1 1 1 1 1 1 1
```

In two's complement notation, there is only one representation for zero because after complementing the bits you add one, which zeroes all the bits again.

One of the interesting, and valuable, features of two's complement notation is that -1 is represented by all bits being set to one. It also follows that the largest positive number that can be represented occurs when all but the sign bit are set. This value is $2(n - 1) - 1$ where n is the number of bits. The largest negative value is $-2(n - 1)$.

Table 3-2 shows sizes and ranges of integer types for our machine. (See Appendix D for the minimum ranges that must be supported by an ANSI-conforming C compiler.)

3.2.1 Unsigned Integers

There are a number of instances where a variable will have to hold only non-negative values. For instance, variables that are used to count things are often restricted to non-negative numbers. The C language allows you to declare that a variable is non-negative only (or unsigned), thereby doubling its positive range (the most significant bit will *not* be a sign bit). A signed **short int** has a range of $-32,767$ to $32,767$, whereas an **unsigned short int** has a range of 0 to 65,535.

To declare an integer variable as being nonnegative only, use the **unsigned** qualifier, as in

```
unsigned int k;
unsigned short m;
unsigned long n;
```

You can also use **unsigned** by itself, as in

```
unsigned p;
```

which is the same as **unsigned int**. The K&R standard supports only **unsigned int**s — the other types of unsigned integers are ANSI extensions. In addition, the ANSI Standard supports the **signed** qualifier, as described in Box 3-1.

Box 3-1: ANSI Feature — *signed* Qualifier

The ANSI Standard recognizes a new keyword called **signed**, which specifically makes a variable capable of holding negative as well as non-negative values. In most cases, variables are signed by default, so that the **signed** keyword is superfluous. The one exception is with the **char** type, which can be either signed or unsigned by default, depending on the whims of the compiler developers. Most compilers use **signed char** as the default. Keep in mind that the **signed** keyword is new and may not be implemented on your compiler.

Type	Size (in bytes)	Value Range
int	4	-2^{31} to $2^{31}-1$
short int	2	-2^{15} to $2^{15}-1$
long int	4	-2^{31} to $2^{31}-1$
unsigned short int	2	0 to $2^{16}-1$
unsigned long int	4	0 to $2^{32}-1$
signed char	1	-2^{7} to $2^{7}-1$
unsigned char	1	0 to $2^{8}-1$

Table 3-2. Size and Range of Integer Types on Our Machine.

3.2.2 Characters and Integers

Most programming languages make a distinction between numeric and character data. The number "5" is a number while the letter "A" is a character. In reality, though, even characters are stored in the computer as numbers. Every character has a unique numeric code. There are various codes, two of the most common being ASCII, which stands for American Standard Code for Information Interchange, and EBCDIC (Extended Binary-Coded Decimal Interchange Code), which is what IBM uses on its larger computers. Appendix G contains a full list of the ASCII character set. The examples in this section assume an ASCII code set since it is the most prevalent in C implementations. For most codes, all character values lie within the range 0 through 255, which means that a character can be represented in a single byte. (Character sets for certain languages, such as *Kanji*, require more than 256 character codes. To represent text using these character sets, you can take advantage of ANSI C's *multibyte character* feature. See Box 3-2 for more information.)

In C, the distinction between characters and numbers is blurred. There is a data type called **char**, but it is really just a 1-byte integer value that can be used to hold either characters or numbers. For instance, after making the declaration

```
char c;
```

you can make either of the following assignments:

```
c = 'A';
c = 65;
```

In both cases, the decimal value 65 is loaded into the variable *c* since 65 is the ASCII code for the letter 'A'. Note that character constants are enclosed in single quotes. The quotes tell the compiler to get the numeric code value of the character. For instance, in the following example, *a* gets the value 5, whereas *b* gets the value 53 since that is the ASCII code for the character "5".

```
char a , b;
a = 5;
b = '5';
```

The following program reads a character from a terminal and then displays the code value of the character. The **%c** format in the *scanf()* call indicates that the data item to be read is a character. The **%d** format in the *printf()* call tells the function to output the character in its integer form.

```
/*   Print the numeric code value of a character */

#include <stdio.h>

main()
{
   char ch;

   printf( "Enter a character:" );
   scanf( "%c", &ch );
   printf( "Its numeric code value is: %d\n", ch );
   exit( 0 );
}
```

Because **char**s are treated as small integers, you can perform arithmetic operations on them. In the following lines, *j* gets the value 131 since 'A' equals 65 and 'B' equals 66.

```
int j;
j = 'A' + 'B';
```

In the ASCII character set, character codes are ordered alphabetically. For example, an uppercase 'A' , for example, is 65, a 'B' is 66, ... a 'Z' is 90. Lowercase letters start at 97 and run through 122. This makes it fairly easy to implement a function that changes a character from uppercase to lowercase:

```
char to_lower( ch )
char ch;
{
   return ch +32;
}
```

However, if you assume an ASCII character set, and add or subtract 32, your program will fail when you run it on a machine that uses EBCDIC or some other character code. To avoid this problem, the C runtime library contains two functions called *toupper()* and *tolower()* that change a character's case. These functions, described in Appendix A, are guaranteed to work the same in all implementations. For maximum portability, therefore, you should use these functions rather than writing your own.

Box 3-2: ANSI Feature — Multibyte Characters

The English character set contains only 26 letters. Even when you consider uppercase and lowercase letters, numerals, and punctuation, the total number of symbols one needs to express something in the English language is relatively small. The ASCII character codes define 128 symbols, which is quite sufficient. Every English character, therefore, can fit in a single byte since a byte allows for 256 unique codes.

Other languages, however, have much larger character sets. The written Japanese language, for example, contains thousands of characters. Obviously, one byte is not sufficient to uniquely represent each character.

To allow for programming in languages other than English, the ANSI Standard supports *multibyte characters*. When multibyte characters are activated, the runtime environment interprets two or more successive bytes as a single character. The actual number of bytes used and the character codes depend on the implementation.

For more information about multibyte characters, refer to the appropriate runtime routines in Appendix A. In particular, Sections A.8 and A.16 describe how to use multibyte characters.

3.3 Different Kinds of Integer Constants

We have already seen a few integer constants, 5, 10, and 2. These are called *decimal* constants since they represent decimal numbers. You can also write *octal* and *hexadecimal* constants. An octal constant is written by preceding the octal value with the digit zero. A hexadecimal constant is written by preceding the value with a zero and an **x** or **X**. Table 3-3 shows some decimal constants and their octal and hexadecimal equivalents.

Note that negative numbers are preceded with a minus sign just as in algebraic notation. (Strictly speaking, negative numbers are really expressions, not constants.) Non-negative numbers may be preceded by an optional plus sign. (The plus sign is an added feature of the ANSI Standard which has a nonintuitive meaning. We discuss its impact in Chapter 5.) Note also that you cannot include a comma or a decimal point in an integer constant.

An octal constant cannot contain the digits 8 and 9 since they are not part of the octal number set. (This restriction was not present in the K&R standard.)

Decimal	Octal	Hexadecimal
3	003	0x3
8	010	0x8
15	017	0xF
16	020	0x10
21	025	0x15
−87	−0127	−0x57
187	0273	0xBB
255	0377	0xff

Table 3-3. Integer Constants.

The *scanf( )* and *printf( )* functions have format specifiers for reading and writing octal and hexadecimal numbers. For octal numbers, the format specifier is **o**; for hexadecimal numbers the format specifier is **x**. The following program reads a hexadecimal number (with or without the **0x** prefix) from the terminal and prints its decimal and octal equivalents.

```
/*  Print the decimal and octal equivalents of a
 *  hexadecimal constant.
 */

#include <stdio.h>

main()
{
    int num;

    printf( "Enter a hexadecimal constant: " );
    scanf( "%x", &num );
    printf( "The decimal equivalent of %x is: %d\n",
            num, num );
    printf( "The octal equivalent of %x is: %o\n",
            num, num );
    exit( 0 );
}
```

The number of bytes allocated for an integer constant varies from machine to machine, depending on the relative sizes of the integer types. In general, an integer constant has type **int** if its value can fit in an **int**. Otherwise, it has type **long int**. More precisely, the ANSI Standard states that the type of an integer constant is the first in the corresponding list in which its value can be represented. The list is shown in Table 3-4.

Form of Constant	List of Possible Types
Unsuffixed decimal	**int, long int, unsigned long int**
Unsuffixed octal or hexadecimal	**int, unsigned int, long int, unsigned long int**
Suffixed by **u** or **U**	**unsigned int, unsigned long int**
Suffixed by **l** or **L**	**long int, unsigned long int**

Table 3-4. Types of Integer Constants.

If a constant is too large to fit into the longest type in its list, the results are unpredictable. Many compilers simply truncate the value and then load it into memory, whereas others produce an error message.

It is also possible to specifically designate that a constant have type **long int** by appending an **l** or **L** to the constant (we recommend that you use an uppercase **L** since it is easy to confuse a lowercase **l** with the digit **1**). For example,

```
55L
0777776L
-0XAAAB321L
```

Note that octal and hexadecimal constants may also be **long**.

Box 3-3: ANSI Feature — *unsigned* Constants

The ANSI Standard allows you to apply the **unsigned** qualifier to a constant. This is done by appending a **u** or **U** to the constant, as in

```
55u
077743U
0xfffu
```

This syntax, though supported by the ANSI Standard, is new, so older compilers may give you an error if you try to use it.

3.3.1 Escape Character Sequences

We have already used the \n escape sequence, which represents a newline. The full list of escape sequences is shown in Table 3-5 (\a and \v are ANSI extensions, though they are available on many older compilers).

\a	(alert)	Produces an audible or visible alert signal.
\b	(backspace)	Moves the cursor back one space.
\f	(form feed)	Moves the cursor to the next logical page.
\n	(newline)	Prints a newline.
\r	(carriage return)	Prints a carriage return.
\t	(horizontal tab)	Prints a horizontal tab.
\v	(vertical tab)	Prints a vertical tab.

Table 3-5. C Escape Sequences.

In addition to the escape sequences listed in Table 3-5, C also supports escape character sequences of the form,

```
\octal-number
        and
\hex-number
```

which translates into the character represented by the octal or hexadecimal number. For example, if ASCII representations are being used, the letter 'a' may be written as '\141' and 'Z' as '\132'. This syntax is most frequently used to represent the null character as '\0'. This is exactly equivalent to the numeric constant zero (0). Note that the octal number does not include the zero prefix as it would for a normal octal constant. To specify a hexadecimal number, you should also leave out the zero so that the prefix is an **x** (uppercase X is not allowed in this context). Support for hexadecimal sequences is an ANSI extension. The ANSI Standard also supports trigraph sequences, as described in Box 3-4.

Box 3-4: ANSI Feature — Trigraph Sequences

Because certain characters used by the C language are not available on every computer keyboard, the ANSI Standard adopted a new format for representing these characters. Trigraph sequences consist of two question marks followed by a third character. During the translation stage, the compiler converts these sequences into a single character, as shown in Table 3-6. For example, the following line of source code:

```
printf( "Print a newline ??/n" );
```

becomes

```
printf( "Print a newline \n" );
```

Note that this feature is not available on older compilers and may, in fact, break existing code that accidentally contains trigraph sequences.

Trigraph Sequence	Resulting Character
??=	# (pound sign)
??(	[(left bracket)
??/	\ (backslash)
??)	] (right bracket)
??'	^ (caret)
??<	{ (left brace)
??!	| (bar)
??>	} (right brace)
??–	~ (tilde)

Table 3-6. ANSI Trigraph Sequences.

Box 3-5: ANSI Feature — *long double* Type

The ANSI Standard supports an additional floating-point type called **long double**. This is a new type so it may not be implemented by many compilers. **long double**s are intended to provide even greater range and precision than **double**s. On many machines, however, **long double** and **double** are synonymous.

The **long double** declaration was added by the ANSI Committee because some architectures support more than two floating types.

3.4 Floating-Point Types

Integers are fine for many occasions but they are inadequate for representing very large numbers and fractions. For this, you need floating-point types. There are two ways to write floating-point constants, the simplest being to place a decimal point in the number. For example,

```
0.356
5.0
0.000001
 .7
7.
```

are all legal examples of floating-point constants. To declare a variable capable of holding one of these values, you use the **float** or **double** keyword. For example,

```
float pi;
double pi_squared;

pi = 3.141;
pi_squared = pi * pi;
```

The word **double** stands for double-precision, because on many machines it is capable of representing about twice as much *precision* as a **float**. The precision refers to the number of decimal places that can be represented. On many machines, a **double** also takes up twice as much memory. A **float** generally requires four bytes, and a **double** generally requires eight bytes, although these sizes are not strict requirements. The internal representation of floating-point values is incorporated into the hardware architecture of each computer and is one of the least standardized aspects of computers. You should read the documentation for your particular compiler to discover the range and precision of **float**s and **double**s (these limits are also listed in the *<limits.h>* header file that comes with the ANSI runtime library).

The following function takes a **double** value as an argument that represents a temperature in Fahrenheit and converts it to Celsius.

```
/* Convert a float value from Fahrenheit to Celsius
 */

double fahrenheit_to_celsius( temp_fahrenheit )
double temp_fahrenheit;
{
  double temp_celsius;

  temp_celsius = (temp_fahrenheit - 32.0) *
              100.0/(212.0 - 32.0);
  return temp_celsius;
}
```

The following function computes the area of a circle, given a radius.

```
/*  Given the radius, find the area of a circle.
 */

#define PI 3.14159

float area_of_circle( radius )
float radius;
{
  float area;

  area = PI*radius*radius;
  return area;
}
```

Note that we use the **#define** feature to create a constant called *PI*. This is better than embedding the numeric constant in the code since the name *PI* is more meaningful than the string of digits 3.14159.

3.4.1 Scientific Notation

Scientific notation is a useful shorthand for writing lengthy floating point values. In scientific notation, a value consists of two parts: a number called the *mantissa* followed by a power of 10 called the *characteristic* (or *exponent*). The letter **e** or **E**, standing for exponent, is used to separate the two parts. The floating-point constant **3e2**, for instance, is interpreted as $3*10^2$, or 300. Likewise, the value **−2.5e−4** is interpreted as $-2.5*10^{-4}$, or −0.00025. The examples in Table 3-7 show some legal and illegal floating-point constants.

Legal	Illegal	
3.141	35	No decimal point or exponent
.3333333333	3,500.45	Commas are illegal
0.3	4E	The exponent sign must be followed
3e2		by a number
5E–5	4e3.6	The exponent value must be an
3.7e12		integer

Table 3-7. Legal and Illegal Floating-Point Constants.

Box 3-6: ANSI Feature — *float* **and** *long double*
constants

By default, all floating-point constants have type **double**. The ANSI
Standard, however, allows you to override this rule by appending an **f** or
F to the constant to make it **float**, or an **l** or **L** to make it **long double**.
For example,

```
3.5      /* A double constant */
3.5f     /* A float constant  */
3.5e3L   /* A long double      */
```

These suffixes are useful for forcing floating-point expressions to be
computed with either single or double precision, as explained in Section
3.9.3.

3.5 Initialization

A declaration allocates memory for a variable, but it does not necessarily store
an initial value at the location (*fixed duration* variables, discussed in Chapter 7,
are an exception). If you read the value of such a variable before making an
explicit assignment, therefore, the results are unpredictable. For example, try the
following program:

```
#include <stdio.h>

main()
{
    int x;

    printf( "The value of x is: %d\n", x );
    exit( 0 );
}
```

The output when you execute this program could be just about anything since *x* gets the value of whatever is left over in memory from the previous program execution. Because you often want a variable to start with a particular value, the C language provides a special syntax for *initializing* a variable. Essentially, you just include an assignment expression after the variable name in a declaration. For example,

```
char ch = 'A';
```

allocates one byte for *ch*, and also assigns the character 'A' to it. The initialization is really just a shorthand for combining a declaration statement and an assignment statement. The previous initialization, for instance, is exactly the same as:

```
char ch;
ch = 'A';
```

3.6 Mixing Types

The C language allows you to mix arithmetic types in expressions with few restrictions. For example, you can write:

```
num = 3 * 2.1;
```

even though the expression on the right-hand side of the assignment is a mixture of two types, an **int** and a **double**. Also, the data type of *num* could be any scalar data type except a pointer.

To make sense out of an expression with mixed types, C performs conversions automatically. These *implicit conversions* make the programmer's job easier but put a greater burden on the compiler, since it is responsible for reconciling mixed types. This can be dangerous since the compiler may make conversions that are unexpected. For example, the expression

```
3.0 + 1/2
```

does not evaluate to 3.5 as you might expect. Instead, it evaluates to 3.0.

Implicit conversions, sometimes called *quiet conversions* or *automatic conversions*, occur under four circumstances:

1. In assignment statements, the value on the right side of the assignment is converted to the data type of the variable on the left side. These are called *assignment conversions*.

2. Whenever a **char** or **short int** appears in an expression, it is converted to an **int**. **unsigned char**s and **unsigned short**s are converted to **int** if the **int** can represent their value; otherwise they are converted to **unsigned int** (see Box 3-7). These are called *integral widening conversions*.

3. In an arithmetic expression, objects are converted to conform to the conversion rules of the operator.

4. In certain situations, arguments to functions are converted. This type of conversion is described in detail in later chapters.

As an example of the first type of conversion, suppose *j* is an **int** in the following statement:

```
j = 2.6;
```

Before assigning the **double** constant to *j*, the compiler converts it to an **int**, giving it an integral value of 2. Note that the compiler truncates the fractional part rather than rounding to the closest integer.

The second type of implicit conversion, called *integral widening* or *integral promotion,* is almost always invisible.

To understand the third type of implicit conversion, we first need to describe briefly how the compiler processes expressions. The discussion that follows is only cursory—we describe expressions in detail in Chapter 5.

3.6.1 Implicit Conversions in Expressions

When the compiler encounters an expression, it divides it into *subexpressions*, where each subexpression consists of one operator and one or more objects, called *operands*, that are bound to the operator. For example, the expression

```
-3 / 4 + 2.5
```

contains three operators: −, /, and +. The operand to − is 3; there are two operands to /, −3 and 4; and there are two operands to +, −3/4 and 2.5.

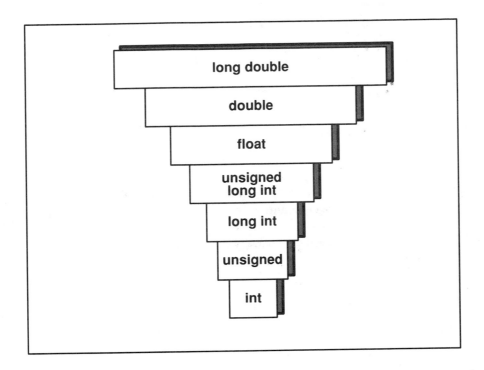

Figure 3-2. Hierarchy of C Scalar Data Types.

The minus operator is said to be a *unary operator* because it takes just one operand, whereas the division and addition operators are *binary operators*. Each operator has its own rules for operand type agreement, but most binary operators require both operands to have the same type. If the types differ, the compiler converts one of the operands to agree with the other one. To decide which operand to convert, the compiler resorts to the hierarchy of data types shown in Figure 3-3 and converts the "lower" type to the "higher" type. For example,

```
1 + 2.5
```

involves two types, an **int** and a **double**. Before evaluating it, the compiler converts the **int** into a **double** because **double** is higher than **int** in the type hierarchy. The conversion from an **int** to a **double** does not usually affect the result in any way. It is as if the expression were written

```
1.0 + 2.5
```

The rules for implicit conversions in expressions can be summarized as follows. Note that these conversions occur *after* all integral widening conversions have taken place.

- If a pair of operands contains a **long double**, the other value is converted to **long double**.

- Otherwise, if one of the operands is a **double**, the other is converted to **double**.

- Otherwise, if one of the operands is a **float**, the other is converted to a **float**.

- Otherwise, if one of the operands is an **unsigned long int**, the other is converted to **unsigned long int**.

- Otherwise, if one of the operands is a **long int**, then the other is converted to **long int**.

- Otherwise, if one of the operands is an **unsigned int**, then the other is converted to **unsigned int**.

In general, most implicit conversions are invisible. They occur without any obvious effect. The following sections describe implicit conversions in more detail.

3.6.2 Mixing Integers

There are four possible sizes of integers—**char**, **short**, **int**, and **long**—and they may be mixed freely in an expression. Due to the integral widening rules, the compiler converts **char**s and **short**s to **int**s before evaluating an expression. This is why Figure 3-3 shows **int** at the bottom of the inverted pyramid—all smaller integer types are converted to **int** or **unsigned int** before an expression is evaluated. For example, in the following program, c and j are expanded to **int**s before the arithmetic expression is evaluated. The constant 8 is already an **int** so it does not need to be converted.

```
main()
{
   char c = 5
   short j = 6;
   int k = 7;

   k = c+j+8;
   exit( 0 );
}
```

Box 3-7: ANSI Feature — Unsigned Conversions

Prior to the ANSI Standard, there was no agreed-upon method for promoting **unsigned char**s and **unsigned short**s. Should they be widened to **int**s or to **unsigned int**s? There was also confusion about converting operands when one was a long unsigned integer and the other was a short signed integer. Should the short unsigned integer be widened to an **unsigned int**, making the result unsigned, or should it be converted to a **signed int**, making the result a signed integer?

Most compilers converted **unsigned char**s and **unsigned short**s to **unsigned int**s, figuring that the unsigned quality was too important to convert away. Likewise, when signed and unsigned objects met in expressions, the result was always unsigned. But this *sign-preserving* strategy sometimes produces strange results. For example, if *a* is an **unsigned short** whose value is 2, then the expression

```
a - 3
```

evaluates to a very large unsigned value rather than the signed value of −1.

To avoid this problem, the ANSI Committee adopted a different conversion method, known as *value-preserving*. This method converts **unsigned char**s and **unsigned short**s to **int**, assuming that the **int** type is larger than **unsigned char** and **unsigned short**, respectively. If **int** is not larger, the object is converted to **unsigned int**. Assuming 16-bit **short**s and 32-bit **int**s in the previous example, *a* would be converted to **int** rather than **unsigned int**, so the result of the expression would be −1.

Note that the difference between sign-preserving and value-preserving rules only becomes manifest when an unsigned type is shorter than an **int**. If both operands are **unsigned int**s, the result is unsigned, so that the expression

```
2u - 3u
```

always evaluates to a large unsigned value.

To convert a **short** 5 to an **int**, all that is required is to add 2 additional bytes of zeroes. The **short** variable with value 5 would be stored in binary form:

```
00000000 00000101
```

After converting it to a four-byte **int**, its representation is

```
00000000 00000000 00000000 000000101
```

Clearly, this does not present any problems since the object retains its value of 5. For negative values, the process is slightly more complicated since the compiler must ensure that the converted value is also negative. It does this by filling the additional bytes with ones rather than zeroes. This is known as *sign extension*. For example, the **short** value –5 is represented in two's complement notation as

```
11111111 11111011
```

To convert it to a **long int** whose value is –5, the compiler adds two bytes filled with ones:

```
11111111 11111111 11111111 11111011
```

Integral *widening* conversions are almost always innocuous. Problems arise, however, when an implicit conversion *shortens* an object. This happens only in assignment conversions. For example, suppose c is a **char**, and you make the assignment

```
c = 882;
```

The binary representation of 882 is

```
00000011 01110010
```

It requires two bytes of storage, but the variable c has only one byte allocated for it, so the two upper bits don't get assigned to c. This is known as *overflow* and the result is not defined by the ANSI Standard for signed types.

Usually, a compiler simply ignores the extra byte, so c would be assigned the rightmost byte:

```
01110010
```

This would erroneously give c the value of 114. It is important, therefore, to make sure that you do not exceed the size limits when you assign values to variables. The principle illustrated for **char**s also applies to **short**s, **int**s, and **long int**s. For **unsigned** types, however, C has well-defined rules for dealing with overflow conditions. When an integer value x is converted to a smaller unsigned integer type, the result is the non-negative remainder of

```
x / (U_MAX+1)
```

where U_MAX is the largest number that can be represented in the shorter unsigned type. For example, if j is an unsigned short, which is two bytes, then the assignment

```
j = 71124;
```

assigns to j the remainder of

```
71124 / (65535+1)
```

The remainder is 5588. Note that for nonnegative numbers, and for negative numbers represented in two's complement notation, this is the same result that you would obtain by ignoring the extra bytes.

3.6.3 Mixing Signed and Unsigned Types

The only difference between signed and unsigned integer types is the way they are interpreted. They occupy the same amount of storage. For example, a **signed char** with bit pattern

```
11101010
```

has a decimal value of –22, assuming two's complement notation. An **unsigned char** with the same binary representation has a decimal value of 234. A problem arises when you mix a signed type with an unsigned type. For example, what is the value of this expression?

```
10u - 15
```

One might expect the result to be –5, but this is not the case. The ANSI Standard states that if one of the operands of a binary expression has type **unsigned int** and the other operand has type **int**, the **int** object is converted to **unsigned int**, and the result is **unsigned**. Using this rule, which is described in more detail in Box 3-7, the value of the expression shown above would be 4,294,967,291 (assuming the machine has 4-byte **int**s and uses two's complement notation). This value is derived from the same bit pattern used to represent –5.

In most cases, the conversion from **signed** to **unsigned** does not cause any problems and goes unnoticed. Where you need to be careful is when you use an **unsigned** expression to control program flow. Although the subject of program flow is discussed in the next chapter, the following example should be clear.

```
main()
{
    unsigned jj;
    int k;

    if (jj-k < 0)  /* This is almost certainly
                    * a bug. */
        foo();
    exit( 0 );
}
```

Translated into English, the program states: "if *jj* minus *k* is less than zero, call the *foo()* function; otherwise, end the program." However, because of unsigned conversion rules, the expression *jj – k* will *never* be less than zero. This is obviously not what is intended by the programmer. Good compilers are able to diagnose these bugs and issue a warning message.

3.6.4 Mixing Floating-Point Values

There are three types of floating-point values—**float, double,** and **long double** (ANSI extension). There is no difficulty with mixing them in an expression. After dividing the expression into subexpressions, the compiler widens the smaller object of each binary pair to match the wider object. If, for example, a binary expression contains a **float** and a **double,** the **float** would be converted to **double.** This would not affect their value in any way and would go unnoticed. It should be pointed out, however, that many computers perform arithmetic with **float**s much faster than with **double**s and **long double**s. You should only use these larger types if you need the greater range or precision.

As is the case with mixing integers, the problem with floating-point conversions occurs when you assign a larger type to a smaller type. There are two potential problems. One is the loss of precision, and the other is an overflow condition. Suppose that on your computer a **double** can represent 10 decimal places and a **float** can only represent 6 decimal places. If *f* is a **float** variable, and you make the assignment

```
f = 1.0123456789
```

the computer rounds the **double** constant value before assigning it to *f.* The value actually assigned to *f,* therefore, might be 1.012346 (if **float**s are only 32 bits long). This probably will not cause any problems unless your program requires great accuracy. If you need more accuracy, you should use **double** or **long double** variables, not **float**s.

A more serious problem occurs when the value being assigned is too large to be represented in the variable. For example, the largest positive number representable by a **float** might be 2e38 (the actual ranges vary from computer to computer). What happens if you try to execute the following assignment?

```
f = 2e40;
```

The behavior is not defined by the ANSI Standard, but on some computers this statement would produce a *runtime error*. A runtime error is an error that occurs while the program is actually executing, as opposed to errors that occur when you compile the program (called *compile-time errors*). Runtime errors are particularly difficult to recover from, so you should go to great pains to avoid them. If there is any chance that an assignment statement will cause a floating-point overflow, you should use a larger floating-point type.

3.6.5 Mixing Integers with Floating-Point Values

It is perfectly legal to mix integers and floating-point values in an expression, to assign a floating-point value to an integer variable, or assign an integer value to a floating-point variable. The simplest case is assignment of an integer to a floating-point variable. In this case, the integer value is implicitly converted to a floating-point type. If the floating-point type is capable of representing the integer, there is no change in value. If f is a **double**, the assignment

```
f = 10;
```

is executed as if it had been written

```
f = 10.0;
```

This conversion is invisible. There are cases, however, where a floating-point type is not capable of exactly representing all integer values. Even though the range of floating-point values is generally greater than the range of integer values, the precision may not be as good for large numbers. In these instances, conversion of an integer to a floating-point value may result in a loss of precision. For example, try running the following example on your computer.

```
#include <stdio.h>

main()
{
   long int j = 2147483600;
   float x;

   x = j;
   printf( "j is %d\nx is %10f\n", j, x );
   exit( 0 );
}
```

The case of mixing integer and floating-point values in expressions is similar. The compiler converts all integers into the largest floating-point type present. If *j* is an **int** and *f* is a **float**, the expression

```
f + j
```

would cause *j* to be quietly converted to a **float**. In the expression

```
f + j + 2.5
```

both *f* and *j* would be converted to **double**s because the constant 2.5 is a **double**.

The most risky mixture of integer and floating-point values is the case where a floating-point value is assigned to an integer variable. First, the fractional part is discarded. Then, if the resulting integer can fit in the integer variable, the assignment is made. In the following statement, assuming *j* is an **int**, the **double** value 2.5 is converted to the **int** value 2 before it is assigned.

```
j = 2.5;
```

This causes a loss of precision which could have a dramatic impact on your program. The same truncation process occurs for negative values. After the assignment

```
j = -5.8;
```

the value of *j* is –5.

An equally serious situation occurs when the floating-point value cannot fit in an integer. For example,

```
j = 999999999999.888888
```

This causes an overflow condition which may halt program execution. As a general rule, it is a good idea to keep floating-point and integer values separate unless you have a good reason for mixing them.

3.7 Explicit Conversions — Casts

The previous section describes quiet conversions that the C language performs under certain circumstances. It is also possible to *explicitly* convert a value to a different type. Explicit conversion is called *casting* and is performed with a construct called a *cast*. To cast an expression, enter the target data type enclosed in parentheses directly before the expression. For example,

```
j = (float) 2;
```

converts the integer 2 to a **float** before assigning it to *j*. Of course, if *j* is an integer, the compiler would implicitly convert the value back to an integer before making the assignment.

Casting is a useful operation in a number of diverse situations. Consider, for example, the following situation:

```
int j = 2, k = 3;
float f;

f = k/j;
```

At first glance, it might appear that the *f* gets assigned the value 1.5. However, a closer look reveals that *f* is actually assigned the value 1.0. This is because the expression

```
k/j
```

contains only **int**s, so there is no reason to "promote" either variable to a floating-point type. The result of an integer expression is always an integer, so the true value 1.5 is truncated to the integer value 1. Then, because it is being assigned to a floating-point variable, the value 1 is converted to 1.0. One way to avoid this problem is to cast either, or both, of the integer variables to floats. For instance,

```
f = (float) j/k;
```

This explicitly converts *j* to a **float**. Then the implicit conversion rules come into play. Because *j* has been converted to a **float**, the system automatically converts *k* to a **float** as well. The result of an expression containing two **float**s is a **float**, so *f* gets assigned the true expression value, which is 1.5.

3.8 Enumeration Types

In addition to integer, floating-point, and pointer types, the scalar types also include *enumeration types*. Other computer languages, such as Pascal, also have enumeration types that enable you to declare variables and the set of named constants that can be legally stored in the variable.

Enumeration types are particularly useful when you want to create a unique set of values that may be associated with a variable. The compiler reports an error if you attempt to assign a value that's not part of the declared set of legal values to an enum variable.

In the following example, we declare two enumeration variables called *color* and *intensity*. *color* can be assigned one of four constant values: *red*, *blue*, *green*, and *yellow*. *intensity* can be assigned one of three constant values: *bright*, *medium*, or *dark*.

```
enum { red, blue, green, yellow } color;
enum { bright, medium, dark } intensity;
```

As shown in our examples, the syntax for declaring enumeration types is to start with the **enum** keyword followed by the list of constant names enclosed in braces, followed by the names of the enum variables. There is another syntax described in Section 8.4 that is slightly more complex.

Because enumeration types were not part of the original K&R standard, their implementation varies from one C compiler to another. Most C compilers issue warning messages when an enum type conflict occurs, although the warning is not required by the ANSI Standard. (In fact, the Standard prohibits compilers from halting compilation due to enum type conflicts.) A good compiler, however, would issue warnings for all of the type conflicts and misleading usages shown below:

```
color = yellow;        /* OK */
color = bright;        /* type conflict */
intensity = bright;    /* OK */
intensity = blue;      /* type conflict */
color = 1;             /* type conflict */
color = blue + green;  /* misleading usage */
```

Constant names in an enum declaration receive a default integer value based on their position in the enumeration list. In most cases, the integer value is not important because you are treating the enumeration as a unique value. Nevertheless, it's helpful to know how the compiler is storing the values.

The default values start at zero and go up by one with each new name. In the declaration of *color*, for instance, *red*, *blue*, *green*, and *yellow* represent the integer values 0, 1, 2, and 3, respectively.

You can override these default values by specifying other values. If you do specify a value, all subsequent default values begin at one more than the last defined value. For example,

```
enum { APPLES, ORANGES = 10, LEMONS, GRAPES = -5,
       MELONS };
```

is the same as

```
enum { APPLES = 0, ORANGES = 10, LEMONS = 11,
       GRAPES = -5, MELONS = -4 };
```

Note that the assigned values need not be in ascending order, though for readability it is a good idea to write them that way.

The compiler need only allocate as much memory as is necessary for an enum value. In our color example, for instance, a good compiler will realize that the potential values of *color* are small enough that only one byte is needed for the variable. This can make a difference when enum variables are embedded in aggregate types, as described in Chapter 8.

3.9 The *void* Data Type

The **void** data type was not an original element of the K&R standard, but in recent years it has become an accepted part of the C language. Prior to the ANSI Standard, however, its semantics were somewhat vague. This section describes the ANSI version of **void**.

The **void** data type has two important purposes. The first is to indicate that a function does not return a value. For instance, you may see a function definition such as

```
void func( a, b )
int a, b;
{
    .
    .
    .
}
```

This indicates that the function does not return any useful value. Likewise, on the calling side, you would declare *func()* as

```
extern void func();
```

This informs the compiler that any attempt to use the returned value from *func()* is a mistake and should be flagged as an error. For example, you could invoke *func()* as follows:

```
func ( x, y );
```

But you cannot assign the returned value to a variable:

```
num = func ( x, y );   /*  This should produce an
                        *  error
                        */
```

The other purpose of **void** is to declare a generic pointer. We defer a discussion of this subject to Chapter 7.

3.10 Typedefs

The C language allows you to create your own names for data types with the **typedef** keyword. Syntactically, a typedef is exactly like a variable declaration except that the declaration is preceded by the **typedef** keyword. Semantically, the variable name becomes a synonym for the data type rather than a variable that has memory allocated for it. For example, the statement

```
typedef long int FOUR_BYTE_INT;
```

makes the name *FOUR_BYTE_INT* synonymous with **long int**. The following two declarations are now identical:

```
long int j;
FOUR_BYTE_INT j;
```

By convention, typedef names are capitalized so that they are not confused with variable names.

There are a number of uses for typedefs. They are especially useful for abstracting global types that can be used throughout a program. This application of typedefs is described in Chapter 8.

Box 3-8: Bug Alert — Confusing *typedef* with *#define*

At first glance, it may seem that the **typedef** keyword duplicates functionality provided by the **#define** directive. After all, we could write

```
#define USHORT unsigned int
```

which would serve the same effect as

```
typedef unsigned int USHORT;
```

In this case, the two versions are indeed similar (though there are some subtle differences), but for more complex type declarations, **#define** is inadequate. Suppose, for example, that you want to define a name that represents pointer to **int**. Using **#define** you would write

```
#define PT_TO_INT int *
```

Then to declare two pointers to **int**s, you would write

```
PT_TO_INT p1, p2;
```

which expands to

```
int *p1, p2;
```

Because the asterisk appears just once, only *p1* is declared as a pointer to an **int**; *p2* is an **int**.

If you use a typedef, this problem does not arise. After declaring

```
typedef int *PT_TO_INT;
```

the declaration

```
PT_TO_INT p1, p2;
```

defines both *p1* and *p2* as pointers to **int**s.

Another use of typedefs is to compensate for differences in C compilers. For example, some non-ANSI C compilers do not support the **unsigned short** type. Using typedefs, you can write the program so that it uses **unsigned short** if it's available, or **unsigned int** when the compiler does not support **unsigned short**. For ANSI-conforming compilers, you would write

```
typedef unsigned short USHORT;
```

For compilers that do not support unsigned short, you would write

```
typedef unsigned int USHORT;
```

Then you would use the typedef name *USHORT* whenever you want to declare an **unsigned short** variable. To compile the program on a different machine, all you need to do is find out whether it supports **unsigned short**, and write the typedef accordingly.

Note that the typedef definition must appear before it is used in a declaration.

3.11 Finding the Address of an Object

As we described earlier, every variable has a unique address that identifies its storage location in memory. For some applications, it is useful to access the variable through its address rather than through its name. To obtain the address of a variable, you use the ampersand (**&**) operator. Suppose, for instance, that *j* is a **long int** whose address is 2486. The statement

```
ptr = &j;
```

stores the address value 2486 in the variable *ptr*. When reading an expression, the ampersand operator is translated as "address of," so you would read this statement as: "Assign the address of *j* to *ptr*." The following program prints the value of the variable called j and the address of j:

```
#include <stdio.h>

main()
{
    int j=1;

    printf( "The value of j is: %d\n", j );
    printf( "The address of j is: %p\n", &j );
    exit( 0 );
}
```

The result is

```
The value of j is: 1
The address of j is: 3634264
```

The address represents the actual location of *j* in memory. The particular address listed above is arbitrary. It happens to be *j*'s address on our computer for a particular execution. On another computer, the value could be different. Note that *printf()* requires a special format specifier (**%p**) to print address values. The **%p** specifier is a relatively new ANSI addition to the C language that may not be supported on older compilers. Many compilers allow you to print an address with the **%d**, **%o**, and **%x** specifiers, but this is not portable since addresses are not guaranteed to be represented in the same fashion as integers.

Note that you cannot use the ampersand operator on the left-hand side of an assignment expression. For instance, the following is illegal since you cannot change the address of an object:

```
&x = 1000;   /* ILLEGAL */
```

3.12 Introduction to Pointers

In the previous example,

```
ptr = &j;
```

the variable *ptr* that holds the address of *j* in our first example cannot be a normal integer variable. To store addresses, you need a special type of variable called a *pointer* variable (by storing an address, it *points* to an object). To declare a *pointer* variable, you precede the variable name with an asterisk. The following declaration, for example, makes *ptr* a variable that can hold addresses of **long int** variables.

```
long *ptr;
```

The data type, **long** in this case, refers to the type of variable that *ptr* can point to. For instance, the following is legal:

```
long *ptr;
long long_var;
ptr = &long_var;   /*  Assign the address of
                    *  long_var to ptr.
                    */
```

But this is illegal:

```
long *ptr;
float float_var;
ptr = &float_var; /* ILLEGAL - because ptr can only
                   * store the address of a long int.
                   */
```

The following program illustrates the difference between a pointer variable and an integer variable:

```c
#include <stdio.h>

main()
{
  int j=1;
  int *pj;

  pj = &j;   /* Assign the address of j to pj */
  printf( "The value of j is: %d\n", j );
  printf( "The address of j is: %p\n", pj );
  exit( 0 );
}
```

The result is

```
The value of j is: 1
The address of j is: 3634264
```

3.12.1 Dereferencing a Pointer

The asterisk, in addition to being used in pointer declarations, is also used to *dereference* a pointer (i.e., get the value stored at the pointer address).   If you have not come across the concept before, the notion of dereferencing can be difficult to grasp at first.   The following program and Figure 3-2 show how dereferencing works.

```c
#include <stdio.h>

main()
{
  char *p_ch;
  char ch1 = 'A', ch2;

  printf( "The address of p_ch is %p\n", &p_ch );

  p_ch = &ch1;
  printf( "The value stored at p_ch is %p\n", p_ch );
  printf( "The dereferenced value of p_ch is %c\n",
          *p_ch );
  ch2 = *p_ch;

  exit( 0 );
}
```

The output from running this program is

```
The address of p_ch is 1004
The value stored at p_ch is 2001
The dereferenced value of p_ch is A
```

This is a roundabout and somewhat contrived example that assigns the character 'A' to both *ch1* and *ch2*. It does, however, illustrate the effect of the dereference (*) operator. Figure 3-2 shows the memory contents at each stage of the program execution. On our machine, the declarations allocate four bytes for *p_ch* (pointer variables must be large enough to hold the highest possible address in the machine so they are often the same size as **long int**s), and one byte each for *ch1* and *ch2*. *ch1* is initialized to 'A'. The first *printf()* call displays the address of the pointer variable *p_ch*. In the next step, *p_ch* is assigned the address of *ch1*, which is also displayed. Finally, we display the dereferenced value of *p_ch* and assign it to *ch2*.

These last steps are the important ones. The expression **p_ch* is interpreted as: "take the address value stored in *p_ch* and get the value stored at that address." This gives us a new way to look at the declaration. The data type in the pointer declaration indicates what type of value results when the pointer is dereferenced. For instance, the declaration

```
float *fp;
```

means that when ʌfp appears as an expression, the result will be a **float** value.

The expression **fp* can also appear on the left side of an expression:

```
*fp = 3.15;
```

In this case, we are storing a value (3.15) at the location designated by the pointer *fp*. Note that this is different from

```
fp = 3.15;
```

which attempts to store the address 3.15 in *fp*. This, by the way, is illegal since addresses are not the same as integers or floating-point values.

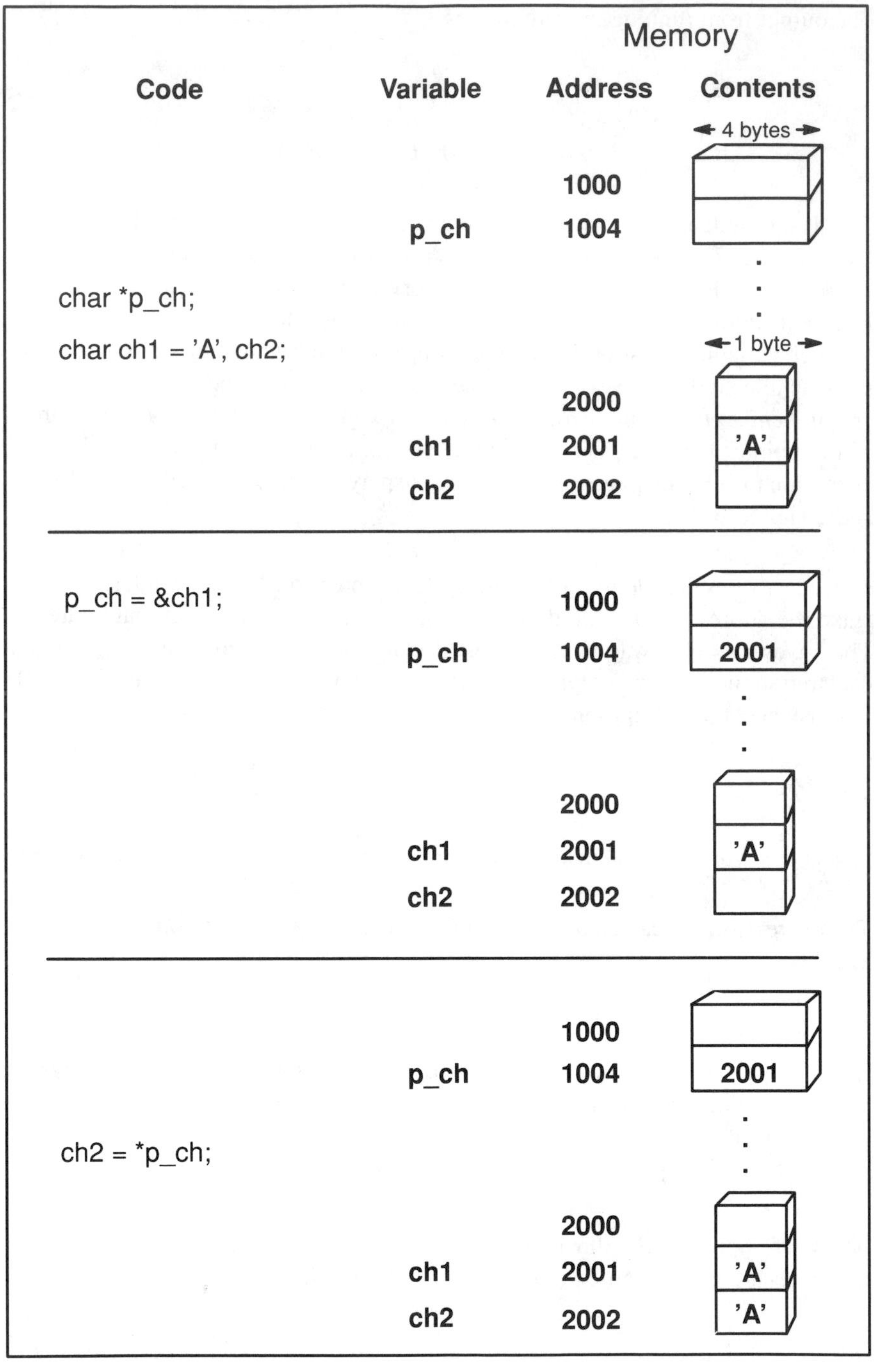

Memory

Code	Variable	Address	Contents

◄ 4 bytes ►

1000

p_ch   1004

char *p_ch;

char ch1 = 'A', ch2;   ◄ 1 byte ►

2000

ch1   2001   'A'

ch2   2002

---

p_ch = &ch1;   1000

p_ch   1004   2001

2000

ch1   2001   'A'

ch2   2002

1000

p_ch   1004   2001

ch2 = *p_ch;

2000

ch1   2001   'A'

ch2   2002   'A'

Figure 3-3. Dereferencing a Pointer Variable.

3.12.2 Initializing Pointers

You can initialize a pointer just as you would any other type of variable. However, the initialization value must be an address. For example, you could write

```
int j;
int *ptr_to_j = &j;
```

However, you cannot reference a variable before it is declared, so the following declarations would be illegal:

```
int *ptr_to_j = &j;
int j;
```

3.12.3 Using Pointers

Pointer variables are used frequently with aggregate types, such as arrays and structures. We have described them in this chapter because they are an important scalar data type with which you should become familiar. In later chapters, we describe the full flexibility and power of C pointers.

Exercises

1. When printing a **float** or **double** with the %f format specifier, how many decimal digits does *printf()* output? Does *printf()* round or truncate the value?

2. After reading the description of *printf()* in Appendix A, write a function that accepts a **double** argument and prints it out, but only prints three decimal digits.

3. Write a program with the following declarations in it that prints out the address of each variable.

```
char c;
int j;
float x;
```

What do the addresses tell you about the way your compiler allocates memory for variables?

4. Write the octal, decimal, and hexadecimal equivalents of the following binary numbers:

```
a)  00010010
b)  01100101
c)  01101011
d)  10111011    (assume two's complement notation)
e)  00111111
f)  00000100 01100100
```

5. Write declarations for the following:

   a) An unsigned long integer.
   b) A double-precision floating-point variable.
   c) A pointer to a **char**.
   d) A **char** initialized to 'x'.
   e) An external function returning an **unsigned int**.

6. Give the binary two's complement representation of the following:

    a)   1
    b)   −1
    c)   255
    d)   256
    e)   511
    f)   512
    g)   513
    h)   127
    i)   128
    j)   −128
    k)   0xFF
    l)   0x7F

7. Give the binary one's complement representation of the numbers listed in Exercise 6.

Chapter 4

Control Flow

"Begin at the beginning," the King said, very
gravely, "and go on till you come to the
end: then stop." — Lewis Carroll, <u>Alice in Wonderland</u>

The programs listed in the previous chapter were architecturally simple because they were *straight line* programs. That is, statements were executed in the order in which they appeared without any branching or repetition. Most programming problems are not so simple. In fact, the great power of programming languages stems from their ability to instruct the computer to perform the same task repeatedly, or to perform a different task if parameters change.   In high-level programming languages, this is accomplished with control flow statements that allow you to alter the sequential flow.   Control flow statements fall into two general categories: *conditional branching* and *looping*. Conditional branching is the ability to decide whether or not to execute code based on the value of an expression. Looping, also called *iteration*, is the ability to perform the same set of operations repeatedly until a special condition is met.

4.1 Conditional Branching

Conditional branching is the most basic control feature of any programming language. It enables a program to make decisions, to decide whether or not to execute a sequence of statements based on the value of an expression. Since the value of the expression may change from one execution to another, this feature allows a program to react dynamically to different data. In C, conditional execution is performed with the **if** and **else** keywords. The syntax is shown in Figure 4-1.

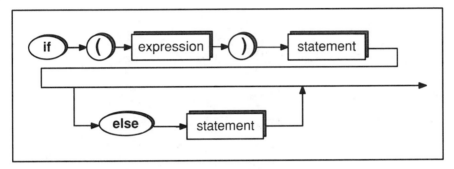

Figure 4-1. Syntax of an **if...else** *Statement.*

The form of an **if** statement is fairly simple. The **if** keyword is followed by an expression enclosed in parentheses. If the expression is "true" (nonzero), the next statement is executed. Otherwise, execution skips over the next statement:

```
if (x)
   statement1; /* Executed only if x is nonzero   */
statement2;    /* Always executed.                 */
```

If the **else** clause is present, the statement following the **else** keyword is executed whenever the **if** expression is "false" (zero):

```
if (x)
   statement1;   /* Executed only if x is nonzero */
else
   statement2;   /* Executed only if x is zero */
statement3;      /* Always executed */
```

This syntax mirrors the syntax we use in everyday language. For example, the sentence, "If the light is red, stop; otherwise, go" would be written in C as

```
if (light == red)
   stop;
else
   go;
```

Note that there is no **then** after the **if** as in other programming languages such as Pascal and FORTRAN.

A common use of the **if** statement is to test the validity of data. Suppose, for example, that you want a program that accepts an integer value from the user and prints the square root of the number. Before calling the *sqrt()* function, which is part of the runtime library, you should make sure that the input value is non-negative:

```
#include <stdio.h>
#include <math.h>    /* Include file for sqrt() */

main()
{
  double num;

  printf( "Enter a non-negative number: " );

/*  The %lf conversion specifier indicates a
 *  data object of type double.
 */
  scanf( "%lf", &num );
  if (num < 0)
    printf( "Input Error: Number is negative.\n" );
  else
    printf( "The square root is: %f\n", sqrt(num));
  exit( 0 );
}
```

Note that the **else** is necessary. If we write the program without the **else**, as shown on the next page, the program will print an error message when the input value is less than zero, but then go ahead and mistakenly try to print the square root.

```
#include <stdio.h>
#include <math.h>

main()
{
  double num;

  printf( "Enter a non-negative number: " );
  scanf( "%lf", &num );
  if (num < 0)
    printf( "Input Error: Number is negative.\n" );
/* Next statement is always executed. */
  printf( "The square root is: %f\n", sqrt( num ) );

  exit( 0 );
}
```

The indentations after **if** and **else** are included for readability, not for functionality. The program could be written

```
#include <stdio.h>
#include <math.h>
main(){double num;
printf("Enter a non-negative number:"
);scanf("%lf", &num);
if (num <
0) printf("Input Error: Number is negative.\n");
else printf("The square root is: %f\n",
sqrt(num)); exit(0);
}
```

Although this program will run correctly, it reflects poor programming style since it is difficult to read. The normal convention is to put the statement following an **if** or **else** on its own indented line. In this book, we always indent two spaces at a time, although some people prefer to indent 3, 4, or even 8 spaces at a time.

4.1.1 Comparison Expressions

Typically, the conditional expression in an **if** statement is a comparison between two values. Altogether, there are six *comparison operators* (sometimes called *relational operators*), as shown in Table 4-1.

<	less than
>	greater than
<=	less than or equal to
>=	greater than or equal to
==	equal to
!=	not equal to

Table 4-1. Relational Operators.

Note especially that the "equal to" comparison operator consists of *two* equal signs. One of the most common mistakes made by beginners and experts alike is to confuse the *equal to* (==) operator with the assignment operator (=). (See Box 4-1 for a discussion of when this confusion is particularly dangerous.)

Relational expressions are often called *Boolean expressions,* in recognition of the nineteenth century mathematician and logician George Boole. Boole reduced logic to a propositional calculus involving only true and false values.

Many programming languages, such as Pascal, have Boolean data types for representing TRUE and FALSE. The C language, however, represents these values with integers. Zero is equivalent to FALSE, and any nonzero value is considered TRUE.

Like the arithmetic operators described in Chapter 3, the relational operators are *binary operators*. The value of a relational expression is an integer, either 1 (indicating the expression is *true*) or 0 (indicating the expression is *false*). The examples in Table 4-2 illustrate how relational expressions are evaluated.

Expression	Value
−1 < 0	1
0 > 1	0
0 == 0	1
1 != −1	1
1 >= −1	1
1 >10	0

Table 4-2. Relational Expressions.

Because Boolean values are represented as integers, it is perfectly legal to write

```
if (j)
    statement;
```

Box 4-1: Bug Alert — Confusing = with ==

One of the most common mistakes made by beginners and experts alike is to use the assignment operator (=) instead of the equality operator (==). For instance,

```
if (j = 5)
   do_something();
```

What is intended, clearly, is that the *do_something()* function should only be invoked if *j* equals five. It should been written

```
if (j == 5)
   do_something();
```

Note that the first version is syntactically legal since all expressions have a value. The value of the expression *j = 5* is 5. Since this is a nonzero value the **if** expression will always evaluate to true and *do_something()* will always be invoked. There are a few C compilers on the market that are able to recognize this bug and issue a warning message.

If *j* is any nonzero value, *statement* is executed; if *j* equals zero, *statement* is skipped. This aspect of the language creates some interesting possibilities. Suppose, for instance, that you want to write a program that reads a character and prints it out if it is a letter of the alphabet, but ignores it if it is not an alphabetic character. Recalling that the runtime library function *isalpha()* returns a nonzero value if its argument is a letter, you could write a program that checks whether the input is an alphabetic character, as shown below.

```
#include <stdio.h>
#include <ctype.h>   /* included for isalpha() */

main()
{
  char ch;

  printf( "Enter a character: " );
  scanf( "%c", &ch );
  if (isalpha( ch ))
    printf( "%c", ch );
  else
   printf( "%c is not an alphabetic character.\n",
         ch );
  exit( 0 );
}
```

Note that the statement

```
if (isalpha( ch ))
```

is exactly the same as

```
if (isalpha( ch ) != 0)
```

The practice of using a function call as a conditional expression is a common idiom in C. It is especially effective for functions that return zero if an error occurs, since you can use a construct such as

```
if (func())
  proceed;
else
  error handler;
```

4.1.2 Compound Statements

Any statement can be replaced by a block of statements, sometimes called a *compound statement*. A compound statement must begin with a left brace { and end with a right brace }. A function body, therefore, is really just a compound statement. Compound statements are particularly useful when used with flow control statements because they allow you to execute a group of statements rather than a single statement. To conditionally execute more than one statement, therefore, surround the group of statements with left and right braces, as shown in the following example:

```c
#include <stdio.h>

main()
{
  double num;

  printf( "Enter a non-negative number: " );
  scanf( "%lf", &num );
  if (num < 0)
    printf( "That's not a non-negative number!\n" );
  else
  {
    printf( "%f squared is: %f\n", num, num^num );
    printf( "%f cubed is: %f\n", num, num*num*num );
  }
  exit( 0 );
}
```

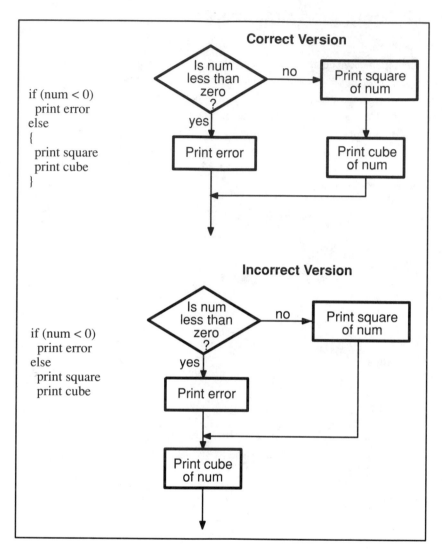

Figure 4-2. Braces Ensure Correct Control Flow.

Box 4-2: Bug Alert — Missing Braces

If we remove the braces after the **else** phrase in the example in Section
4.1.2, the program takes on a different meaning, although it is still a syntactically legal program.

```
#include <stdio.h>

main()
{
  double num;

  printf("Enter a non-negative number: ");
  scanf( "%lf", &num );
  if (num < 0)
   printf("That's not a non-negative number\n");
  else
   printf("%f squared is: %d\n", num, num*num);
   printf("%f cubed is: %d\n", num,num*num*num);
  exit( 0 );
}
```

The indentation is misleading here because it implies that both the square
and the cube of *num* will be printed if, and only if, *num* is not less than
zero. Actually, though, only the first statement after the **else** is part of the
flow-control logic. The other *printf()* statement is always executed, regardless of *num*'s value. Figure 4-2 shows the logic of the two versions.

This example illustrates the important point that *the compiler is oblivious
to formatting*. The compiler recognizes syntax, such as spelling and
punctuation, but it completely ignores indentations, comments, and other
formatting aids. The formatting is entirely for humans.

4.1.3 Nested *if* Statements

A single **if** statement enables the program to choose one of two paths. Frequently, however, you need to specify subsequent branching. After making decision 1,
you need to make decision 2, then decision 3, etc. This type of program flow
requires a construct called a *nested* **if** statement. Suppose, for example, that you
want to write a function that accepts three integers, and returns the one that has
the smallest value. Using nested **if** statements, you could write the function
shown in Figure 4-3.

The **else** phrases, except for the last one, are all necessary to provide correct
conditional execution. It is a worthwhile exercise to draw a program flow
diagram with the **else** phrases omitted. Note that when an **else** is immediately
followed by an **if**, they are usually placed on the same line. This is commonly
called an **else if** statement, although it is really an **if** statement nested within an
else phrase.

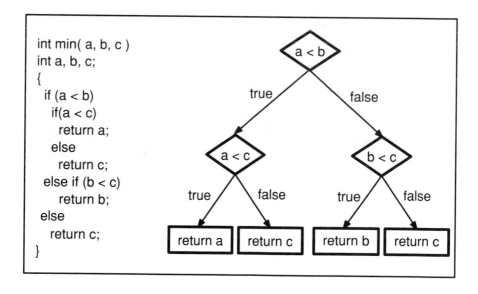

Figure 4-3. Logic of a Nested **if** *Statement.*

Box 4-3: Bug Alert — The Dangling else

Nested **if** statements create the problem of matching each **else** phrase to the right **if** statement. This is often called the *dangling* **else** problem. In the *min()* function, for example, note that the first **else** is associated with the second **if**. The general rule is

*An **else** is always associated with the nearest previous **if**.*

Each **if** statement, however, can have only one **else** phrase. The next **else** phrase in *min()*, therefore, corresponds to the first **if** because the second **if** has already been matched up. The final **else** phrase corresponds to the third **if** statement (which is written as an **else if**).

It is important to format nested **if**s correctly to avoid confusion. An **else** phrase should always be at the same indentation level as its associated **if**.

4.2 The *switch* Statement

When there are many paths in a program, **if-else** branching can become so convoluted that it is difficult to follow. These situations are usually prime candidates for use of the **switch** statement. The **switch** statement allows you to specify an unlimited number of execution paths based on the value of a single expression. For example, the following function has five branches based on the value of *input_arg*.

```
int switch_example( input_arg )
char input_arg;
{
  switch ( input_arg )
  {
    case 'A':   return 1;
    case 'B':   return 2;
    case 'C':   return 3;
    case 'D':   return 4;
    default :   return -1;
  }
}
```

The function returns 1, 2, 3, or 4 depending on whether *input_arg* is 'A', 'B', 'C', or 'D', respectively. If *input_arg* is anything else, the function returns –1. The same function can be written using **if**s and **else**s:

```
int switch_example( input_arg )
char input_arg;
{
  if (input_arg == 'A')
    return 1;
  else if (input_arg == 'B')
    return 2;
  else if (input_arg == 'C')
    return 3;
  else if (input_arg == 'D')
    return 4;
  else
    return -1;
}
```

Note that we line up all the **else if** statements at the same indentation level to emphasize that it is a multibranching construct. Even with this formatting, though, the version using **switch** is considerably more readable. In addition, **switch** statements often result in more efficient machine code.

4.2.1 Syntax of a *switch* Statement

The formal syntax of a **switch** statement is shown in Figure 4-4. The expression immediately after the **switch** keyword must be enclosed in parentheses and must be an integral expression. That is, it can be **char**, **short**, **int**, or **long**, but not **float**, **double**, or **long double**. (Note: the K&R standard requires the expression to be of type **int**.) The expressions following the **case** keywords must be integral constant expressions, meaning they may not contain variables.

The semantics of the **switch** statement are straightforward. The **switch** expression is evaluated, and if it matches one of the **case** labels, program flow continues with the statement that follows the matching **case** label. If none of the **case** labels match the **switch** expression, program flow continues at the **default** label, if it exists. (Strictly speaking, the **default** label need not be the last label, though it is good style to put it last.) No two **case** labels may have the same value.

An important feature of the **switch** statement is that program flow continues
from the selected case label until another control flow statement is encountered
or the end of the **switch** statement is reached. That is, the compiler executes any
statements following the selected **case** label until a **break, goto,** or **return**
statement appears. The **break** statement explicitly exits the **switch** construct,
passing control to the statement following the **switch** statement. Since this is
usually what you want, you should almost always include a **break** statement at
the end of the statement list following each **case** label.

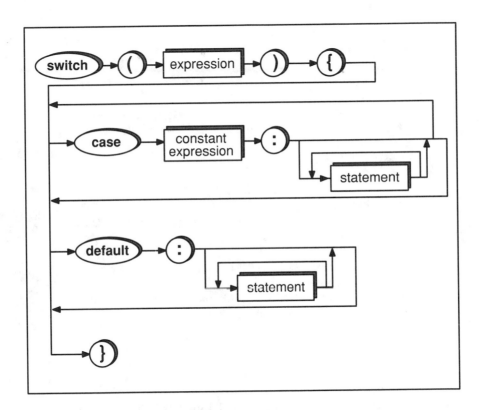

Figure 4-4. Syntax of a **switch** *Statement.*

The *print_error()* function shown on the following page, for example, prints an
error message based on an error code passed to it.

```
/*   Prints error message based on error_code.
 *   Function is declared with void because it
 *   doesn't return anything.
 */

#include <stdio.h>
#define ERR_INPUT_VAL 1
#define ERR_OPERAND 2
#define ERR_OPERATOR 3
#define ERR_TYPE 4

void print_error( error_code )
int error_code;
{
  switch (error_code)
  {
    case   ERR_INPUT_VAL:
            printf("Error: Illegal input value.\n");
            break;
    case   ERR_OPERAND:
            printf("Error: Illegal operand.\n");
            break;
    case   ERR_OPERATOR:
            printf("Error: Unknown operator.\n");
            break;
    case   ERR_TYPE:
            printf("Error: Incompatible data.\n");
            break;
    default: printf("Error: Unknown error code %d\n",
                    error_code);
            break;
  }
}
```

The **break** statements are necessary to prevent the function from printing more than one error message. The last **break** after the default case isn't really necessary, but it is a good idea to include it anyway for consistency's sake. If, at some later date, you change **default** to a specific case and add other cases below it, you needn't worry about forgetting to include the **break**.

We could write a superior version of the *print_error()* function by using enumeration constants instead of **#define**d constants. The declaration of *error_code* would be

```
typedef enum {
  ERR_INPUT_VAL,
  ERR_OPERAND,
  ERR_OPERATOR,
  ERR_TYPE
} ERROR_SET;

ERROR_SET error_code;
```

The typedef declaration makes *ERROR_SET* a synonym for the declaration of enumeration constants. If we want to add new error codes, we need merely invent a new name and add it to the list. The enum declaration ensures that each name will be given a unique value. Moreover, a quality compiler will perform type consistency checking to ensure that you use *error_code* in a meaningful way. Note also that the name *ERROR_SET* is much more descriptive than **int**. Typically, the typedef declaration would be placed in a header file where it can be accessed by other source files.

Sometimes you want to associate a group of statements with more than one case value. To obtain this behavior, you can enter consecutive case labels. The following function, for instance, returns 1 if the argument is a punctuation character, or zero if it is anything else.

```
/*  This function returns 1 if the argument is a
 *  punctuation character.  Otherwise, it returns
 *  zero.
 */

is_punc( arg )
char arg;
{
  switch (arg)
  {
    case '.':
    case ',':
    case ':':
    case ';':
    case '!':  return 1;
    default :  return 0;
  }
}
```

As a more practical example of the **switch** statement, consider the following function which accepts three arguments—two operands and an operator—and returns the value of the binary expression. Later, we'll use this function as part of a calculator program that performs simple arithmetic on expressions entered from the terminal.

```
/*  This function evaluates an expression, given
 *  the two operands and the operator.
 */
#include "err.h" /*  contains the typedef
                  *  declaration of ERR_CODE.
                  */
double evaluate( op1, operator, op2 )
double op1, op2;
char operator;
{
  extern void print_error();

  switch(operator)
  {
    case '+':  return op1 + op2;
    case '-':  return op1 - op2;
    case '*':  return op1 * op2;
    case '/':  return op1 / op2;
    default :  /* Illegal operator */
               print_error( ERR_OPERATOR );
               exit( 1 );
  }
}
```

Note that we use the *print_error()* function listed previously if the second argument is not one of the four operators. The *exit()* function, described in Appendix A, is a library function that exits the current program and returns control to the operating system. You should always have a normal *exit()* (argument equal to zero) in your *main()* function. In addition, *exit()* is useful in situations such as this one where it is difficult to recover from an error. In this case, we return a non-zero value to indicate an abnormal exit. How the operating system reacts to different values returned from *exit()* varies from one implementation to another.

4.3 Looping

Looping, or *iteration*, directs the computer to perform the same set of operations over and over until a specified condition is met. The C language contains three statements for looping:

- The **while** statement

- The **do...while** statement

- The **for** statement

The following sections describe each in detail.

4.3.1 The *while* Statement

The syntax of a **while** statement is shown in Figure 4-5. The semantics are as follows. First, the *expression* is evaluated. If it is a nonzero value (i.e., true), *statement* is executed. After *statement* is executed, program control returns to the top of the **while** statement, and the process is repeated. This continues indefinitely until the expression evaluates to zero (false), at which time program flow jumps to the point immediately following *statement*. The statement, which is often a compound statement, is called the *body*.

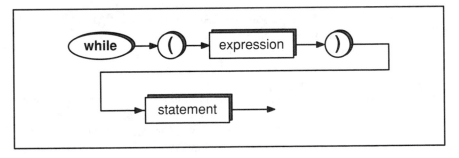

*Figure 4-5. Syntax of a **while** Statement.*

Figure 4-6 shows the flow of control for a simple **while** statement. So long as *x* is less than *y*, the program continues to execute the **while** loop. With each pass through the loop, however, *x* is incremented by one. When it is no longer less than *y*, control flows to the next statement.

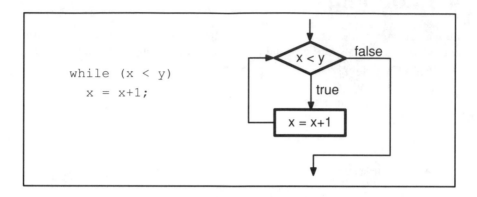

*Figure 4-6. Flow Control of a **while** Statement.*

Because the incrementing operation occurs so frequently, the C language has a special increment operator called **++**. The **while** statement shown above, for example, would normally be written

```
while (x < y)
   x++;
```

The **++** operator is described in more detail in the next chapter.

As an example of using the **while** statement, suppose you want to read characters from the terminal. The *scanf()* statement is one way to read data, but it requires that you know what type of data is being entered so you can use the correct format specifier. To read data when you don't know the data type, you can use the *getchar()* function, which reads a single character from your terminal and returns it as an **int**. Repeated calls to *getchar()* enable you to read a string of characters, one at a time. When *getchar()* reaches the end of the input, it returns a special value called *EOF*. *EOF* is a constant name defined in the header file *<stdio.h>*. Its value is –1 for many implementations, but you should always use the macro name itself rather than the constant in case an implementation uses a different value.

The following program combines *getchar()* and the **while** statement to read a string of characters from the terminal and count the number of spaces. The loop terminates when the *getchar()* function reads a newline, represented by the **\n** escape sequence.

```
#include <stdio.h>

main()
{
  int ch, num_of_spaces = 0;

  printf( "Enter a sentence:\n" );

  ch = getchar();
  while (ch != '\n')
  {
    if (ch == ' ')
      num_of_spaces++;
    ch = getchar();
  }
  printf( "The number of spaces is %d.\n",
          num_of_spaces );
  exit( 0 );
}
```

Note that we make an assignment to *ch* before entering the **while** loop. This is to ensure that its initial value, which would otherwise be random, is not accidentally a space or newline character. Note also that the statement part of the **while** loop is actually a compound statement. A typical execution of the program would be

```
Enter a sentence:
```
How many spaces does this sentence have?
```
The number of spaces is 6.
```

Note, however, that the program does not analyze your input until you press the newline or RETURN key. This is because computers employ a temporary storage area called a *buffer* for keyboard input. This allows you to edit your input before it is processed. Once you enter a newline character, the computer sends the entire buffer to the executing program. The *getchar()* function then reads the buffer one character at a time. Chapter 11 describes buffers and I/O in more detail.

4.3.2 The *do...while* Statement

One important characteristic of the **while** statement is that the test condition is at the top of the loop. This means that if the condition is false (or zero) the first time, the **while** body will never be executed. But there are certain situations where you need to execute the body at least once. These situations are not common, but when they do occur, you should use the **do...while** statement,

which has the form shown in Figure 4-7. The only difference between a
do...while and a regular **while** loop is that the test condition is at the bottom of
the loop. This means that the program always executes *statement* at least once
(the first time through). Then, depending on the value of *expression*, it may loop
back to **do**, or it may continue with the next statement.

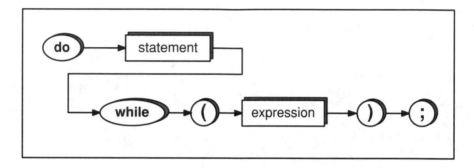

*Figure 4-7. Syntax of a **do...while** Statement.*

Using **do...while** instead of **while**, the previous program would be written

```
#include <stdio.h>

main()
{
  int ch, num_of_spaces = 0;

  printf( "Enter a sentence:\n" );
  do
  {
    ch = getchar();
    if (ch == ' ')
      num_of_spaces++;
  } while (ch != '\n');

  printf( "The number of spaces is %d.\n",
          num_of_spaces );
  exit( 0 );
}
```

Note that in this version it is not necessary to include the initial assignment of *ch*
because the **do...while** statement guarantees that at least the first character will
be fetched.

4.3.3 The *for* Statement

The last, but certainly not the least, of the iterative statements is the **for** statement. The **for** statement is designed as a shorthand for a particularly common looping situation—when you need to initialize one or more variables before entering the loop, and you need to change the value of one or more variables each time through the loop. The syntax of a **for** statement is shown in Figure 4-8.

The **for** statement operates as follows:

1. First, *expression1* is evaluated. This is usually an assignment expression that initializes one or more variables.

2. Then *expression2* is evaluated. This is the conditional part of the statement.

3. If *expression2* is false, program control exits the **for** statement and flows to the next statement in the program. If *expression2* is true, *statement* is executed.

4. After *statement* is executed, *expression3* is evaluated. Then the statement loops back to test *expression2* again.

Note that *expression1* is evaluated only once, whereas *expression2* and *expression3* are evaluated on each iteration.

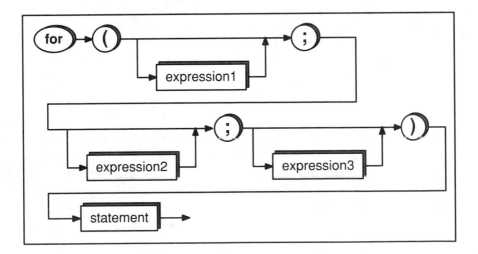

Figure 4-8. Syntax of a **for** *Statement.*

The easiest way to understand the **for** statement is to compare it to a **while** statement, as shown below. The statement

```
for  (expr1; expr2; expr3)
    statement;
```

is the same as

```
expr1;
while ( expr2 )
{
  statement;
  expr3;
}
```

Though difficult to grasp at first, the **for** statement is probably the most frequently used of all the iterative statements. An example should make its operation clearer. The following function returns the factorial of its argument:

```
long int factorial( val )
int val;
{
  int j, fact = 1;

  for (j=2; j <= val; j++)
    fact = fact*j;
  return fact;
}
```

If you're having trouble understanding how this function works, try rewriting it using a **while** statement in place of the **for** statement. As another example, consider the following function, which converts a string of digits typed from the keyboard into an integer.

```
/*  This function reads a string of digits from
 *  the terminal and produces the string's integer
 *  value.
 */

#include <stdio.h>
#include <ctype.h>

int make_int()
{
  int num=0, digit;

  digit = getchar();
  for ( ; isdigit( digit ); digit = getchar())
  {
    num = num * 10;
    num = num + (digit - '0');
  }
  return num;
}
```

The expression

```
digit - '0'
```

converts the character from its code to its real numeric value. Note that it only works if the codes for zero through ten are continuous and ascending. Fortunately, this is the case with all the common codes, including ASCII and EBCDIC. In ASCII, for instance, the decimal code for '5' is 53 and the code for '0' is 48. So, if *digit* is '5', the expression

```
digit - '0'
```

evaluates to

```
53 - 48
```

which is 5.

Another way to write this function, using **while** instead of **for**, would be

```c
#include <stdio.h>
#include <ctype.h>

int make_int()
{
    int num=0, digit;

    digit = getchar();
    while (isdigit( digit ))
    {
        num = num * 10;
        num = num + digit - '0';
        digit = getchar();
    }
    return num;
}
```

From a software engineering standpoint, the **for** version has the advantage that the operation performed after each loop—getting the next character—is right in the looping statement itself, clearly visible. For a short program such as this one, it probably doesn't make much difference. But for large programs, where the loop may contain a page or more of source code, the **for** statement makes it easy to find out which variable is changing with each iteration.

In both versions, we call *getchar()* twice, which is unfortunate. If we want to change the *getchar()* call to a different function call, we need to change both occurrences. Yet another way to write this function, which is superior to both of the previous versions, takes advantage of the fact that an assignment expression yields a value. In this version, shown on the following page, we call *getchar()* only once.

```
#include <stdio.h>
#include <ctype.h>

int make_int()
{
   int num=0, digit;

   while (isdigit( digit = getchar() ))
   {
      num = num * 10;
      num = num + (digit - '0');
   }
   return num;
}
```

The assignment to *digit* and the test of *digit* are combined in a single expression. This is probably the simplest version, and the way most experienced C programmers would write the loop. Later in this chapter, we'll return to this function and revise it so that we can use it in a calculator program.

4.3.4 Omitting Expressions

Note from the syntax diagram (Figure 4-8) that it is legal to omit any or all of the three expressions in a **for** statement. However, you must include the two semicolons. In practice, it is common to omit *expression1* or *expression3*, but *expression2* is almost always included since it is the test condition. Also, there is usually no reason to omit *both expression1* and *expression3* since that would result in the same functionality as a **while** statement. The following function, which prints a specified number of newlines, does not use *expression1* since there is no need to make assignments before the loop is entered. The only variable, *newline_num*, gets its value from the calling function.

```
#include <stdio.h>

void pr_newline( newline_num )
int newline_num;
{
   for (; newline_num > 0; newline_num--)
      printf( "\n" );
}
```

Note that "—" is analogous to "++". The expression,

```
newline_num--
```

is equivalent to:

```
newline_num = newline_num - 1
```

Box 4-4: Bug Alert — Off-by-One Errors

A common programming error is to iterate through a loop the wrong number of times. Usually, when you're off, you're off by one because you have used the wrong relational operator (e.g., < instead of <=). Off-by-one errors are especially pernicious because they usually do not produce a compile-time or runtime error. Instead, the program runs smoothly but produces erroneous results. For example, the following function attempts to compute the factorial of its argument:

```
long factorial( arg )
long arg;
{
  long fact = 1, j;

  for (j=1; j < arg; j++)
    fact = fact * j;
  return fact;
}
```

This function actually returns the factorial of *arg–1* because the conditional expression is

```
j < arg
```

instead of

```
j <= arg
```

The best way to avoid off-by-one errors is to think through the problem clearly and determine exactly when the loop will terminate. Also, after writing a function like *factorial( )*, you should test it with known values to make sure it works. This is another reason for keeping functions small— the smaller they are, the easier they are to test.

4.3.5 Null Statements

Just as it is possible to omit one of the expressions in a **for** loop, it is also possible to omit the body of the **for** loop. This is useful when the loop's work is being performed by the expressions. For example, the following function reads spaces from the terminal and discards them. A space is defined by the runtime library *isspace()* function as space characters, tabs, and newlines.

```
#include <stdio.h>
#include <ctype.h> /* Header file for isspace(). */

void skip_spaces()
{
   int c;

   for (c = getchar(); isspace( c ); c = getchar())
      ;   /* Null Statement */
   ungetc( c, stdin );   /*   Put the nonspace
                          *   character back in the
                          *   buffer.
                          */
}
```

The *ungetc()* function is a library function that places a character in the input buffer. It takes two arguments. The first is the character to be replaced, and the second is the stream in which it is to be deposited. The macro name *stdin* is defined in *<stdio.h>* and represents the standard input stream, usually your terminal. The *ungetc()* function is particularly useful in situations like this one where it is necessary to read one more character than you want to process. In the case of *skip_spaces()*, for example, it is necessary to read the first nonspace character to know where the spaces end. The *ungetc()* function places this nonspace character back in the input buffer so that it is the character read by the next *getchar()* call.

There is no need for a statement in the **for** loop, so we use a *null statement*, which is just a lone semicolon. It is a good idea to put the semicolon on a separate line to make it more visible since it is potentially misleading. For example, if we place the semicolon on the same line, as shown below, a casual reader might assume that the *ungetc()* function is the body of the **for** loop.

```
#include <stdio.h>

void skip_spaces()
{
   int c;
   for (c = getchar(); isspace( c ); c = getchar());
     ungetc( c,stdin );
}
```

This program can also be written using a **while** loop instead of a **for** loop:

```
#include <stdio.h>

void skip_spaces()
{
   while (isspace( c = getchar() ))
     ;   /* Null Statement */
   ungetc( c,stdin );
}
```

In this version, the argument to *isspace()* is the expression

```
c = getchar()
```

Box 4-5: Bug Alert — Misplaced Semicolons

A common programming mistake is to place a semicolon immediately after a control flow statement—for instance, writing

```
if (j == 1);
   j = 0;
```

instead of

```
if (j == 1)
   j = 0;
```

Placing a semicolon after the test condition causes the compiler to execute a null statement whenever the **if** expression is true. It is as if you had written

```
if (j == 1)
   ;   /* null statement */
j = 0;
```

As a result, *j* gets assigned zero regardless of whether *j* equals one. Note that the null statement is syntactically legal, so the misplaced semicolon does not cause a compiler error.

So *c* is first assigned the value of the next input character, and then *c* is passed as an argument to *isspace()*. If *c* is a space, *isspace()* returns a nonzero value making the loop condition true. The body of the loop, however, is a null statement, so control returns to the top of the loop where the process is repeated. When *c* is not a space, *isspace()* returns zero, making the test condition false, and program control flows to the *ungetc()* call.

4.4 Nested Loops

Just as it is possible to nest **if** statements to any depth, it is also possible to nest looping statements. The key point to remember with nested loops is that the inner loops must finish before the outer loops can resume iterating. Consider the following program which prints a multiplication table up to 10. (The \t format is a special escape sequence that causes the computer to print a tab.)

```
#include <stdio.h>

/* print a multiplication table using nested loops
*/

main()

{
   int j, k;
   printf("    1  2  3  4  5  6  7  8  9  10\n");
   printf("    --------------------------------\n");
   for (j = 1; j <= 10; j++)   /* outer loop */
   {
      printf( "%5d|", j );
      for (k=1; k <= 10; k++)   /* inner loop */
         printf( "%5%d", j*k );
      printf( "\n" );
   }
   exit( 0 );
}
```

The output would be

```
        1    2    3    4    5    6    7    8    9   10
   ----------------------------------------------------
  1|     1    2    3    4    5    6    7    8    9   10
  2|     2    4    6    8   10   12   14   16   18   20
  3|     3    6    9   12   15   18   21   24   27   30
  4|     4    8   12   16   20   24   28   32   26   40
  5|     5   10   15   20   25   30   35   40   45   50
  6|     6   12   18   24   30   36   42   48   54   60
  7|     7   14   21   28   35   42   49   56   63   70
  8|     8   16   24   32   40   48   54   64   72   80
  9|     9   18   27   36   45   54   63   72   81   90
 10|    10   20   30   40   50   60   70   80   90  100
```

For each value of j, the program first prints j, then loops through ten values of k, printing $j*k$ for each iteration, and then prints a newline. Proper indentation becomes especially important with nested loops. The indentation in our program, for example, makes it readily apparent that the statement

```
        printf( "%5d", j*k );
```

belongs to the innermost **for** loop. The **%5d** conversion specifier forces *printf()* to output 5 characters for each number. If the number requires fewer characters, it is preceded with padding spaces. See Appendix A for more information about *printf()*.

The following example is a variation on the *make_int()* function. This new function, however, is capable of parsing floating-point values as well as integers. It utilizes many of the constructs we have discussed, including nested loops. Note that the **for** loop is nested in a **while** loop, which is itself nested within an **if** statement.

```c
#include <stdio.h>
#include <ctype.h>

#define DECIMAL_POINT '.'

double parse_num()
{
  int c, j, digit_count = 0;
  double value = 0, fractional_digit;

  while (isdigit( c = getchar()) )
  {
    value = value * 10;
    value = value + (c - '0');
  }

/*  When c is not a digit, test to see if it is a
 *  decimal point.
 */
  if (c == DECIMAL_POINT) /* if yes, get
                           * fraction
                           */
    while (isdigit( c = getchar() ))
    {
      digit_count++;
      fractional_digit = c - '0';
      for (j=0; j < digit_count; j++)
        fract_digit = fractional_digit/10;
      value = value + fractional_digit;
    }
  ungetc( c, stdin );
  return value;
}
```

4.5 A Simple Calculator Program

Using the functions from this chapter and Chapter 3, we can write a simple calculator program, as shown below.

```
#include <stdio.h>

main()
{
  extern double parse_num(), evaluate();
  extern void skip_spaces();
  double op1, op2, answer;
  int operator;

  printf( "Enter <number> <op> <number><newline>: " );
  skip_spaces();
  op1 = parse_num();
  skip_spaces();
  operator = getchar();
  skip_spaces();
  op2 = parse_num();
  answer = evaluate( op1, operator, op2 );
  printf( "%f\n", answer );
  exit( 0 );
}
```

When executed, this program enables you to type a simple arithmetic expression which is then calculated. For example,

```
Enter <number> <op> <number><newline>: 3.1*2
6.2
```

The *skip_spaces()* function allows you to enter any number of spaces between the operands and operator. Note, however, that the program cannot handle complicated expressions, such as,

```
3*(2.3+4.5)/8.1
```

In Chapter 12, we expand the program so that it can handle complex expressions such as this one.

It is worth noting that *scanf()* has the *parse_num()* and *skip_spaces()* functionality built into it. So you could rewrite the preceding program more simply, as follows. (The **%lf** format specifier indicates a **double** variable.)

```
#include <ctype.h>
#include <stdio.h>

main()
{
  double op1, op2, answer, evaluate();
  char operator;

  printf( "Enter <number> <op> <number><newline>: ");
  scanf( "%lf %c %lf", &op1, &operator, &op2 );
  answer = evaluate( op1, operator, op2 );
  printf( "%f\n", answer );
  exit( 0 );
}
```

We can make the program even more efficient by passing the result of *evaluate()* directly to *printf()*, without storing it in the variable *answer:*

```
#include <ctype.h>
#include <stdio.h>

main()
{
  double op1, op2, evaluate();
  char operator;

  printf( "Enter <number> <op> <number><newline>: ");
  scanf( "%lf %c %lf", &op1, &operator, &op2 );
  printf( "%f\n", evaluate( op1, operator, op2 ) );
  exit( 0 );
}
```

4.6 The *break* and *continue* Statements

You have already seen the **break** statement in connection with the **switch** statement. In that context, it prevents program flow from falling through to the next case value. Another way of looking at it is that the **break** statement prematurely terminates the **switch** statement, causing program control to flow to the next statement after the **switch**. This is also **break**'s purpose when used within a looping statement.

Suppose you want to process 50 characters or an entire line, whichever comes first. You could write

```
for (cnt = 0; cnt < 50; cnt++)
{
  c = getchar();
  if (c == '\n')
    break;
  else
    /*  process character */
          .

          .

          .

}
/* program continues here after break statement */
```

As soon as a newline character is encountered, the **break** statement is executed, and program control flows to the statement following the **for** loop. Otherwise, the loop iterates until *cnt* equals 50.

break statements should be used with caution since they force program control to jump discontinuously to a new place. Too many **break** statements can make a program difficult to follow. There is usually another way to write the code without using **break**. We talk more about some of these methods in the following chapter. There is, however, no equally good substitute for using the **break** statement in a **switch** construct.

The **continue** statement provides a means for returning to the top of a loop earlier than normal. It is particularly useful when you want to bypass the remainder of the loop for some reason. Suppose you want to modify the *make_int()* function so that it skips nondigit characters, as shown on the following page. If the input is A3b–45C, for example, the function would return 345.

```
#include <stdio.h>
#include <ctype.h>

int mod_make_int ()
{
  int num = 0, digit;

  while ((digit = getchar()) != '\n')
  {
    if (isdigit( digit ) == 0)
      continue;
    num = num * 10;
    num = num + (digit - '0');
  }
  return num;
}
```

The **if** statement checks to see whether *digit* is in fact a digit. If it isn't, the **continue** statement is executed. This returns the program to the top of the **while** loop, where it reads in the next character.

As with **break** statements, **continue** statements should be used judiciously since they break up the natural control flow. However, they are much preferred over **goto** statements.

4.7 The *goto* Statement

Few programming statements have produced as much debate as the **goto** statement. The **goto** statement is necessary in more rudimentary languages, but its use in high-level languages is generally frowned upon. Nevertheless, most high-level programming languages, including C, contain a **goto** statement for those rare situations where it can't be avoided.

The purpose of the **goto** statement is to enable program control to jump (or perhaps leap) to some other spot. The destination spot is identified by a *statement label*, which is just a name followed by a colon. The label must be in the same function as the **goto** statement that references it. The program on the following page illustrates how the **goto** statement works.

```
#include <stdio.h>
#include <math.h>   /* for sqrt() function */

main()
{
  int num;

  scanf( "%d", &num );
  if (num < 0)
    goto bad_val;
  else
  {
    printf( "The square root of num is %f",
            sqrt( num ) );
    goto end;
  }

bad_val: printf( "Error: Negative Value.\n" );
         exit( 1 );
end: exit( 0 );
}
```

As with most usages of **goto**, this program can be written in a much better fashion without using **goto** (see the version at the beginning of this chapter). It is difficult, in fact, to describe any general conditions where a **goto** statement should be used. There are, however, specific instances where a **goto** statement makes the code more efficient or enhances readability. For a full discussion of these cases, we recommend the 1968 paper by E. W. Dijkstra, entitled *Goto Statement Considered Harmful*. In general, you should not use **goto**s unless you have a very good reason for doing so.

4.8 Infinite Loops

An infinite loop is a loop that does not contain a terminating condition or a loop in which the terminating condition is never reached. In most instances, infinite loops are produced by bugs in the program. For example,

```
for (j=0; j < 10; j++)
{
     .

     .
  j = 1;
}
```

This loop will never finish because *j* is reassigned the value on each iteration.

On the other hand, there are certain situations where you *want* an infinite loop. There are a number of ways to write infinite loops, but the two most common are

```
while (1)
    statement;
```

and

```
for (;;)
    statement;
```

Both statements have equivalent functionality, so the choice is a matter of aesthetics. To get out of an infinite loop, you need to abort the program manually. Sometimes this is what you want. For example, we can rewrite the calculator program with an infinite loop:

```
#include <ctype.h>
#include <stdio.h>

main()
{
   double op1, op2, answer, evaluate();
   char operator;

   while(1)
   {
     printf( "Enter <number> <op> <number>\
<newline>: ");
     scanf( "%lf %c %lf", &op1, &operator, &op2 );
     answer = evaluate( op1, operator, op2 );
     printf( "%f\n", answer );
   }
}
```

The *while(1)* loop causes the program to run continuously until you abort it. On most systems, you can abort a program by typing CTRL-C.

Exercises

1. Every computer is limited in the amount of precision it can represent for floating-point numbers. At some point, where *epsilon* is very small, the following expression will be *true*:

```
1.0 == 1.0 + epsilon
```

Write a program to find the largest value of *epsilon* on your computer. Note that the value of *epsilon* may be different for **float**s and **double**s. Find both values (and the value for **long double**s if your compiler supports them). Also, use 1.0 not 0.0 to test *epsilon* because most computers have special hardware instructions for handling zero arithmetic.

2. Rewrite the following program without using **break**, **continue**, or **goto**:

```
/* Count the number of a's in input */

#include <stdio.h>
#include <ctype.h>

main()
{
   int num_a = 0;
   char c;
   c = getchar();
   while (1)
   {
     if (c == '\n')
       break;
     if (isdigit( c ))
       continue;
     if (c == 'a')
       goto add_num_a;
get_next_char: c = getchar();
     goto end_loop;
add_num_a: num_a++;
     goto get_next_char;
end_loop: ;
   }
   exit( 0 );
}
```

3. Write two programs that return the number of *x*'s returned by *getchar()*.
    Write the first one using only **if** and **goto** statements. Write the second one
    using only **while**, **break**, and **continue**. Which version is better? Why?

4. Write a function that accepts an integer number and writes that number of
    spaces. Using this function, write a program that reads characters from
    standard input, and echoes them to standard output, but replaces tabs with
    five spaces.

5. Many programs that require moving character data from one place to
    another use a *checksum* mechanism to ensure that the data is transferred
    correctly. The checksum technique requires a function that sums the code
    values of all the characters being sent. If the letters *a, b,* and *c* are being
    sent, for instance, the sum would be 294 because the ASCII values of these
    characters are 97, 98, and 99. The sending part of the program would then
    send this sum value along with the characters. The receiving part of the
    program computes the sum of the characters it receives and compares it
    with the sum from the sending component. If the sums match, there is a
    high probability that the data was transferred correctly. Write a *checksum()*
    function that returns the sum of a line entered from the keyboard. Use an
    unsigned integer to store the sum so that the value will behave predictably
    if an overflow occurs.

6. Write two versions of a function that classifies its **char** argument as one of

    WHITE_SPACE (space, '\n', '\r', or '\t')
    PUNCTUATION (',!;:().')
    ALPHA (a – z, A – Z)
    NUMERIC (0 – 9)
    UNKNOWN (anything else)

    For the first version, use only **if, else,** and **return** statements. For the
    second version, use only **switch** and **return** statements. Which version is
    better? Why?

7. Write a program that prints out the letters from a to z, and A to Z, and their
    integer values.

8. Expand the program in Exercise 7 so that it prints out the integer values in
    decimal, octal, and hexadecimal format.

Chapter 5

Operators and Expressions

We must either institute conventional forms of
expression or else pretend that we have nothing to express.
— George Santayana, Soliloquies in England

Operators are the verbs of the C language that let you calculate values. C's rich set of operators is one of its distinguishing characteristics. You have already seen a number of C operators in the preceding chapters, such as + (addition), / (division), < (less than), and = (assignment). The operator symbols are composed of one or more special characters. If an operator consists of more than one character, you must enter the characters without any intervening spaces:

```
x <= y    /* legal expression */
x < = y   /* illegal expression */
```

In this chapter, we take another look at the previously mentioned operators and introduce some new ones. We also describe expressions in greater detail.

You can think of operators as verbs and of *operands* as the subject and object of those verbs. An *expression* consists of one or more operands and zero or more operators linked together to compute a value. For instance,

```
a + 2
```

is a legal expression that results in the sum of *a* and *2*. The variable *a* all by itself is also an expression, as is the constant *2*, since they both represent a value. There are four important types of expressions:

- *Constant expressions* contain only constant values. For example, the following are all constant expressions:

```
5
5 + 6 * 13 / 3.0
'a'
```

- *Integral expressions* are expressions that, after all automatic and explicit type conversions, produce a result that has one of the integer types. If *j* and *k* are integers, the following are all integral expressions:

```
j
j * k
j / k + 3
k - 'a'
3 + (int) 5.0
```

- *Float expressions* are expressions that, after all automatic and explicit type conversions, produce a result that has one of the floating-point types. If *x* is a **float** or **double**, the following are floating-point expressions:

```
x
x + 3
x / y * 5
3.0
3.0 - 2
3 + (float) 4
```

- *Pointer expressions* are expressions that evaluate to an address value. These include expressions containing pointer variables, the "address of" operator (&), string literals, and array names. If *p* is a pointer and *j* is an **int**, the following are pointer expressions:

```
p
&j
p + 1
"abc"
(char *) 0x000fffff
```

The meaning of pointer arithmetic (such as *p + 1*) is described in the next chapter.

Class of operator	Operators in that class	Associativity	Precedence
primary	() [] -> .	Left–to–Right	**HIGHEST**
unary	**cast operator** **sizeof** **& (address of)** *** (dereference)** **– +** **~ ++ — !**	Right–to–Left	
multiplicative	*** / %**	Left–to–Right	
additive	**+ –**	Left–to–Right	
shift	**<< >>**	Left–to–Right	
relational	**< <= > >=**	Left–to–Right	
equality	**== !=**	Left–to–Right	
bitwise AND	**&**	Left–to–Right	
bitwise exclusive OR	**^**	Left–to–Right	
bitwise inclusive OR	**|**	Left–to–Right	
logical AND	**&&**	Left–to–Right	
logical OR	**||**	Left–to–Right	
conditional	**? :**	Right–to–Left	
assignment	**= += –= *=** **/= %= >>= <<=** **&= ^=**	Right–to–Left	
comma	**,**	Left–to–Right	**LOWEST**

Table 5-1. Precedence and Associativity of C Operators.

5.1 Precedence and Associativity

All operators have two important properties called *precedence* and *associativity*. Both properties affect how operands are attached to operators. Operators with higher precedence have their operands *bound*, or *grouped*, to them before operators of lower precedence, regardless of the order in which they appear. For example, the multiplication operator has higher precedence than the addition operator, so the two expressions

```
2 + 3 * 4
3 * 4 + 2
```

both evaluate to 14—the operand 3 is grouped with the multiplication operator rather than the addition operator because the multiplication operator has higher precedence. If there were no precedence rules, and the compiler grouped operands to operators in left–to–right order, the first expression,

```
2 + 3 * 4
```

would evaluate to 20. Table 5-1 lists every C operator in order of precedence.

In cases where operators have the same precedence, associativity (sometimes called *binding*) is used to determine the order in which operands are grouped with operators. Grouping occurs in either *right–to–left* or *left–to–right* order, depending on the operator. Right–to–left associativity means that the compiler starts on the right of the expression and works left. Left–to–right associativity means that the compiler starts on the left of the expression and works right. For example, the plus and minus operators have the same precedence and are both left–to–right associative:

```
a + b - c;  /* add a to b, then subtract c */
```

The assignment operator, on the other hand, is right-associative:

```
a = b = c;  /* assign c to b, then assign b to a */
```

5.1.1 Parentheses

The compiler groups operands and operators that appear within the parentheses first, so you can use parentheses to specify a particular grouping order. For example,

```
/*   subtract 3 from 2, then multiply that by 4 --
 *   result is -4
 */
(2 - 3) * 4

/*   multiply 3 and 4, then subtract from 2 --
 *   result is -10
 */
2 - (3 * 4)
```

In the second case, the parentheses are unnecessary since multiplication has a higher precedence than addition. Nevertheless, parentheses serve a valuable stylistic function by making an expression more readable, even though they may be redundant from a semantic viewpoint. It is a good idea to enclose all but the simplest expressions in parentheses. This ensures that the expression is evaluated correctly, and it enables you and others to decipher an expression without referring to the precedence table.

In the event of nested parentheses, the compiler groups the expression enclosed by the innermost parentheses first. Figure 5-1 shows how a compiler might group and evaluate the expression

```
1 + ((3 + 1) / (8 - 4) - 5)
```

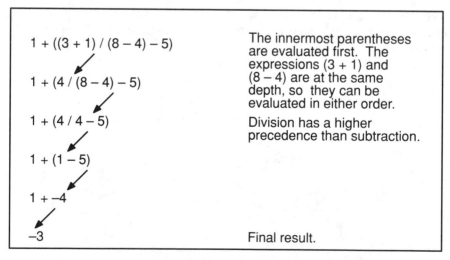

Figure 5-1. Evaluation of an Expression Enclosed by Parentheses.

One way to evaluate expressions is to go through the process shown in Figure 5-1, evaluating each subexpression in order. Another method that many compilers use is to create a *tree structure* as shown in Figure 5-2. Each operator, called a *node*, points to its operands, called *leaves*. The compiler evaluates the expression beginning at the bottom of the inverted tree. As each operator–operands combination is evaluated, the result is placed in the operator node, becoming an operand for the operator at the next higher level.

Note that there are two subexpressions at the very bottom of the tree. The compiler is free to evaluate them in any order—one compiler may evaluate *(3 + 1)* first while another evaluates *(8 – 4)* first. This is true of most operators, although there are a few for which the operands must be evaluated in left–to–right order.

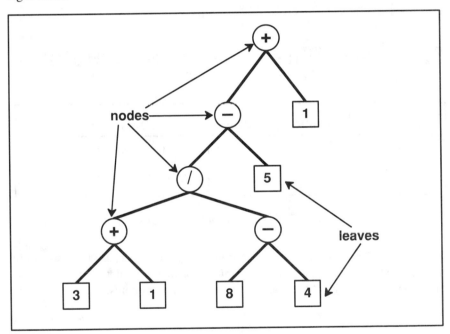

Figure 5-2.   Representation of an Expression as an Inverted Binary Tree.

5.1.2 Order of Evaluation

An important point to understand is that precedence and associativity have little to do with *order of evaluation*, another important property of expressions. The order of evaluation refers to the actual order in which the compiler evaluates operators. Note that this is independent of the order in which the compiler groups operands to operators. For most operators, the compiler is free to evaluate subexpressions in any order it pleases. It may even reorganize the expression, so long as the reorganization does not affect the final result. For example, given the expression

```
(2 + 3) * 4
```

the compiler might first add 2 and 3 and then multiply by 4. On the other hand, a compiler is free to reorganize the expression into

```
(2 * 4) + (3 * 4)
```

since this gives the same result.

The order of evaluation can have a critical impact on expressions that contain side effects, as explained in Box 5-2. Moreover, reorganization of expressions can sometimes cause overflow conditions.

5.2 Unary Plus and Minus Operators

Operator	Symbol	Form	Operation
unary minus	–	–x	negation of x
unary plus	+	+x	value of operand

Table 5-2. Unary Arithmetic Operators.

The plus and minus operators are called *unary* operators because they take only one operand. The operand can be any integer or floating-point value. The type of the result is the type of the operand after integral promotions.

The unary plus sign is an ANSI feature not found in older compilers. The result is the value of the operand after integral promotions. In other words, it doesn't have any effect except to promote small integer types.

The minus operator does just what you would expect—it returns the negation of its argument. If *m* equals 5, *–m* equals –5. On the other hand, if *m* equals –5, *–m* equals 5. In short, the expression

```
-e
```

is a shorthand for the expression

```
0 - (e)
```

where *e* is any integer or floating-point expression.

Do not confuse the unary minus operator with the binary subtraction operator. Even though they use the same symbol, they are different operators. For example,

```
j = 3 - -x
```

is interpreted as

```
j = (3 - (-x));
```

The first dash is a subtraction operator; the second is a unary minus sign. Note that the space between the two dashes prevents them from being interpreted as a decrement operator.

5.3 Binary Arithmetic Operators

Operator	Symbol	Form	Operation
multiplication	*	x * y	x times y
division	/	x / y	x divided by y
remainder	%	x % y	remainder of x divided by y
addition	+	x + y	x plus y
subtraction	–	x – y	x minus y

Table 5-3. Binary Arithmetic Operators.

Most of the arithmetic operators should already be familiar to you. The only new one is the remainder (%) operator. The multiplication, division, and remainder operators are called *multiplicative operators* and have a higher precedence than the *additive operators* (addition and subtraction). The operands to the multiplicative operators must be of integral or floating-point type. The additive operators accept operands whose type is integral, floating-point, or pointer. All of the arithmetic operators bind from left to right (see Table 5-1). Looking at the third example in Table 5-4, note that the subexpression

```
3 / 4
```

evaluates to zero because it is an integer expression—the fractional part of the result is truncated.

Also note that if the right operand of a division expression is zero, the results are undefined.

Given the following declarations:
 	
`int m = 3, n = 4;`
`float x = 2.5, y = 1.0;`		

Expression	**Equivalent Expression**	**Result**
m + n + x + y m + x * n + y x / y + m / n x − y * m + y / n x / 0	(((m + n) + x) + y) ((m + (x * n) + y)) (x / y) + (m / n) (x − (y * m)) + (y / n) x / 0	10.5 14.0 2.5 −0.25 undefined

Table 5-4. Examples of Expressions Using Arithmetic Operators.

5.3.1 The Remainder Operator — %

Unlike the other arithmetic operators, which accept both integer and floating-point operands, the remainder operator (sometimes called the *modulus* operator) accepts only integer operands. The resulting value is the remainder of the first operand divided by the second operand. For example, the expression

```
9 % 5
```

has a value of 4 because 5 goes into 9 once with a remainder of 4. The expression

```
10 % 5
```

has a value of zero because 5 goes into 10 evenly. If either operand is negative, the remainder can be negative or positive, depending on the implementation (see Box 5-1). The ANSI Standard requires the following relationship to exist between the remainder and division operators:

a equals `a%b + (a/b) * b` for any integral values of *a* and *b*

As with division expressions, the result of a remainder expression is undefined if the right operand is zero.

A frequent application of the remainder operator is to perform some action at regular intervals. The following program, for example, reads a line of input and prints it out, inserting a newline after every five characters.

```c
#include <stdio.h>

main()
{
    int c, j = 0;

    printf( "Enter string to be squished: " );
    while ((c = getchar()) != '\n')
    {
        if (j%5 == 0)       /* if j goes into 5 evenly */
            printf( "\n" );
        putchar( c );
        j++;
    }
    exit( 0 );
}
```

If this program were called *breakline*, execution would look like the following:

```
$ breakline
Needless redundancy is the hobgoblin...

Needl
ess r
edund
ancy
is th
e hob
gobli
n...
```

Note that the program outputs a newline at the very beginning. This is because j is initialized to zero, and dividing any number into zero always results in zero, with zero remainder.

To make this program more general and useful, you could turn it into a function whose argument is the interval value. This improved function appears on the following page.

```
#include <stdio.h>

void break_line( interval )
int interval;
{
  int c, j = 1;

  while ((c = getchar()) != '\n')
  {
    putchar( c );
    if (j%interval == 0)
      printf( "\n" );
    j++;
  }
}
```

Note that in this version we initialize *j* to one rather than zero and place the *putchar()* function before the interval test. This prevents the function from outputting an initial newline. This function would be useful as part of a text formatter that supports adjustable line lengths. A drawback of this function, however, is that there is no provision against inserting a newline in the middle of a word. We leave it as an exercise to correct this deficiency.

5.4 Arithmetic Assignment Operators

Operator	Symbol	Form	Operation
assign	=	a = b	put the value of b into a
add–assign	+=	a += b	put the value of a+b into a
subtract–assign	–=	a –= b	put the value of a–b into a
multiply–assign	*=	a *= b	put the value of a*b into a
divide–assign	/=	a /= b	put the value of a/b into a
remainder–assign	%=	a %= b	put the value of a%b into a

Table 5-5. Arithmetic Assignment Operators.

The assign operator (=) should be familiar. It causes the value of the right-hand operand to be written into the memory location of the left-hand operand. In addition, an assignment expression itself has a value, which is the same value that is assigned to the left-hand operand. The left-hand operand, sometimes called an *lvalue*, must refer to a memory location.

Box 5-1: Bug Alert — Integer Division and Remainder

When both operands of the division operator (/) are integers, the result is an integer. If both operands are positive and the division is inexact, the fractional part is truncated:

5/2	evaluates to	2
7/2	evaluates to	3
1/3	evaluates to	0

If either operand is negative, however, the compiler is free to round the result either up or down:

−5/2	evaluates to	−2 or −3
7/−2	evaluates to	−3 or −4
−1/−3	evaluates to	0 or −1

By the same token, the sign of the result of a remainder operation is undefined by the C Standard:

−5 % 2	evaluates to	1 or −1
7 % −4	evaluates to	3 or −3

Obviously, you should avoid division and remainder operations with negative numbers since the results can vary from one compiler to another.

If the sign of the remainder is important to your program's operations, you should use the runtime library *div()* function, which computes the quotient and the remainder of its two arguments. The sign of both results is determined in a guaranteed and portable manner. (See the description of *div()* in Appendix A for more information.)

As mentioned previously, the assign operator has right–to–left associativity, so the expression

```
a = b = c = d = 1;
```

is interpreted as

```
(a = (b = (c = (d = 1))));
```

First 1 is assigned to *d*, then *d* is assigned to *c*, then *c* is assigned to *b*, and finally *b* is assigned to *a*. The value of the entire expression is 1. This is a convenient syntax for assigning the same value to more than one variable. Note, however, that each assignment may cause quiet conversions, so

```
int j;
double f;
f = j = 3.5;
```

assigns the truncated value 3 to both *f* and *j*. On the other hand,

```
j = f = 3.5;
```

assigns 3.5 to *f* and 3 to *j*.

In addition to the simple assign operator, the C language supports five additional assignment operators that combine assignment with each of the arithmetic operations. The equivalences are shown in Figure 5-3.

For example, the expression

```
j = j * 5;
```

can be written

```
j *= 5;
```

One of the main reasons for using the arithmetic assignment operators is to avoid spelling mistakes and make code more readable. For example, the expression,

```
op_big_x_dimension_3 = op_big_x_dimension_3 * 2;
```

can be written:

```
op_big_x_dimension_3 *= 2;
```

The second version is easier to read and to write and contains fewer opportunities for spelling errors. This issue becomes even more important when referencing structure and union members, as described in Chapter 8.

In addition, use of the arithmetic assignment operators sometimes produces more efficient object code. The increased efficiency is due to the fact that some computers have special machine instructions to perform arithmetic-assign combinations. A good compiler will usually rewrite an expression for you to take advantage of this feature.

Another feature of the arithmetic assignment operators is that if the lvalue contains side effects, the side effects occur only once. This feature has special significance for arrays, as explained in the next chapter. See Box 5-2 for more information about side effects.

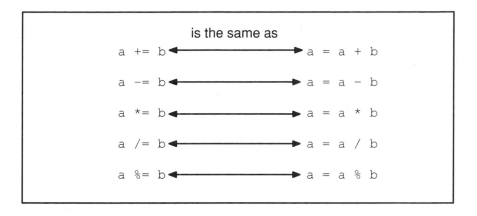

*Figure 5-3.   Arithmetic Assignment Operator Equivalences. These
            equivalences are true so long as a has no side effects.*

As shown in Table 5-1, the assign operators have relatively low precedence.
This leads to interesting consequences. For example, the following two expressions are *not* the same:

```
j = j * 3 + 4;
j *= 3 + 4;
```

The addition operator has higher precedence than the assign operator, and the
multiplication operator has higher precedence than the addition operator, so the
two expressions are interpreted as follows:

Table 5-6 gives some more examples of expressions using these operators.

Given the following declarations:

```
int m = 3, n = 4;
float x = 2.5, y = 1.0;
```

Expression	Equivalent Expression	Result
m + = n + x − y	m = (m + ((n + x) − y))	8
m /= x ∗ n + y	m = (m / ((x∗ n) + y))	0
n %= y + m	n = (n % (y + m))	0
x += y −= m	x = (x + (y = (y − m)))	0.5

Table 5-6.   Examples of Expressions Using Arithmetic Assignment
            Operators.

5.5 Increment and Decrement Operators

In the previous chapter, we introduced the increment and decrement operators as shorthands for adding 1 to and subtracting 1 from a variable. As Table 5-7 indicates, there are actually two versions of each operator. If the operator comes after the variable, it is called a *postfix* operator. If it comes before the lvalue expression, it is called a *prefix* operator. The difference between the two types of operators is subtle but can be very important, as we explain in this section.

Operator	Symbol	Form	Operation
postfix increment	++	a++	get value of a, then increment a
postfix decrement	−−	a−−	get value of a, then decrement a
prefix increment	++	++a	increment a, then get value of a
prefix decrement	−−	−−a	decrement a, then get value of a

Table 5-7. The Increment and Decrement Operators.

Like the unary minus operator, the increment and decrement operators are unary. The operand must be a scalar lvalue—it is illegal to increment or decrement a constant or a structure. It is legal to increment or decrement pointer variables, but the meaning of adding one to a pointer is different from that of adding one to an arithmetic value. We describe pointer arithmetic in the next chapter.

The postfix increment and decrement operators fetch the current value of the variable and store a copy of it in a temporary location. The compiler then increments or decrements the variable. The temporary copy, which has the variable's value *before* it was modified, is used in the expression. For example

```
main ()
{
   int j = 5, k = 5;

   printf ( "j: %d\t k: %d\n", j++, k-- );
   printf ( "j: %d\t k: %d\n", j, k );
   exit ( 0 );
}
```

The result is

```
j: 5      k: 5
j: 6      k: 4
```

In the first *printf()* call, the initial values of *j* and *k* are used, but once they have been used they are incremented and decremented, respectively.

In contrast, the *prefix* increment and decrement operators modify their operands *before* they fetch the values:

```
main ()
{
   int j = 5, k = 5;

   printf ( "j: %d\t k: %d\n", ++j, --k );
   printf ( "j: %d\t k: %d\n", j, k );
   exit ( 0 );
}
```

The result of this version is

```
j: 6      k: 4
j: 6      k: 4
```

In many cases, you are interested only in the side effect, not in the result of the expression. In these instances, it doesn't matter which operator you use. For example, as a stand-alone assignment, or as the third expression in a for loop, the side effect is the same whether you use the prefix or postfix versions:

```
x++;
```

is equivalent to

```
++x;
```

and the statement

```
for (j = 0; j <= 10; j++)
```

is equivalent to

```
for (j = 0; j <= 10; ++j)
```

Box 5-2: Bug Alert — Side Effects

The increment and decrement operators, and the assignment operators, cause *side effects*. That is, they not only result in a value but also change the value of a variable. A problem with side effect operators is that it is not always possible to predict the order in which the side effects occur. Consider the following statement:

```
x = j * j++;
```

The C language does not specify which multiplication operand is to be evaluated first. One compiler may evaluate the left-hand operand first, while another evaluates the right-hand operand first. The results are different in the two cases. If j equals 5 and the left-hand operand is evaluated first, the expression will be interpreted as

```
x = 5 * 5;    /* x is assigned 25 */
```

If the right-hand operand is evaluated first, the expression becomes

```
x = 6 * 5;    /* x is assigned 30 */
```

Statements such as this one are nonportable and should be avoided. The side effect problem also crops up in function calls because the C language does not guarantee the order in which arguments are evaluated. For example, the function call

```
f( a, a++ )
```

is not portable because compilers are free to evaluate the arguments in any order they choose.

To prevent side effect bugs, follow this rule: *If you use a side effect operator in an expression, do not use the affected variable anywhere else in the expression.* The ambiguous expression above, for instance, can be made unambiguous by breaking it into two assignments:

```
x = j * j;
++j;
```

You need to be careful, however, when you use the increment and decrement operators within an expression. Consider the rendition of the *break_line()* function:

```
#include <stdio.h>

void break_line( interval )
int interval;
{
   int c, j=0;

   while ((c = getchar()) != '\n')
   {
      if ((j++ % interval) == 0)
         printf( "\n" );
      putchar( c );
   }
}
```

This works because we use the postfix increment operator. If we were to use the prefix increment operator, the function would break the first line one character early.

5.5.1 Precedence of Increment and Decrement Operators

Note in Table 5-1 that the increment and decrement operators have the same precedence but bind from right to left. So the expression

```
--j++
```

is evaluated as

```
--(j++)
```

This expression is illegal because *j++* is not an lvalue as required by the — operator. In general, you should avoid using multiple increment or decrement operators together. Table 5-8 shows a number of expressions involving increment and decrement operators.

Given the following declarations: int j = 0, m = 1, n = -1;		
Expression	**Equivalent Expression**	**Result**
m++ – –j m += ++j * 2 m++ * m++	(m++) – (–j) m = (m + ((++j)* 2) (m++) * (m++)	2 3 implementation- dependent

Table 5-8.   Examples of Expressions Using the Increment and
Decrement Operators.

5.6 Comma Operator

Operator	**Symbol**	**Form**	**Operation**
comma	,	a , b	evaluate a, evaluate b, result is b

Table 5-9. The Comma Operator.

The comma operator allows you to evaluate two or more distinct expressions wherever a single expression is allowed. The result is the value of the rightmost operand. The comma operator is one of the few operators for which the order of evaluation is specified. The compiler must evaluate the left-hand operand first.

Although the comma operator is legal in a number of situations, it leads to confusing code in many of them. By convention, therefore, the comma operator is used primarily in the first and last expressions of a **for** statement. For instance,

```
for (j = 0, k = 100; k - j > 0; j++, k--);
```

In this example, both *j* and *k* are initialized before the loop is entered. After each iteration, *j* is incremented and *k* is decremented. It is equivalent to the following **while** loop.

```
j = 0;
k = 100;
while (k - j < 0)
{
    .
    .
    .
    j++;
    k--;
}
```

Note that this code could also be written

```
j = 0, k=100;
while (k - j < 0)
{
    .
    .
    .
    j++, k--;
}
```

Some programmers use the comma operator in this context, but we feel it is better style to place each assignment on its own line to avoid confusion.

There is also a temptation to fit as much as possible into the **for** expressions. For example, the *break_line()* function could be written

```
#include <stdio.h>

break_line( interval )
int interval;
{
    int c, j;

    for (c=getchar(), j = 0; c != EOF; j++
                                    , putchar(c)
                                    ,c = getchar())
        if (j%interval == 0)
            printf( "\n" );
}
```

Although this is more compact, it is not better since it is harder to read. In particular, you should be wary about entering multiple assignments in the third expression of a **for** loop.

5.7 Relational Operators

Operator	Symbol	Form	Result
greater than	>	a > b	1 if a is greater than b; else 0
less than	<	a < b	1 if a is less than b; else 0
greater than or equal to	>=	a >= b	1 if a is greater than or equal to b; else 0
less than or equal to	<=	a <= b	1 if a is less than or equal to b; else 0
equal to	==	a == b	1 if a is equal to b; else 0
not equal to	!=	a != b	1 if a is not equal to b; else 0

Table 5-10. The Relational Operators.

These operators should be familiar from the previous chapter. In this chapter, we discuss some of the ramifications of the precedence and associativity rules when applied to these operators. Note first that all of these operators have lower precedence than the arithmetic operators. The expression

```
a + b * c < d / f
```

is evaluated as if it had been written

```
(a + (b * c)) < (d / f)
```

Box 5-3: Bug Alert — Comparing Floating-Point Values

It is very dangerous to compare floating-point values for equality because floating-point representations are inexact for some numbers. For example, the following expression, though algebraically true, will evaluate to false on most computers:

```
(1.0/3.0 + 1.0/3.0 + 1.0/3.0) == 1.0
```

This evaluates to 0 (false) because the fraction *1.0/3.0* contains an infinite number of decimal places (3.33333...). The computer is only capable of holding a limited number of decimal places, so it rounds each occurrence of 1/3. As a result, the left-hand side of the expression does not equal 1.0 exactly.

To avoid bugs caused by inexact floating-point representations, you should refrain from using strict equality comparisons with floating-point types.

Among the relational operators, the first four in Table 5-10 have the same precedence. The == and != operators have lower precedence. All of the relational operators have left–to–right associativity. Table 5-11 illustrates how the compiler parses complex relational expressions.

Given the following declarations: `int j = 0, m = 1, n = -1;` `float x = 2.5, y = 0.0;`		
Expression	**Equivalent Expressions**	**Result**
j > m m / n < x j <= m >= n j <= x == m − x + j == y > n > m x += (y >= n) ++j == m != y * 2	j > m (m / n) < x ((j <= m) >=n) ((j <= x) == m) ((−x) + j) == ((y > n) >= m) x = (x + (y >= n)) ((++j) == m) != (y * 2)	0 1 1 1 0 3.5 1

Table 5-11.   *Examples of Expressions Using the Relational Operators.*

5.8 Logical Operators

Operator	**Symbol**	**Form**	**Result**
logical AND	&&	a && b	1 if a and b are nonzero; else 0
logical OR	||	a || b	1 if a or b is nonzero; else 0
logical negation	!	! a	1 if a is zero; else 0

Table 5-12.   *The Logical Operators.*

In algebra, the expression

    x < y < z

is true if y is greater than x and less than z. Unfortunately, this expression has a very different meaning in C, since it is evaluated as

    (x < y) < z

The subexpression (x < y) is evaluated first and results in either 0 and 1. So in C, the expression is true if x is less than y and z is greater than 1, or if x is not less than *y* and *z* is greater than zero. To obtain the algebraic meaning, you must rewrite the expression using relational operators.

The logical AND operator (&&) and the logical OR operator (||) evaluate the truth or falseness of pairs of expressions. The AND operator returns TRUE only if both expressions are TRUE. The OR operator returns TRUE if *either* expression is TRUE. To test whether *y* is greater than *x* and less than *z*, you would write

```
(x < y) && (y < z)
```

The logical negation operator (!) takes only one operand. If the operand is TRUE, the result is FALSE; if the operand is FALSE, the result is TRUE.

Recall that in C, TRUE is equivalent to any nonzero value and FALSE is equivalent to zero. Table 5-13 shows the logical tables for each operator, along with the numerical equivalent. Note that all of the operators return 1 for TRUE and 0 for FALSE.

Operand	Operator	Operand	Result
zero	&&	zero	0
nonzero	&&	zero	0
zero	&&	nonzero	0
nonzero	&&	nonzero	1
zero	||	zero	0
nonzero	||	zero	1
zero	||	nonzero	1
nonzero	||	nonzero	1
	!	zero	1
NA	!	nonzero	0

Table 5-13. Truth Table for C's Logical Operators.

The operands to the logical operators may be integers or floating-point objects. The expression

```
1 && –5
```

results in 1 because both operands are nonzero. The same is true of the expression

```
0.5 && –5
```

Logical operators (and the comma and conditional operators) are the only operators for which the order of evaluation of the operands is defined. The compiler must evaluate operands from left to right. Moreover, the compiler is guaranteed *not* to evaluate an operand if it's unnecessary. For example, in the expression

```
if ((a != 0) && (b/a == 6.0))
```

if *a* equals zero, the expression *(b/a == 6)* will *not* be evaluated. This rule can have unexpected consequences when one of the expressions contains side effects (see Box 5-4).

Table 5-14 shows a number of examples that use relational and logical operators. Note that the logical NOT operator has a higher precedence than the others. The AND operator has higher precedence than the OR operator. Both the logical AND and OR operators have lower precedence than the relational and arithmetic operators.

Given the following declarations:		
`int j = 0, m = 1, n = -1;` `float x = 2.5, y = 0.0;`		
Expression	**Equivalent Expression**	**Result**
j && m	(j) && (m)	0
j < m && n < m	(j < m) && (n < m)	1
m + n || ! j	(m + n) || (!j)	1
x * 5 && 5 || m / n	((x * 5) && 5) || (m / n)	1
j <= 10 && x >= 1 && m	((j <= 10) && (x >= 1)) && m	1
!x || !n || m + n	((!x) || (!n)) || (m + n)	0
x * y < j + m || n	((x * y) < (j + m)) || n	1
(x > y) + !j || n++	((x > y) + (!j)) || (n++)	1
(j || m) + (x || ++n)	(j || m) + (x || (++n))	2

Table 5-14. Examples of Expressions Using the Logical Operators.

A complex relational expression is normally used as the conditional part of a looping statement, or in an **if** statement. Linking expressions with the logical AND operator is equivalent to using nested **if** statements. The expression

```
if ((a < b) && (b < c))
    stmt;
```

is functionally equivalent to

```
if (a < b)
   if (b < c)
     stmt;
```

Box 5-4: Bug Alert — Side Effects in Relational Expressions

Logical operators (and the conditional and comma operators) are the only operators for which the order of evaluation of the operands is defined. For these operators, a compiler must evaluate operands from left to right. However, a compiler evaluates only as much of a relational expression as it needs to determine the result. In many cases, this means that the compiler does not need to evaluate the entire expression. For instance, consider the following expression:

```
if ((a < b) && (c == d))
```

The compiler begins by evaluating *(a < b)*. If *a* is not less than *b*, the compiler knows that the entire expression is false, so it will not evaluate *(c == d)*. This can cause problems if some of the expressions contain side effects:

```
if ((a < b) && (c == d++))
```

In this case, *d* is incremented only when *a* is less than *b*. This may or may not be what the programmer intended. In general, you should avoid using side effect operators in relational expressions.

This is true so long as there is no **else** present. However, the sequence

```
if ((a < b) && (b < c))
    stmt1;
else
    stmt2;
```

is not the same as

```
if (a < b)
    if (b < c)
        stmt1;
    else
        stmt2;
```

To get the same functionality, you would have to write

```
if (a < b)
    if (b < c)
        stmt1;
    else
        stmt2;
else
    stmt2;
```

In situations that don't involve an **else**, you can use either form. Given that you can write the expression either way, which should you use? The relational expression is more maintainable because it is easy to add **else** clauses at a later date. In terms of readability, the two versions are about the same. The relational expression version is easier to read because it groups all the necessary conditions together. It also avoids some of the readability problems associated with deeply nested **if** statements. On the other hand, relational expressions can themselves be difficult to read if they become too long.

One way to decide whether a relational expression is too complex is to employ the so-called "telephone test." This involves reading aloud the relational expression. For instance, the previous example would be read as "if a is less than b and b is less than c." If you can understand the expression as you read it, then it passes the test and you can use it. If, on the other hand, you find yourself losing the thread, it is probably better to break it up into nested expressions. Most important, you should be consistent. If you like one style better than another, use it throughout your programs. Don't switch back and forth.

5.9 Bit-Manipulation Operators

The bit-manipulation operations enable you to access specific bits within an object and to compare the bit sequences of pairs of objects. The operands for all the bit-manipulation operators must be integers.

Operator	Symbol	Form	Result
right shift	>>	x >> y	x shifted right y bits
left shift	<<	x << y	x shifted left y bits
bitwise AND	&	x & y	x bitwise ANDed with y
bitwise inclusive OR	|	x | y	x bitwise ORed with y
bitwise exclusive OR (XOR)	^	x ^ y	x bitwise exclusive ORed with y
bitwise complement	~	~x	bitwise complement of x

Table 5-15. The Bit-Manipulation Operators.

5.9.1 Shift Operators

The two shift operators, << and >>, enable you to shift the bits of an object a specified number of places to the left or the right. The operands must have integral type, and the automatic integral promotions are performed for each operand. After these promotions, the right-hand operand is converted to an **int**. The type of the result is the type of the promoted left-hand operand.

Consider the examples in Table 5-16 (these examples assume that an **int** is 16 bits and that two's complement notation is used for negative numbers).

Expression	Binary Model of Left Operand		Binary Model of Result		Result Value
5 << 1	00000000	00000101	00000000	00001010	10
255 >> 3	00000000	11111111	00000000	00011111	31
8 << 10	00000000	00001000	00100000	00000000	2^{13}
1 << 15	00000000	00000001	10000000	00000000	-2^{15}

Table 5-16. Examples Using the Shift Operators.

Shifting to the left is equivalent to multiplying by powers of two:

$$x << y \quad \text{is equivalent to} \quad x * 2^y$$

Shifting nonnegative integers to the right is equivalent to dividing by powers of two:

$$x >> y \quad \text{is equivalent to} \quad x / 2^y$$

Note that as bits are moved to the right or left, the vacant bits are filled with zeroes. This is the rule when a positive value is shifted. When a negative value is shifted to the right, however, the vacant bits can be filled with ones or zeroes, depending on the implementation, as shown in Table 5-17.

Expression	Binary Model of Left Operand		Binary Model of Result		Result Value
−5 >> 2	11111111	11111011	00111111	11111110	$2^{13}-1$
−5 >> 2	11111111	11111011	11111111	11111110	−2

Table 5-17.   Shifting Negative Numbers. Some implementations fill the vacant bits with zeroes, while others fill them with ones.

The first version, in which vacant bits are filled with zeroes, is called a *logical shift*. The second version is called an *arithmetic shift* because it retains the arithmetic value.   The ANSI Standard does not specify whether a compiler should perform a logical or arithmetic shift for signed objects. If the left operand is **unsigned**, however, the compiler must perform a logical shift. For example,

```
(unsigned) -5 >> 2
```

always results in 2!#–1 on a machine where **int**s are 16 bits long. Use the *(unsigned)* cast for portability. Also, make sure that the right operand is not larger than the size of the object. For example, the following produces unpredictable and nonportable results because most **int**s have fewer than 50 bits:

```
10 >> 50
```

You will also get unpredictable results if the shift count (the second operand) is a negative value.

5.9.2 Logical Bitwise Operators

The logical bitwise operators are similar to the Boolean operators, except that they operate on every bit in the operand(s). For instance, the bitwise AND operator (**&**) compares each bit of the left operand to the corresponding bit in the right operand. If both bits are one, a one is placed at that bit position in the result. Otherwise, a zero is placed at that bit position.

When constants are used in expressions with bitwise operators, they are usually written in hexadecimal notation to make it easier to see the value of each bit. Each digit in a hexadecimal number represents four bits. By memorizing the sixteen possible combinations (see Table 5-18), you can quickly convert from binary to hexadecimal and *vice versa*.

Decimal	Hex	Binary	Octal
0	0	0000	0
1	1	0001	1
2	2	0010	2
3	3	0011	3
4	4	0100	4
5	5	0101	5
6	6	0110	6
7	7	0111	7
8	8	1000	10
9	9	1001	11
10	A	1010	12
11	B	1011	13
12	C	1100	14
13	D	1101	15
14	E	1110	16
15	F	1111	17

Table 5-18.   Decimal, Hexadecimal, Binary, and Octal Versions of the Integers 0 Through 15.

Table 5-19 shows some examples of the bitwise AND operator.

Expression	Hexadecimal Value	Binary Representation	
9430 5722	0x24D6 0x165A	00100100 00010110	11010110 01011010
9430 & 5722	0x0452	00000100	01010010

Table 5-19.   The Bitwise AND Operator.

The bitwise inclusive OR operator (|) places a 1 in the resulting value's bit position if either operand has a bit set at the position (see Table 5-20).

Expression	Hexadecimal Value	Binary Representation	
9430 5722	0x24D6 0x165A	00100100 00010110	11010110 01011010
9430 | 5722	0x36DE	00110110	11011110

Table 5-20.   Examples Using the Bitwise Inclusive OR Operator.

The bitwise EXCLUSIVE OR (XOR) operator (^) sets a bit in the resulting value's bit position if either operand (but not both) has a bit set at the position (see Table 5-21).

Expression	Hexadecimal Value	Binary Representation	
9430	0x24D6	00100100	11010110
5722	0x165A	00010110	01011010
9430 ^ 5722	0x328C	00110010	10001100

Table 5-21. Example Using the XOR Operator.

The bitwise complement operator (~) reverses each bit in the operand (see Table 5-22).

Expression	Hexadecimal Value	Binary Representation	
9430	0x24d6	00100100	11010110
~9430	0xdb29	11011011	00101001

Table 5-22. Example Using the Bitwise Complement Operator.

The bit-manipulation operators are frequently used to implement a programming technique called *masking*, which allows you to access a specific bit or a group of bits. This is particularly useful for compressing information. Suppose, for instance, that you have a test consisting of 32 yes/no questions. Since each question has only two possible answers, you can store the answer to each in a single bit. The answers for the entire test can be stored in a 32-bit **int**, as shown in the following code.

```c
#include <stdio.h>

long get_answers()
{
  long answers = 0;
  int j;
  char c;

  for (j=0; j <= 31; j++)
  {
    scanf( "%c", &c );
    if (c == 'y' || c == 'Y')
      answers |= 1 << j;
  }
  printf( "Answers entered = (%lx)", answers );
  return answers;
}
```

Note particularly how the correct bit is set for each yes answer. With each iteration through the **for** loop, j is incremented, so the expression

```
1 << j
```

moves the set bit one position to the left:

Value of j	Value of 1 << j
0	00000000 00000000 00000000 00000001
1	00000000 00000000 00000000 00000010
2	00000000 00000000 00000000 00000100
3	00000000 00000000 00000000 00001000
4	00000000 00000000 00000000 00010000
5	00000000 00000000 00000000 00100000
.	.
.	.

By ORing this expression with *answer*, we can set all the bits that have an answer of 'y' or 'Y'. For example if the test answers are,

y n n n y n y y n n y n y n y y y y n y n n n y n y n y n n n y y

The bit pattern of *answer* will be (with high-order bits on the left)

1 1 0 0 0 1 0 1 0 1 0 0 0 1 0 1 1 1 0 1 0 1 0 0 1 1 0 1 0 0 0 1

This is one general use of the bitwise OR—to set one or more bits in an object. Having arranged the bits in *answer*, we need a way to compare *answer* to the correct answers. This is accomplished with the exclusive OR operator:

```
/*   correct answers are:
 *        nnyy ynyn nyyy yynn nnyn yyyy ynyy nyny
 *        0011 1010 0111 1100 0010 1111 1011 0101
 */

#define CORRECT_ANSWERS 0x3A7C2FB5

double grade_test( answers )
long int answers;
{
   extern int count_bits();
   long wrong_bits;
   double grade;

   wrong_bits = answers ^ CORRECT_ANSWERS;
   grade = 100 * ((32 - count_bits( wrong_bits )) /
                    32.0);
   return grade;
}
```

The XOR operator compares *answers* to *CORRECT_ANSWERS* and sets a bit in *wrong_bits* only when the operands differ. Hence, *wrong_bits* has bits set for each wrong answer. To obtain the grade, we subtract the number of wrong answers from the total to get the number of right answers. Then we divide the number of right answers into the total. Finally, we multiply by 100. If there were ten wrong answers, for example, the expression would be

```
100 * ((32.0 - 10) / 32.0)
```

which reduces to

```
100 * (22.0 / 32.0)
```

for a grade of 69.

We still need to write a *count_bits()* function that counts the number of bits set in *wrong_answers*. This function is similar to *get_answers()*, but instead of using the OR operator to *set* bits, we use the AND operator to *read* bits.

```
int count_bits( long_num )
long int long_num;
{
    int j, count = 0;

    for (j = 0; j <= 31; j++)
        if (long_num & (1 << j))
            ++count;
    return count;
}
```

Now we can invoke all of these functions from a *main()* function to form an executable program:

```
#include <stdio.h>

main()
{
    extern double grade_test();
    extern long int get_answers();
    double grade;

    printf( "Enter the answers:\n" );
    grade = grade_test( get_answers() );
    printf( "The grade is %3.0f\n", grade );
    exit( 0 );
}
```

Note that the argument to *grade_test()* is itself a function. It is functionally the same as

```
temp = get_answers();
grade = grade_test( temp );
```

but in the nested version, we do not need to declare a temporary variable temp. This makes the function somewhat cleaner and more efficient.

The format specifier **%3.0f** directs *printf()* to output at least three digits of the value, but to round the decimal digits.

If this program is called *grade*, typical execution, with three incorrect answers, would look like the following:

```
$ grade
Enter the answers:
ynynyynyyyyynynynnyyyyynnynnyyny
The grade is   91
```

A major drawback of this program is that it works only when there are exactly 32 questions and answers. We leave it as an exercise to modify the program so that it works for any number of questions, where the number of questions and answers is entered by the user. (For more than 32 questions, you need to use an array, described in the next chapter.)

5.10 Bitwise Assignment Operators

Operator	Symbol	Form	Operation
right–shift–assign	**>>=**	a >>= b	Assign a>>b to a.
left–shift–assign	**<<=**	a <<= b	Assign a<<b to a.
AND–assign	**&=**	a &= b	Assign a&b to a.
OR–assign	**|=**	a |= b	Assign a|b to a.
XOR–assign	**^=**	a ^= b	Assign a^b to a.

Table 5-23. The Bitwise Assignment Operators.

The bitwise assignment operators are analogous to the arithmetic assignment operators. For example, the assignment

```
x = x << 2;
```

can be written

```
x <<= 2;
```

5.11 Cast Operator

Operator	Symbol	Form	Operation
cast	**(type)**	(type) e	Convert e to type.

Table 5-24. The Cast Operator.

We introduced the cast operator in Chapter 3. It enables you to convert a value to a different type. One of the uses of casts, as we remarked in Chapter 3, is to promote an integer to a floating-point number to ensure that the result of a division operation is not truncated, as illustrated in the following example:

```
/*  Result is 1 because fractional part is truncated
 */
3 / 2

/*  Result is 1.5 because the 3 is converted to a
 *  float
 */
(float) 3 / 2
```

Note that the cast operator has very high precedence, so the preceding expression is parsed as if it had been written

```
((float) 3) / 2
```

Another use of the cast operator is to convert function arguments. Suppose you want to write a program that prints the powers of 2 up to 2^{31}. The runtime library function *pow()* will do the trick, but it expects its arguments to be of type **double**. If your variables are integers, you need to cast them to **double** before you pass them as arguments, as shown in the following example.

```
#include <stdio.h>
#include <math.h>

main()
{
    int j;
    long k;

    for (j = 0; j < 32; j++)
    {
        k = (int) pow( 2.0 , (double) j );
        printf( "%4d\t\t%13lu\n", j, k );
    }
    exit( 0 );
}
```

If we pass *j* without casting it to **double**, the program will fail. The *pow()* function is expecting a **double** object and interprets whatever object is passed as if it were a **double**. If the object being passed is actually an **int**, you will get unpredictable results. (The ANSI Standard supports a new syntax for declaring the types of arguments that makes this sort of cast unnecessary. This syntax, called prototyping, is described in Chapter 9.)

The value returned by *pow()* is a **double**, so we cast it to **int** before assigning it to *j*. This cast is actually unnecessary since the compiler automatically converts right-hand expressions of an assignment. Nevertheless, the explicit cast serves an important documentation function by emphasizing that a conversion is taking place. We discuss argument-passing conventions in more detail in Chapter 9.

The most frequent and important uses of casts involve pointers and data initialization. We cover both of these topics in later chapters.

5.12 *sizeof* operator

Operator	Symbol	Form	Operation
sizeof	**sizeof**	sizeof(t) or sizeof x	Return the size, in bytes, of data type t or expression x.

*Table 5-25. The **sizeof** Operator.*

The **sizeof** operator accepts two types of operands: an expression or a data type. However, the expression may not have type function or **void** or be a bit field (described in Chapter 8). Moreover, the expression itself is not evaluated—the compiler determines only what type the result would be. Any side effects in the expression, therefore, will not have an effect. The result type of the **sizeof** operator is either **int**, **long**, **unsigned int**, or **unsigned long**, depending on your compiler. The ANSI Standard requires it to be **unsigned**.

If the operand is an expression, **sizeof** returns the number of bytes that the result occupies in memory:

```
/*  Returns the size of an int (4 if ints are four
 *  bytes long)
 */
sizeof(3 + 5)

/*  Returns the size of a double (8 if doubles are
 *  eight bytes long)
 */
sizeof(3.0 + 5)
```

For expressions, the parentheses are optional, so the following is legal:

```
sizeof x
```

By convention, however, the parentheses are usually included.

The operand can also be a data type, in which case the result is the length in bytes of objects of that type:

```
sizeof(char)     /* 1 on all machines */
sizeof(short)    /* 2 on our machine */
sizeof(float)    /* 4 on our machine */
sizeof(int *)    /* size of a pointer to an integer
                  * (4 bytes on our machines)    */
```

The parentheses are required if the operand is a data type. Note that the results of most **sizeof** expressions are implementation dependent. The only result that is guaranteed is the size of a **char**, which is always 1.

In general, the **sizeof** operator is used to find the size of aggregate data objects such as arrays and structures. This use of **sizeof** is discussed in Chapters 6 and 8.

You can also use the **sizeof** operator to obtain information about the sizes of objects in your C environment. The following, for example, prints the sizes of the basic data types:

```
#include <stdio.h>

main()
{
  printf( "TYPE\t\tSIZE\n\n" );
  printf( "char\t\t%d\n", sizeof(char) );
  printf( "short\t\t%d\n", sizeof(short) );
  printf( "int\t\t%d\n", sizeof(int) );
  printf( "float\t\t%d\n", sizeof(float) );
  printf( "double\t\t%d\n" sizeof(double) );
  exit( 0 );
}
```

5.13 Conditional Operator (? :)

Operator	Symbol	Form	Operation
conditional	**?:**	a ? b : c	if a is nonzero result is b; otherwise result is c.

Table 5-26. The Conditional Operator.

The conditional operator is the only ternary (three operands) operator. The conditional operator is really just a shorthand for a common type of **if...else** branch. The **if...else** expression

```
if (x < y)
   z = x;
else
   z = y;
```

can be written

```
z = ((x < y) ? x : y);
```

The first operand is the test condition. It must have scalar type. The second and third operands represent the final value of the expression. Only one of them is selected, depending on the value of the first operand. The second and third operands can be of any data type, so long as the two types are compatible according to the normal conversion rules. For example, if the second operand is an **int** and the third is a **double**, the result type is **double** regardless of which one is selected (i.e., if the **int** is selected, it is converted to a **double**).

The conditional operator is difficult to read and should be used with care. In certain situations, however, it is handy. For example, in the following statement, we print *j* if *j* is greater than zero; otherwise we print *k*:

```
printf( "Here is %d", j > 0 ? j : k );
```

Without the conditional operator, this would have to be written

```
if (j > 0)
    printf( "Here is %d", j );
else
    printf( "Here is %d", k );
```

We need to duplicate the print statement, which leads to redundant code. The version using the conditional operator, therefore, is better in this case.

5.14 Memory Operators

There are several operators that enable you to access and dereference memory locations. We introduced some of them in Chapter 3, and we list them all in this chapter (Table 5-27) for completeness, but we defer discussing them in detail until Chapters 6 and 8.

Operator	Symbol	Form	Operation
address of	&	&x	Get the address of x.
dereference	*	*a	Get the value of the object stored at address a.
array elements	[]	x[5]	Get the value of array element 5.
dot	.	x.y	Get the value of member y in structure x.
right–arrow	!	p -> y	Get the value of member y in the structure pointed to by p.

Table 5-27. The Memory Operators.

Exercises

1. Enclose the following expressions in parentheses the way a C compiler would evaluate them. (Hint: use Table 5-1).

    a) a = b * c == 2;
    b) a = f(x) && a > 100;
    c) a == b && x != y;
    d) a = b += 2 + f(2);
    e) a = s . f + x . y;
    f) a = b >> 2 + 4;
    g) a = b && a > z ? x = y : z;
    h) a = * ++ * p;
    i) a = b ^ c & d;

2. Suppose that you want to build a 4-byte **long int** out of four calls to a routine called *getbyte()* which returns a 1-byte value. Write a single expression that represents such an integer, given that the first call to *getbyte()* gets the high-order byte and the next calls get subsequently lower-order bytes. Is your expression portable? If not, is it possible to make it portable?

3. What is the output of the following program?

    ```
    main()
    {
       short i = 0;
       printf( "%d\n", (i + 1) * (i = 1) );
       exit( 0 );
    }
    ```

    Is this program portable? Explain.

4. Which of the following *printf()* calls give a unique portable result?

    ```
    main()
    {
       printf( "%x\n", ~0 >> 1 );
       printf( "%x\n", (unsigned) ~0 >> 1 );
       printf( "%x\n", (long) 1 << 32 );
       exit( 0 );
    }
    ```

5. Write a function called *circular_shift(a, n)*, which takes *a*, which is an **unsigned long int**, and shifts it left *n* positions, where the high-order bits are reintroduced as low-order bits. For example if the binary representation of *a* is

    ```
    00010110 00111010 01110010 11100101
    ```

    then the call

    ```
    circular_shift(a, 5)
    ```

    should return a **long int** whose binary representation is

    ```
    11000111 01001110 01011100 10100010
    ```

6. Using shift operators, determine the largest **int** value that your computer can represent.

7. Write a function that accepts an **int** and prints its binary representation. (Hint: use the **sizeof** operator to ensure that your function works no matter how big an **int** is.)

8. Write a function that reads a number in binary form and converts it to hexadecimal form.

9. Which of the following expressions are not portable? Why?

    ```
    a)  x++ * ++y
    b)  x = ++y - x++
    c)  x++ / (y - y)
    d)  -3/x * y
    e)  y = (unsigned) x >> 4
    f)  y = x >> 4
    g)  y >>= x
    h)  foo(j++, j++)
    ```

10. Write a function called *pack()* that accepts four **char**s and packs them into a **long int**. The function definition should be

    ```
    long int pack( a, b, c, d )
    char a, b, c, d;
    ```

11. Modify the *breakline()* function so that it does not print a newline in the middle of a word.

12. Modify the *grade* program so that it works with any number of questions and answers less than or equal to 32. Have the user input the number of answers.

Chapter 6

Arrays and Pointers

"Curiouser and curiouser!" said Alice. — Lewis Carroll,
<u>Alice in Wonderland</u>

We have already introduced pointers as one of the scalar data types. In this chapter, we examine them more closely and introduce an aggregate type called an *array*. Arrays and pointers are closely related in C. Together, they represent some of the most powerful features of the C language and probably account, as much as anything, for C's popularity.

In C, *an array is a collection of identically typed variables stored contiguously in memory.*

Each variable in an array is called an *element* and can be accessed by giving the array name plus an index expression called a *subscript*. A subscript value of 0 identifies the initial element, a value of 1 identifies the next element, and so forth.

The most basic purpose of arrays is to store large amounts of related data that share the same data type. Suppose that you want to analyze the temperature fluctuations over the course of a year. To write such a program, you first need to store the average temperature for each day. This requires 365 memory locations. Obviously, it would be extremely tiresome to declare 365 variables, each with a unique name. Arrays provide a solution to this problem.

6.1 Declaring an Array

You declare an array by placing a pair of brackets after the array name. To specify the size of an array, enter the number of elements within the brackets. Figure 6-1 shows the syntax of an array declaration, where *array size* is an integer expression. Array *initializers* are described in Section 6.3.

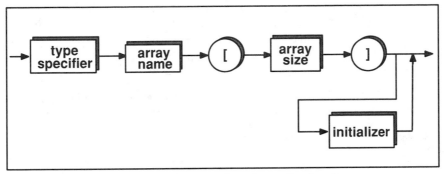

Figure 6-1. Syntax of an Array Declaration.

For the array to hold temperatures, you can write

```
int daily_temp[365];
```

This creates an array called *daily_temp* with 365 integer elements. You can then enter the temperatures of each day with assignment statements, such as

```
daily_temp[0] = 38;
daily_temp[1] = 43;
daily_temp[2] = 27;
        .
        .
```

The objects on the left side of the assignment expressions are called *array element references* since they reference a single array element. Note that subscripts begin at 0, not 1. The highest legal subscript, therefore, is always one less than the array's size. For the *daily_temp[]* array, the last element is *daily_temp[364]*.

Because subscripts begin with zero, it is confusing to identify members with words such as "first," "second," and "third." Does the "third" element refer to the element with subscript 3 or subscript 2? To avoid this confusion, we always refer to elements by their subscript number. Also, the element with subscript 0 is referred to as the *initial element*.

It may seem confusing to have arrays begin at 0 instead of 1, but it reflects C's philosophy of staying close to the computer architecture. Zero is a much more natural starting point for computers, even though it may be a bit more inconvenient for people. In other languages, such as FORTRAN 77, arrays begin with subscript 1. While the FORTRAN method may be more intuitive, it is often more costly because the compiler must subtract 1 from each subscript reference to get the true internal address of an element. The C method can produce more efficient code. Also, as you will see later in this chapter, the C method makes it very easy to access array elements through pointers.

It is important to keep in mind the difference between an array declaration and an array element reference. Though they look the same, they have different functions. In a declaration, the subscript defines the size of the array. In an array element reference, the subscript determines which element of the array is to be accessed. For instance,

```
/*  This is a declaration -- the 4 specifies the
 *  number of elements in the array.
 */
int ar[4];

/*  This is an array element reference -- the 2
 *  specifies the particular element to access.
 */
ar[2] = 0;
```

Returning to our daily temperature example, suppose we want to write a program that gives us the average temperature for the year. To simplify the problem, let us assume that you have already assigned temperature values for every element in the array. The program could be written as follows:

```
#include <stdio.h>
#define DAYS_IN_YEAR 365

main()
{
   int j, sum=0;
   int daily_temp[DAYS_IN_YEAR];

/* Assign values to daily_temp[] here. */

   for (j=0; j < DAYS_IN_YEAR; ++j)
     sum += daily_temp[j];
   printf( "The average temperature for the year is\
%d.\n", sum/DAYS_IN_YEAR );
   exit( 0 );
}
```

The variable *j* is used to subscript the array. After fetching an element and adding it to *sum*, the function increments *j* so that the next element can be accessed. When all 365 elements have been summed, the **for** loop ends and the *printf()* function outputs the average.

6.2 How Arrays Are Stored in Memory

To see how arrays are stored in memory, consider the array *ar*, which is declared and assigned values by the following statements:

```
int ar[5];    /* declaration */
ar[0] = 15;
ar[1] = 17;
ar[3] = ar[0] + ar[1];
```

The storage for this array is shown in Figure 6-2. We show the array starting at address 1000, but it could start anywhere in memory. The actual number of bytes allocated for each element depends on how large an **int** is on your computer. Our machine allocates four bytes for an **int**.

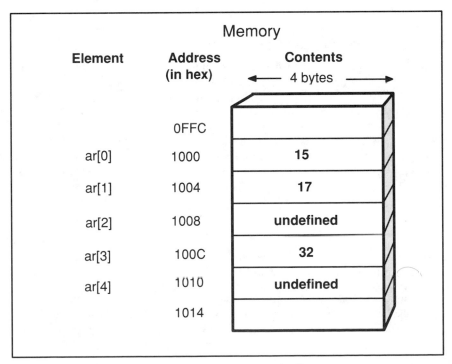

Figure 6-2. Storage of an Array.

Note that *ar[2]* and *ar[4]* have *undefined* values. This means that their values are unpredictable. The contents of these memory locations are whatever is left over from the previous program execution. In the programming world, undefined values are often called "garbage" or "trash," and they produce some of the most pesky bugs because they can cause different results each time the program is executed. They may have harmless values, such as zero, most of the time; yet in rare circumstances, they may acquire harmful values that cause the program to fail. Frequently, these bugs are not noticed until after the product has been shipped to customers and the harmful values turn up at a customer site. To avoid this type of bug, you can initialize arrays, as described in the next section.

You can find the size in bytes of an array by using the **sizeof** operator. For example, the expression

```
sizeof(ar)
```

evaluates to 20 because the array consists of five 4-byte **int**s. Note that you use the array name without a subscript reference to get the size of the entire array. If you include a subscript, you get the size of a single element. For example,

```
sizeof(ar[0])
```

evaluates to 4.

6.3 Initializing Arrays

To initialize an array prior to the ANSI Standard, you had to declare the array outside a function or precede the array declaration with the **static** keyword (see Box 6-1). Both of these methods give the array a quality called *fixed duration*, which is discussed in Chapter 7.

By default, arrays with fixed duration have all of their elements initialized to zero. You can assign different initial values by enclosing specific values in braces following the array declaration. The values must be constant expressions that can be automatically converted to the array type. For example,

```
static int a_ar[5];
static int b_ar[5]={1, 2, 3.5, 4, 5};
```

results in the storage patterns shown in Figure 6-3. Note that the floating-point 3.5 is converted to the integer value 3.

It is incorrect to enter more initialization values than there are elements in the array; the compiler should report an error when you try. If you enter fewer initialization values than elements, the remaining elements are initialized to zero. The declaration

```
static int c_ar[5]={1,2,3};
```

results in the following initial values:

```
c_ar[0] = 1
c_ar[1] = 2
c_ar[2] = 3
c_ar[3] = 0
c_ar[4] = 0
```

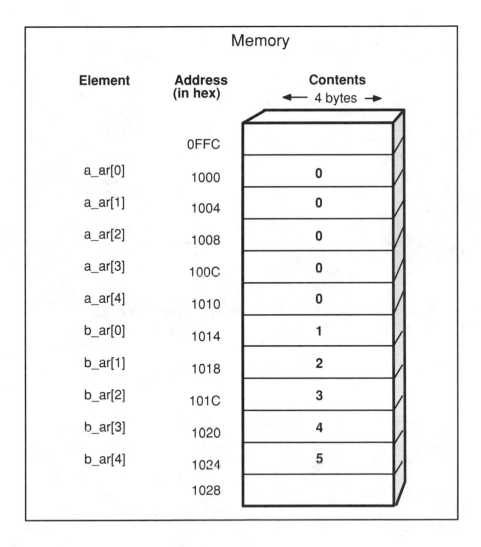

Figure 6-3. Initialization of Arrays.

When you enter initial values, you may omit the array size—the compiler auto-matically figures out how many elements are in the array based on how many initial values are present. For instance,

```
static char d_ar[]={'a' , 'b' , 'c' , 'd'};
```

creates a four-element array of **char**s with initial values:

```
d_ar[0] = 'a'
d_ar[1] = 'b'
d_ar[2] = 'c'
d_ar[3] = 'd'
```

Box 6-1: ANSI Feature — Initialization of Arrays

Most older C compilers require an array to have fixed duration to be initialized. This means that the declaration must occur outside a function or be preceded by the **static** keyword. The ANSI Standard, however, permits *automatic* arrays to be initialized as well. Automatic variables, described in detail in Chapter 7, are variables declared within a function and without the **static** keyword.

The rules for initializing automatic arrays are similar to the rules for initializing fixed arrays. As with fixed arrays, the uninitialized elements in an automatic array are initialized to zero. However, if no initializer is present, none of the elements receive a default initial value (as is the case with the old semantics). The initialization values must be constant ex-pressions.

Because this feature is not supported by many compilers, our examples are confined to the old syntax. If your compiler supports initialization of dynamic arrays, however, you should use them where applicable since they can produce more efficient code. The next chapter describes the difference between fixed and dynamic variables in greater detail.

6.4 Array Example: Encryption and Decryption

Because computers are used to store all sorts of private information, a great deal of effort goes into making them secure against intruders. On large computer systems, every file has a protection status that controls who can access the file and what they can do to it. Users, and sometimes groups of users, have passwords that they must enter to log onto a computer. These measures provide various levels of protection, but none of them give total security.

A more robust security technique is to encode files. Every character is translated into a code character so that the file looks like gibberish to someone who doesn't know the code. The following program illustrates a simple encoding function that uses an array.

```
/*  Return a coded value for a character
 */
#define ILLEGAL_VAL -1

char encode( ch )
char ch;
{
    static unsigned char encoder[128] = { 127, 124,
  121, 118, 115,112, 109, 106,103, 100, 97, 94, 91,
  88, 85, 82, 79, 76, 73, 70, 67, 64, 61, 58, 55,
  52, 49, 46, 43, 40, 37, 34, 31, 28, 25, 22, 19,
  16, 13,10, 7, 4, 1, 126, 123, 120, 117, 114, 111,
  108, 105, 102, 99, 96, 93, 90, 87, 84, 81, 78, 75,
  72, 69, 66, 63, 60, 57, 54, 51, 48, 45, 42, 39,
  36, 33, 30, 27, 24, 21, 18, 15, 12, 9, 6, 3, 125,
  122, 119, 116, 113, 110, 107, 104, 101, 98, 95, 92,
  89, 86, 83, 80, 77, 74, 71, 68, 65, 62, 59, 56,
  53, 50, 47, 44, 41, 38, 35, 32, 29, 26, 23, 20,
  17, 14, 11, 8, 5, 2, 0
    };

/* Test for illegal character. */
  if (ch > 127)
    return ILLEGAL_VAL;
  else
    return encoder[ch];   /* Return coded character.*/
}
```

First we set up a 128-element array initialized with random numbers from 0 through 127. Each element must have a unique value. Our array initialization actually follows a simple pattern, but ideally the pattern should be harder to perceive. Real encoders use an algorithm to create the translation array. The more complex the algorithm, the more difficult it is for would-be spies to break the code.

After initializing the array, we test the input argument to make sure that it is a legal character (remember that **unsigned char** objects have a range of 0 through 255). If *ch* is greater than 127, it is not a printable character so we return –1 to signify an input error. If *ch* is less than or equal to 127, we use it as a subscript expression and return the element referenced by that subscript. For every value of *ch* from 0 through 127, there is a unique translation code. If *ch* equals 0, for instance, the function returns 127; if *ch* equals 1, the function returns 124. To see how it works, consider the following program that invokes *encode( )*.

```
#include <stdio.h>

main()
{
  char c[5];
  int i;

  c[0] = encode('W');
  c[1] = encode('h');
  c[2] = encode('a');
  c[3] = encode('t');
  c[4] = encode('?');

  for (i=0; i<5; ++i)
    printf( "%d\t", c[i] );
  exit( 0 );
}
```

If your computer uses the ASCII representation of characters, program execution results in the following:

```
w        D       Y                  B
```

The phrase "What?" is coded as "wDY B" (the space between Y and B is an unprintable character). If your computer uses some other form of character representation, such as EBCDIC, the program will still work, but it will print different characters. Anyone trying to read a file that contains these encoded characters will be very confused, to say the least. Of course, authorized readers need a decoder that has a reverse translation table to translate the file back to its original form.

6.5 Pointer Arithmetic

The C language allows you to add and subtract integers to and from pointers. If p is a pointer, the expression

```
p+3
```

is perfectly legal, meaning three objects after the object that p points to. Since p holds an address, performing arithmetic on p generates a new address value. However, rather than simply adding 3 to p, the compiler multiplies the 3 by the size of the object that p points to. This is called *scaling*.

Suppose, for example, that the address value held by p is 1000. If p is declared as a pointer to a 4-byte **long int**, the 3 in $p+3$ is multiplied by 4. The value of $p+3$, therefore, is 1012. On the other hand, if p is declared as a pointer to a **char**, $p+3$ would equal 1003. In this way, the expression $p+3$ always means 3 objects after p, regardless of the type of object that p points to.

6.5.1 Pointer Subtraction

It is legal to subtract one pointer value from another, provided that the pointers point to the same type of object. This operation yields an integral value that represents the number of objects between the two pointers. If the first pointer represents a lower address than the second pointer, the result is negative. For example,

```
&a[3]  -  &a[0]
```

evaluates to 3, but

```
&a[0]  -  &a[3]
```

evaluates to –3.

It is also legal to subtract an integral value from a pointer value. This type of expression yields a pointer value. The following examples illustrate some legal and illegal pointer expressions:

```
long *p1, *p2;
int j;
char *p3;

p2 = p1 + 4;   /* legal */
j = p2 - p1;   /* legal -- j is assigned 4  */
j = p1 - p2;   /* legal -- j is assigned -4 */
p1 = p2 - 2;   /* legal -- compatible pointer types */
p3 = p1 - 1;   /* ILLEGAL -- different pointer types*/
j = p1 - p3;   /* ILLEGAL -- different pointer types*/
```

6.5.2 Null Pointer

The C language supports the notion of a *null pointer*—that is, a pointer that is guaranteed not to point to a valid object. A null pointer is any pointer assigned the integral value zero. For example,

```
char *p;

p = 0;   /* make p a null pointer */
```

In this one case—assignment of zero—you do not need to cast the integral expression to the pointer type.

Null pointers are particularly useful in control-flow statements since the zero-valued pointer evaluates to false, whereas all other pointer values evaluate to true. For example, the following **while** loop continues iterating until p is a null pointer:

```
char *p;
   .
   .
while (p)
{
   .
/* iterate until p is a null pointer */
   .
}
```

This use of null pointers is particularly prevalent in applications that use arrays of pointers, as described later in this chapter.

6.6 Passing Pointers as Function Arguments

As we mentioned in Chapter 3, the compiler complains if you try to mix different types of pointers. The one exception to this rule occurs when you pass pointers as arguments. In the absence of function prototyping (described in Chapter 9), the compiler does not check to make sure that the type of the actual argument is the same as the type of the formal argument. If the types are different, strange behavior can result. The following program shows what can happen if you pass a pointer to one type but declare it as a pointer to a different type on the receiving side.

```
#include <stdio.h>

void clr( p )
long *p;
{
    *p = 0;   /* Store a zero at location p. */
}

main()
{
  static short s[3] = {1, 2, 3};

  clr( &s[1] );   /* Clear element 1 of s[]. */
  printf( "s[0]=%d\ns[1]=%d\ns[2]=%d\n", s[0],
          s[1], s[2] );
  exit( 0 );
}
```

First we assign the values 1, 2, and 3 to *s[0]*, *s[1]*, and *s[2]*, respectively. Then we send the address of element 1 to the *clr()* function, which sets the element equal to 0. The values of *s[0]*, *s[1]*, and *s[2]* should now be 1, 0, and 3. The output, however, is

```
s[0]=1
s[1]=0
s[2]=0
```

The problem is that the pointer *p* in the *clr()* function is declared as a pointer to a **long** integer. When zero gets assigned to the address of *p*, four bytes are zeroed. *s[1]*, which is a **short** integer, is only two bytes long, so two extra bytes get cleared. Because arrays are stored contiguously in memory, the two extra bytes are the ones allocated for *s[2]*. Figure 6-4 shows what transpires. It is worth taking some time to understand this example since it illustrates an important concept in the C language.

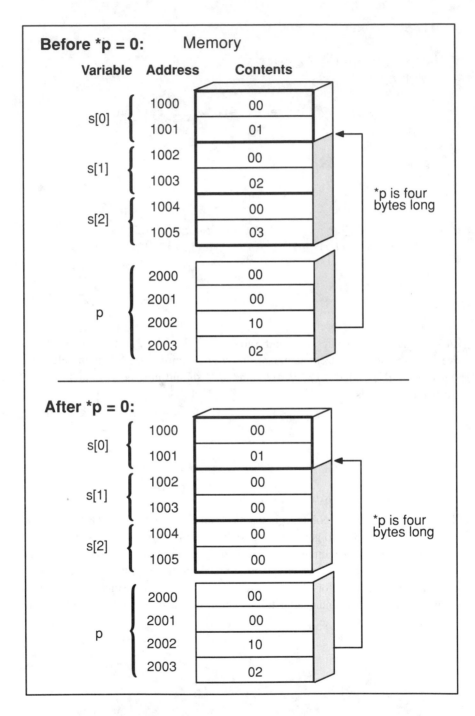

Figure 6-4. Passing the Wrong Pointer Type. Because *p points to* a **long int**, *four bytes are set to zero.*

6.7 Accessing Array Elements Through Pointers

One way to access array elements is to enter the array name followed by a subscript. Another way is through pointers. The declarations

```
short ar[4];
short *p;
```

create an array of four variables of type **short**, called *ar[0], ar[1], ar[2],* and *ar[3],* and a variable named *p* that is a pointer to a **short**. Using the "address of" operator (&), you can now make the assignment,

```
p = &ar[0];
```

which assigns the address of array element 0 to *p*. If we dereference *p*,

```
*p
```

we get the value of element *ar[0]*.

Until the value of *p* is changed, the expressions *ar[0]* and **p* refer to the same memory location. Due to the scaled nature of pointer arithmetic, the expression

```
*(p+3)
```

refers to the same memory contents as

```
ar[3]
```

In fact, for any integer expression *e*,

```
*(p+e)
```

is the same as

```
ar[e]
```

This brings us to the first important relationship between arrays and pointers: *Adding an integer to a pointer that points to the beginning of an array, and then dereferencing that expression, is the same as using the integer as a subscript value to the array.*

The second important relationship is that an array name that is not followed by a subscript is interpreted as a pointer to the initial element of the array. That is, the expressions

```
ar
```

and

```
&ar[0]
```

are exactly the same. Combining these two relationships, we arrive at the following important equivalence:

ar[n] is the same as *(ar + n)

This relationship is unique to the C language and is one of C's most important features. When the C compiler sees an array name, it translates it into a pointer to the initial element of the array. Then the compiler interprets the subscript as an offset from the *base address* position. For example, the compiler interprets the expression *ar[2]* as a pointer to the first element of *ar*, plus an offset of 2 elements. Due to scaling, the offset determines how many elements to skip, so an offset of 2 means skip two elements. The two expressions

```
ar[2]
*(ar+2)
```

are equivalent. In both cases, *ar* is a pointer to the initial element of the array and 2 is an offset that tells the compiler to add two to the pointer value.

Because of this interrelationship, pointer variables and array names can be used interchangeably to reference array elements. It is important to remember, however, that the values of pointer variables can be changed whereas array names cannot be changed. This is because an array name by itself is not a variable—it refers to the address of the array variable. You cannot change the address of variables. This means that a naked array name (one without a subscript or indirection operator) cannot appear on the left-hand side of an assignment statement. For instance,

```
float ar[5], *p;

p = ar;            /* legal -- same as p= &ar[0]      */
ar = p;            /* illegal -- you may not assign   */
                   /*              to an array address */
&p = ar;           /* illegal -- you may not assign   */
                   /*            to a pointer address  */
ar++;              /* illegal -- you may not          */
                   /*    increment an array address   */
ar[1] = *(p+3);    /* legal -- ar[1] is a variable    */
p++;               /* legal -- you may increment a    */
                   /*            pointer variable      */
```

This difference between pointers and arrays is an important distinction to grasp. We encounter this distinction again when we describe character strings later in this chapter. In the above examples, note that scaling allows you to use the increment and decrement operators to point to the next or previous element of an array.

6.8 Passing Arrays as Function Arguments

In C, an array name that appears as a function argument is interpreted as the address of the first element of the array. For instance,

```
main()
{
  extern float func();
  float x, farray[5];
       .
       .
  x = func( farray ); /* Same as func(&farray[0]) */
       .
       .
}
```

On the receiving side, you need to declare the argument as a pointer to the initial element of an array. There are two ways to do this:

```
func( ar )
float *ar;
{

     .
     .

}
```

or

```
func( ar )
float ar[];
{

     .
     .

}
```

The second example declares *ar* to be an array of indeterminate size. You may omit the size specification because no storage is being allocated for the array. The array has already been created in the calling routine, and what is being passed is really a pointer to the first element of the array. Since the compiler knows that array expressions result in pointers to the first element of the array, it converts *ar* into a pointer to a **float**, just like the first declaration. Functionally, therefore, the two versions are equivalent. In terms of readability, however, the second version may be superior since it emphasizes that the object being passed is the base address of an array. In the first version, there is no way of knowing whether *ar* points to a single **float** or to the beginning of an array of **floats**.

It is also legal to declare the size of the array in an argument declaration:

```
func( ar )
float ar[6];
{
      .


      .

}
```

However, the compiler uses the size information only for bounds checking (if the compiler supports this feature). (See Box 6-2 for more about bounds checking.) Also, you must specify all but the first dimension size of a multidimensional array. This is described in Section 6.10.

The choice of declaring a function argument as an array or as a pointer has no effect on the compiler's operation (unless your compiler supports bounds checking)—it is purely for human readability.. (This may change in the future. See Box 9-1 for a discussion about ANSI's future plans for array parameters.) To the compiler, *ar* simply points to a **float**; it is *not* an array. Because of the pointer-array equivalence, however, you can still access *ar* as if it were an array. But you cannot find out the size of the array in the calling function by using the **sizeof** operator on the argument. For example,

```
#include <stdio.h>

main()
{
   void print_size();
   float f_array[10];

   printf( "The size of f_array is: %d\n",
           sizeof(f_array) );
   print_size( f_array );
   exit( 0 );
}

void print_size( arg )
float arg[];
{
   printf("The size of arg is: %d\n", sizeof(arg) );
}
```

On our computer, the results of running this program are

```
The size of f_array is: 40
The size of arg is: 4
```

The variable *f_array* is an array of ten 4-byte **float**s, so the value 40 is its correct size in bytes. The variable *arg*, on the other hand, is converted to a pointer to a

float. On our machine, pointers are four bytes long, so the size of *arg* is 4. Because it is impossible for the called function to deduce the size of the passed array, it is often a good idea to pass the size of the array along with the base address. This enables the receiving function to check array boundaries:

```
#define MAX_SIZE 1000

void foo( f_array, f_array_size );
float f_array[];
int f_array_size;
{
    .
    .
    .
    if (f_array_size > MAX_SIZE)
    {
      printf( "Array too large.\n" );
      exit( 1 );
    }
    .
    .
    .
```

You can obtain the number of elements in an array by dividing the size of the array by the size of each element. On the calling side, you would write

```
foo( f_array, sizeof(f_array)/sizeof(f_array[0]) );
```

Note that this expression works regardless of the type of element in *f_array[]*.

6.9 Sorting Algorithms

Sorting a list of objects into alphabetical or numerical order is a common programming operation and is a classic application of arrays. Although the idea of sorting is simple enough, it turns out that the process can be complicated. There are numerous sorting algorithms, and the mathematical analyses for deciding which are the most efficient are the subject of many lengthy volumes.

In this section, we show one of the simpler algorithms, called a *bubble sort*. The idea behind a bubble sort is to compare adjacent elements, starting with the first two, and interchange them if the first is larger than the second. After comparing the first two elements, we compare the second and third, then the third and fourth, and so on until we reach the end of the array. Comparing all the adjacent pairs is termed a *pass*. If in the first pass we need to interchange any of the pairs, we need to make another pass. We keep making passes until the array is in sorted order.

Box 6-2: Bug Alert — Walking Off the End of an Array

Unlike many programming languages, C does not require compilers to *check array bounds*. (A few compilers include options that let you check anyway.) This means that you can attempt to access elements for which no memory has been allocated. The results are unpredictable. Sometimes you will access memory that has been allocated for other variables. Sometimes you will attempt to access special protected areas of memory and your programs will abort. Usually this type of error occurs because you are off by one in testing for the end of the array. For example, consider the following program, which attempts to initialize every element of an array to zero:

```
main()
{
  int ar[10], j;

  for (j=0; j <= 10; j++)
    ar[j] = 0;
}
```

Since we have declared *ar[]* to hold ten elements, we can validly refer to elements 0 through 9. Our **for** loop, however, has an off-by-one bug in it. The loop runs from 0 through 10, so element 10 also gets assigned zero. Since there is no element 10, the compiler overwrites a portion of memory, very likely the portion of memory reserved for *j*. This will produce an infinite loop because *j* will be reset to zero.

You can avoid this type of error by keeping your functions small and testing each one after it is written. This way, you can catch these bugs early before they become a major problem.

To see exactly what is happening we have added a couple of *printf()* statements that show the current status of the array before each pass.

```
/*   Sort an array of ints in ascending order using
 *   the bubble sort algorithm.
 */


#define FALSE 0
#define TRUE 1
#include <stdio.h>
                                     ovd
void bubble_sort( list, list_size )
int list[], list_size;
{
   int j, k, temp, sorted = FALSE;
   while ( !sorted )
   {
      sorted = TRUE;    /* assume list is sorted */

/* Print loop: not part of bubble sort algorithm */
      for (k = 0; k < list_size; k++)
         printf( "%d\t", list[k] );
      printf( "\n" );
/* End of print loop */

      for (j = 0; j < list_size -1; j++)
      {
         if (list[j] > list[j+1])
         {
/* At least 1 element is out of order */
            sorted = FALSE;
            temp = list[j];
            list[j] = list[j+1];
            list[j+1] = temp;
         }
      } /* end of for loop */
   } /* end of while loop */
}
```

The function accepts two parameters, a pointer to the first element of an array of **int**s and an **int** representing the size of the array.

The following program calls *bubble_sort()* with a 10-element array.

```
main()
{
  int i;
  static int list[] = { 13, 56, 23, 1, 89, 58,
                          20, 125, 86, 3};

  bubble_sort( list, sizeof(list)/sizeof(list[0]));
  exit( 0 );
}
```

Note how we pass the number of elements in the array using the **sizeof** operator. This is a useful technique in C because it is portable. We can add new elements to the array, and the size of the array elements can vary, but we never need to change the function call. Program execution results in the following output:

13	56	23	1	89	58	20	125	86	3
13	23	1	56	58	20	89	86	3	125
13	1	23	56	20	58	86	3	89	125
1	13	23	20	56	58	3	86	89	125
1	13	20	23	56	3	58	86	89	125
1	13	20	23	3	56	58	86	89	125
1	13	20	3	23	56	58	86	89	125
1	13	3	20	23	56	58	86	89	125
1	3	13	20	23	56	58	86	89	125

The bubble sort is not very efficient, but it's a simple algorithm that illustrates array manipulation. The standard runtime library contains a much more efficient sorting function called *qsort()*. We describe how to use *qsort()* in Chapter 9.

6.10 Strings

One of the most common uses of arrays is to store strings of characters. A string is an array of characters terminated by a *null character*. A null character is a character with a numeric value of zero. It is represented in C by the escape sequence: **'\0'**. A *string constant*, sometimes called a *string literal*, is any series of characters enclosed in double quotes. It has a data type of *array of char*, and each character in the string takes up one byte. In addition, the compiler automatically appends a *null character* to designate the end of the string.

6.10.1 Declaring and Initializing Strings

To store a string in memory, you need to declare an array of type **char**. You may initialize an array of **char**s with a string constant. For example,

```
static char str[] = "some text";
```

The array is one element longer than the number of characters in the string to accommodate the trailing null character. *str[]*, therefore, is ten characters in length. If you specify an array size, you must allocate enough characters to hold the string. In the following example, for instance, the first four elements are initialized with the characters 'y', 'e', 's', and '\0'. The remaining six elements receive the default initial value of zero:

```
static char str[10] = "yes";
```

The following statement, however, is illegal:

```
static char str[3] = "four";   /* illegal */
```

Some compilers, including those that conform to the ANSI Standard, allow you to specify an array size that does not include the trailing null character. The following declaration causes the compiler to allocate four characters, initialized to 'f', 'o', 'u', and 'r':

```
static char str[4] = "four"; /* no trailing null */
```

You may also initialize a **char** pointer with a string constant. The declaration

```
char *ptr = "more text";
```

also creates an array of characters initialized with "more text," but it is subtly different from the preceding declaration. Both declarations allocate the same amount of storage for the string and initialize the memory locations with the same values, but the pointer declaration creates an additional 4-byte variable for the pointer (see Figure 6-5).

All subsequent uses of the array name refer to the address of the array's initial element. This address, as we said before, cannot be changed. The pointer is a *variable* that is initialized with the address of the array's initial element. However, you can assign a different address value to the pointer. In this case, the address with which it was initialized will be lost.

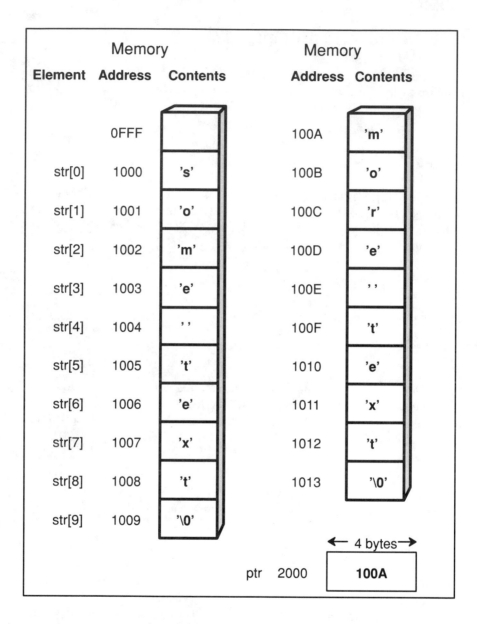

Figure 6-5. Storage of a String.

6.10.2 String Assignments

The reason you can initialize a pointer with a string constant is that a string is an array of **char**s, so C treats string constants like other arrays—it interprets a string constant as a pointer to the first character of the string. This means that you can assign a string constant to a pointer that points to a **char.** However, you must be careful about allocating enough memory for the string, as shown below.

```
main()
{
  char array[10];
  char *ptr1 = "10 spaces";
  char *ptr2;

  array = "not OK"; /* cannot assign to an address */
  array[5] = 'A';    /* OK */
  ptr1[5] = 'B';     /* OK */
  ptr1 = "OK";
  ptr1[5] = 'C';         /* questionable due to prior  */
                         /* assignment */
  *ptr2 = "not OK";  /* type mismatch */
  ptr2 = "OK";
  exit( 0 );
}
```

This example highlights many of the problems that beginners have with pointers, arrays, and strings, so we'll discuss each assignment in detail.

```
array = "not OK";
```
        array represents the address of the initial element of the array, so it cannot be changed. Note, however, that the operand types agree because the string "not OK" is interpreted as a pointer to the first character, *n*.

```
array[5] = 'A';
```
        This is a simple assignment to element 5 of the *array[]* array.

```
ptr1[5] = 'B';
```
        ptr1 is a pointer to a **char** that has been initialized to point to the string "*10 spaces*," which exists somewhere in memory. Because of the pointer-array equivalence, this assignment changes the value of element 5, so that *ptr1* now points to a string whose contents are "*10 spBces.*" Note that this assignment does not change the value of *ptr1*.

```
ptr1 = "OK";
```
        This assignment changes the value of *ptr1* so that it now points to a string "*OK*," which exists somewhere else in memory.

```
ptr1[5] = 'C';
```

Due to the prior assignment, *ptr1* points to a string whose contents are "OK." Including the terminating null character, this string takes up three bytes of memory. This assignment attempts to assign a value to a memory location 3 bytes beyond the terminating null character in "OK," thereby accessing memory whose contents are unknown. This will not produce a compile-time error, but it will very likely produce a runtime error or erroneous results.

```
*ptr2 = "not OK";
```

In this case, we are attempting to assign a value to the **char** which *ptr2* points to. The string is interpreted as the address of the first character *n*, so this assignment is attempting to assign an address value to a **char**. According to the ANSI Standard, this is illegal — address values may be assigned only to pointer variables. Older compilers may accept this syntax, but they should at least issue a warning.

```
ptr2 = "OK";
```

This assignment illustrates that you can assign a string to a **char** pointer even if you have not initialized the pointer. There is no difference between this statement and the statement

```
ptr1 = "OK";
```

6.10.3 Strings vs. Chars

It is important to recognize the difference between string constants and character constants. In the following two declarations, one byte is allocated for *ch* but *two* bytes are allocated for the string *"a"* (an extra byte for the terminating null character), plus additional memory is allocated for the pointer *ps*.

```
char ch = 'a';   /* One byte is allocated for 'a' */

/*  In the following declaration, two bytes are
 *  allocated for "a", plus an implementation-
 *  defined number of bytes are allocated for
 *  the pointer ps.
 */
char *ps = "a";
```

It is legal to assign a character constant through a dereferenced pointer:

```
*p = 'a';
```

But it is incorrect to assign a string to a dereferenced **char** pointer:

```
*p = "a";   /* INCORRECT */
```

Since a string is interpreted as a pointer to a **char** and a dereferenced pointer has the type of the object that it points to, this assignment attempts to assign a pointer value to a **char** variable. This is illegal. By the same token, it is legal to assign a string to a pointer (without dereferencing it), but it is incorrect to assign a character constant to a pointer:

```
p = "a";   /* OK */
p = 'a';   /* Illegal - p is a pointer, not a char.
            */
```

The last assignment attempts to assign a **char** value to a pointer variable. An ANSI-conforming compiler should issue an error. Some older compilers merely report a warning.

The crucial observation to be made is that initializations and assignments are not symmetrical: You can write

```
char *p = "string";
```

but not

```
*p = "string";
```

Note that this is true of assignments and initializations of all data types, not just character arrays. For instance,

```
float f;
float *pf = &f;   /* OK */

*pf = &f;   /* ILLEGAL */
```

6.10.4 Reading and Writing Strings

You can read and write strings with the *printf()* and *scanf()* functions by using the %s format specifier. For *scanf()*, the data argument should be a pointer to an array of characters that is long enough to store the input string. The input string is terminated by any space character. After reading in the input characters, *scanf()* automatically appends a null character to make it a proper string. On the *printf()* side, the data argument should be a pointer to a null-terminated array of characters. *printf()* outputs successive characters until it reaches a null character. The following program reads a string from the standard input device and then prints it out ten times.

```
#include <stdio.h>
#define MAX_CHAR 80

main()
{
  char str[MAX_CHAR];
  int i;

  printf(" Enter a string: ");
  scanf( "%s", str );
  for (i = 0; i < 10; ++i)
    printf( "%s\n", str );
  exit( 0 );
}
```

Note that we can use the array name as the data argument because a naked array name is really a pointer to the initial element of the array. One drawback of this program is that it can fail if the input string is more than *MAX_CHAR* characters. We leave it as an exercise to the reader to remove this deficiency.

In addition to *printf()* and *scanf()*, the C runtime library contains many functions that manipulate strings. In this section, we show some sample source code for a few of them to illustrate some of the concepts behind arrays and pointers.

6.10.5 The String Length Function

Probably the simplest string function is *strlen()*, which returns the number of characters in a string, not including the trailing null character. Using arrays, *strlen()* can be written

```
int strlen( str )
char str[];
{
  int i=0;
  while (str[i])
     ++i;
  return i;
}
```

We test each element of *str*, one by one, until we reach the null character. If *str[i]* is the null character, it will have a value of zero, making the **while** condition false. Any other value of *str[i]* makes the **while** condition true. Once the null character is reached, we exit the **while** loop and return *i*, which is the last subscript value and, conveniently, the length of the string.

You could also write the function using a **for** statement instead of a **while** statement:

```
int strlen( str )
char str[];
{
   int i;
   for (i=0; str[i]; ++i)
      ;             /* null statement in for body */
   return i;
}
```

The pointer version of *strlen()* would be

```
int strlen( str )
char *str;
{
   int i;

   for (i = 0; *str++; i++)
      ;  /* null statement */
   return i;
}
```

The expression

```
*str++
```

illustrates a common idiom in C. Since the ++ operator has the same precedence as the * operator, associativity rules take effect. Both operators bind from right to left, so the expression causes the compiler to

1. Evaluate the post-increment (++) operator. Because ++ is a *post*-increment operator, the compiler passes *str* to the next operator but makes a note to increment *str* after the entire expression is complete.

2. Evaluate the indirection (*) operator, applied to *str*.

3. Complete the expression by incrementing *str*.

Box 6-3: ANSI Feature — String Concatenation

The ANSI Standard states that two adjacent string literals will be concatenated into a single null-terminated string. For example, the statement

```
printf( "one.." "two..." "three\n" );
```

is treated as if it had been written

```
printf( "one..two...three\n" );
```

Note that the terminating null characters of the string(s) are not included in the concatenated string. This feature is particularly useful with regard to macros that expand to string literals, as described in Chapter 10. String concatenation can also be used to break up long strings that would otherwise require the continuation character. For example, the statement

```
printf( "This is a very long string that\
cannot fit on one line\n" );
```

can be written

```
printf( "This is a very long string that"
        "cannot fit on one line\n" );
```

As this example illustrates, string concatenation (combined with the fact that the compiler ignores the spaces between tokens) gives you greater formatting flexibility.

6.10.6 String Copy Function

The following function, called *strcpy()*, copies a string from one array to another.

```
void strcpy( s1, s2 )
char s1[], s2[];
{
  int i;

  for (i=0; s1[i]; ++i)
    s2[i] = s1[i];
  s2[++i] = '\0';
}
```

Note that we need to explicitly append a null character because the loop ends before the terminating null character is copied. Note also that we must use the prefix increment operator in the expression

```
s2[++i]
```

We can rewrite this function using pointers as follows:

```
void strcpy( s1, s2 )
char *s1, *s2;
{
   int i;

   for (i=0; *(s1+i); ++i)
     *(s2+i) = *(s1+i);
   s2[++i] = '\0';
}
```

Due to the array–pointer relationship described earlier, your compiler should produce exactly the same code for both the array and pointer versions. The choice of which version to use, therefore, revolves around readability. We feel that the array version is more straightforward. Although both versions are perfectly fine and will work correctly, a superior version that runs faster on most machines is the following:

```
void strcpy( s1, s2 )
char *s1, *s2;
{
   while (*s2++ = *s1++)
     ; /* null statement */
}
```

This version utilizes just about all of the shortcuts that C provides. Instead of adding an offset to the string pointer, we just increment it with the post-increment operator. The result of the assignment is used as the test condition for the **while** loop. Remember that even an assignment expression has a value. If *s2 equals zero (which it will on the terminating null character), the entire assignment expression will equal zero and the **while** loop will end. By using the assignment expression as the test condition, we no longer need an extra statement to assign the terminating null character. Note that we use a postfix increment operator instead of a prefix operator. If we used ++ before the variable

```
(*(++s1))
```

the function would not work because it would always skip the initial element.

We say this version is "superior," but perhaps we should qualify this term. This version is superior in the sense that it produces the most efficient machine code. At first blush, it may seem less readable than our first version because so many things are happening at once. To an experienced C programmer, however, it is more readable because seasoned C programmers are familiar with the techniques being used. Very often, there is a give–and–take relationship between readability and efficiency. The decision as to which quality is more important depends to a large degree on your application and your resources. If you have unlimited CPU power and memory, the question of efficiency should take a backseat to readability. If it is important that your program runs fast and occupies a small amount of memory, you may have to make some sacrifices to readability. The efficient version of *strcpy()* illustrates the power and elegance of the C language. Do not be discouraged, though, if you feel uncomfortable with this version. Like any foreign language, the C language is full of idioms that take time to learn.

6.10.7 Pattern Matching

The next program is a pattern-matching function. Though not part of many C libraries, this is nevertheless a common and useful function. (In the ANSI C runtime library, this function is called *strstr()*, but we call it *pat_match()*.) It accepts two arguments, both pointers to character strings. It then searches the first string for an occurrence of the second string. If it is successful, it returns the byte position of the occurrence; if it is unsuccessful, it returns −1. For example, if the first string is: "Everybody complains about the weather but nobody ever does anything about it" and the second string is "the weather," the function would return 26 because "the weather" starts at element 26 of the first string.

```
#include <stdio.h>

/* Return the position of str2 in str1; -1 if not
 * found.
 */
int pat_match( str1, str2 )
char str1[], str2[];
{
    int j, k;

    for (j=0; j < strlen(str1); ++j)
    {
/*  test str1[j] with each character in str2[].  If
 *  equal, get next char in str1[].  Exit loop if we
 *  get to end of str1[], or if chars are equal.
 */
        for (k=0; (k < strlen(str2) && (str2[k] ==
             str1[k+j])); k++);

/*  Check to see if loop ended because we arrived at
 *  end of str2.  If so, strings must be equal.
 */
        if (k == strlen( str2 ))
            return j;
    }
    return -1;
}
```

There are two loops, one nested within the other. The outer loop increments *j* until it reaches the end of *str1*. The inner loop compares the current character in *str1* with the first character in *str2*. If they are equal, it tests the next character in each string. The loop ends either when the characters in the two strings no longer match or when there are no more characters in *str2*. If the loop ends because there are no characters left, the strings match and we return *j*, which is the byte position in *str1*. If the loop ends because the strings do not match, we jump back to the outer loop and test the next character in *str1*. If we reach the end of *str1* without a match, we return –1.

The value –1 is convenient as a failure indicator because there is no possibility of ambiguity. If the pattern match is successful, a non-negative number will be returned. You will find that most functions in the C library return either –1 or 0 as a failure signal. In this example, we cannot return 0 for failure because 0 will be returned if the pattern match is successful on the initial element of *str2*.

The *pat_match()* function has a serious flaw. It calls *strlen()* with each iteration of the **for** loop. This is a waste of computer cycles since the string length never changes. We can remove this problem by storing the string length in a variable:

```
#include <stdio.h>

/* Return the position of str2 in str1; -1 if not
 * found.
 */
pat_match( str1, str2 )
char str1[], str2[];
{
   int j, k;
   int length1 = strlen( str1 );
   int length2 = strlen( str2 );

   for (j=0; j < length1; ++j)
   {
      for (k=0; k < length2; k++)
        if (str2[k] != str1[k+j])
           break;
      if (k == length2)
         return j;
   }
   return -1;
}
```

This second version requires two extra variables, but the savings in CPU effort are well worth the extra memory allocation. An even more efficient version of this function is shown on the following page. Again, while it is more efficient, it may be less readable to you. However, the more programs you see that use these idioms and shortcuts, the more readable they will become.

```
/* Return the first occurrence of str2 in str1
 * using pointers instead of arrays;   return -1
 * if no match is found.
 */
pat_match( str1, str2 )
char *str1, *str2;
{
  char *p, *q, *substr;

/* Iterate for each character position in str1 */
  for (substr = str1; *substr; substr++)
    {
      p = substr;
      q = str2;
    /* See if str2 matches at this char position */
      while (*q)
        if (*q++ != *p++)
          goto no_match;

  /* Only arrive here if every char in str2
   * matched. Return the number of characters
   * between the original start of str1 and the
   * current character position by using pointer
   * subtraction.
   */
      return substr - str1;

  /* Arrive here if while loop couldn't match str2.
   * Since this is the end of the for loop, the
   * increment part of the for will be executed
   * (substr++), followed by the check for
   * termination (*substr), followed by this loop
   * body.  We have to use goto to get here because
   * we want to break out of the while loop and
   * continue the for loop at the same time.  Note
   * that the semicolon is required after the label
   * so that the label prefixes a statement (albeit
   * a null one).
   */
      no_match: ;
    }
/* We arrive here if we have gone through every
 * character of str1 and did not find a match.
 */
  return -1;
}
```

To show how to use *pat_match()*, we need to write a *main()* routine that reads in a string and a pattern to be matched. However, we can't use *scanf()* and *%s* because *scanf()* stops assigning characters to the array as soon as a space character is encountered. If a string or pattern contains a space, the program won't work. Fortunately, there is another runtime routine, called *gets()*, that reads a string from your terminal (including spaces) and assigns the string to a character array. The *gets()* function takes one argument, which is a pointer to the character array. Characters are read from the terminal until a linefeed or end-of-file is encountered. When you use this function, be sure to make your character array large enough to hold the longest possible input string. The following example shows how we might call *pat_match()*.

```
#include <stdio.h>

main()
{
   char first_string[100] , pattern[100];
   int pos;

   printf( "Enter str: " );
   gets( first_string );
   printf( "Enter pattern to be matched: " );
   gets( pattern );
   pos = pat_match( first_string, pattern );
   if (pos == -1)
      printf( "The pattern was not matched.\n" );
   else
      printf( "The pattern was matched at position\
%d\n", pos );
   exit( 0 );
}
```

A typical execution of the program would be

```
Enter str: To be or not to be, that is the question.
Enter pattern to be matched: to be
The pattern was matched at position 13
```

The first "To be" is not matched because the "T" is capitalized: the pattern matching function is case sensitive.

In addition to the string functions used in the previous examples, there are many others in the Standard Library (see Table 6-1).

strcpy()	Copies a string to an array.
strncpy()	Copies a portion of a string to an array.
strcat()	Appends one string to another.
strncat()	Copies a portion of one string to another.
strcmp()	Compares two strings.
strncmp()	Compares two strings up to a specified number of characters.
strchr()	Finds the first occurrence of a specified character in a string.
strcoll()	Compares two strings based on an implementation-defined collating sequence.
strcspn()	Computes the length of a string that does not contain specified characters.
strerror()	Maps an error number with a textual error message.
strlen()	Computes the length of a string.
strpbrk()	Finds the first occurrence of any specified characters in a string.
strrchr()	Finds the last occurrence of any specified characters in a string.
strspn()	Computes the length of a string that contains only specified characters.
strstr()	Finds the first occurrence of one string embedded in another.
strtok()	Breaks a string into a sequence of tokens.
strxfrm()	Transforms a string so that it is a suitable as an argument to *strcmp()*.

Table 6-1. String Functions in the Standard Library. See Appendix A for a more complete description of these routines.

6.11 Multidimensional Arrays

An array of arrays is a *multidimensional array* and is declared with consecutive pairs of brackets. For instance,

```
/*  In the following, x is a 3-element array of
 *  5-element arrays.
 */
int x[3][5];

/*  In the following, x is a 3-element array of
 *  4-element arrays of 5-element arrays.
 */
char x[3][4][5];
```

Although a multidimensional array is stored as a one-dimensional sequence of elements, you can treat it as an array of arrays. For example, consider the following 5 × 5 "magic square." It is called magic because the rows, columns, and diagonals all have the same sum.

17	24	1	8	15
23	5	7	14	16
4	6	13	20	22
10	12	19	21	3
11	18	25	2	9

To store this square in an array, we could make the following declaration:

```
static int magic[5][5] = { {17 , 24 ,  1 ,  8 , 15 },
                           {23 ,  5 ,  7 , 14 , 16 },
                           { 4 ,  6 , 13 , 20 , 22 },
                           {10 , 12 , 19 , 21 ,  3 },
                           {11 , 18 , 25 ,  2 ,  9 }
                         };
```

In the initialization, each row of values is enclosed by braces.

To access an element in a multidimensional array, you specify as many sub-scripts as are necessary. Multidimensional arrays are stored in row-major order, which means that the last subscript varies fastest. For example, the array de-clared as

```
int ar[2][3]={ { 0, 1, 2 },
               { 3, 4, 5 }
             };
```

is stored as shown in Figure 6-6.

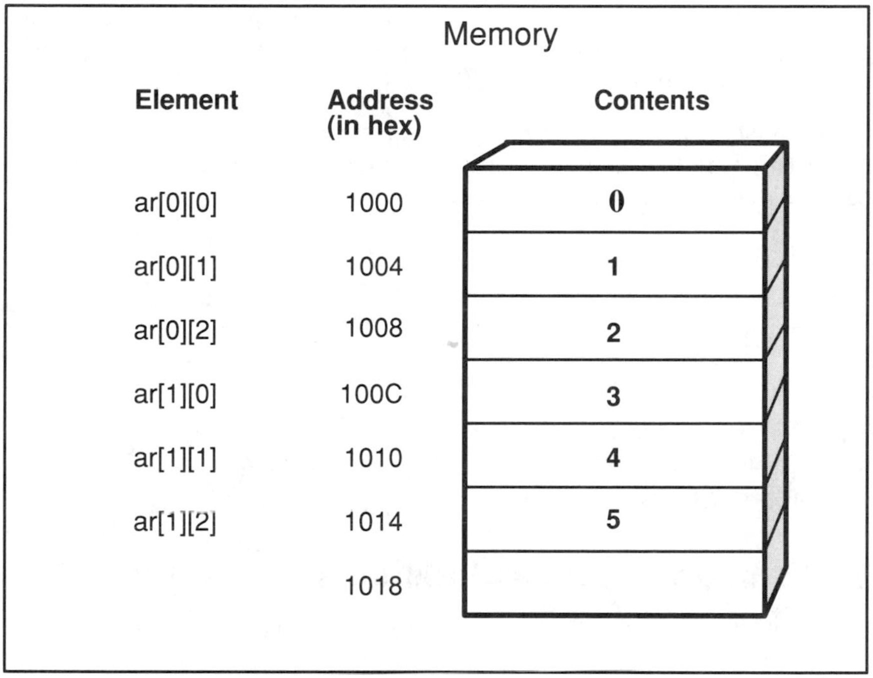

Figure 6-6.   Storage of a Multidimensional Array.

The array reference

```
ar[1][2]
```

is interpreted as

```
*(ar[1] + 2)
```

which is further expanded to

```
*(*(ar+1)+2)
```

Recall that *ar* is an array of arrays. When *(ar+1)* is evaluated, therefore, the 1 is scaled to the size of the object, which in this case is a 3-element array of **int**s (which we assume are four bytes long), and the 2 is scaled to the size of an **int**:

```
*(int *)( (char *)ar + (1*3*4)) + (2*4))
```

We put in the *(char *)* cast to turn off scaling because we have already made the scaling explicit. The *(int *)* cast ensures that we get all four bytes of the integer when we dereference the address value. After doing the arithmetic, the expression becomes

```
*(int *) ( (char *)ar + 20 )
```

The value 20 has already been scaled so it represents the number of bytes to skip. If *ar* starts at address 1000, as in our picture, *ar[1][2]* refers to the **int** that begins at address 1014 (hex value), which is 5.

If you specify fewer subscripts than there are dimensions, the result is a pointer to the base type of the array. For example, given the two-dimensional array declared above, you could make the reference

```
ar[1]
```

which is the same as

```
&ar[1][0]
```

The result is a pointer to an **int**.

The ANSI Standard places no limits on the number of dimensions an array may have, although implementations may impose a limit. They are required, however, to support at least six dimensions.

6.11.1 Initializing a Multidimensional Array

When initializing a multidimensional array, you may enclose each row in braces. If there are too few initializers, the extra elements in the row are initialized to zero. Consider the following example:

```
static int examp[5][3] = { { 1 , 2 , 3 },
                           { 4 },
                           { 5 , 6 , 7 } };
```

This example declares an array with five rows and three columns, but only the first three rows are initialized, and only the first element of the second row is initialized. Pictorially, this declaration produces the following array:

```
1 2 3
4 0 0
5 6 7
0 0 0
0 0 0
```

If we do not include the inner brackets, as in

```
static int examp[5][3] = {  1 ,  2 ,  3 ,
                                 4 ,
                            5 ,  6 ,  7 };
```

the result is

```
1 2 3
4 5 6
7 0 0
0 0 0
0 0 0
```

Obviously, the initializer in this example is very misleading. To enhance readability and clarity, you should always enclose each row of initializers in its own set of braces, as we did in the first example.

As with one-dimensional arrays, if you omit the size specification of a multidimensional array, the compiler automatically determines the size based on the number of initializers present. In the case of multidimensional arrays, however, it is important to remember that you are really declaring an array of arrays. That is, you are declaring an array where each element is itself an array. You may omit the number of elements in the outermost array you are declaring because the compiler can figure this out based on the number of initializers present. From a syntactic point of view, this means that you may only omit the *first* size specification, but you must specify the other sizes. For example,

```
static int a_ar[][3][2] = {{{1, 1}, {0,0}, {1,1}},
                           {{0, 0}, {1,2}, {0,1}}
                          }
```

results in a 2-by-3-by-2 array because there are twelve initializers. Each element in the array *a_ar* is itself a 3-by-2 array. If we added another initializer, the compiler would allocate space for a 3-by-3-by-2 array, initializing the extra elements to zero. The following declaration is illegal because the compiler has no way of knowing what shape the array should be:

```
/*   ILLEGAL
 */
static int b_ar[][] = { 1, 2, 3, 4, 5, 6 };
```

Should the compiler create a 2-by-3 array or a 3-by-2 array? There's no way to tell. However, if you specify the size of each array other than the first, the declaration becomes unambiguous.

**Box 6-4: Bug Alert — Referencing Elements in a
                Multidimensional Array**

One of the most common mistakes made by beginning C programmers—
especially those familiar with another programming language—is to use a
comma to separate subscripts,

```
ar[1,2] = 0;   /* Legal, but probably wrong */
```

instead of

```
ar[1][2] = 0; /* Correct */
```

The comma notation is used in some other languages, such as FORTRAN
and Pascal. In C, however, this notation has a very different meaning
because the comma is a C operator in its own right. The first statement
above causes the compiler to evaluate the expression *1* and discard the
result; then evaluate the expression *2*. The result of a comma expression
is the value of the rightmost operand, so the value 2 becomes the subscript to *ar*. As a result, the array reference accesses element 2 of *ar*.

If *ar* is a two-dimensional array of **int**s, the type of *ar[2]* is a pointer to
an **int**, so this mistake will produce a type incompatibility error. This can
be misleading since the real mistake is using a comma instead of brackets.

6.11.2 Passing Multidimensional Arrays as Arguments

To pass a multidimensional array as an argument, you pass the array name as you
would a single-dimension array. The value passed is a pointer to the initial
element of the array, but in this case the initial element is itself an array. On the
receiving side, you must declare the argument appropriately, as shown in the
example on the following page.

```
f1()
{
  int ar[5][6][7];
          .
          .
  f2( ar );
          .
          .
}

f2( received_arg )
int received_arg[][6][7];
{
          .
          .
}
```

Again, you may omit the size of the array being passed, but you must specify the size of each element in the array. Most compilers don't check bounds, so it doesn't really matter whether you specify the first size. For example, the compiler would interpret the declaration of *received_arg* as if it had been written

```
int (*received_arg)[6][7];
```

Another way to pass multidimensional arrays is to explicitly pass a pointer to the first element, and pass the dimensions of the array as additional arguments. In our example, what gets passed is actually a pointer to a pointer to a pointer to an **int**.

```
f1()
{
  int ar[5][6][7];
          .
          .
  f2( ar, 5, 6, 7 );
          .
          .

f2( received_arg, dim1, dim2, dim3 )
int ***received_arg;
int dim1, dim2, dim3;
{
          .
          .
}
```

The advantage of this approach is that you need not know ahead of time the shape of the multidimensional array. The disadvantage is that you need to perform the indexing arithmetic manually to access an element. For example, to access *ar[x][y][z]* in *f2()*, you would need to write

```
*((int *)received_arg + x*dim3*dim2 + y*dim2 + z)
```

Note that we need to cast *received_arg* to a pointer to an **int** because we are performing our own scaling. Although this method requires considerably more work on the programmer's part, it gives more flexibility to *f2()* since it can accept three-dimensional arrays of any size and shape. Moreover, it is possible to define a macro that simplifies the indexing expression. However, we defer a discussion of complex macros to Chapter 10.

6.11.3 Multidimensional Array Example

The following function is a practical example of how multidimensional arrays are used. The purpose of the function is to determine the resulting data type of a binary expression. The function takes two arguments, which are integers representing the data types of the operands. It returns an integer representing the result type. You may want to review Chapter 3 if you have forgotten how C determines the data types of expressions.

```
#include <stdio.h>

typedef enum {SPECIAL = -2, ILLEGAL, INT, FLOAT,
              DOUBLE, POINTER, LAST} TYPES;

TYPES type_needed( type1, type2 )
TYPES type1, type2;
{
    static TYPES result_type[LAST][LAST] = {
/*              int         float       double      pointer
 */
/*  int */    INT,        DOUBLE,     DOUBLE,     POINTER,
/*float */    DOUBLE,     DOUBLE,     DOUBLE,     ILLEGAL,
/*double */   DOUBLE,     DOUBLE,     DOUBLE,     ILLEGAL,
/*pointer*/   POINTER,    ILLEGAL,    ILLEGAL,    SPECIAL
                                                       };
    TYPES result = result_type[type1][type2];

    if (result == ILLEGAL)
      printf( "Illegal pointer operation.\n" );
    return result;
}
```

All of the work is done by the array declaration. Each data type is assigned an integer value with the **enum** declaration; then we set up a matrix of return types. If *type1* is an **int** and *type2* is a **float,** the return type is *DOUBLE* (as is the case on most pre-ANSI compilers—the result type is **float** on ANSI compilers). Because of the way we have set up the two-dimensional array, all we need to do is input the two types as subscripts and the referenced element gives us the return type.

This function illustrates a number of important programming concepts that are worth reviewing. First, note that we use an **enum** to define constants for all of the return data types. This way, we can add new types without worrying about what integer value is used to represent them. The **enum** declaration ensures that each constant name will have a unique integer value and that *LAST* will represent the total number of types. Note that we use *LAST* to specify the size of the array.

Also, we use comments and formatting techniques to make the array as readable as possible. The computer itself doesn't care how it is formatted. We could write the declaration as follows and the program would work exactly the same, but it would be harder to understand and maintain.

```
char return_type[4][4] = { 0, 2, 2, 3, 3, 1, 2, -1,
                           2, 2, 2, -1, 3, -1,-1,-2
                         };
```

Finally, we should say a word about the *SPECIAL* case when both operands are pointers. This expression is legal only if the pointers point to the same type of object and if the operator is a minus sign, in which case the result is an **int**. To make this function perfect, therefore, we would need to determine what type of pointers the operands are and what the operator is.

6.12 Arrays of Pointers

In certain situations, it is useful to employ an array of pointers. Consider the following declaration:

```
char *ar_of_p[5];
```

The variable *ar_of_p[]* is a 5-element array of pointers to characters, *not* a pointer to a 5-element array of characters. This is because the array element operator [] has higher precedence than the dereferencing operator *. We discuss complex declarations such as this one in more detail in Chapter 9.

So far the pointers have not been assigned any values, so they point to random addresses in memory. But you can make assignments such as

```
char *ar_of_p[5];
char c0 = 'a';
char c1 = 'b';

ar_of_p[0] = &c0;
ar_of_p[1] = &c1;
```

These declarations and assignments cause the compiler to do two things. First it must allocate two bytes somewhere in memory for the variables *c0* and *c1*. Then it assigns the addresses of these variables to *ar_of_p[0]* and *ar_of_p[1]*. Figure 6-7 shows the storage relationship. The addresses in the figure are arbitrary. The only thing that is guaranteed is that *ar_of_p[0]* and *ar_of_p[1]* will contain the addresses of *c0* and *c1* and that *c0* and *c1* will be initialized to 'a' and 'b'.

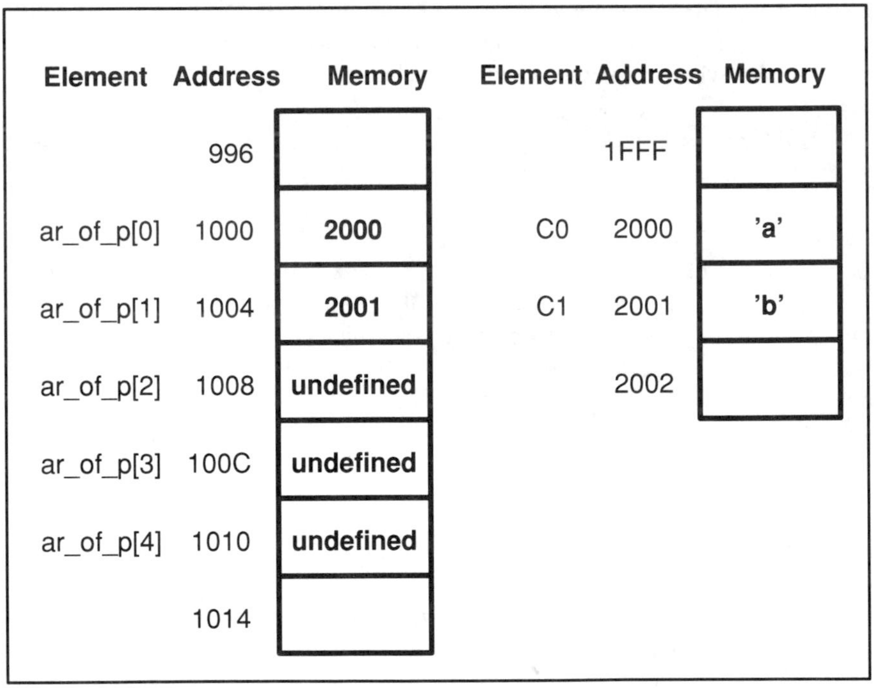

Element	Address	Memory		Element	Address	Memory
	996				1FFF	
ar_of_p[0]	1000	**2000**		C0	2000	'a'
ar_of_p[1]	1004	**2001**		C1	2001	'b'
ar_of_p[2]	1008	**undefined**			2002	
ar_of_p[3]	100C	**undefined**				
ar_of_p[4]	1010	**undefined**				
	1014					

Figure 6-7. Array of Pointers.

Arrays of pointers are frequently used to access arrays of strings. The following function, for example, takes an integer (from 1 to 12) representing a month as its input and prints the name of the month.

```c
#include <stdio.h>

void print_month( m )
int m;
{
    static char *month[13] = { "Badmonth", "January",
                "February", "March", "April", "May",
                "June", "July", "August", "September",
                "October", "November", "December"
                        };
    if (m > 12)
    {
        printf( "Illegal month value.\n" );
        exit( 1 );
    }
    printf( "%s\n", month[m] );
}
```

The variable *month* is a 13-element array of pointers to **char**s. Because of the
initialization, each pointer actually points to the initial element of a string.
Figure 6-8 shows how this would be stored in memory. Note that the month
names are not necessarily contiguous, as shown by the gap between "February"
and "March." The characters making up each name must be contiguous, but the
names themselves can be placed anywhere the compiler sees fit.

Note that the array contains 13, not 12, elements, and that the initial element is
initialized to "Badmonth." The reason we have this extra pointer with a useless
value is so that we don't have to subtract anything from the subscript. We could
just as easily declare a 12-element array and then change the *printf()* statement to

```c
printf( "%s\n",month[m-1] );
```

We prefer the first version, though, because it is more straightforward. It is a
fairly common practice to discard the initial element of an array when the
subscript values start naturally at 1. The only drawback to doing this is that you
must allocate an extra element that is never used. But doing arithmetic on a
subscript expression also has its price. Additional arithmetic operations usually
translate into extra machine code that makes the program run more slowly. The
extra instructions also take up more memory, so you don't even save memory by
using element zero. Like many stylistic issues, the question of whether to declare
an extra unused element is a question of readability and efficiency. The correct
answer depends on the machine code produced by your compiler, the computer
resources at your disposal, and your own aesthetic inclinations.

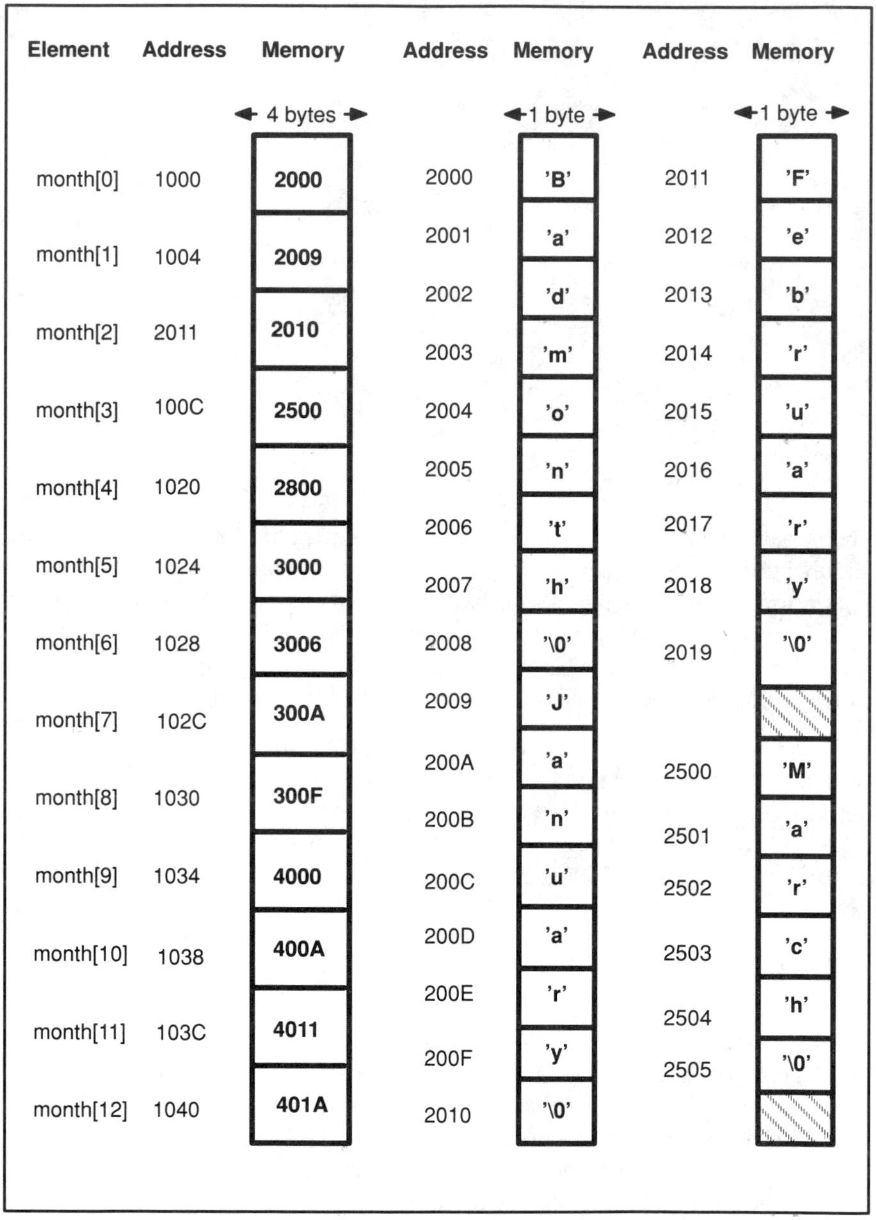

Element	Address	Memory	Address	Memory	Address	Memory
		◄ 4 bytes ►		◄1 byte ►		◄1 byte ►
month[0]	1000	2000	2000	'B'	2011	'F'
month[1]	1004	2009	2001	'a'	2012	'e'
			2002	'd'	2013	'b'
month[2]	2011	2010	2003	'm'	2014	'r'
month[3]	100C	2500	2004	'o'	2015	'u'
			2005	'n'	2016	'a'
month[4]	1020	2800	2006	't'	2017	'r'
month[5]	1024	3000	2007	'h'	2018	'y'
month[6]	1028	3006	2008	'\0'	2019	'\0'
month[7]	102C	300A	2009	'J'		
			200A	'a'	2500	'M'
month[8]	1030	300F	200B	'n'	2501	'a'
month[9]	1034	4000	200C	'u'	2502	'r'
month[10]	1038	400A	200D	'a'	2503	'c'
			200E	'r'	2504	'h'
month[11]	103C	4011	200F	'y'	2505	'\0'
month[12]	1040	401A	2010	'\0'		

Figure 6-8. Storage of an Array of Pointers to Strings.

The *print_month()* function would be more useful if, instead of printing the month, it returned it. The calling function could then do with it what it wished. To write this version, we need to declare a function that returns a pointer to a **char**.

```
#include <stdio.h>

char *month_text( m )
int m;
{
   static char *month[13] = { "Badmonth", "January",
              "February", "March", "April", "May",
              "June", "July", "August", "September",
              "October", "November", "December"
                           };
   if (m > 12)
   {
     printf( "Illegal month value.\n" );
     exit( 1 );
   }
   return month[m];
}
```

6.13 Pointers to Pointers

A pointer to a pointer is a construct used frequently in sophisticated programs. To declare a pointer to a pointer, precede the variable name with two successive asterisks. For instance,

```
int **p;
```

declares *p* to be a pointer to a pointer to an **int**. To dereference the pointer and access the **int**, you also need to use two asterisks. For example,

```
j = **p;
```

assigns an integer to *j*.

Consider the following series of declarations:

```
int r = 5;
int *q = &r;
int **p = &q;
```

These declarations result in the storage pattern shown in Figure 6-9. Both *q* and *r* are pointers, but *q* contains the address of an **int**, whereas *p* contains the address of a pointer to an **int**.

We can assign values to *r* in three ways, as shown in the following statements:

```
r = 10;        /* Direct assignment */
*q = 10;       /* Assignment with one indirection */
**p = 10;      /* Assignment with two indirections */
```

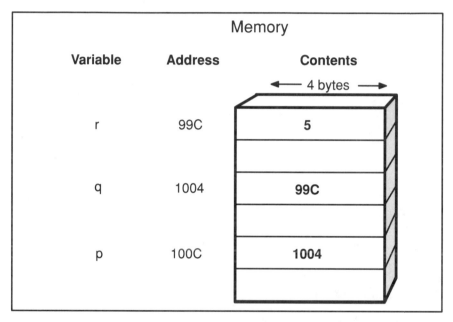

Figure 6-9. A Pointer to a Pointer.

As an example of when you might use a pointer to a pointer, suppose you want to write a spelling checker. The function takes a string as input and compares it to an internal dictionary to see if it matches. If it does match, a null pointer is returned; if it doesn't, a pointer to the spelling of the closest match is returned. To make the program more useful (and illustrate pointers to pointers), though, let's write it so that it tests not only English words, but French words as well.

One way to do this is to create a two-dimensional array of pointers. The first subscript selects the English or French dictionary; the second subscript selects a particular word in one of the dictionaries. In addition to accepting a string as an argument, the function takes another argument that indicates the language of the input string. These parameters are put in a header file that we call *spell.h*:

```
typedef enum { FRENCH, ENGLISH, LANG_NUM } LANGUAGE;
extern char *check_spell();
#define NULL (char *) 0
```

The function might look like the following example.

```c
#include "spell.h"
#define MAX_WORDS 50
/* Dictionary in alphabetic order
 * with NULL as last entry.
 */
  static char *dict[LANG_NUM][MAX_WORDS] = {
     { "aardvark", "abacus", "abash", "abbot",
       "abhor", "able", "abort", "about", NULL
     },
     { "abeille", "absence", "absurde", "accepter",
       "accident", "accord", "achat", "acheter",
         NULL
     } };

/* Return NULL pointer if str is found in
 * dictionary. Otherwise, return a pointer to
 * the closest match
 */
char *check_spell( str, language )
char *str;
LANGUAGE language;
{
  int j, diff;

  /* Iterate over the words in the dictionary */
  for (j=0; dict[language][j] != NULL; ++j)
    {
      diff = strcmp( str, dict[language][j] );
 /* Keep going if str is greater than dict entry */
      if (diff > 0)
         continue;
      if (diff == 0)
         return NULL; /* Match! */

      /* No match, return closest spelling */
      return dict[language][j];
    }

  /* Return last word if str comes after last
   * dictionary entry
   */
  return dict[language][j-1];
```

To save space and energy, we entered only the first few words of the dictionary. Normally, the dictionary would be stored in a file so you would not need to enter the words in an initialization. The function *strcmp()*, which is part of the C library, compares two strings and returns zero if they are equal and the difference between the first two differing chars if they are not equal. If *strcmp()* returns zero, the input string must be equal to one of the strings in the dictionary, so we return *NULL*. If the input string doesn't match any of the strings in the dictionary, we assume that it is misspelled and return a pointer to the closest spelling.

Note that we need to include a null pointer as the last element in the initialization list. This is because the **for** loop iterates based on the value of *dict[language][j]*, which is a pointer to a string of **char**s. So long as *dict[language][j]* is a valid pointer, the loop will continue to iterate. When *dict[language][j]* is a null pointer (i.e., all words in the array are exhausted), the loop will terminate. Without a null pointer to terminate the loop, *j* would be incremented beyond the reserved storage for the array, causing unpredictable behavior.

By using the language selector (*language*), we cut our work in half since we need to check the words in only one of the dimensions. We can make the function even more efficient by introducing a pointer to a pointer. One of the areas of inefficiency in the current version is the element reference *dict[language][j]*. In order to evaluate this expression, the compiler has to do a fair amount of arithmetic, determining the offset values and scaling them to the proper size. By eliminating one or both of the subscript operators, we can make the function more efficient.

```
#include "spell.h"
#define MAX_WORDS 50
/* Dictionary in alphabetic order
 * with NULL as last entry.
 */
  static char *dict[LAST_LANG][MAX_WORDS] = {
      { "aardvark","abacus", "abash", "abbot",
        "abhor", "able", "abort", "about", NULL
      },
      { "abeille", "absence", "absurde", "accepter",
        "accident", "accord", "achat", "acheter",
         NULL
      } };

/* Return NULL pointer if str is found in
 * dictionary. Otherwise, return a pointer to
 * the closest match. This time use pointers
 * instead of array references
 */
char *check_spell( str, language )
char *str;
LANGUAGE language;
{
  int diff;
  char **z;

/* Iterate over dictionary entries */
  for (z = dict[language]; *z; z++)
     {
       diff = strcmp( str, *z)
  /* Keep going if str is greater than dict entry */
       if (diff > 0)
          continue;
       if (diff == 0)
          return NULL; /* Match! */

     /* No match, return closest spelling */
       return *z;
     }

  /* Return last word if str comes after last
   * dictionary entry
   */
  return z[-1];
}
```

The variable *z* is declared to be a pointer to a pointer to a **char**. It is used to hold the addresses of the elements of *dict[language]*. Recall that *dict[]* is an array of arrays, so *z* points to an element of one of two arrays, either *dict[ENGLISH]* or *dict[FRENCH]*. The **for** statement then increments *z* directly instead of using a subscript. If the function does not find a match, it returns *z, where *z* is the pointer to the current dictionary entry. This is the same algorithm as the first version; all we have done is to take the array address expression, &*dict[language][j]*, and put it in z.

This second version of *check_spell()* may seem like a lot of trouble to go through just to eliminate some subscripts, and in a sense it is. But it illustrates one of C's strengths: there is almost always something you can do to make a program more efficient. This type of improvement—removing subscripts so the compiler can avoid excessive pointer arithmetic—is called *strength reduction*.

Exercises

1. Modify the *avg_temp()* function so that it prints the average temperature for each month. Use an array to store the number of days in each month.

2. Write a function that initializes *encoder[]* with random values. Use the *rand()* and *srand()* functions described in Chapter 12, and make sure that all the elements have a unique value from 0 through 127.

3. Given the following declarations and assignments, what do these expressions evaluate to?

    ```
    static int ar[]={10, 15, 4, 25, 3, -4};
    int *p;
    p = &ar[2];
    ```

    a) *(p+1)
    b) p[-1]
    c) (ar-p)
    d) ar[*p++]
    e) *(ar+ar[2])

4. What's wrong with the following code?

    ```
    int j, ar[5] = {1, 2, 3, 4, 5 };
    for (j=1; i < 5; ++j)
       printf( "%d\n", ar[j] );
    ```

5. Modify the bubble sort program so that instead of actually rearranging the elements of an array, it stores the correct order in another array called *ord[]*. For example, if an original 5-element sequence is

    ```
    13   25   11 2   14
    ```

    then the values of *ord[]* after sorting should be

    ```
    ord[0] = 2
    ord[1] = 4
    ord[2] = 1
    ord[3] = 0
    ord[4] = 3
    ```

6. Write a function called *merge_arrays()* that takes two sorted arrays and merges them into one sorted array. The function header should be

    ```
    void merge_arrays()
    double *a, *b, *c;
    ```

    where *a* and *b* are pointers to the two sorted arrays and *c* is a pointer to the resulting merged array.

7. Modify *merge_arrays()* so that it eliminates duplicate entries.

8. Write a function called *strcat()* that appends one string to another. The function should accept two arguments that are pointers to *str1* and *str2* and return a pointer to the first character in *str1*. Make sure to overwrite the null character in *str1*.

9. Rewrite the *strlen()* function using pointers and increment operators to make it as efficient as possible.

10. Revise *pat_match()* so that it is *not* case sensitive.

11. Are the declarations

    ```
    char s[10];
    ```

    and

    ```
    char *s;
    ```

    the same? If not, show how they are different by writing a program where they cannot be interchanged.

12. The names of many high-tech companies all sound similar. They start with roots such as "Com," "Data," "Inter," and end with suffixes such as "graph," "dex," and "mation." Come up with some more beginnings and endings, and write a program using *rand()* that randomly puts the two together to form company names.

13. Modify the program in Section 6.10.4 so that it does not fail if the input string is more than MAX_CHAR characters.

14. Modify the *result_type()* function so that it works correctly for the SPECIAL case. (Hint: you will need to add an additional argument to the function.)

15. Write a function that sorts an array of character strings into alphabetical order. Note that this is really a two-dimensional array of **char**s.

16. Given the following declarations, what do these expressions evaluate to?

```
static int a[2][3] = { { -3, 14, 5 },
                       { 1, -10, 8 }
                     };
static int *b[] = { a[0] , a[1] };
int *p = b[1];
```

a) *b[1]
b) *(++p)
c) *(*(a+1)+1)
d) *(—p–2)

17. Which of the following expressions are equivalent to a[j][k]?

a) *(a[j] + k)
b) **(a[j+k])
c) (*(a+j))[k]
d) (*(a+k))[j]
e) *((*(a+j)) + k)
f) **(a+j) + k
g) *(&a[0][0] + j + k)

Chapter 7

Storage Classes

*Memory: what wonders it performs in preserving and
storing up things gone by, or rather, things that are!* —
Plutarch, <u>Morals: On the Cessation of Oracles</u>

Most large programs are written by teams of programmers. After they design the
general outline of the program together, each programmer goes off and writes an
isolated piece of the program. When everyone is finished, all the pieces are
linked together to form the complete program. For this process to work, there
must be a mechanism to ensure that variables declared by one programmer don't
conflict with unrelated variables of the same name declared by another programmer. On the other hand, there is usually some data that needs to be shared
between different source files, so there must also be a mechanism that ensures
that some variables declared in different files *do* refer to the same memory
locations and that the computer interprets those locations in a consistent fashion.
In C, you define whether a variable is to be shared, and which portions of code
can share it, by designating its *scope*.

*"Scope" is the technical term that denotes the region of the C source text in
which a name's declaration is active.*

Another property of variables is *duration*, which describes the lifetime of a
variable's memory storage. Variables with *fixed duration* are guaranteed to
retain their value even after their scope is exited. There is no such guarantee for
variables with *automatic duration*.

Collectively, the scope and duration of a variable is called its *storage class*. This chapter describes storage classes in detail.

Consider the following program segment:

```
void func()
{
   int j;
   static int ar[]={1,2,3,4};
       .
       .

}
```

There are two variables, *j* and *ar*. Both have *block scope* because they are declared within a block. They can be referenced, or "seen," only by statements within the block. Variables with block scope are often called *local* variables.

Variable *j* has *automatic duration* (the default for variables with block scope), whereas *ar* has *fixed duration* because it is declared with the **static** keyword. This means that *j* has memory allocated to it automatically and may have a new address each time the block is entered. *ar*, on the other hand, has memory allocated for it just once and keeps its original address for the duration of the program.

The next section describes fixed and automatic variables in more detail. We use the term "fixed" as opposed to the more common term "static" so as not to confuse the concept with the keyword. The **static** keyword *does* give a variable static duration but it also has scoping implications not usually associated with static variables.

7.1 Fixed vs. Automatic Duration

As the names imply, a fixed variable is one that is stationary, whereas an automatic variable is one whose memory storage is automatically allocated during program execution. This means that a fixed variable has memory allocated for it at program start-up time, and the variable is associated with a single memory location until the end of the program. An automatic variable has memory allocated for it whenever its scope is entered. The automatic variable refers to that memory address only as long as code within the scope is being executed. Once the scope of the automatic variable is exited, the compiler is free to assign that memory location to the next automatic variable it sees. If the scope is reentered, a new address is allocated for the variable. There is no way to ensure that an automatic variable will retain its value from one scope entry to another.

Local variables (those whose scope is limited to a block) are automatic by default, but you can make them fixed by using the keyword **static** in the declaration. The **auto** keyword explicitly makes a variable automatic, but it is rarely used since it is redundant.

7.1.1 Initialization of Variables

The difference between fixed and automatic variables is especially important for
initialized variables. Fixed variables are initialized only once, whereas automatic variables are initialized each time their block is reentered. Consider the
following program:

```
void increment()
{
    int j=1;
    static int k=1;

    j++;
    k++;
    printf( "j: %d\tk: %d\n", j, k );
}

main()
{
    increment();
    increment();
    increment();
}
```

The *increment()* function increments two variables, *j* and *k*, both initialized to 1.
j has automatic duration by default, while *k* has fixed duration because of the
static keyword. The result of running the program is

```
j: 2        k: 2
j: 2        k: 3
j: 2        k: 4
```

When *increment()* is called the second time, memory for *j* is reallocated and *j* is
reinitialized to 1. *k*, on the other hand, has still maintained its memory address
and is *not* reinitialized, so its value of 2 from the first function call is still
present. No matter how many times we call *increment()*, the value of *j* will
always be 2, while *k* will increase by 1 with each invocation.

We can summarize this observation with the following rule: *an automatic variable, when declared with an initializer, is reinitialized every time its block is
reentered; a fixed variable is initialized only once at program start-up time.*

Another important difference between automatic and fixed variables is that automatic variables are not initialized by default whereas fixed variables get a default initial value of zero. If we rewrite the previous program without initializing the variables, we get

```
void increment()
{
   int j;
   static int k;

   j++;
   k++;
   printf( "j: %d\tk: %d\n", j, k );
}

main()
{
   increment();
   increment();
   increment();
}
```

Executing the program on our machine results in

```
j: 3604481     k: 1
j: 3604481     k: 2
j: 3604481     k: 3
```

The values of *j* are random because the variable is never initialized. With each invocation of *increment()*, *j* receives a new memory allocation and acquires whatever "garbage" value happens to be at the new location. Because most compilers use a stack-frame implementation, the garbage values may, in this simple example, be the same each time. The C language, however, does not guarantee this. If you use a more complicated calling sequence, the results will be different. A helpful compiler will issue a warning if you attempt to use an uninitialized automatic variable before you have made an assignment to it.

Another difference between initializing variables with fixed and automatic duration is the kinds of expressions that may be used as an initializer. For scalar variables with automatic duration, the initializer may be any expression so long as all of the variables in the expression have been previously declared. For example, all of the following declarations are legal.

```
{
    int j = 0, k = 1;
    int m = j + k;
    float x = 3.141 * 2.3;
          .
          .
```

The next series of declarations is illegal because *j* and *k* appear in an expression before they are declared:

```
{
    /*  The following assignment is illegal because j
     *  and k have not yet been declared.
     */
    int m = j + k;

    /*  j and k are declared now, but it's too late.
     */
    int j = 0, k = 1;
          .
          .
```

The rules for initializing variables with fixed duration are stricter. The initialization must be a constant expression, which means that it may *not* contain variable names. For example,

```
    int j = 10 * 4;   /* OK */
    int k = j;        /* NOT OK */
```

7.1.2 Using Variables with Fixed Duration

A common use of fixed variables is to keep track of how many times a function is invoked and to change the function's execution at regular intervals. As an example, suppose you have a program that formats an input text file and writes the formatted output to another file. One of the functions in the program is *print_header()*, called at the beginning of each new page. However, you want it to write a different header depending on whether the page is even-numbered or odd-numbered. The following version shows a possible solution that makes use of a fixed variable.

```
#define ODD 0
#define EVEN 1

print_header( chap_title )
char *chap_title;
{
  static char page_type = ODD;

  if (page_type == ODD)
  {
    printf( "\t\t\t\t%s\n\n", chap_title );
    page_type = EVEN;
  }
  else
  {
    printf( "%s\n\n", chap_title );
    page_type = ODD;
  }
}
```

The variable *page_type* acts as a toggle switch, alternating between ODD and EVEN. When the page number is odd, the function prints the string pointed to by *chap_title* on the right side of the page; when the page is even, the *chap_title* string appears on the left side. Note that the program depends on *page_type* having fixed duration. If *page_type* had automatic duration, it would get reinitialized to zero with each invocation and the function would always print odd-numbered headers.

7.2 Scope

As stated earlier, the scope of a variable determines the region over which you can access the variable by name. There are four types of scope: *program, file, function,* and *block*.

- *Program scope* signifies that the variable is active among different source files that make up the entire executable program. Variables with program scope are often referred to as *global variables*.

- *File scope* signifies that the variable is active from its declaration point to the end of the source file.

- *Function scope* signifies that the name is active from the beginning to the end of the function.

- *Block scope* signifies that the variable is active from its declaration point to the end of the block in which it is declared. A block is any series of statements enclosed in braces. This includes compound statements as well as function bodies.

In general, the scope of a variable is determined by the location of its declaration. Variables declared within a block have block scope; variables declared outside of a block have file scope if the **static** keyword is present, or program scope if **static** is not present; only **goto** labels have function scope.

The four scopes are arranged hierarchically as shown in Figure 7-1. A variable with program scope is also active within all files, functions, and blocks that make up the program. Likewise, a variable with file scope is also active within all functions and blocks in the file, but is not active in other parts of the program. At the bottom of the hierarchy is block scope, the most limiting case.

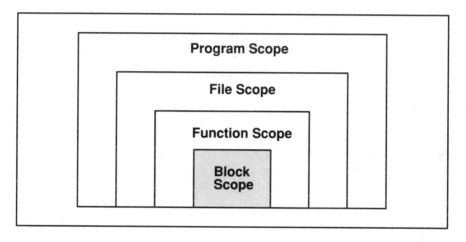

Figure 7-1.   Hierarchy of Active Regions (Scopes).

The program fragment below shows variables with all four types of scope:

```
int i;          /* Program scope */
static int j;   /* File scope */

func( k )       /* Program scope */
int k;          /* Block scope */
{
    int m;      /* Block scope */

    start:      /* Function scope */
        .
        .
```

Note that function parameters have block scope. They are treated as if they are the first declarations in the top-level block (see Box 7-1).

The C language allows you to give two variables the same name, provided they have different scopes. For example, the two functions below both use a variable called *j*, but because they are declared in different blocks, they do not conflict.

```
func1()
{
   int j;
     .
     .
     .
}

func2()
{
   int j;
     .
     .
     .
}
```

It is also possible for variables with the same name to have different scopes that overlap. In this event, the variable with the smaller scope temporarily "hides" the other variable. For instance,

```
int j=10;      /* Program scope */
main()
{
    int j;      /* Block scope -- hides global j */
    for (j=0; j < 5; ++j)
       printf( "j: %d", j );
}
```

There are two *j*'s, one with program scope and the other with block scope. Although they have the same name, they are distinct variables. The *j* with block scope temporarily hides the other *j*, so the result of running the program is

```
j: 0
j: 1
j: 2
j: 3
j: 4
```

The *j* with program scope retains its value of 10.

7.2.1 Block Scope

A variable with block scope cannot be accessed outside its block. This limitation is really an advantage since it protects the variable from inadvertent side effects. By limiting the region over which variables can be seen, you reduce the complexity of a program, making it more readable and maintainable. Block scoping allows you to write sections of code without worrying about whether your variable names conflict with names used in other parts of the program. Also, readers of your program know that the variable's use is limited to a small region.

It is also possible to declare a variable within a nested block. This temporarily hides any variables of the same name declared in outer blocks. This feature can be useful when you want to add some debugging code into a function. By creating a new block and declaring variables within it, you eliminate the possibility of naming conflicts. In addition, if you delete the debugging code at a later date, you need not look at the top of the function to find variable declarations that also need to be deleted.

In the following example, we add some debugging code that prints the values of the first ten elements of an array.

```
foo()
{
   int ar[20];
   int j;
         .

         .
/* Begin debug code */
{
   /* This j does not conflict with other j's.*/
   int j;
   for (j=0; j <= 10; ++j)
     printf( "%d\t", ar[j] );
}
/* End debug code */
      .

      .

   }
```

Although variable hiding is useful in situations such as these, it can also lead to errors that are difficult to detect. Consequently, you should use the name-hiding feature judiciously.

7.2.2 Function Scope

The only names that have function scope are **goto** labels. Labels are active from the beginning to the end of a function. This means that labels must be unique within a function. Different functions, however, may use the same label names without creating conflicts.

Box 7-1: ANSI Note — Scope of Function Arguments

According to the ANSI Standard, the scope of function arguments is the same as the scope of variables declared at the top level. This makes it illegal to hide a function argument by declaring a top-level block scope argument with the same name. For instance,

```
func( a )
int a;
{
    int a;     /* This is illegal */
    .
    .
}
```

In older compilers this syntax may be legal, but we can think of no reason for using it. In fact, it can be a troublesome bug. Many compilers issue a warning when they encounter this syntax.

7.2.3 File and Program Scope

Giving a variable *file scope* makes the variable active throughout the rest of the file. So if a file contains more than one function, all of the functions following the declaration are able to use the variable. To give a variable file scope, declare it outside a function with the **static** keyword.

Variables with program scope, called *global variables*, are visible to routines in other files as well as their own file. To create a global variable, declare it outside a function without the **static** keyword. In the following program segment, *j* has program scope and *k* has file scope. Both variables can be accessed by routines in the same file, but only *j* can be accessed by routines in other files.

```
int j;
static int k;

main()
{
    .
    .
```

Variables with file scope are particularly useful when you have a number of functions that operate on a shared data structure, but you don't want to make the data available to other functions. A file that contains this group of functions is often called a *module*. The linked-list functions in Chapter 8 illustrate a good use of a variable with file scope.

Box 7-2: Bug Alert — The Dual Meanings of static

One of the most confusing aspects about storage-class declarations in C is that the **static** keyword seems to have two effects depending on where it appears. In a declaration within a block, **static** gives a variable fixed duration instead of automatic duration. Outside a function, on the other hand, **static** has nothing to do with duration. Rather, it controls the scope of a variable, giving it file scope instead of program scope.

One way of reconciling these dual meanings is to think of **static** as signifying both file scoping and fixed duration. Within a block, the stricter block scoping rules override **static**'s file scoping, so fixed duration is the only manifest result. Outside a function, duration is already fixed, so file scoping is the only manifest result.

7.3 Global Variables

In general, you should try to avoid global variables as much as possible. They make a program hard to maintain because they increase a program's complexity. If you are attempting to understand someone else's code, the **static** keyword signifying file scope is a boon since it ensures that you need only look in the current source file to see all interactions of the variable. If the **static** keyword is absent, you must assume the worst and look at every source file that is part of the program to see if the variable is used. This can be a frustrating and needless exercise.

Global variables also create the potential for conflicts between modules. Two programmers working on separate parts of a large project may choose the same name for different global variables. The problem won't surface until the entire program is linked together, at which time it may be difficult to fix.

When you need to share data among different routines, it is usually better to pass the data directly, or pass pointers to a shared memory area. The one advantage of global variables is that they produce faster code. In most cases, however, the increase in execution speed comes at the expense of a significant decrease in maintainability. Such trade-offs of execution speed for maintainability should be made only at the end of a project when it is clear that performance is a problem.

Because global names must be recognized not only by the compiler but also by the linker or binder, their naming rules are a little different. The ANSI Standard guarantees only that the first six characters of a global name will be recognized. Also, a compiler may suspend the case-sensitivity rule for global names. This is an unfortunate restriction, but it is necessary to support older systems. Note, however, that even though the compiler may recognize only the first six characters, you are not restrained from adding additional characters to make the name more meaningful. Just make sure that the first six characters are unique.

7.3.1 Definitions and Allusions

Up to now, we have assumed that every declaration of a variable causes the compiler to allocate memory for the variable. However, memory allocation is produced by only one type of declaration, called a *definition*. Global variables permit a second type of declaration, which we call an *allusion*. An allusion looks just like a definition, but instead of allocating memory for a variable, it informs the compiler that a variable of the specified type exists but is defined elsewhere. In fact, we have already used allusions in some of our examples to declare functions defined elsewhere. For example,

```
main()
{
    extern int f();    /* Allusion to f() */
    extern float g();  /* Allusion to g() */
        .
        .
```

Global variables follow the same rules as functions. Whenever you want to use global variables defined in another file, you need to declare them with allusions. For example, the following program contains allusions to *j* and *array_of_f[]*.

```
void func()
{
    extern int j;               /* An allusion */
    extern float array_of_f[];  /* An allusion */
        .
        .
```

The **extern** keyword tells the compiler that the variables are *defined* elsewhere. The purpose of the allusion is to enable the compiler to perform type checking. For any global variable, there may be any number of allusions but only one definition among the source files making up the program.

The rules for creating definitions and allusions are one of the least standardized features of the C language because they involve not just the C compiler, but the linker and loader as well. This section describes the ANSI rules. Box 7-3 describes two other common strategies.

To *define* a global variable according to the ANSI Standard, you need to make a declaration with an initializer outside a function. The presence or absence of the **extern** keyword has no effect. For instance, the following code defines two global variables, one local variable, and alludes to one global variable:

```
int j=0;                    /* Global Definition */
extern float x = 1.0;  /* Global Definition */
func()
{
   int k = 0;        /* Local Definition   */
   extern int j;     /* Allusion to global variable */
   .
   .
```

If you omit an initializer, the compiler produces either an allusion (if **extern** is specified) or a *tentative definition* (if **extern** is not present). A tentative definition is a declaration that can become either a definition or an allusion depending on what the remainder of the source file contains. If no real definition for the variable occurs (i.e., one with an initializer) in the remainder of the source file, the tentative definition becomes a real definition, initialized to zero. Otherwise, if there is a real definition in the source file, the tentative definition becomes an allusion. In the following example, *j* is a tentative definition that becomes a real definition, and *k* is a tentative definition that becomes an allusion.

```
int j;    /* Tentative Definition */
int k;    /* Tentative Definition */

f()
{
    .

    .
}

int j = 1; /*   Real definition of j makes the
           *   tentative definition an allusion.
           *
           *   There is no real definition of k,
           *   so the tentative definition becomes
           *   a real definition.
           */
```

Typically, you put all allusions in a header file which can be included in other source files. This ensures that all source files use consistent allusions. Any change to a declaration in a header file is automatically propagated to all source files that include that header file.

Box 7-3: Non-ANSI Strategies for Declaring Global Variables

K&R Strategy

This strategy, sometimes called the "omitted-**extern** strategy," is the simplest. Regardless of scope, if a declaration contains the **extern** keyword, it is an allusion and not a definition. A global definition is produced by declaring a variable outside a block, *without* the **extern** keyword. For instance, the following segment contains one definition (j) and two allusions (k and m).

```
int j;
extern int k;
func()
{
   extern int m;
        .
        .
```

The presence or absence of an initializer does not affect whether the declaration is a definition or an allusion, but some compilers will not allow you to include an initializer with an allusion. Those that allow an initializer ignore it. Global variables defined without an initializer are automatically initialized to zero.

UNIX Strategy

This technique, adopted by the C compiler for UNIX, uses the presence or absence of an initializer to determine whether a declaration is a definition or an allusion. For declarations occurring outside a block, there are three possibilities:

1. If **extern** is present, the declaration is an allusion. It is illegal to include both **extern** and an initializer.

2. If **extern** is not present and the declaration includes an initializer, the declaration is a definition.

(*continues*)

Box 7-3 (continued):

3. If **extern** is not present and the variable is not initialized, a "common" definition (as in FORTRAN) is emitted. If, in the entire set of source files, there is one definition and one or more common definitions of a variable, the common definitions become allusions. If there are no real definitions and only common definitions, the linker itself provides a definition for the variable and resolves the common definitions as if they were allusions.

The UNIX method is similar to the ANSI method. The essential difference is that the ANSI method decides whether to make a tentative definition a real definition or an allusion based on whether any definitions exist in the current source file. The UNIX method delays this decision until link time so that it can see if the variable is defined in other modules.

A Portable Strategy

If you want your programs to run on a wide range of computers, you should use the following method, which is compatible with the ANSI Standard, the K&R standard, and UNIX compilers.

– To *define* a global variable, omit the **extern** keyword and include an initializer.

– To *allude* to a global variable, include **extern** but omit an initializer.

For instance, to define *j* in header file *foo.h* and reference it in file *prog.c*, you would write

    File foo.h:

```
int j=0;
          .
          .
```

    File prog.c:

```
extern int j;
        foo()
        {
          .
          .
```

7.4 The *register* **Specifier**

The **register** keyword enables you to help the compiler by giving it suggestions about which variables should be kept in registers. To understand the purpose of register variables, it is necessary to understand how registers work in computers.

Every computer has a limited number of registers, which are storage areas within the CPU. Each register is capable of holding a unit of data (typically two or four bytes) and arithmetic calculations are processed using these registers. For example, on a hypothetical machine the simple statement

```
j = k+m;
```

might cause the compiler to load two registers, call them r0 and r1, with the values stored in *k* and *m*. The computer then adds the two registers and writes the result to the memory location occupied by j.

Operations involving registers are generally faster than memory operations. If you could store every variable in its own register, your program would run somewhat faster. Unfortunately, computers usually have far fewer registers than there are variables. As a result, the compiler must try to figure out the optimal strategy for assigning values to registers so as to minimize memory accesses. This is one of the most difficult jobs compilers perform, and it is often what separates a good compiler from a bad one.

The **register** keyword is designed to help the compiler decide which variables to store in registers. However, it is only a hint, not a directive—the compiler is free to ignore it. The degree of support for **register** varies widely from one compiler to another. Some compilers store all variables defined as **register** in a register until all of the computer's registers are filled. Other compilers ignore **register** altogether. Still others contain some type of intelligence that tries to determine whether it really is best to store a **register** variable in a register. All of these variations are within the ANSI Standard.

Since a variable declared with **register** might never be assigned a memory address, it is illegal to take the address of a **register** variable (registers are not addressable). This is true regardless of whether the variable is actually assigned to a register. You should get a compile error if you ever try to take the address of a variable declared with **register**.

A typical case where you might use **register** is when you use a counter in a loop. In fact, we can rewrite our *strlen()* example from Chapter 6 to make use of the **register** feature.

```
int strlen( p )
register char *p;
{
  register int len = 0;

  while (*p++)
    len++;
  return len;
}
```

Note that this does not guarantee that *p* or *len* will be kept in registers throughout the duration of the function's execution, but it makes it more likely. In theory, there is no limit to the number of variables that you can declare with **register**. In practice, however, compilers recognize only the first *n* **register** declarations. After that, they interpret a **register** declaration as a regular **auto** declaration. You should read the documentation for your particular compiler to find out how you can best utilize the **register** keyword.

Box 7-4: ANSI Feature — The *const* Storage-Class Modifier

The **const** keyword, borrowed from the C++ language developed by Bjarne Stroustrup, specifies that the variable may not be modified in any way following its initialization. For instance, after declaring *str[]*,

```
const char str[10] = "Constant";
```

you cannot change any of the values in the array *str[]*. The statement

```
str[0] = 'a';
```

would be illegal and should be reported as an error by the compiler. The rule, however, does not necessarily apply to non-**const** pointers that point to **const** objects. If you make the additional declaration

```
char *p = &str[5];
```

then the statement

```
*p = 'm';
```

may or may not be legal, depending on the compiler. Ideally, this should be illegal, but in many cases it is impossible for the compiler to diagnose this error.

(continues)

Box 7-4 (continued):

You can use **const** in place of a **#define** directive. For instance,

```
const long double pi = 3.1415926535897932385;
```

One unusual aspect concerning the **const** keyword is that it may appear between the pointer symbol (*****) and the variable name, as in

```
int *const const_ptr;
```

This means that the pointer *const_ptr* is a constant — it must point to the same object as long as it exists. Contrast this to the similar-looking declaration

```
int const *ptr_to_const
```

which says that the object which *ptr_to_const* points to cannot change. *ptr_to_const* itself can be assigned a different address, although it must be an address of an object declared with **const**. That is, *ptr_to_const* can only point to objects of type **const int**.

The main purpose of **const** is to ensure that read-only data is not modified. This is particularly useful when passing pointer arguments to functions. By declaring the argument with **const**, you can ensure that the called function will not change the object pointed at by the pointer. In the following example, the declaration of *q* as a pointer to a **const** object guarantees that the *strcpy()* function will not change the object that *q* points to.

```
char *strcpy(p, q)
char *p;
const char *q;
{
    .
    .
}
```

The **const** feature is also useful to some computer manufacturers in determining which parts of data can be "burned" into ROMs (Read-Only Memories). ROMs are essential for systems that do not have some other storage medium, such as disk storage, available. In addition, ROMs are considerably less expensive than read–and–write memory boards.

Box 7-5: ANSI Feature — The *volatile* Storage-Class Modifier

The **volatile** keyword, which is not supported by older compilers, informs the compiler that the variable can be modified in ways unknown to the C compiler. This usually applies to variables that are mapped to a particular memory address (i.e., device registers). In these cases, it is crucial that an expression or a series of statements be executed exactly as they are written rather than being reordered for optimization purposes. For instance, suppose *KEYBOARD* in the following function is a device register that accepts characters from the keyboard.

```
void get_two_kbd_chars()
{
    extern char KEYBOARD;
    char c0, c1;

    c0 = KEYBOARD;
    c1 = KEYBOARD;
}
```

The purpose of the function is to read a character from the keyboard and store it in *c0*, then read the next character and store it in *c1*. However, the C compiler, unaware that the value of *KEYBOARD* can be changed outside the block, is likely to store the value of *KEYBOARD* in a register and then assign that register to *c0* and *c1*. In other words, it will compile the program as if it had been written

```
void get_two_kbd_chars()
{
    extern char KEYBOARD;
    char c0, c1
    register char temp;

    temp = KEYBOARD;
    c0 = temp;
    c1 = temp;
}
```

Obviously, this is not what was intended since the same character will be assigned to both *c0* and *c1*. To ensure that *KEYBOARD* is read twice, you must declare it as **volatile**:

```
extern volatile char KEYBOARD;
```

(*continues*)

Box 7-5 (continued):

Another situation where normal optimization techniques can change the meaning of a program is in loop-invariant expressions. For instance, using *KEYBOARD* again, suppose we have the function

```
void read_ten_chars()
{
    extern char KEYBOARD;
    int x;
    char c;

    for (x=0; x < 10; x++)
    {
      c = KEYBOARD;
      copy( c );
    }
}
```

The purpose of the function is to read 10 successive characters from the keyboard and pass each to a function called *copy()*. To the compiler, however, it looks like an inefficient program because c will be assigned the same value 10 times. To optimize the program, the compiler may translate it as if it had been written like this:

```
{
    extern char KEYBOARD;
    int x;
    char c;

    c = KEYBOARD;   /* The invariant expression is
                        removed from the loop. */
    for (x=0; x < 10; x++)
      copy( c );
}
```

As a result, the same character is sent to *copy()* each time. Once again, declaring *KEYBOARD* with **volatile** ensures that the expression is not extracted from the loop.

The **volatile** modifier is often used in a cast expression. The following statement assigns the contents of hexadecimal address 20 to the variable c. The **volatile** keyword in the cast ensures that the assignment will not be optimized in any way.

```
c = (*(volatile char *) 0x20);
```

7.5 Summary of Storage Classes

So far we have described the *semantics* of storage classes—how they affect variables. But we have glossed over some of the details about *syntax*—how storage classes are specified. In this section, we summarize the ANSI rules for the syntax and semantics of the storage-class keywords.

There are four *storage-class specifiers* (**auto**, **static**, **extern**, and **register**) and two *storage-class modifiers* (**const** and **volatile**). Any of the storage class keywords may appear before or after the type name in a declaration, but by convention they come before the type name. The semantics of each keyword depends to some extent on the location of the declaration. Omitting a storage class specifier also has a meaning, as described below. Table 7-1 summarizes the scope and duration semantics of each storage class specifier.

auto	The **auto** keyword, which makes a variable automatic, is legal only for variables with block scope. Since this is the default anyway, **auto** is somewhat superfluous and is rarely used.
static	The **static** keyword may be applied to declarations both within and outside a function (except for function arguments), but the meaning differs in the two cases. In declarations within a function, **static** causes the variable to have fixed duration instead of the default automatic duration. For variables declared outside a function, the **static** keyword gives the variable file scope instead of program scope.
extern	The **extern** specifier may be used for declarations both within and outside a function (except for function arguments). For variables declared within a function, it signifies a global allusion. For declarations outside a function, **extern** denotes a global definition. In this case, the meaning is the same whether you specify **extern** or not.
register	The **register** keyword may be used only for variables declared within a function. It makes the variable automatic but also passes a hint to the compiler to store the variable in a register whenever possible. You should use the **register** keyword for automatic variables that are accessed frequently. Compilers support this feature at various levels. Some don't support it at all, while others support as many as 20 concurrent register assignments.

omitted   For variables with block scope, omitting a storage
                                class specifier is the same as specifying **auto**. For
                                variables declared outside of a function, omitting the
                                storage class specifier is the same as specifying **ex-
                                tern**. It causes the compiler to produce a global
                                definition.

const   The **const** specifier guarantees that you cannot
                                change the value of the variable.

volatile   Declaring a variable with the **volatile** specifier causes
                                the compiler to turn off certain optimizations. This is
                                especially useful for device registers and other data
                                segments that can change without the compiler's
                                knowledge.

Place Where Declared / Storage Class Specifier	Outside a Function	Within a Function	Function Arguments
auto or register	NOT ALLOWED	scope: *block* duration: *automatic*	scope: *block* duration: *automatic*
static	scope: *file* duration: *fixed*	scope: *block* duration: *fixed*	NOT ALLOWED
extern	scope: *program* duration: *fixed*	scope: *block* duration: *fixed*	NOT ALLOWED
No storage-class specifier present	scope: *program* duration: *fixed*	scope: *block* duration: *dynamic*	scope: *block* duration: *automatic*

Table 7-1. Semantics of Storage-Class Specifiers.

The syntax for storage-class keywords is rather loose, allowing some declarations that have little or no meaning. For example, it is legal to declare a variable with both **register** and **volatile,** although it is unclear how a compiler would interpret it. The only real syntactic restriction is that a declaration may include at most one storage-class specifier. But either or both modifiers may be used. The following, for example, is perfectly legal and even has a reasonable meaning:

```
{
    extern const volatile char real_time_clock;
        .
        .
```

It is an allusion to a variable of type **char** that is both **const** and **volatile.**

7.6 Dynamic Memory Allocation

Fixed variables provide a means for reserving memory for the duration of a program, while automatic variables cause the system to allocate memory when each block is entered. Both of these approaches assume that you know how much memory you need ahead of time when you write the source code. Frequently, however, the amount of memory required by a program hinges on the input. For example, consider the *bubble_sort()* function in the previous chapter. Suppose you want to write another function that reads a list of numbers entered from the keyboard and then calls *bubble_sort()* to put them in order. To make the function as useful as possible, it should work no matter how many numbers you enter. But if the amount of input varies from one execution to another, how large an array should you declare to store the input?

There are two solutions to this problem. The simplest is to pick a maximum value and declare an array of that size. For instance, if you decide to set a limit of 100 input values, you would declare a 100-element array, as shown in the example on the following page.

```
#include <stdio.h>
#define MAX_ARRAY 100

main()
{
  extern void bubble_sort();
  int list[MAX_ARRAY], j, sort_num;

  printf("How many values are you going to enter? ");
  scanf( "%d", &sort_num );
  if (sort_num > MAX_ARRAY)
  {
    printf( "Too many values -- %d is the maximum\n",
            MAX_ARRAY );
    sort_num = MAX_ARRAY;
  }
  for (j=0; j < sort_num; j++)
    scanf( "%d", &list[j] );
  bubble_sort( list, sort_num );
  exit( 0 );
}
```

There are two basic problems with this solution. First, you need to set an arbitrary maximum. This isn't good because there may be a future time when you want to exceed this limit. The second, related problem is that the higher the maximum, the more memory is wasted. If you declare an array with 100 4-byte **int**s but use only ten of them, you are wasting 360 (90*4) bytes. 360 wasted bytes isn't too bad, but suppose you set the maximum at 1000. Then the number of wasted bytes would be 3,960, or almost 4K. On a small computer, this is a significant amount of memory.

The other solution takes advantage of runtime library functions that enable you to allocate memory on the fly. There are four *dynamic memory allocation* functions:

malloc()	Allocates a specified number of bytes in memory. Returns a pointer to the beginning of the allocated block.
calloc()	Similar to *malloc()*, but initializes the allocated bytes to zero. This function also allows you to allocate memory for more than one object at a time.
realloc()	Changes the size of a previously allocated block.
free()	Frees up memory that was previously allocated with *malloc()*, *calloc()*, or *realloc()*.

Each of these functions is described in detail in Appendix A. The following
function shows how you might use *malloc()* to get space for data to sort.

```
#include <stdio.h>

main()
{
   extern void bubble_sort();
   int *list, sort_num, j;

   printf("How many numbers are you going to enter?");
   scanf( "%d", &sort_num );
   list = (int *) malloc( sort_num * sizeof(int) );
   for( j=0; j < sort_num; j++)
      scanf( "%d", list + j );
   bubble_sort( list, sort_num );
   exit( 0 );
}
```

The argument to *malloc()* is the size in bytes of the block of memory to be
allocated—in this case, the number of elements times the size of each element.
malloc() returns a pointer to the beginning of the allocated block. We cast the
result to a pointer to an **int** because on most older compilers *malloc()* returns a
pointer to a **char** (see Box 7-6). Using *calloc()*, the storage allocation statement
would be

```
      list = (int *) calloc( sort_num, sizeof(int) );
```

The *calloc()* function takes two arguments: the first is the number of objects to
reserve memory for, and the second is the size of each object.

Note that the functions using *malloc()* and *calloc()* depend on the fact that all the
elements are stored contiguously. If they weren't, the expression *list + j* would
not necessarily retrieve the next value. The only reason they are stored together
is that they are allocated in a single block. If you were to allocate each element
individually, the operating system would be free to spread the elements around.
For instance, the statements

```
   p1 = (int *) malloc( sizeof(int) );
   p2 = (int *) malloc( sizeof(int) );
   p3 = (int *) malloc( sizeof(int) );
```

allocates memory for three **int**s, but there is no guarantee about the relative
locations of the three objects. *p1* might point to address 10,000, while *p2* points
to address 5,000. Therefore, you cannot allocate memory for each individual
element and expect them to be contiguous. You must know ahead of time the
total size of the block that is required. There is a technique to get around this
limitation called a *linked list*. We describe linked lists in the next chapter.

Box 7-6: ANSI Feature — Generic Pointers

The memory allocation functions are implemented differently in the
ANSI Standard than in the K&R standard and most previous versions of
C. Prior to the ANSI standard, the memory allocation functions would
return a pointer to a **char** that designated the beginning of the allocated
region. It was the programmer's responsibility to cast the returned pointer to a pointer of the correct type. The ANSI version makes use of the
void data type by returning a pointer to a **void**. The **void** pointer is a
generic pointer that is automatically cast to the correct type when it is
assigned a pointer value. The following example shows how the new
version of *malloc()* differs from the old version.

Old Call to malloc()

```
        .
        .
    int num, *pt;
        .
        .
    pt = (int *) malloc( sizeof(num) );
        .
        .
```

ANSI Call to malloc()

```
    #include <stdlib.h>
        .
        .
    int num, *pt;
        .
        .
    pt = malloc( sizeof(num) );
        .
        .
```

You do not need to cast the function result in the ANSI version. The cast,
though redundant in the ANSI version, is not illegal, so old code will still
work with the new memory-management functions. You must, however,
include the header file *stdlib.h* because it contains function prototypes
(described in Chapter 10). Because the new syntax, without the cast, will
not work on older compilers, we use the old version in our examples.

Exercises

1. For all of the following declarations, state which ones are definitions and which ones are allusions:

```
int j;
float x = 1.0;
extern char *p = "string";
static int a;

char *f1( arg1, arg2 )
register int arg1;
double arg2;
{
   extern float x;
   extern char *p2;
   static long int big_int;
   register long r1;
   unsigned u1;



          .

          .

}

int j = 0;
```

2. Write declarations for the following. Include braces to make it clear whether the declaration appears inside or outside a block.

   a) An automatic local **int**.
   b) A fixed local **float**.
   c) A global pointer to a **char**, initialized with a null pointer.
   d) An **int** with file scope.
   e) A register **int** argument.
   f) A constant **double**.
   g) A constant pointer to a **double**.
   h) A pointer to a constant **char**.
   i) A volatile **int**.

3. What are the initialized values of the variables in the following program?
    Also identify all of the following declarations as definitions, tentative defi-
    nitions, or allusions.

```
static int s = 2;
int x = 3;
extern int x1;

main()
{
   static float j = x + 5;
   float j1 = x + x1;
   static float x2;
   float x3;
   register int s2;
}

extern int x4 = 3
```

4. Write a function that prints out *n* asterisks, where *n* represents the number
    of times it has been called. If it is called four times, for instance, the output
    will be

```
*
* *
* * *
* * * *
```

Chapter 8

Structures and Unions

Art and science cannot exist but in minutely organized particulars. — William Blake, <u>To the</u> <u>Public</u>

Arrays are good for dealing with groups of identically typed variables, but they are unsatisfactory for managing groups of differently typed data. To service groups of mixed data, you need to use an aggregate type called a *structure*. (Other languages, such as Pascal, call this data type a *record*.) Another aggregate type, called a *union* (similar to a *variant record* in Pascal), enables you to interpret the same memory locations in different ways.

8.1 Structures

We are all familiar with the ubiquitous forms that ask for our name, date of birth, and social security number. The purpose of this information is usually obscure, but we can assume that, like most other information, it eventually finds its way into a computer memory bank. Years later, it comes back to haunt us when we fail to pay a parking ticket or when we apply for a loan. It is reasonable to ask how this not-so-innocuous information is stored in the computer.

The first piece of information (your name) is clearly a character array. The second and third pieces of information can be treated as either character arrays or integers, or even as arrays of integers. For this discussion, we treat the date as three integers, one each for day, month, and year. We treat the social security number as an 11-element character array (ten characters for digits and one for the terminating null character). You cannot put all of the information in a single array because arrays contain only one type of data. You can, however, store this information in separate variables. For instance, you might write

```
char name[19], ssnum[11];
short day, month, year;
```

You could then enter data with the following assignments:

```
strcpy( name, "John Doe" );
strcpy( ssnum, "0132222456" );
day = 26;
month = 11;
year = 1957;
```

Storing the data in this fashion gets the information into the computer but creates a strange organization. The information about one person is scattered about memory instead of being grouped together. The arrangement becomes even worse if you adjust the data structure to accommodate information about more than one person. In this case, you would need to make each piece of information an array. To store data about 1000 people, you would write

```
char name[1000][19], ssnum[1000][11];
short month[1000], day[1000], year[1000];
```

A more natural organization would be to create a single variable that contains all three pieces of data. C enables you to do this with a data type called a *structure*. A structure is like an array except that each element can have a different data type. Moreover, the elements in a structure, called *fields* or *members*, have names instead of subscript values. We like to think of structures as arrays with personality. To declare a structure to hold one's vital statistics, you would write

```
struct vitalstat
{
    char  vs_name[19], vs_ssnum[11];
    short vs_month, vs_day, vs_year;
} ;

struct vitalstat vs;
```

There are two declarations: the first declares a structure *template* called *vitalstat*; the second declares an actual variable called *vs* with the *vitalstat* form. It is a good idea to include a unique prefix for each member name so that the members are not confused with members of other structures that may have similar names. The storage for *vs* on our machine is shown in Figure 8-1. Note that the fields are stored consecutively in the order they are declared. *Contiguity*, however, is not required. As we describe later in this chapter, it is possible for structures to contain gaps between members.

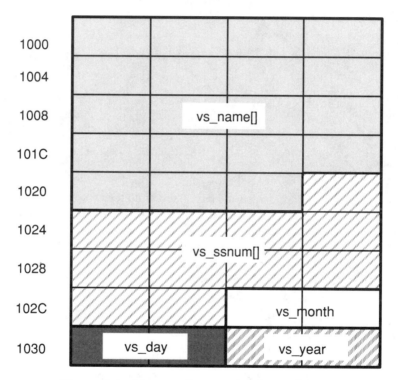

Figure 8-1. Memory Storage for the vs *Structure.*

The name *vitalstat* is called a *tag name*. It represents a new, user-defined data type, but no storage is allocated for it. You can use the tag name over and over again within a program to create additional variables with the same fields. For instance, you could write

```
struct vitalstat vsa[1000], *pvs;
```

The variable *vsa[]* is an array with 1000 members; each member is itself a structure containing the fields *vs_name[]*, *vs_ssnum[]*, *vs_day*, *vs_month*, and *vs_year*. The variable *pvs* is a pointer to a structure with these fields. You could make the assignment

```
pvs = &vsa[10];
```

which makes *pvs* point to element 10 of the array.

The syntax of a structure declaration can be fairly complex. The form of declaration we have used—declaring a tag name and then using the tag name to declare actual variables—is one of the most common. It is also possible to declare a structure without using a tag name, as in

```
struct
{
    char  vs_name[19], vs_ssnum[11];
    short vs_month, vs_day, vs_year;
} vs;
```

This is useful if you want to declare a single structure type to be used in one place only. You can also declare a tag name and variables together:

```
struct vitalstat
{
    char  vs_name[19], vs_ssnum[11];
    short vs_month, vs_day, vs_year;
} vs, *pvs, vsa[10];
```

A final method, which is the one we use most often, is to define a **typedef** name. For instance,

```
typedef struct
{
    char  vs_name[19], vs_ssnum[11];
    short vs_month, vs_day, vs_year;
} VITALSTAT;
```

In this case, the type *VITALSTAT* represents the entire structure declaration, including the **struct** keyword. Note that we use all capital letters for the **typedef** name to keep it distinct from regular variable names and tag names. To declare a variable with this structure, you would write

```
VITALSTAT vs;
```

A tag name or **typedef** enables you to define the data structure just once even though you may use it over and over again. Typically, structure definitions are placed in a header file where they can be accessed by multiple source files.

8.1.1 Initializing Structures

You can initialize a structure in the same manner as you initialize arrays. Follow the structure variable name with an equal sign, followed by a list of initializers enclosed in braces. Each initializer should agree in type with the corresponding field in the structure. For instance,

```
VITALSTAT vs = { "George Smith", "002340671",
                 3 , 5, 1946,
              };
```

The ANSI Standard allows you to initialize both automatic and fixed structures, but the K&R standard and most older C compilers allow you to initialize only fixed structures. Also, you may not include an initializer in a declaration that contains only a tag name or is a typedef since these types of declarations create templates but do not allocate storage. The following, for instance, is invalid:

```
typedef struct
{
    int a;
    float b;
} s = { 1, 1.0 };   /* Initializer is not allowed
                     * in a typedef
                     */
```

8.1.2 Referencing Structure Members

Having declared a structure, you need a way to access the fields. There are two methods, depending on whether you have the structure itself or a pointer to the structure. Each method uses a special operator. If you have the structure itself, you can enter the structure name and field name separated by the dot (.) operator. For instance, to assign the date March 15, 1987 to *vs*, you would write

```
vs.vs_month = 3;
vs.vs_day = 15;
vs.vs_year = 1987;
```

The referenced field expression is just like any other variable, so you can use *vs.vs_month* anywhere you would normally use a **short** variable. The following statement, for instance, is perfectly legal:

```
if (vs.vs_month > 12 || vs.vs_day > 31)
  printf( "Illegal Date.\n" );
```

The other way to reference a structure member is indirectly through a pointer to the structure. Declaring pointers to structures is the same as declaring pointers to other kinds of objects:

```
VITALSTAT *pvs;   /* Declare a pointer to a
                     structure of type VITALSTAT */
```

To reference a member through a pointer, use the right-arrow operator (–>), which is formed by entering a dash followed by a right angle bracket. For example,

```
if (pvs->vs_month > 12 || pvs->vs_day > 31)
  printf( "Illegal Date.\n" );
```

The right-arrow operator is actually a shorthand for dereferencing the pointer and using the dot operator. That is,

```
pvs->vs_day
```

is the same as

```
(*pvs).vs_day
```

8.1.3 Arrays of Structures

Since a structure is a data object, it is possible to create arrays of structures. An array of structures is declared by preceding the array name with the structure typedef name:

```
VITALSTAT vsa[10];
```

The following function counts the number of people in a particular age group. We assume that the array of structures has already been filled with data and a pointer to the beginning of this array is passed as an argument. The second argument is the number of elements in the array. We also assume that the include file called *v_stat.h* contains the declaration of *VITALSTAT*.

```
#include "v_stat.h"      /*   Contains declaration of
                          *   VITALSTAT typedef name.
                          */
int agecount( vsa, size, low_age, high_age,
              current_year )
VITALSTAT vsa[];
int size, low_age, high_age, current_year;
{
   int i, age, count = 0;

   for (i = 0; i < size; ++i)
   {
      age = current_year - vsa[i].vs_year;
      if (age >= low_age && age <= high_age)
         count++;
   }

   return count;
}
```

As we noted in Chapter 6, indexing into an array is not as efficient as using a pointer to an array since indexing involves an additional multiplication. The computer must multiply the index by the size of the array element and add the resulting offset to the base of the array. You can avoid some of this arithmetic by assigning a pointer to the base of the array. Then you need only increment the pointer for each iteration. This is an optimization called *strength reduction,* which is performed automatically by some compilers.

Rewriting *agecount()* using pointers and the –> operator, we get the function shown on the following page.

```
#include "v_stat.h"   /*  Contains declaration
                       *  of VITALSTAT typedef name.
                       */
int agecount( vsa, size, low_age, high_age,
              current_year )
VITALSTAT vsa[];
int size, low_age, high_age, current_year;
{
   int i, age, count = 0;

   for (i = 0; i < size; ++vsa, ++i)
   {
     age = current_year - vsa->vs_year;
     if (age >= low_age && age <= high_age)
       count++;
   }

   return count;
}
```

The only difference between this version and the earlier version is that we increment *vsa* directly instead of incrementing an index variable. The declaration of *vsa* remains the same due to C's array-passing conventions. Recall from Chapter 6 that C converts an argument declared as an array into a pointer to the array type. In both versions, therefore, *vsa* is a pointer to a *VITALSTAT* structure. You could also declare it as

```
VITALSTAT *vsa;
```

Note that pointer scaling enables us to use the increment operator to move the pointer down the array. In this case, *vsa* points to a 36-byte structure, so it is incremented 36 bytes on each iteration.

One stylistic problem with the pointer version of *agecount()* is that it changes the value of the formal parameter *vsa*. This is perfectly legal, but it is a dangerous practice in general because it makes the function less maintainable. The problem is that you or another programmer may expand the function later on and use *vsa* again, expecting that it will still point to the beginning of the array. But instead, it will point to the last element of the array.

Maintaining a program is easier if you can assume that formal parameters maintain their initial value throughout the function. In this particular case, assigning to formal parameters isn't too big a problem because the function is small and relatively simple. For larger, more complex functions, however, you should avoid assigning into formal parameters. The simplest solution is to create temporary variables initialized with the values of the formal parameters, as shown in the following version of *agecount()*:

```c
#include "v_stat.h"   /*  Contains declaration
                        *  of VITALSTAT typedef name.
                        */
int agecount( vsa, size, low_age, high_age,
              current_year )
VITALSTAT vsa[];
int size, low_age, high_age, current_year;
{
   int age, count = 0;
   VITALSTAT *p = vsa, *p_last = &vsa[size];

   for ( ; p < p_last; ++p)
   {
     age = current_year - p->vs_year;
     if (age >= low_age && age <= high_age)
        count++;
   }

   return count;
}
```

8.1.4 Nested Structures

When one of the fields of a structure is itself a structure, it is called a *nested structure*. Nested structures are common in C programming because they enable you to create data hierarchies. For instance, we can rewrite the *VITALSTAT* structure as

```c
typedef struct
{
    char vs_name[19], vs_ssnum[11];
    struct
    {
      short vs_day;
      short vs_month;
      short vs_year;
    } vs_birth_date;
} VITALSTAT;
```

We replace the three fields representing the date of birth with a structure containing these fields. The storage allocation is the same, but instead of accessing the year as

```
vs.vs_year
```

we access it as

```
vs.vs_birth_date.vs_year
```

The second reference is more readable since *vs_birth_date.vs_year* is more meaningful than *vs_year*.

Another way to declare nested structures is with **typedef**s. We can rewrite the previous declaration as

```
typedef struct
{
  char day;
  char month;
  short year;
} DATE;

typedef struct
{
  char vs_name[19], vs_ssnum[11];
  DATE vs_birth_date;
} VITALSTAT;

VITALSTAT vsa[1000];
```

Note that we also changed day and month to be chars because all possible values for these members can be represented in eight bits. Having defined a new structure type called *DATE*, we can put it in a header file (*date.h*) and use this structure template in other ways. For this reason, we did not include the *vs_* prefix in the field names. For instance, in another program we might write

```
#include "date.h"

typedef struct
{
  DATE d;
  char event[20];
} CALENDAR;

CALENDAR holiday = {
            { 12, 25, 1986 },
            { "Christmas" }
                };
```

Note that when you initialize a nested structure, you should enclose it in braces, just as you would if you were initializing a multidimensional array. Theoretically, there is no limit to the number of levels you may nest structures. Eventually, though, the field references become rather hard to read since they contain all of the intermediary structures.

Box 8-1: ANSI Feature — *struct* and *union* Name Spaces

The ANSI Standard requires C compilers to create a separate *naming space* within each structure and union, so that two or more structures or unions can have components with the same name. For example,

```
struct s1 {
   int a,b;
};

struct s2 {
   float a,b;
};
```

This feature is an extension to the K&R standard, so it may not be available on older compilers. Moreover, for stylistic reasons, you should avoid giving different variables the same name unless there is a very good reason for doing so.

Tag names, member names, and variable names are all distinct, so a tag, a member, and a variable may have the same name without a conflict arising. The following, for example, is legal:

```
struct x { int x;} x;
```

Again, you should be careful not to abuse this capability.

8.1.5 Self-Referencing Structures

A structure or union may not contain instances of itself, but it may contain pointers to instances of itself. For example,

```
struct s {
   int a,b;
   float c;
   struct s *pointer_to_s;     /* This is legal */
};
```

As this example illustrates, you are permitted to declare pointers to structures that have not yet been declared. This feature enables you to create self-referential structures and also to create mutually referential structures and unions, as shown in the following example.

```
struct s1 {
   int a;
   struct s2 *b;
};
struct s2 {
   int a;
   struct s1 *b;
};
```

Each structure contains an integer as the first component and a pointer to the other structure as the second component. The compiler allows you to declare a *pointer* to struct *s2* before *s2* is ever declared. This situation, known as *forward referencing*, is one of the few instances in the C language where you may use an identifier before it has been declared.

Note that forward references are not permitted within typedefs. The following produces a syntax error:

```
typedef struct
   { int a;
     FOO *p;   /* Error because FOO is not
               * yet declared.
               */
   } FOO;
```

8.1.6 Alignment of Structure Members

Some computers require that any data object larger than a char must be assigned an address that is a multiple of a power of two. For instance, the Motorola 68000 CPU requires that all objects larger than a **char** be stored at even addresses. Normally, these alignment restrictions are invisible to the programmer. However, they can create *holes*, or *gaps*, in structures. Consider how a compiler would allocate memory for the following structure:

```
struct ALICN_EXAMP
{
   char mem1;
   short mem2;
   char mem3;
} s1;
```

If the computer has no alignment restrictions, *s1* would be stored as shown in Figure 8-2.

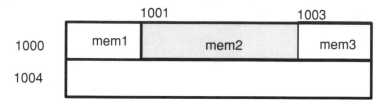

Figure 8-2. Allocation Without Alignment Restrictions.

If the computer requires objects larger than a **char** to be stored at even addresses, *s1* would be stored as shown in Figure 8-3. This storage arrangement results in a 1-byte hole between *mem1* and *mem2* and following mem3. The trailing gap is necessary so that in an array of *ALIGN_EXAMP* structures, each element would begin at an even address.

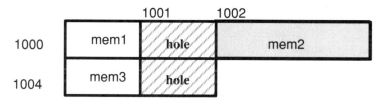

Figure 8-3. Allocation with Alignment Restrictions.

Note that you can avoid these holes by rearranging the member declarations:

```
struct ALIGN_EXAMP
{
   char mem1, mem3;
   short mem2;
} s1;
```

Because structures can be allocated differently on different machines, you should be careful about accessing them in a portable manner. One way to avoid portability problems is to make sure that all members are *naturally aligned*. Natural alignment means that an object's address is evenly divisible by its size. For example, all 2-byte objects would have an even address and all 4-byte objects would have addresses divisible by four. Natural alignment is the strictest alignment requirement that any computer imposes, so if all members of a structure are naturally aligned, the structure will be portable from one computer to another. You can control the alignment of members by using bit fields, as described in the next section. You can also promote portability by accessing members by their names rather than through unions or offsets from pointers.

Box 8-2: ANSI Feature — *offsetof* **Macro**

The ANSI Standard provides a method of determining the byte offset of any non-bitfield structure member. The macro takes two arguments: the type of the structure and the member name:

offsetof(*type, member-name*)

and expands to an integral byte offset. The exact type of the result is specified by a macro called *size_t* that is defined in the *stddef.h* header file. Consider the following example:

```
#include <stddef.h>

typedef struct
{
  char widgetName[MAX_NAME];
  int widgitCount
  enum WIDGET_TYPE widgetType;
}  WIDGET_INFO;

...
size_t typeOffset = offsetof( WIDGET_INFO,
                              widgetType );
```

The variable *typeOffset* now contains an integer value representing the offset of member *widgetType*. This information can be very helpful in determining how a compiler aligns members.

Though this feature is an extension to the K&R standard, many compilers have supported some form of this construct for years.

8.1.7 Bit Fields

The smallest data type that C supports is **char**, which is usually 8 bits long. But in structures, it is possible to declare a smaller object called a *bit field*. Bit fields behave like other integer variables, except that you cannot take the address of a bit field and you cannot declare an array of bit fields.

The syntax for declaring a bit field is shown in Figure 8-4.

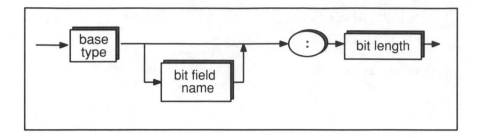

Figure 8-4. Syntax of Bit Field Declarations.

The base type may be **int**, **unsigned int**, or **signed int**. If the bit field is declared as **int**, the implementation is free to decide whether it is an **unsigned int** or a **signed int**. For portable code, use the **signed** or **unsigned** qualifier. (Many compilers allow you to use **enum**s, **char**s, and **short**s as the base type.)

Bit fields may be named or unnamed. Unnamed fields cannot be accessed and are used only as padding. As a special case, an unnamed bit field with a width of zero causes the next structure member to be aligned on the next **int** boundary.

The *bit length* is an integer constant expression that may not exceed the length of an **int**. On machines where **int**s are 16 bits long, for example, the following is illegal:

```
int too_long : 17;
```

The compiler allocates at least a **char**'s worth of memory and possibly more. The precise number of bits allocated is implementation dependent, but the compiler must allocate at least as many bits as are specified by the bit field length, and the length must be an even multiple of **char**s. Consecutive bit fields are packed into the allocated space until there is no room left. Assuming your compiler allocates 16-bits for a bit field, the following declarations would cause *a*, *b*, and *c* to be packed into a single 16-bit object (see Figure 8-5).

```
struct
{
    int a : 3;
    int b : 7;
    int c : 2;
} s;
```

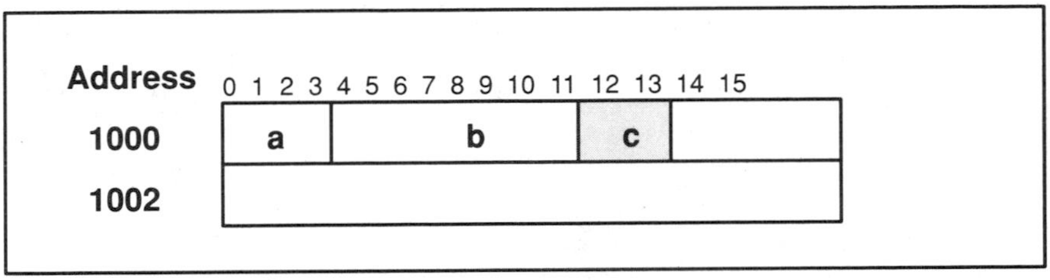

Address 0 1 2 3 4 5 6 7 8 9 10 11 12 13 14 15

1000   a   b   c

1002

Figure 8-5. Storage of Three Consecutive Bit Fields.

However, each implementation is free to arrange the bit fields within the object in either increasing or decreasing order, so a compiler might arrange the bit fields as shown in Figure 8-6.

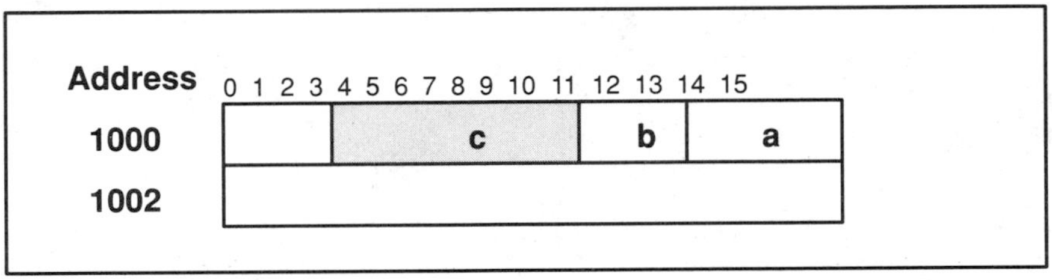

Address 0 1 2 3 4 5 6 7 8 9 10 11 12 13 14 15

1000   c   b   a

1002

Figure 8-6. Alternative Storage of Three Consecutive Bit Fields.

Also, if a bit field would straddle an **int** boundary, a new memory area may be allocated, depending on your compiler. For instance, the declaration

```
struct
{
   int a : 10;
   int b : 10;
} s;
```

might cause a new 16-bit area of memory to be allocated for *b*, as shown in Figure 8-7. As a result, 32 bits would be allocated, even though only 20 are used. If you are using bit fields to save storage space, you should try to arrange the fields to avoid gaps.

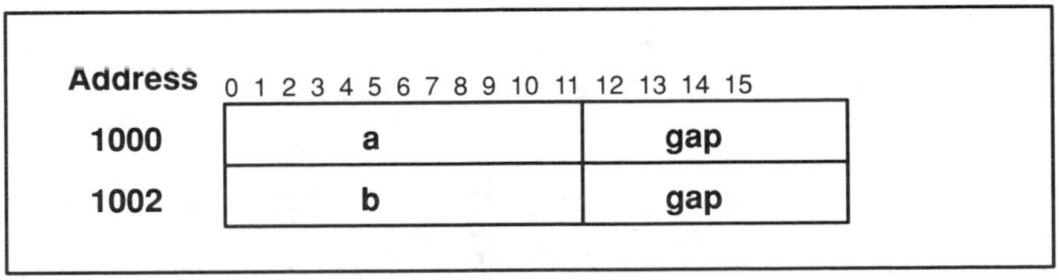

Address 0 1 2 3 4 5 6 7 8 9 10 11 12 13 14 15

1000   a   gap

1002   b   gap

Figure 8-7. Storage of Two Consecutive Bit Fields.

Box 8-3: Bug Alert — Passing Structures *vs.* Passing Arrays

Passing structures is *not* the same as passing arrays. This inconsistency in the C language can cause confusion.

To pass an array in C, you simply specify the array name without a subscript. The compiler interprets the name as a pointer to the initial element of the array so it really passes the array by reference. There is no way to pass an array by value (except to embed it in a structure and pass the structure by value).

With structures, however, the structure name is interpreted as the entire structure, not as a pointer to the beginning of the structure. If you use the same syntax that you use with arrays, therefore, you will get different semantics. For example,

```
int ar[100];
struct tag st;
        .
        .
func( ar );  /* Passes a pointer to the first
                element of ar[] */
func( st );  /* Passes an entire structure */
```

The inconsistency follows through to the receiving side. For example, the following two array versions are the same:

```
func( ar )
int ar[];  /* ar is converted to a pointer
              to an int */

func( ar )
int *ar;   /* ar is a pointer to an int */
```

But the following two structure versions are very different:

```
func( st )
struct tag st;  /* st is an entire
                   structure */

func( st )
struct tag *st;  /* st is a pointer to
                    a struct */
```

As the preceding discussion indicates, the implementation of bit fields varies somewhat from one compiler to another. Consequently, you should use bit fields with care—they are inherently nonportable. There are two situations where the use of bit fields are valid: 1) when efficient use of memory or data storage is a serious concern and 2) when you need to map a structure to a predetermined organization. The second situation occurs when somebody else has defined a structure that contains objects smaller than **char**s and you need to manipulate this externally created structure.

As an example of using bit fields to save space, consider our DATE structure. Since a day value cannot exceed 31 and a month value cannot exceed 12, we can rewrite the *DATE* structure using bit fields as

```
struct DATE
{
   unsigned int day : 5;
   month : 4;
   year : 11;
};
```

Only 20 bits are needed for the three fields. Due to the bit field allocation rules, however, some compilers would allocate 24 bits while others would allocate 32 bits. Figures 8-8 and 8-9 show two possible allocation schemes for an array of *DATE* structures. Figure 8-8 assumes that the compiler packs bit fields to the nearest **char** and allows bit fields to span **int** boundaries. Note that each array element must begin at a **char** boundary. Figure 8-9 assumes that **int**s are 16 bits and that the compiler does not allow bit fields to span **int** boundaries.

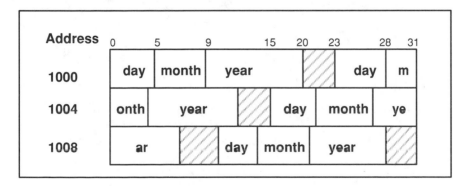

Figure 8-8.   *Storage of the* DATE *Structure with Bit Fields. This figure assumes that the compiler packs bit fields to the nearest* **char** *and allows fields to span* **int** *boundaries.*

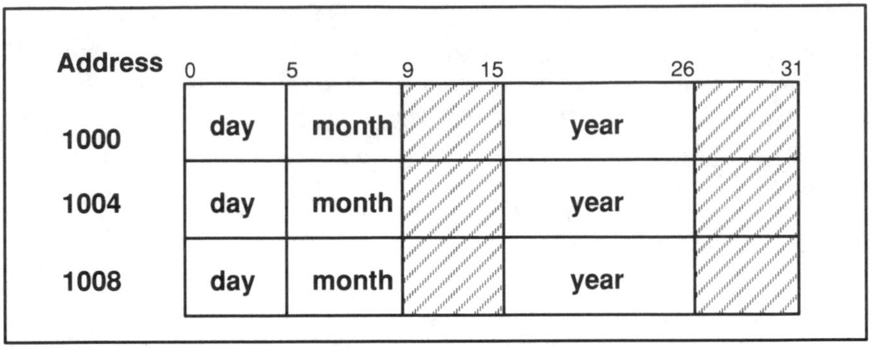

Figure 8-9.   *Alternative Storage of the* DATE *Structure with Bit Fields.*
                This figure assumes that the compiler packs bit fields to
                the nearest **short** *and does not allow fields to span* **int**
                boundaries.

8.1.8 Passing Structures as Function Arguments

There are two ways to pass structures as arguments: pass the structure itself
(called *pass by value*) or pass a pointer to the structure (called *pass by reference*).
The two methods are shown in the following example.

```
VITALSTAT vs;
    .
    .
    .
func( vs );    /*  Pass by value -- Passes an entire
               *   copy of the structure.
               */
func( &vs );   /*  Pass by reference -- Passes the
               *   address of a structure.
               */
    .
    .
    .
```

Passing the address of a structure is usually faster because only a single pointer is copied to the argument area. Passing by value, on the other hand, requires that the entire structure be copied. There are only two circumstances when you should pass a structure by value:

- The structure is very small (i.e., approximately the same size as a pointer).

- You want to guarantee that the called function does not change the structure being passed. (When an argument is passed by value, the compiler generates a copy of the argument for the called function. The called function can only change the value of the copy, not the value of the argument on the calling side. This is described in greater detail in Chapter 9.)

In all other instances, you should pass structures by reference. (Note: passing structures by value, though supported in almost all C compilers, is not part of the original K&R standard. It is required by the ANSI Standard.)

Depending on which method you choose, you need to declare the argument on the receiving side as either a structure or a pointer to a structure:

```
func ( vs )
VITALSTAT vs;    /*  Pass by value -- the argument
                 *   is a structure .
                 */
```

or

```
func ( pvs )
VITALSTAT *pvs;    /* Pass by reference -- the
                   * argument is a pointer to
                   * a structure.
                   */
```

Note that the argument-passing method you choose determines which operator you should use in the function body—the dot operator if a structure is passed by value and the right-arrow operator if the structure is passed by reference.

8.1.9 Returning Structures

Just as it is possible to pass a structure or a pointer to a structure, it is also possible to return a structure or a pointer to a structure. (Returning a structure is not supported in the original K&R standard but is a common extension supported by most C compilers.) The declaration of the function's return type must agree with the actual returned value. For example,

```
struct tag f()    /* Define a function that returns */
{                 /* a struct */
   struct tag st;
     .
     .
   return st;     /* Return an entire struct */
}

struct tag *f1() /* Define a function that returns */
                 /* a pointer to a struct */
{
   static struct tag pst;
     .
     .
   return &pst;   /* Return the address of a struct */
}
```

As with passing structures, you generally want to return pointers to structures because it is more efficient. Note, however, that if you return a pointer to a structure, the structure must have fixed duration. Otherwise, it will cease to be valid once the function returns.

One situation where returning structures is particularly useful is when you want to return more than one value. The **return** statement can only send back one expression to the calling routine, but if that expression is a structure or a pointer to a structure, you can indirectly return any number of values. The following function, for instance, returns the sine, cosine, and tangent of its argument. The functions *sin()*, *cos()*, and *tan()* are part of the runtime library. Each accepts an argument measured in radians and returns the corresponding trigonometric value. If the argument is too large, however, the results will not be meaningful.

```
#include <stdio.h>
#include <math.h>   /* include file for trig */
                    * functions */
#define too_large 100 /* Differs from one machine
                       *  to another. */
typedef struct
{
  double sine, cosine, tangent;
} TRIG;

TRIG *get_trigvals( radian_val )
double radian_val;
{
  static TRIG result;

/*  If radian_val is too large, the sine, cosine
 *  and tangent values will be meaningless.
 */
  if (radian_val > TOO_LARGE)
  {
    printf( "Input value too large -- cannot \
return meaningful results\n" );
    return NULL; /* return null pointer --
                  * defined in stdio.h.
                  */
  }

  result.sine = sin( radian_val );
  result.cosine = cos( radian_val );
  result.tangent = tan( radian_val );
  return &result;
}
```

8.1.10 Assigning Structures

Although it is not supported in the original K&R standard, most compilers (and the ANSI Standard) allow you to assign a structure to a structure variable, provided they share the same structure type. The code extract on the following page shows some examples of structure assignments.

```
struct {
        int a;
        float b;
    } s1, s2, sf(), *ps;
        .
        .
        .
s1 = s2;
s2 = sf();
ps = &s1;
s2 = *ps;

        .

        .
```

This feature may not be available on older compilers. To assign structures using older versions of C, you need to use the *memcpy()* runtime library function. See Appendix A for more information about this function.

8.2 Linked Lists

In our examples up to now, we have used an array of structures to handle groups of data. This is a valid approach when you know beforehand exactly how many structures you are manipulating. When the number is unknown, however, arrays can be extremely costly since they force you to allocate enough memory for the worst-case situation. This memory is reserved and unavailable for other uses even if you use only a fraction of the array elements. Moreover, if you need to access more memory than you initially allocated, your program will fail.

The obvious solution is to be able to allocate memory for new structures as needed. C allows you to do this through the runtime library routines *malloc()* and *calloc()*, described in Chapter 7. But successive calls to these routines will not guarantee that the structures will be placed contiguously in memory. What is needed, therefore, is a technique for connecting all the structures together.

The most common way to do this is through a construct called a *linked list*. A linked list is a chain of structures that are linked one to another, like sausages. In the simplest linked-list scheme, each structure contains an extra member which is a pointer to the next structure in the list.

Revising our earlier *vitalstat* example to make a linked list, you would write

```
typedef struct vitalstat
{
    char  vs_name[19], vs_ssnum[11];
    unsigned int vs_day :    5,
                   vs_month : 5,
                   vs_year : 11;
    struct vitalstat *vs_next;
} VITALSTAT;
```

Pictorially, a linked list looks like Figure 8-10. This is a *singly* linked list because it goes in only one direction. There are also *doubly* linked lists, in which each structure contains two pointers, one to the next element and one to the previous element. The following discussion and examples, however, are confined to singly linked lists.

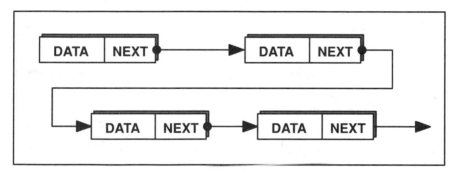

Figure 8-10. A Singly Linked List.

In a typical linked-list application, you need to perform the following operations:

- Create a list element

- Add elements to the end of a list

- Insert elements in the middle of a list

- Remove an element from a list

- Find a particular element in a list

Each of these tasks (except the last one) can be written as a self-contained and generalized function that will work no matter how the structures are configured.

8.2.1 Creating a Linked-List Element

To create a linked-list element, all you need to do is allocate memory for the structure and return a pointer to this memory area.

```
#include "v_stat.h"

ELEMENT *create_list_element()
{
  ELEMENT *p;

  p = (ELEMENT *) malloc( sizeof( ELEMENT ) );
  if (p == NULL)
  {
    printf( "create_list_element: malloc failed.\n");
    exit( 1 );
  }
  p->next = NULL;
  return p;
}
```

To make the function as general as possible, we use the name *ELEMENT*, which gives no clue about the actual type of data being manipulated. For this function to work for the *vitalstat* structure, we would need to include the following typedefs in *v_stat.h*.

```
#define NULL (void *) 0

typedef struct vitalstat
{
    char  vs_name[19], ssnum[11];
    unsigned int vs_day :    5,
                 vs_month : 5,
                 vs_year : 11;
    struct vitalstat *next;
} VITALSTAT;

typedef struct vitalstat ELEMENT;
```

ELEMENT becomes synonymous with s*truct vitalstat*. Note in the declaration of *create_list()* that it returns a value of type *ELEMENT* *. Note also that you must use a tag name rather than a **typedef** to declare the pointer *next*. This self-referencing is legal if you identify the structure by its tag name, but not if you identify it by a **typedef** name. This is because the typedef name is not defined until the end of the declaration.

8.2.2 Adding Elements

The *create_list_element()* function allocates memory, but it doesn't link the element to the list. For this, we need an additional function, which we call *add_element()*:

```
#include "v_stat.h"

static ELEMENT *head

void add_element ( e )
ELEMENT *e;
{
  ELEMENT *p;

/*  If the first element (the head) has not been
 *  created, create it now.
 */
  if (head == NULL)
  {
    head = e;
    return;
  }

/*  Otherwise, find the last element in the list */
  for (p = head; p->next != NULL; p = p->next);
    ;  /* null statement */

  p->next = e;
}
```

This function has a number of interesting aspects worth noting. The variable *head* serves as a pointer to the beginning of the linked list. It is declared with file scope so that it will be available to a number of functions. However, all functions that use *head* must exist in the same source file.

The purpose of the **for** loop is to find the last element of the list. It goes through each element testing to see whether *p.next* is *NULL* or not. If not, *p.next* must point to another element. When *p next* does equal *NULL*, we have found the end of the list and we end the **for** loop. The assignment

```
p->next = e;
```

appends a new structure to the end of the list. The argument, *e*, is a pointer to a structure that has been allocated by the calling function.

To create a linked list containing ten *vitalstat* structures, you could write

```
#include "v_stat.h"
static ELEMENT *head;

main()
{
  for (j=0; j < 10; ++j)
    add_element( create_list_element() );
}
```

8.2.3 Inserting an Element

To insert an element in a linked list, you must specify where you want the new element inserted. The following function accepts two pointer arguments, *p* and *q*, and inserts the structure pointed to by *p* just after the structure pointed to by *q*. (See Figure 8-11.)

```
/*  Insert p after q */
#include "v_stat.h"

void insert_after( p, q )
ELEMENT *p, *q;
{
/*  Perform sanity check on arguments.
 *  If p and q are the same or NULL, or if p
 *  already follows q, report.
 */
  if (p == NULL || q == NULL || p == q ||
      q->next == p)
  {
    printf( "insert_after: Bad arguments\n" );
    return;
  }

  p->next = q->next;
  q->next = p;

}
```

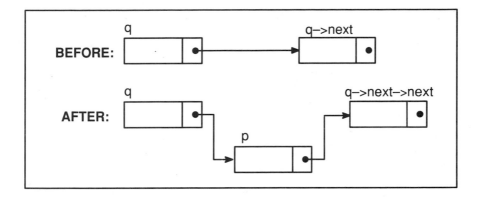

Figure 8-11. Linked-List Insertion.

8.2.4 Deleting an Element

Deleting an element in a singly linked list is a little trickier since you need to find the element before the one you are deleting so that you can bond the list back together after removing one of the links. You also need to use the *free()* function, described in Chapter 7, to free up the memory used by the deleted element. Figure 8-12 illustrates the operation of the *delete_element()* function.

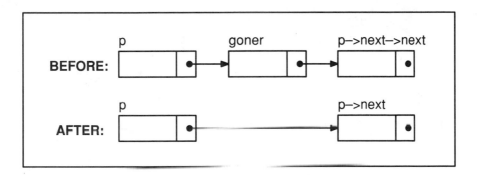

Figure 8-12. Linked-List Deletion.

```
#include "v_stat.h"

static ELEMENT *head;

void delete_element( goner )
ELEMENT *goner;
{
  ELEMENT *p;

  if (goner == head)
   head = goner->next;
  else
  {        /* Find element preceding the one to be
            * deleted
            */
    for (p = head; (p != NULL) && (p->next != goner);
         p = p->next)
      ; /* null statement */
    if (p == NULL)
    {
      printf( "delete_element: can't find element in\
list.\n" );
      return;
    }
    p->next = p->next->next;
  }
  free( goner );
}
```

The right-arrow operator binds from left to right, so the expression

```
p->next->next
```

is evaluated as if it had been written

```
(p->next)->next
```

8.2.5 Finding an Element

There is no easy way to create a general-purpose *find()* function because you usually search for an element based on one of its data fields, which depends on the structure being used. To write a general-purpose *find()* function, you need to use *pointers to functions*, which are described in the next chapter.

The following function, based on the *vitalstat* structure, searches for an element whose *vs_name* field matches the argument.

```
#include "v_stat.h"

static ELEMENT *head;

ELEMENT *find( name )
char *name;
{
   for (p = head; p != NULL; p = p->next)
     if (strcmp( p->vs_name, name ) == 0)
        return p;
   return NULL;
}
```

8.3 Unions

Unions are similar to structures except that the members are overlaid one on top of another, so members share the same memory. For example, the following declaration results in the storage shown in Figure 8-13.

```
typedef union
{
   struct
   {
     char c1, c2;
   } s;
   long j;
   float x;
} U;

U example;
```

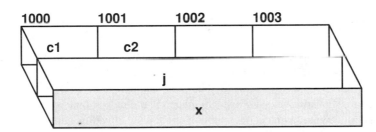

Figure 8-13. Example of Union Memory Storage.

The compiler always allocates enough memory to hold the largest member, and all members begin at the same address. The data stored in a union depends on which union member you use. For example, the assignments

```
example.s.c1 = 'a';
example.s.c2 = 'b';
```

would result in the storage shown in Figure 8-14.

1000	1001	1002	1003
'a'	'b'		

Figure 8-14. Storage in example Union After Assignment.

But if you make the assignment

```
example.j = 5;
```

it would overwrite the two characters, using all four bytes to store the integer value 5.

Unions obey the same syntactic rules as structures. You can access elements with either the dot operator or the right-arrow operator; you can declare bit fields, and you can use tag names.

There are two basic applications for unions:

- Interpreting the same memory in different ways.

- Creating flexible structures (called *variant records* in Pascal) that can hold different types of data.

8.3.1 Interpreting Data Differently

As an example of interpreting data differently, consider the common communications problem where data comes over the line byte by byte. Unions provide a way of grouping bytes together so that they can be reconstructed into their original form. For instance, suppose *get_byte()* is a function that returns a single byte from a communications device. An eight-byte **double** value can be extracted from the communications device through eight successive calls to *get_byte()* as shown in the following function.

```
union doub
{
  char c[8];
  double val;
};

double get_double()
{
  extern char get_byte();
  int j;
  union doub d;

  for (j=0; j < 8; j++)
    d.c[j] = get_byte();

  return d.val;
}
```

We store each successive character in the next element of *c[]*. Then when we want the **double** value, we access the union using the *val* member.

One area of confusion among many C programmers is the difference between conversions using unions and conversions using casts. Accessing a union through different members does not affect the actual bits in memory in any way. The compiler simply uses different interpretations for the bits. Likewise, a cast does not affect the bits in storage. But instead of interpreting them differently, it converts the value they represent into the target type. The following example should make this clearer.

```
main()
{
  union {
          long long_element;
          float float_element;
        } u;
  long lng_var;
  float flt_var;
  lng_var = u.long_element = 10;

  printf( "The value of lng_var cast to a float \
is: %f\n", (float) lng_var );

  printf( "The value of float_element after\n\
assignment to long_element is: %f\n\n",
          u.float_element );

  flt_var = u.float_element = 3.555;

  printf( "The value of flt_var cast to a long \
is: %d\n", (long) flt_var );

  printf( "The value of long_element after an \n\
assignment to float_element is: %d\n",
          u.long_element );
}
```

The results are

```
The value of lng_var cast to a float is: 10.000000
The value of float_element after
assignment to long_element is: 0.000000

The value of flt_var cast to a long is 3
The value of long_element after an
assignment to float_element is: 1074557091
```

In a cast, the compiler makes every attempt to preserve the true value. So when casting a **long** to a **float**, the compiler simply adds a fractional part equal to zero. And when casting a **float** to a **long**, the compiler truncates the fractional part. In a union, on the other hand, the compiler ignores the true value — it is interested only in the bit sequence. The values we receive from the program are machine dependent since they depend on the way our system stores **long**s and **float**s. Both casts and unions are powerful tools, but it is important not to confuse the two.

Box 8-4: ANSI Feature — Initializing Unions

The K&R standard states that variables of union type may *not* be initialized. However, the ANSI Standard allows unions to be initialized by assigning the initialization value to the first union component:

```
union init_example
{
  int i;
  float f;
};


/* Assigns 1 to test.i */
union init_example test = {1};
```

If the first component of a union is a structure, the entire structure may be initialized as in

```
union u
{
  struct { int i; float f; } S;
  char ch[6];
};


/*  Assigns 1 to test.2.S.i and 1.0 to
 *  test2.S.f
 */
union u test2 = { 1 , 1.0 };
```

8.3.2 Variant Records

The other application of unions is in creating a single structure that can hold different types of values. For example, suppose you want to add three additional pieces of information to the *vitalstat* structure:

- Are you a U.S. citizen?

- If not a U.S. citizen, what is your nationality?

- If you are a U.S. citizen, in what city were you born?

One way to add this information is to declare three new fields:

```
struct vitalstat
{
    struct vitalstat *next;
    char   name[19], ssnum[11];
    unsigned int vs_day  :    5,
                 vs_month : 4,
                 vs_year : 11;
    unsigned UScitizen : 1;   /* Bit field for U.S.
                                    citizenship */
    char nationality[20];
    char city_of_birth[20];
};
```

Note, however, that one of these new members will always be empty. If the *UScitizen* bit is set, nationality will be empty; if *UScitizen* is zero, *city_of_birth* will be empty. Since these two fields are mutually exclusive, you can have them overlap in memory by declaring a union:

```
struct vitalstat
{
    struct vitalstat *next;
    char name[19], ssnum[11];
    unsigned int vs_day :    5,
                 vs_month : 4,
                 vs_year : 11;
    unsigned UScitizen : 1;   /* Bit field for U.S.
                                    citizenship */
    union {
            char nationality[20];
            char city_of_birth[20];
          } location;
};
```

This saves us 20 bytes of memory for each structure. For a large array of structures, this can result in significant savings. The following functions show how you would use the *UScitizen* member to decide which union member to access. The key function is *get_city_info()*; the other two functions— *double_check()* and *is_yes()*—are general-purpose functions for processing user input. These functions make use of the runtime function *fgetc()*, which reads a string from the specified file or device. For more information about *fgetc()*, you can read about it in Appendix A.

```c
#include <stdio.h>
#include "v_stat2.h"   /* includes location union */
#define TRUE 1
#define FALSE 0

/*  Remove trailing newline (if any), and see if
 *  user typed the right entry.
 */
static int double_check( s )
char *s;
{
  int last_char = strlen( s ) - 1;

  if (s[last_char] == '\n')
    s[last_char] = 0;
  printf( "Is '%s' correct? (Y or N) ", s );
  return is_yes();
}

static int is_yes()
{
  char answer[64];

  while (1)
  {
    fgets( answer, sizeof(answer), stdin );

    switch (answer[0])
    {
      case 'y':
      case 'Y':  return TRUE;
      case 'n':
      case 'N': return FALSE;
      default : printf( "Please answer Y or N\n");
    }
  }
}
```

```
void get_city_info( pvs )
VITALSTAT *pvs;
{
  int answered = FALSE;

  printf("Are you a U.S. citizen? ");
  pvs->UScitizen = is_yes();

  while (!answered)
    if (!pvs->UScitizen)
    {
      printf("What is your nationality?");
      fgets(pvs->location.nationality,
            sizeof(pvs->location.nationality), stdin);
      answered = double_check(
                          pvs->location.nationality );
    }
  else  /* UScitizen */
  {
    printf("Enter city of birth: ");
    fgets(pvs->location.city_of_birth,
          sizeof(pvs->location.city_of_birth), stdin);
      answered = double_check(
                      pvs->location.city_of_birth );
  }
}
```

Note that the union member accessed depends on the value of *UScitizen*. This is typical of variant records, in which one member serves as a selector of union members.

8.4 *enum* **Declarations**

Just as it is possible to declare tag names for structures and unions, it is also possible to declare tag names for **enum** types. For instance, the declaration

```
enum types { INT, LONG_INT, FLOAT, DOUBLE, POINTER };
```

defines the tag name *types*, which can then be used in future declarations. For example,

```
enum types t1;
enum types *ptypes;     /* pointer to types enum */
enum types ar_types[5]; /* array of types enums */
enum types f_types();   /* function returning types
                         * enum
                         */
```

You can also use a typedef:

```
typedef enum {
            INT, LONG_INT, FLOAT, DOUBLE, POINT-
ER
            } TYPES;
```

```
Now you can make the declarations:
```

```
TYPES t1;
TYPES *ptypes;     /* pointer to TYPES enum */
TYPES ar_types[5]; /* array of TYPES enums */
TYPES f_types();   /* function returning TYPES
                    * enum */
```

As with typedefs of structures and unions, enum typedefs are generally placed in a header file where they can be accessed by multiple source files.

Exercises

1. In many commercial applications, integers are represented in a form
   called BCD (Binary-Coded Decimal). In BCD form, each digit is
   represented by 4 bits. An 8-digit integer, for example, would require
   32 bits. Write two functions: one that converts integers into BCD
   format and another that converts BCD integers into their original form.
   Use bit fields to store each BCD digit.

2. Write a function that accepts two pointers, each to a linked list, and
   concatenates the two lists, attaching the second list to the first.

3. A *stack* is a special kind of list that has the following two properties:

   - You can only add elements at the end of the list. This is called *pushing*.

   - You can only remove elements from the end of the list. This is called
     popping.

   Write two functions, *push()* and *pop()*, that perform these stack tasks.

4. Stacks are called first in, last out (FILO) queues because the first
   element pushed onto the stack is always the last one popped. Using
   push(), *pop()*, and any other functions you need, write a program that
   reads a line from the terminal and determines whether or not it is a
   palindrome. A palindrome is a string that is the same spelled forward
   or backward. For example, "Able was I ere I saw Elba."

5. The ANSI *offsetof* macro uses an interesting set of C pointer and
   casting expressions. The macro typically looks something like

   ```
   #define offsetof(t, m)  (size_t)&((t*)0->m)
   ```

   Explain exactly why the code above produces the byte offset of a
   structure member. Can you think of a different way to perform *offsetof*?

Chapter 9

Functions

You are fond of argument, and now you fancy that I am a bag full of arguments. — Socrates, Theoetus

We have been using functions throughout the previous chapters and have discussed in passing some of their essential features. In this chapter, we take a more rigorous look at them and introduce some new topics, including pointers to functions, recursion, and a new ANSI feature called *prototyping*.

9.1 Passing Arguments

Arguments to a function are a means of passing data to the function. Many programming languages pass arguments *by reference*, which means they pass a pointer to the argument. As a result, the called function can actually change the value of the argument. In C, arguments are passed *by value*, which means that a copy of the argument is passed to the function. The function can change the value of this *copy*, but cannot change the value of the argument in the calling routine. Figure 9-1 shows the difference. Note that the arrows in the call-by-reference picture point in both directions, whereas the call-by-value arrows go in only one direction. The argument that is passed is often called an *actual argument*, while the received copy is called a *formal argument* or *formal parameter*.

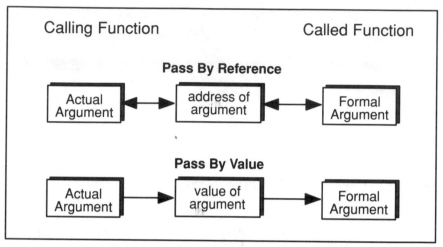

Figure 9-1. Pass By Reference vs. Pass By Value. In Pass By Reference, the actual and formal arguments refer to the same memory area; in Pass By Value, the formal argument is a copy of the actual argument.

Because C passes arguments by value, a function can assign values to the *formal* arguments without affecting the *actual* arguments. For example,

```
#include <stdio.h>

main()
{
   extern void f();
   int a = 2;

   f( a );              /* pass a copy of "a" to "f()" */
   printf( "%d\n", a );
   exit(0);
}

void f( received_arg )
int received_arg;
{
   received_arg = 3; /* Assign 3 to argument copy */
}
```

In the example above, the *printf()* function prints 2, not 3, because the formal argument, *received_arg* in *f()*, is just a copy of the actual argument *a*. C matches actual arguments in the call to the corresponding formal arguments in the function definition, regardless of the names used. That is, the first actual argument is matched to the first formal argument, the second actual argument to the second formal argument, and so on. For correct results, the types of the corresponding actual and formal arguments should be the same.

If you do want a function to change the value of an object, you must pass a pointer to the object and then make an assignment through the dereferenced pointer. The following, for example, is a function that swaps the values of two integer variables.

```
/* Swap the values of two int variables */

void swap( x, y )
   int *x, *y;
{
   register int temp;

   temp = *x;
   *x = *y;
   *y = temp;
}
```

To call this function, you need to pass two addresses:

```
main()
{
   int a = 2, b = 3;

   swap( &a, &b );
   printf( "a = %d\t b = %d\n", a, b );
}
```

Executing this program yields

```
a = 3    b = 2
```

The pass-by-value method explains the purpose of the address of operator in *scanf()* calls. When you write

```
scanf( "%d", &num );
```

the two arguments tell the function what type of data to read (**%d** indicates an integer) and where to store it (at the address of *num*). If you passed the variables themselves, there would be no way for *scanf()* to make assignments to them. By passing the addresses, you give *scanf()* access to the variables so it can assign them values.

9.2 Declarations and Calls

Functions can appear in a program in three forms:

Definition
A declaration that actually defines what the function does, as well as the number and type of arguments.

Function Allusion
Declares a function that is *defined* elsewhere. A function allusion specifies what kind of value the function returns. (With the new prototyping feature, discussed in Box 9-1, it is also possible to specify the number and types of arguments in a function allusion.)

Function Call
Invokes a function, causing program execution to jump to the invoked function. When the called function returns, execution resumes at the point just after the call.

9.2.1 Function Definition Syntax

Figure 9-2 shows the formal syntax of a function definition. You can specify any number of arguments, including zero. The return type defaults to **int** if you leave it blank. However, even if the return type is **int**, you should specify it explicitly to avoid confusion.

If the function does not return an **int**, you *must* specify the true return type. If the function does not return any value, you should specify a return type of **void**. Before **void** became a common feature of C compilers, it was a convention to leave off the return type when there was no return value. The return type would default to **int**, but the context in which the function was used would usually make it clear that no meaningful value was returned. With modern C compilers, however, there is no excuse for omitting the return type. If your compiler does not support **void**, you should circumvent the deficiency by defining a preprocessor macro that changes **void** to **int**:

```
#define void int
```

Not only does this make it possible to declare functions returning **void**, thus aiding readability, but it also opens an avenue of upward mobility. If at a later date you use a compiler that supports **void**, all you need to do is remove the preprocessor definition. No other change to the source code is required.

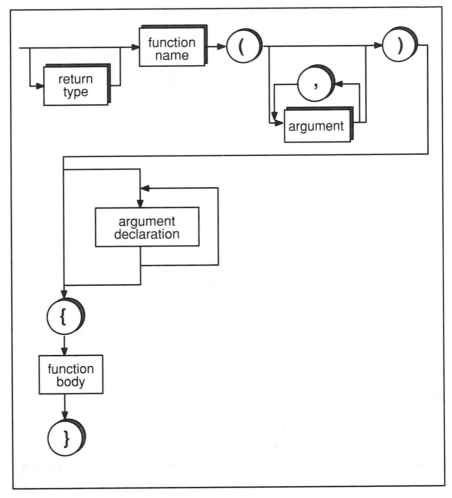

Figure 9-2. Syntax of a Function Definition.

9.2.2 Argument Declarations

Argument declarations obey the same rules as other variable declarations, with the following exceptions:

- The only legal storage class is **register**.

- **char**s and **short**s are converted to **int**s; **float**s are converted to **double**s. (With the new ANSI prototyping feature, you can disable these automatic conversions.)

- A formal argument declared as an array is converted to a pointer to an object of the array type.

- A formal argument declared as a function is converted to a pointer to a function.

- You may not include an initializer in an argument declaration.

It is legal to omit an argument declaration, in which case the argument type defaults to **int**. This is considered very poor style, however.

There is a new syntax invented by ANSI that allows you to declare the type of arguments when you list the parameters. For example, instead of writing

```
int f( a, b, c )
    int a;
    char *b;
    float c;
{
    .
    .
}
```

you could write

```
int f( int a, char *b, float c )
{
    .
    .
}
```

This is consistent with the new prototyping syntax described in Box 9-1. However, since it is a new feature, you should make sure your compiler supports it before using it.

9.2.2.1 The Function Body

The body of a function is delimited by a set of right and left braces. The only type of statement allowed outside a function body is a declaration.

The body of a function can be empty, which can be useful in the design stages of a software product. One of the first tasks in designing a large program is to define a set of high-level operations that correspond to functions. During this stage, it can be useful to have a function that does nothing but return, in order to serve as a placeholder for future functionality. These are called *stubs*. The following, for instance, is a legal C function that does nothing but return when called.

```
void operation1(){}
```

Later, you can fill in the function with some meaningful code.

9.2.2.2 Return Values

Functions can return only a single value directly via the **return** statement. The return value can be any type except an array or function. This means that it is possible to indirectly return more than a single value by passing a pointer to an aggregate type. It is also possible to return a structure or union directly, though this is not generally recommended because it is inefficient.

The syntax for a **return** statement is shown in Figure 9-3.

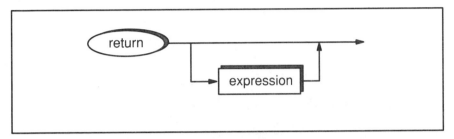

*Figure 9-3. Syntax of a **return** Statement.*

Many C programmers enclose the return expression in parentheses. The parentheses, however, are optional, and we find that they enhance readability only when the return value is a complicated expression.

A function may contain any number of **return** statements. The first one encountered in the normal flow of control is executed and causes program control to be returned to the calling routine. If there is no **return** statement, program control returns to the calling routine when the right brace of the function is reached. In this case, the value returned is undefined.

The return value must be assignment-compatible with the type of the function. This means that the compiler uses the same rules for allowable types on either side of an assignment operator to determine allowable return types. For example, if *f()* is declared as a function returning an **int**, it is legal to return any arithmetic type, since they can all be converted to an **int**. It would be illegal, however, to return an aggregate type or a pointer since these are incompatible types. The following example shows a function that returns a **float**, and some legal return values.

```
float f()
{
   float f2;
   int a;
   char c;

   f2 = a;      /* OK, quietly converts a to float */
   return a;    /* OK, quietly converts a to float */
   f2 = c;      /* OK, quietly converts c to float */
   return c;    /* OK, quietly converts c to float */
}
```

The C language is more picky about matching pointers. In the following example, *f()* is declared as a function returning a pointer to a **char**. Some legal and illegal **return** statements are shown below:

```
char *f()
{
  char **cpp, *cp1, *cp2, ca[10];
  int *ip1, *ip2;

  cp1 = cp2;        /* OK, types match */
  return cp2;       /* OK, types match */
  cp1 = *cpp;       /* OK, types match */
  return *cpp;      /* OK, types match */

/* An array name without a subscript gets converted
 * to a pointer to the first element.
 */
  cp1 = ca;   /* OK, types match */
  return ca;  /* OK, types match */

  cp1 = *cp2; /* Error, mismatched types      */
              /* (pointer to char vs. char ) */
  return *cp2;/* Error, mismatched types      */
              /* (pointer to char vs. char ) */
  cp1 = ip1;  /* Error, mismatched pointer types */
  return ip1; /* Error, mismatched pointer types */
  return;     /* Produces undefined behavior --  */
              /* should return (char *)          */
}
```

Note in the last statement that the behavior is undefined if you return nothing. The only time you can safely use **return** without an expression is when the function type is **void**.

9.2.3 Function Allusions

A function allusion is a declaration of a function that is defined elsewhere, usually in a different source file. The main purpose of the function allusion is to tell the compiler what type of value the function returns. With the new ANSI prototyping feature, it is also possible to declare the number and types of arguments that the function takes. This feature is discussed in Box 9-1. The remainder of this section describes the old function allusion format. Note that this older syntax will still work with ANSI-conforming compilers.

By default, all functions are assumed to return an **int**. You are only strictly required, therefore, to include function allusions for functions that do not return an **int**. However, it is good style to include function allusions for all functions that you call. It makes it possible for a reader to determine what functions are called merely by looking at the declaration section, rather than having to wade through the entire routine. By the same token, you should *not* include function allusions to functions that are not called since this can be misleading. (Sometimes this is unavoidable, particularly when you include a header file that contains allusions to many functions, only a few of which you actually use.)

The syntax for a function allusion is shown in Figure 9-4. If you omit the storage class, it defaults to **extern**, signifying that the function definition may appear in the same source file or in another source module. The only other legal storage class is **static**, which indicates that the function is defined in the same source file. The data type in the function allusion should agree with the return type specified in the definition. If you omit the type, it defaults to **int**. Note that if you omit *both* the storage class and the data type, the expression is a function *call* if it appears within a block; if it appears outside a block, it is an allusion.

```
f1();   /* Function allusion -- default type is int
*/

main()
{
    .
    .
    f2(); /* Function call */
    .
    .
```

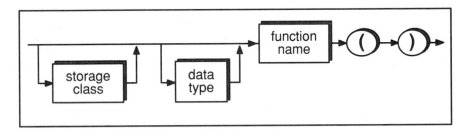

Figure 9-4. Syntax of a Function Allusion.

Typically, a function allusion appears at the head of a block with other declarations. You can mix function allusions with declarations of other variables. For example, the following statement declares a pointer to a **float**, an array of **float**s, and a function returning a **float**.

```
extern float *pflt, arr_flt[10], func_flt();
```

Though the previous declarations are legal, it is better from a stylistic viewpoint to keep function declarations separate from declarations of variables:

```
extern float func_flt();
extern float *pflt, arr_flt[10];
```

The scope of a function allusion follows the same rules as other variables. Functions alluded to within a block have block scope; functions alluded to outside a block have file scope.

Note, however, that the default storage class rules are different for functions than for other variables. For example, in the following declaration, the storage class of *pflt* and *arr_flt[]* defaults to **auto**, whereas the storage class of *func_flt()* defaults to **extern**.

```
{
    float func_flt();
    float *pflt, arr_flt[10];
              .

              .
```

If this declaration appeared outside a block, *pflt* and *arr_flt[]* would be global definitions, whereas *func_flt()* would still be a function allusion.

9.2.4 Function Calls

A *function call*, also called a *function invocation*, passes program control to the specified function. The syntax for a function call is shown in Figure 9-5. A function call is an expression and can appear anywhere an expression can appear. Unless they are declared as returning **void**, functions always return a value that is substituted for the function call. For example, if *f()* returns 1, the statement

```
a = f()/3;
```

is equivalent to

```
a = 1/3;
```

It is also possible to call a function without using the return value. The statement

```
f ();
```

calls the function *f()* but does not use the return value. If *f()* returns 1, the statement is equivalent to

```
1;
```

which is a legal C statement, although it is a *no-op* (no operation is performed, assuming *f()* has no side effects).

Normally, you would ignore the return value only if the function returns **void**. However, if you want to ignore a real return value, it is better to cast it to **void**. For example,

```
(void) f ();
```

is functionally equivalent to

```
f ();
```

but it makes it clear to you and others that you are deliberately ignoring the return value. Of course, we frequently break this rule when we call *printf()* and *scanf()*, which both return values. The return value of *scanf()* can, in fact, be very useful since it returns the number of objects that are actually assigned values. Stylistically, we should probably cast these functions to **void** when we ignore the return value. In some cases, however, it is better to follow familiar conventions, even if they are not stylistically perfect.

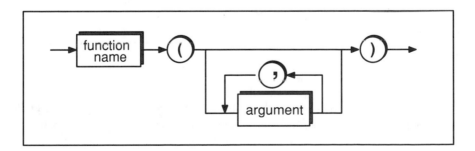

Figure 9-5. Syntax of a Function Call.

9.2.4.1 Automatic Argument Conversions

In the absence of prototyping, all scalar arguments smaller than an **int** are converted to **int**, and all **float** arguments are converted to **double**. If the formal argument is declared as a **char** or **short**, the receiving function assumes that it is getting an **int**, so the receiving side converts the **int** to the smaller type. If the formal argument is declared as a **float**, the receiving function assumes that it is getting a **double**, so it converts the received argument to **float**. This means that every time a **char**, **short**, or **float** is passed, at least one conversion takes place on the sending side where the argument is converted to **int** or **double**. In addition, the argument may also be converted again on the receiving side if the formal argument is declared as a **char**, **short**, or **float**.

Consider the following:

```
{
   char a;
   short b;
   float c;

   foo( a, b, c );   /* a and b are promoted to ints,
                      * and c is promoted to double.
                      */

               .
               .
               .
   foo( x, y, z )
      char x;    /* Received arg is converted from int
                        to   char. */
      short y;   /* Received arg is converted from int
                     to short. */
      float z;   /*   Received arg is converted from
                        double to float */
   {
               .
               .
```

Note that these conversions are invisible. So long as the types of the actual arguments match the types of the formal arguments, the arguments will be passed correctly. However, as discussed in Box 9-1, these conversions can affect the efficiency of your program. Prototyping enables you to turn off automatic argument conversions.

Box 9-1: ANSI Feature — Function Prototypes

Function prototyping is a feature introduced to the C language by Bjarne Stroustrup of AT&T and adopted by the ANSI committee. (The prototyping feature is part of the C++ language, documented in *The C++ Programming Language*.) Function prototypes enable function allusions to include data type information about arguments. This has two main benefits:

- The compiler checks that the types of the actual arguments in the function call are compatible with the types of the formal arguments specified in the function allusion.

- Automatic argument conversions are no longer required. Floating types need not be converted to **double** and small integers need not be widened to **int**. This can significantly speed up algorithms that make intensive use of small integer or floating-point data.

The format for declaring function prototypes is the same as the old function allusion syntax except that you can enter types for each argument. For example, the function allusion

```
extern void func( int, float, char * );
```

declares a function that accepts three arguments—an **int**, a **float**, and a pointer to a **char**. The argument types may optionally include argument names. For example, the previous declaration could also be written

```
extern void func( int a, float b, char *pc );
```

The argument names have no meaning other than to make the type declarations easier to read and write. No storage is allocated for them, and the names do not conflict with real variables with the same name.

If you attempt to call this function with

```
func( j, x );
```

the compiler should report an error since the call contains only two arguments whereas the prototype specifies three arguments. Also, if the argument types cannot be converted to the types specified in the prototype, a compilation error occurs. The rules for converting arguments are the same as for assignments (see Chapter 3). The following, for example, should produce an error because the compiler cannot automatically convert a pointer to a **float**.

(continues)

Box 9-1 (continued):

```
{
    extern void f( int * );
    float x;

    f( x );  /*  ILLEGAL -- cannot convert a float
             *  to a pointer
             */
        .
        .
```

If the compiler can quietly convert an argument to the type of its proto-type, it does so. In the following example, for instance, *j* is converted to a **float** and *x* is converted to a **short** before they are passed.

```
{
    extern void f( float, short );
    double x;
    long j;
        .
        .

    f( j, x );   /* OK -- long is converted to
             .       * float, and double is converted
             .       * to short.
                     */
```

Without prototyping, this example would produce erroneous results be-cause *f()* would treat *j* as a **float** and *x* as a **short**. Prototyping ensures that the right number of arguments are passed, and it prohibits you from passing arguments that cannot be quietly converted to the correct type. On the other hand, it does quietly convert arguments when it can. This could result in unexpected conversions that lead to erroneous results. Of course, this error is just as likely to occur without prototypes. Prototypes give you type checking for certain types of data, particularly pointers, but not for integer and floating-point types.

To declare a function that takes no arguments, use the **void** type specifier:

```
    extern int f( void )   /*  This function takes no
                           *  arguments.
```

Box 9-1 (continued):

Future Feature: Nonoverlapping Arrays

A problem with pointers and the C language is that fast computers employing multiple processors or vector units to speed up processing cannot easily use array arguments in the C language. This is because arguments declared as arrays are converted to pointer types, and few restrictions are placed on what data items the pointer may point to. The ANSI standard warns that future versions of C may distinguish between arguments declared as "pointer to" and arguments declared as "array of." In particular, each parameter declared as an array will be constrained to reference only a single array, and no other array parameter may overlap it. This will allow a compiler to generate optimized code for processing arrays. Consider the following example:

```
/* may "vectorize" under future versions of C */
vadd( float vec1[], float vec2[], float vec3[])
{
  int a;
  for (a = 0; a < 32; a++)
    vec1[a] = vec2[a] + vec3[a];
}
```

Under existing rules, the compiler must assume the worst, that *vec1* overlaps with *vec2* or *vec3* such that early assignmentss to ***vec1*** affect later references to *vec2* or *vec3*. This forces the compiler to generate conventional sequential code for *vadd*. In the future, a compiler will be able to generate a single vector add instruction to simultaneously add all of *vec2* and *vec3* followed by a single vector store to *vec1*, or assign a different processor to each loop of the *for* statement.

If you write code with array references that overlap and you want to be sure that it is executed sequentially on parallel or vector machines, you should use pointer notation in your declarations.

Prototyping a Variable Number of Arguments

If a function accepts a variable number of arguments (*printf()*, for example), you can use the ellipsis token " ". The prototype for *printf()* is

```
int printf( const char *format, ... );
```

This indicates that the first argument is a character string and that there is an unspecified number of additional arguments. See Section A.12 for more information about referencing arguments to functions that take a variable number of arguments.

9.3 Pointers to Functions

Pointers to functions are a powerful tool because they provide an elegant way to call different functions based on the input data. Before discussing pointers to functions, however, we need to describe more explicitly how the compiler interprets function declarations and invocations.

The syntax for declaring and invoking functions is very similar to the syntax for declaring and referencing arrays. In the declaration

```
int ar[5];
```

the symbol *ar* is a pointer to the initial element of the array. When the symbol is followed by a subscript enclosed in brackets, the pointer is indexed and then dereferenced. An analogous process occurs with functions. In the declaration

```
extern int f();
```

the symbol *f* by itself is a pointer to a function. When a function is followed by a list of arguments enclosed in parentheses, the pointer is dereferenced (which is another way of saying the function is called). Note, however, that just as *ar* in

```
int ar[5];
```

is a *constant* pointer, so, too, *f* in

```
extern int f();
```

is a *constant* pointer. Hence, it is illegal to assign a value to *f*. To declare a *variable* pointer to a function, you must precede the pointer name with an asterisk. For example,

```
int (*pf)();   /* pf is a pointer to a function
               * returning an int.
               */
```

declares a pointer variable that is capable of holding a pointer to a function that returns an **int**. The parentheses around **pf* are necessary for correct grouping. Without them, the declaration

```
int *pf()
```

would make *pf* a function returning a pointer to an **int**.

9.3.1 Assigning a Value to a Function Pointer

To obtain the address of a function, you merely enter a function name without the argument list enclosed in parentheses. For example,

```
{
   extern int f1();
   int (*pf)(); /* Declare pf as "pointer to
                  * function returning int" */

   pf = f1; /* assign address of f1 to pf */
   .
   .
   .
```

If you include the parentheses, then it is a function call. For example, if you write

```
pf = f1();   /* ILLEGAL -- f1 returns an int,
             * but pf is a pointer */
```

you should get a compiler error because you are attempting to assign the returned value of *f1()* (an **int**) to a pointer variable, which is illegal. If you write

```
pf = &f1();   /* ILLEGAL -- cannot take the address
              * of a function result. */
```

the compiler will attempt to assign the address of the returned value. This too is illegal. Lastly, you could write

```
pf = &f1;   /* ILLEGAL -- &f1 is a pointer to
            * a pointer, but pf is a pointer to
            * an int.
            */
```

On older C compilers, this would also cause a compile error (or warning) because the compiler would interpret *f1* as an address of a function, and the **address of (&)** operator attempts to take the address of an address. C does not permit this. Even if it did, the result would be a pointer to a pointer to a function which is incompatible with a simple pointer to a function. (The ANSI Standard allows this syntax by ignoring the **&** operator.)

We point out all of these *wrong* ways of assigning a pointer to a function because nearly everyone, in their initial stages of learning C, tries one or more of these possibilities.

9.3.2 Return Type Agreement

The other important point to remember about assigning values to function pointers is that the return types *must* agree. If you declare a pointer to a function that
returns an **int**, you must assign the address of a function that returns an **int**, not
the address of a function that returns a **char**, a **float**, or some other type. If the
types don't agree, you should receive a compile-time error. The following
example shows some legal and illegal function pointer assignments.

```
extern int if1(), if2(), (*pif)();
extern float ff1(), (*pff)();
extern char cf1(), (*pcf)();

main()
{
   pif = if1; /* Legal -- types match */
   pif = cf1; /* ILLEGAL -- type mismatch */
   pff = if2; /* ILLEGAL -- type mismatch */
   pcf = cf1; /* Legal -- types match */
   if1 = if2; /* ILLEGAL -- Assign to a constant */
}
```

9.3.3 Calling a Function Using Pointers

To dereference a function pointer, thereby calling a function, you use the same
syntax you use to declare the function pointer, except this time you include
parentheses and possibly arguments. For example,

```
{
   extern int f1();
   int (*pf)();
   int answer;

   pf = f1;
   answer = (*pf)(a); /* Calls function f1() with
                       *   argument a
                       */
        .
        .
        .
```

As with the declaration, the parentheses around `*pf` in the function call are essential to override default precedence rules. Without them, *pf* would be a function returning a pointer to an **int**, rather than a pointer to a function. Note that the value of a dereferenced function pointer is whatever it was declared to be. In our case, we declared *pf* with the statement

```
int (*pf)();
```

signifying that when it is dereferenced, it will evaluate to an **int**.

One peculiarity about dereferencing pointers to functions is that it does not matter how many asterisks you include. For example,

```
(*pf)(a)
```

is the same as

```
(****pf)(a)
```

This odd behavior stems from two rules: first, that a function name by itself is converted to a pointer to the function; and second, that parentheses change the order of evaluation. The parentheses cause the expression

```
****pf
```

to be evaluated before the argument list. Each time *pf* is dereferenced, it is converted back to a pointer because the argument list is still not present. Only after the compiler has exhausted all of the indirection operators does it move on to the argument list. The presence of the argument list makes the expression a function call.

It follows from this logic that you can dereference a pointer to a function *without* the indirection operator. That is,

```
pf(a)
```

should be the same as

```
(*pf)(a)
```

This is, in fact, the case according to the ANSI Standard. Older compilers, however, may not support this syntax. We recommend the second version because it is more portable and reminds us that *pf* is a pointer variable.

9.3.4 A Generalized Sort Routine

A common use of pointers to functions is to provide a mechanism for performing a number of similar operations without needlessly duplicating code. Suppose, for example, that you want to sort an array of **int**s in both ascending and descending order. One possibility is to write one function to do the sort in ascending order and another to do it in descending order. However, these two functions would be almost identical. It would be more efficient to change only what needs to be changed without duplicating everything else.

```c
#define FALSE 0
#define TRUE 1

void bubble_sort( list, list_size )
  int list[], list_size;
{
  int j, k, temp, sorted = FALSE;

  while (!sorted)
  {
    sorted = TRUE;    /* assume list is sorted */
    for (j = 0; j < list_size - 1; j++)
      if (list[j] > list[j+1])
      {
        temp = list[j];
        list[j] = list[j+1];
        list[j+1] = temp;
        sorted = FALSE;
      }
  } /* end of while loop */
}
```

Our *bubble_sort()* program from Chapter 5 is shown above. It is clear that the statement that we need to change to make it a *descending* sort is the expression

```c
list[j] > list[j+1]
```

If we change the "greater than" operator to "less than"

```c
list[j] < list[j+1]
```

the function will sort in descending order.

Rather than rewriting the entire program to make this one change, we can simply remove this expression and make it into a function called *compare()*. Then we change the statement in *bubble_sort()* to

```
if ( compare(list[j], list[j+1] )
```

If the sort is in ascending order, *compare()* should return 1 when *list[j]* is greater than *list[j+1]*; otherwise it should return 0. For descending sorts, the return value should be reversed. So we need two compare functions:

```
/* Compare two integers and return 1 if a is
 * greater than b -- use for ascending sorts.
 */

int compare_ascend( a, b )
int a,b;
{
  return a > b;
}

/* Compare two integers and return 1 if a is less
 * than b -- use for descending sorts.
 */

int compare_descend( a, b )
   int a,b;
{
  return a < b;
}
```

This doesn't completely solve the problem, however. We have abstracted the differences between an ascending and descending sort into two small functions, but we haven't created a mechanism to select one of these functions dynamically. We could change the *compare()* call in the *bubble_sort()* function to either *compare_ascend()* or *compare_descend()*, but how can we make it choose one or the other depending on which sort we desire?

The solution lies in pointers to functions. Specifically, we need to make *com pare* a pointer to a function capable of pointing to either *compare_ascend()* or *compare_descend()*. Then we can add another argument to *bubble_sort()* indicating whether the sort is to be in ascending or descending order. To declare *compare* as a pointer to a function that returns an **int**, you would write

```
int (*compare)();
```

Using *compare* as a pointer to a function, we can rewrite *bubble_sort()* as follows:

```
#define FALSE 0
#define TRUE 1

void bubble_sort( list, list_size, compare )
  int list[], list_size;
  int (*compare)();
{
  int j, k, temp, sorted = FALSE;

  while (!sorted)
  {
    sorted = TRUE;    /* assume list is sorted */
    for (j = 0; j < list_size-1; j++)
      if ((*compare)( list[j], list[j+1]) )
      {
        temp = list[j];
        list[j] = list[j+1];
        list[j+1] = temp;
        unsorted = 1;
      }
  } /* end of while loop */
}
```

This makes the program smaller and more straightforward. Note that we do not need to declare *compare_ascend()* and *compare_descend()* because the address of one or the other is being passed directly to *bubble_sort()*. However, this puts a burden on the calling function since it must know the addresses of these two functions. For example, you might call *bubble_sort()* as follows to sort an array in descending order:

```
main()
{
  extern void bubble_sort();
  extern int compare_ascend(), compare_descend();
  static int list[] = {1, 0, 5, 444, -332, 76 };
#define LIST_SIZE (sizeof(list)/sizeof(list[0]))

  bubble_sort( list, LIST_SIZE, compare_descend );
  exit( 0 );
}
```

To pass a pointer to *compare_descend()*, we just enter the function name without the parentheses.

Since sorting is such a common task, it probably makes sense to put all the declarations for the sort function into a header file. For example, we could create a file called *sort.h* that contains the following:

```
#define ASCEND compare_ascend
#define DESCEND compare_descend

extern void bubble_sort();
extern int compare_ascend(), compare_descend();
```

Rewriting the *main()* function using this header file, we get

```
#include "sort.h"

main()
{
   static int list[] = {1, 0, 5, 444, -332, 76 };
#define LIST_SIZE (sizeof(list)/sizeof(list[0]))

   bubble_sort( list, LIST_SIZE), DESCEND );
   exit( 0 );
}
```

This is superior to the previous version for a number of reasons. First, it makes it easier to call *bubble_sort()* from other functions since all you need to do is include the header file. Second, it hides the names and data types of the comparison functions. If, for some reason, you want to change the names at a later date, you need only change the header file to broadcast the change to all source files. Without the header file, you would need to search through every module to find all the places where *compare_ascend()* and *compare_descend()* are declared and invoked.

It may seem that we have gone to a lot of trouble just to make *bubble_sort()* general enough to sort in either ascending or descending order. Wouldn't it have been easier, after all, to write two separate functions? The answer is probably yes. In this particular instance, it is questionable whether it is really worth generalizing *bubble_sort()*. We did it more to illustrate some important principles and techniques than to improve our code. The runtime library, however, contains a much more generalized sort function called *qsort()* which makes more practical use of pointers to functions. Not only can it sort objects in a user-defined order, but it can also sort objects of any data type. See Section A.14.5 for more about *qsort()*.

9.3.5 Returning Pointers to Functions

A function may return a pointer to a function. However, you must declare the type of the function properly. For example, the following declares a function that returns a pointer to a function that returns an **int**.

```
int (*f( x, y ))()    /* f is a function with
                       * arguments x and y, returning
                       * a pointer to a function
                       * returning an int.
                       */
    float x, y;
{
           .
           .
```

As an example of when you might use this construct, consider the case where you need to sort many files of data. We already mentioned that there are several sorting algorithms, each of which is best with certain types of data. A *quicksort*, for example, is very fast with randomly arranged data but is inefficient if the data is already largely sorted. For data that is already in approximately sorted order, a *merge sort* is one of the most efficient algorithms. If the array to be sorted is very large, on the other hand, a *heap sort* might be best since it requires the minimum amount of memory. (See *Computing Algorithms* by Donald Knuth for a detailed discussion.)

Suppose, then, that we have three functions—*quick_sort()*, *merge_sort()*, and *heap_sort()*—and another function, called *best_sort()*, which is capable of sampling an array to determine which sort method is most efficient for a particular set of data. We can write *best_sort()* so that it returns a pointer to one of the three sort functions:

```
void (* best_sort(list))( )
   float list[];
{
   extern void quick_sort(), merge_sort(),
              heap_sort();
   /*  Analyze data */
   /* If quick sort is best */
     return quick_sort;

   /* Else if merge sort is best */
     return merge_sort;

   /* Else if heap sort is best */
     return heap_sort;
}
```

To sort an array, you would invoke one of the sort functions as shown below:

```
void sort_array( list )
float list[];
{
   extern void (* best_sort())();

   (best_sort( list ))( list );
}
```

Note that the argument *list* appears twice — once for the *best_sort()* function and once for the sorting function whose address *best_sort()* returns.

There are, of course, other ways to perform the same functionality without using pointers to functions. One advantage of using pointers, however, is that we remove all decision making from the *sort_array()* function. If we want to add new sorting functions, the only routine we need to change is *best_sort()*.

One thing you must be careful about when using pointers to functions is to make sure that assignment types agree with declaration types. This can become difficult as declarations become more and more complex. In the following example, we attempt to return a pointer to a function that returns a pointer to a function that returns an **int**, when what is expected is simply a pointer to a function that returns an **int**. It is worth spending a few moments to make sure that you understand this example. We discuss complex declarations such as these in more detail in Section 9.6.

```
int (*f())()          /* f is a function that returns
                       * a pointer to a function that
                       * returns an int.
                       */
{
   extern int f1();   /*  f1 is a function that returns
                       *  an int.
                       */
   extern int (* f2())();   /*  f2 is a function that
                            *   returns a pointer to a
                            *   function that returns
                            *   an int.
                            */
   int (*pf)(); /*  pf is a pointer to a function
                 *   that returns an int
                 */

   pf = f1;     /* OK, types match.                        */
   return f1;   /* OK  types match.                        */
   pf = f2;     /* Error, mismatched pointer types. */
   return f2;   /* Error, mismatched pointer btypes */
}
```

9.4 Recursion

A recursive function is one that calls itself. For example,

```
void recurse()
{
   static count = 1;

   printf("%d\n", count);
   count++;
   recurse();
}

main()
{
   extern void recurse();

   recurse();
}
```

What will this program do? First it prints the value of *count*, which is 1; then it increments *count*; then it calls itself. The second time through, *count* equals 2. This repeats *ad infinitum*. The output will be

```
1
2
3
4
5
.
.
.
```

At some point, the computer will run out of stack memory, and the program will abort with a runtime error. This illustrates an important point about recursive programming: you must include a stop point or the program will run forever (or until it runs out of memory). For example, we can modify the previous function so that it calls itself only three times:

```
void recurse()
{
   static count = 1;

   if (count > 3)
      return;
   else
   {
      printf( "%d\n", count );
      count ++;
      recurse();
   }
}

main()
{
   extern void recurse();

   recurse();
}
```

The condition that ends the recursion (count being greater than 3) is called the *base case*. Note that the program would not end if *count* were *automatic* rather than *fixed* because it would dynamically create a new variable called *count* and reinitialize it to 1 with each call. This is an important aspect of recursion: for each new call, the compiler creates a whole new set of automatic variables. Even though they have the same name, they refer to different memory areas.

9.4.1 The Return Value in Recursive Calls

Using fixed variables is one way to control recursion. Another method is to use the input value. The program below, for example, uses recursion to compute the sum of integers from 1 to *n*.

```
int sum(n)
int n;
{
   if (n <= 1)
      return n;
   else
      return (n + sum(n-1));
}
```

It is useful to step through the function, observing what value gets returned with each call. If we pass the function the value 5, the call trace shown in Figure 9-6 occurs.

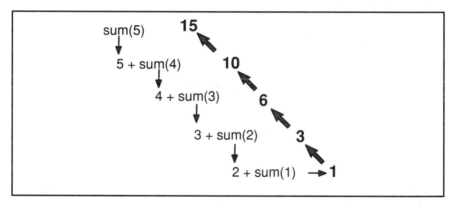

Figure 9-6. Recursion. Call trace of sum() function when argument is 5.

Note that no call returns until all of its subcalls have returned. In our example, this doesn't occur until *n* is less than or equal to 1, at which time the function *unwinds* itself. First it returns 1, which is added to 2, returning the value 3, which is added to 3 to return 6, which is added to 4 to return 10, which is added to 5 to return 15.

Recursive programs are difficult to conceptualize at first, but they are very powerful. They form the basis of artificial intelligence languages such as LISP and Prolog.

You can always use looping constructs to get the same effect as recursion, but the program is often much simpler and easier to read when implemented recursively. Recursion, however, is not necessarily more efficient since the computer must allocate additional stack space for each call. If the recursion is deep enough, the program will run out of stack memory and abort.

9.5 The *main()* Function

All C programs must contain a function called *main()*, which is always the first function executed in a C program. When *main()* returns, the program is done. The compiler treats the *main()* function like any other function, except that at runtime the host environment is responsible for providing two arguments. The first, usually called *argc* by convention, is an **int** that represents the number of arguments that are present on the command line when the program is invoked; the second, called *argv* by convention, is an array of pointers to the command line arguments.

The following program uses *argc* and *argv[]* to print out the list of arguments supplied to it when it is invoked:

```c
/* echo command line arguments */
main( argc, argv )
int argc;
char *argv[];
{
  while (--argc > 0)
    printf( "%s ", *++argv );
  printf( "\n" );
  exit( 0 );
}
```

In UNIX systems, there is a program like this called *echo*. So, if you write at the command line

```
echo Alan Turing was a father of computing.
```

the system prints

```
Alan Turing was a father of computing.
```

Note that a pointer to the command itself is stored in *argv[0]*. This is why we use the prefix increment operator rather than the postfix operator to increment *argv*. Otherwise, the name of the command, *echo*, would be printed first.

When you invoke a program, each command line argument must be separated by one or more spaces. Note that the command line arguments are always passed to *main()* as character strings. If the arguments are intended to represent numeric data, you must explicitly convert them. Fortunately, there are several functions in the runtime library that convert a string into its numeric value. The function *atoi()*, for example, converts a string into an **int**, and *atof()* converts a string into a **float**. The following program takes two arguments and returns the first to the power of the second:

```
#include <math.h>

main( argc, argv )
int argc;
char *argv[];
{
   float x, y;

   if (argc < 3)
   {
      printf( "Usage: power <number>\n" );
      printf( "Yields arg1 to arg2 power\n" );
      return;
   }
   x = atof( *++argv );
   y = atof( *++argv );
   printf( "%f\n", pow( x, y ) );
}
```

The *pow()* function is part of the runtime library. We show more examples of using the command line arguments when we discuss file I/O in Chapter 11.

9.6 Complex Declarations

Declarations in C have a tendency to become complex, making it difficult to determine exactly what is being declared. The following declaration, for instance, declares *x* to be a pointer to a function returning a pointer to a 5-element array of pointers to **int**s:

```
int *(*(*x)())[5];
```

One way to avoid complex declarations such as this one is to create intermediate typedefs, as shown on the following page.

```
typedef int *AP[5];/* 5-element array of pointers
                    * to ints.
                    */
typedef AP *FP();  /* Function returning pointer to
                    * 5-element array of pointers
                    * to ints.
                    */
FP *x               /* Pointer to function returning
                    * pointer to 5-element array of
                    * pointers to ints.
                    */
```

The main reason that complex declarations look so forbidding in C is that the pointer operator is a *prefix* operator, whereas the array and function operators are *postfix* operators. As a result, the variable becomes sandwiched between operators. To compose and decipher complex declarations, you must proceed inside-out, adding asterisks to the left of the variable name and parentheses and brackets to the right of the variable name. It is also important to remember the following two binding and precedence rules:

1. The array operator [ ] and function operator () have a higher precedence than the pointer operator (*).

2. The array and function operators group from left to right, whereas the pointer operator groups from right to left.

9.6.1 Deciphering Complex Declarations

The best strategy for deciphering a declaration is to start with the variable name by itself and then add each part of the declaration, starting with the operators that are closest to the variable name. In the absence of parentheses to affect binding, you would add all of the function and array operators on the right side of the variable name first (since they have higher precedence) and then add the pointer operators on the left side. The declaration

```
char *x[];
```

would be deciphered through the following steps:

1. x[] is an **array**.

2. *x[] is an **array** of **pointers**.

3. char *x[] is an **array** of **pointers** to **char**s.

Parentheses can be used to change the precedence order. For example,

```
int (*x[]) ();
```

would be decomposed as follows:

1.   x[] is an **array**.

2.   (*x[ ]) is an **array** of **pointers**.

3.   (*x[ ])() is an **array** of **pointers** to **functions**.

4.   int (*x[ ])() is an **array** of **pointers** to **functions** returning **int**s.

If this declaration had been written without the parentheses as

```
int *x[] ();
```

it would have been translated as

an **array** of **functions** returning **pointers** to **int**s

which is an illegal declaration since arrays of functions are invalid.

9.6.2 Composing Complex Declarations

To compose a declaration, you perform the same process. For example, to declare a **pointer** to an **array** of **pointers** to **functions** that return **pointers** to **arrays** of **structures** with tag name S, you could use the following steps:

1.   (*x) is a **pointer**.

2.   (*x)[] is a **pointer** to an **array**.

3.   (*(*x)[]) is a **pointer** to an **array** of **pointer**s.

4.   (*(*x)[])() is a **pointer** to an **array** of **pointer**s to **function**s.

5.   (*(*(*x)[])()) is a **pointer** to an **array** of **pointer**s to **function**s returning **pointer**s.

6.   (*(*(*x)[])())[] is a **pointer** to an **array** of **pointer**s to **function**s returning **pointer**s to **array**s.

7.   struct S (*(*(*x)[])())[] is a **pointer** to an **array** of **pointer**s to **function**s returning **pointer**s to **array**s of **structure**s with tag name S.

Note that we add parentheses for binding each time we add a new pointer operator.

`int i;`	An **int**
`int *p;`	A pointer to an **int**
`int a[];`	An array of **int**s
`int f();`	A function returning an **int**
`int **pp;`	A pointer to a pointer to an **int**
`int (*pa)[];`	A pointer to an array of **int**s
`int (*pf)();`	A pointer to a function returning an **int**
`int *ap[];`	An array of pointers to **int**s
`int aa[][];`	An array of arrays of **int**s
`int af[]();`	An array of functions returning **int**s (ILLEGAL)
`int *fp();`	A function returning a pointer to an **int**
`int fa()[];`	A function returning an array of **int**s (ILLEGAL)
`int ff()();`	A function returning a function returning an **int** (ILLEGAL)
`int ***ppp;`	A pointer to a pointer to a pointer to an **int**
`int (**ppa)[];`	A pointer to a pointer to an array of **int**s
`int (**ppf)();`	A pointer to a pointer to a function returning an **int**
`int *(*pap)[];`	A pointer to an array of pointers to **int**s
`int (*paa)[][];`	A pointer to an array of arrays of **int**s
`int (*paf)[]();`	A pointer to an array of functions returning **int**s (ILLEGAL)
`int *(*pfp)();`	A pointer to a function returning a pointer to an **int**
`int (*pfa)()[];`	A pointer to a function returning an array of **int**s (ILLEGAL)
`int (*pff)()();`	A pointer to a function returning a function returning an **int** (ILLEGAL)
`int **app[];`	An array of pointers to pointers to **int**s
`int (*apa[])[];`	An array of pointers to arrays of **int**s
`int (*apf[])();`	An array of pointers to functions returning **int**s
`int *aap[][];`	An array of arrays of pointers to **int**s
`int aaa[][][];`	An array of arrays of arrays of **int**s
`int aaf[][]();`	An array of arrays of functions returning **int**s (ILLEGAL)
`int *afp[]();`	An array of functions returning pointers to **int**s (ILLEGAL)
`int afa[]()[];`	An array of functions returning arrays of **int**s (ILLEGAL)
`int aff[]()();`	An array of functions returning functions returning **int**s (ILLEGAL)
`int **fpp();`	A function returning a pointer to a pointer to an **int**
`int (*fpa())[];`	A function returning a pointer to an array of **int**s
`int (*fpf())();`	A function returning a pointer to a function returning an **int**
`int *fap()[];`	A function returning an array of pointers to **int**s (ILLEGAL)
`int faa()[][];`	A function returning an array of arrays of **int**s (ILLEGAL)
`int faf()[]();`	A function returning an array of functions returning **int**s (ILLEGAL)
`int *ffp()();`	A function returning a function returning a pointer to an **int** (ILLEGAL)

Table 9-1. Legal and Illegal Declarations in C.

Exercises

1. Modify the echo program so that it prints out the arguments in capital letters if the –c or –C switch is present when the program is executed. (Note that the switch should be the first argument and should not be echoed.)

2. Enhance the program obtained from Exercise 1 so that it will work even if the switch is not the first argument.

3. Write a recursive version of *strlen()*. Is the recursive version better or worse than the iterative version in Chapter 5? Explain your answer.

4. Write a recursive version of *strcpy()*. Is the recursive version better or worse than the iterative version in Chapter 5? Explain your answer.

5. Write a recursive function that computes the greatest common divisor of two positive integers.

6. Write an iterative version of Exercise 5.

7. Write a recursive function that accepts a pointer to a string as its argument, turns the string into a linked list of characters, and returns a pointer to the first character in the list.

8. Write a recursive function that counts the number of elements in a linked list. The argument should be a pointer to the first element of the list, and the return value should be an **int**.

9. Write a recursive function that prints the data value of each element in a linked list.

10. Write a recursive function that accepts two pointers, each to a linked list, and concatenates the two lists, attaching the second list to the first.

11. Using pointers to functions, write a general *find()* function for linked lists. (See Chapter 9 for an example of a specialized *find()* function.)

12. Decipher the following declarations. Which are legal and which are illegal? Why?

    a) *(*x())[]
    b) *(**x)[]
    c) (*(*(*x())[])())
    d) **x[]()
    e) *(x[])[]
    f) *(*(x())())

13. Write prototypes for functions that take the following arguments:

    a) Two arguments: a **float** and a pointer to a **char**.
    b) Two arguments: a pointer to an array of **int**s and a pointer to a function returning an **unsigned long**.
    c) One argument: a pointer to a function returning a pointer to a **char**.
    d) Three Arguments: a pointer to **struct** of type S, a pointer to an array of **char**s, and a pointer to an array of functions returning pointers to functions returning **int**s.
    e) Two arguments: a **char** and an **enum** declared as

        enum boolean { FALSE, TRUE};

14. Write a function to multiply two arrays and store the result into a third array so that it might vectorize on a future ANSI compiler.

Chapter 10

The C Preprocessor

If language be not in accordance with the truth of things, affairs cannot be carried on to success. — Confucious, Analects

You can think of the C preprocessor as a separate program that runs before the compiler, with its own simple, line-oriented grammar and syntax. In previous chapters, we introduced two preprocessor directives—the **#define** command for naming a constant and the **#include** command for including additional source files. This chapter discusses both of these directives in greater detail and also describes other preprocessor directives that have not been mentioned yet. Briefly, the preprocessor gives you the following capabilities:

- Macro processing.

- Inclusion of additional C source files.

- "Conditional compilation," which enables you to conditionally compile sections of C source contingent on the value of an arithmetic expression.

All preprocessor directives begin with a pound sign (#), which must be the first nonspace character on the line. They may appear anywhere in the source file— before, after, or intermingled with regular C language statements.

Unlike C statements, a macro command ends with a newline, not a semicolon (see Box 10-2). To span a macro over more than one line, enter a backslash immediately before the newline, as in

```
#define LONG_MACRO "This is a very long macro that\
spans two lines."
```

Box 10-1: ANSI Feature — Flexible Formatting of Preprocessor Lines

Older compilers have strict requirements concerning the format of preprocessor commands. The pound sign must appear in column 1, and no space is allowed between the pound sign and the preprocessor command. The ANSI Standard removes both of these restrictions. The only constraint imposed by the ANSI Standard is that the pound sign must be the first nonspace or nontab character. The following commands, for example, are supported by the ANSI Standard but may be illegal on older compilers.

```
 #      include <stdio.h>
    # include <ctype.h>
```

10.1 Macro Substitution

A *macro* is a name that has an associated text string, called the *macro body*. By convention, macro names that represent constants should consist of uppercase letters only. This makes it easy to distinguish macro names from variable names, which should be composed of lowercase characters. In the following example, *BUF_LEN* is the macro name and *512* is the macro body.

```
#define BUFF_LEN (512)
```

When a macro name appears outside its definition it is replaced with its macro body. The act of replacement is referred to as *macro expansion*. For example, having defined *BUFF_LEN*, you might write

```
char buf[BUFF_LEN];
```

During the preprocessing stage, this line of code would be translated into

```
char buf[(512)];
```

Box 10-2: Bug Alert — Ending a Macro Definition With a Semicolon

One of the most common bugs is to place a semicolon at the end of a macro definition, as in

```
#define SIZE 10;
```

The semicolon becomes part of the replacement string, so that a statement like

```
x = SIZE;
```

expands to

```
x = 10;;
```

This programming error will actually go unnoticed by the compiler, which will interpret the second semicolon as a null statement. The following, however, will cause a compile-time parsing error:

```
int array[SIZE];
```

What makes this bug so difficult to find is that the line on which the error is reported looks perfectly legal. The most pernicious example of this type of bug occurs when the resulting syntax, after replacement, is legal but is semantically different from what was intended. For example,

```
#define GOOD_CONDITION (var == 1);
        .
        .
while GOOD_CONDITION
    foo();
```

This expands to

```
while (var == 1);
    foo();
```

The semicolon after *(var == 1)* is interpreted as a null statement and, more important, as the body of the **while** loop. As a result, the call to *foo()* is *not* part of the **while** body. If *var* equals one, you will get an infinite loop.

Most compilers have a command line option that lets you execute just the preprocessor. This makes it much easier to find this type of bug because you can inspect the source code after all of the macros have been expanded.

The simplest and most common use of macros is to represent numeric constant values. It is always bad practice to write constants in a source file since the constant's purpose is lost. For example, consider the following:

```
static char in_buf[256];
main()
{
        .
        .
    for (a = 0; a < 256 ; a++)
        in_buf[a] = getchar();
        .
        .
```

The two occurrences of 256 seem innocuous enough, but if the occurrences are far apart in a large program, perhaps even in separate files, it becomes difficult to maintain the program. If you want to change the array size, you need to find every 256 in the program and then make sure that it's the right 256. A better way to write the function is

```
#define MAX_INPUT_BUFFER_SIZE 256

static char in_buf[MAX_INPUT_BUFFER_SIZE];
main()
{
        .
        .
    for (a = 0; a < MAX_INPUT_BUFFER_SIZE ; a++)
        in_buf[a] = getchar();
        .
        .
```

As with choosing names for variables, it is important to choose a macro name that corresponds to its use. According to the ANSI Standard, macro names are unique up to at least 31 characters, so you should use as many characters as it takes to describe the macro's function.

The preceding example illustrates a simple form of a macro, in which the macro serves as a name for a constant. There is another form of macros that is similar to a C function in that it takes arguments that can be used in the macro body. The syntax for this type of macro is shown in Figure 10-1.

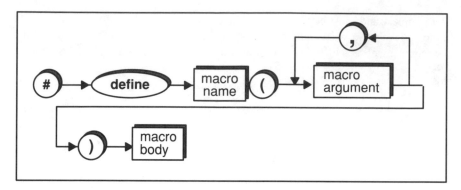

Figure 10-1. Syntax of a Function-like Macro.

For example, you could write

```
#define MUL_BY_TWO(a) ((a) + (a))
```

Then you can use *MUL_BY_TWO* in your program just as you would use a function. For example, the macro invocation

```
j = MUL_BY_TWO(5);
```

is translated by the preprocessor into

```
j = ((5) + (5));
```

The actual argument *5* is substituted for the formal argument *a* wherever it appears in the macro body. The parentheses around *a* and around the macro body are necessary to ensure correct binding when the macro is expanded (see Box 10-7). There is actually some justification for this macro since it reduces a multiplication operation into an addition operation, which is faster.

Note that macro arguments are not variables—they have no type, and no storage is allocated for them. Consequently, macro arguments do not conflict with variables that have the same name. The following, for example, is perfectly legal:

```
j = MUL_BY_TWO(a-1);
```

which, after expansion, becomes

```
j = ((a-1) + (a-1));
```

In general, macros execute more quickly than functions because there is none of the function overhead involved in copying arguments and maintaining stack frames. When trying to speed up slow programs, therefore, you should be on the lookout for small, heavily used functions that can be implemented as macros. For example, one of our first functions in this book (Chapter 3) was a function that converts a letter from uppercase to lowercase. Assuming an ASCII character set, we can rewrite it as

```
#define TO_LOWER(c) ((c) - ('a' - 'A'))
```

Converting functions to macros will have a noticeable impact on execution speed only if the function is called frequently.

Box 10-3: Bug Alert — Using = to Define a Macro

A common mistake made in defining macros is to use the assignment operator as if you were initializing a variable. Instead of writing

```
#define MAX 100
```

you write

```
#define MAX = 100
```

This type of mistake can lead to obscure bugs. For example, the expression

```
for (j=MAX; j > 0; j--)
```

would expand to

```
for (j== 100; j > 0; j--)
```

Suddenly, the assignment is turned into a relational expression. The expression is legal, so the compiler will not complain, making the error difficult to track down.

10.1.1 No Type Checking for Macro Arguments

From an operational point of view, the macro *MUL_BY_TWO* may seem identical to the following function:

```
int mul_by_two( a )
int a;
{
  return a+a;
}
```

However, there is one significant difference—there is no type checking for macros. In the function version of *mul_by_two*, you must pass an integral value, and the function must return an **int**. In the macro version, you can substitute any type of value for *a*.

Suppose, for example, that *f* is a **float** variable. If you write

```
f = MUL_BY_TWO( 2.5 );
```

the preprocessor translates it into

```
f= ((2.5) + (2.5));
```

which assigns the value 5.0 to *f*. In contrast, if you write

```
f = mul_by_two( 2.5 );
```

the compiler takes one of two actions, depending on whether function prototypes are being used. In the presence of prototyping, the compiler converts 2.5 into an **int**, giving it a value of 2; adds two and two together, and returns 4 instead of 5.0. Without function prototypes, the compiler passes a double-precision 2.5 to the function, which interprets it as an **int**. This produces unpredictable results.

Box 10-4: Bug Alert — Space Between Left Parenthesis and Macro Name

Note in Figure 10-1 that the left parenthesis must come immediately after the macro name, without any intervening spaces. Insertion of a space usually results in a compile-time error, but occasionally obscure bugs can result. Consider the following macro:

```
#define neg_a_plus_f(a)  -(a) + f
```

The expression

```
j = neg_a_plus_f(x);
```

expands to

```
j = -(x) + f;
```

But watch what happens if we accidentally insert a space between the left parenthesis and the macro name in the definition:

```
#define neg_a_plus_f (a)  (-(a) + f)
```

Now, the expression expands to

```
j = (a) -(a) + f(x);
```

If *a* is a variable name and *f* is a function name, this will look like a perfectly legal expression to the compiler.

The lack of type checking for macro arguments can be a powerful feature if used with care. Consider the following macro, which returns the lesser of two arguments:

```
#define min( a, b ) ((a) < (b) ? (a) : (b))
```

Note that this works regardless of whether *a* and *b* are integers or floating-point values. It is extremely difficult to write an equivalent function that works for all data types.

Another difference between macros and functions is that the preprocessor checks to make sure that the number of arguments in the definition is the same as the number of arguments in the invocation. The C compiler does this type of checking for functions only if you use the ANSI prototyping syntax in the function declaration. For example, the statement

```
MUL_BY_TWO(x, y);
```

would produce a compile-time error. The analogous statement

```
mul_by_two(x, y);
```

would produce a compile-time error only if the function is declared with the ANSI prototyping syntax. Otherwise, this statement would compile without errors but would produce unpredictable results when executed.

10.1.2 Removing a Macro Definition

Once defined, a macro name retains its meaning until the end of the source file, or until it is explicitly removed with an **#undef** directive. The most typical use of **#undef** is to remove a definition so you can redefine it (see Section 10.2.1).

According to the ANSI Standard and most existing C compilers, it is illegal to redefine a macro without an intervening **#undef** statement, unless the two definitions are the same. This is a useful rule because it enables you to define the same macro in different header files. If you include multiple header files (and hence, multiple definitions of the same macro), your compiler will complain only if the definitions conflict.

Box 10-5: ANSI Feature — Using a Macro Name in Its Own Definition

Most older C compilers don't allow you to use a macro name in the body of its own definition. The following definition, for example, would fail because the compiler would try to expand *sqrt* in the body:

```
#define sqrt(x) ( (x < 0) ? sqrt(-x) : sqrt(x) )
```

The ANSI Standard supports this syntax but states that if a macro name appears in its own definition, it will *not* be expanded. This avoids the problem of infinite expansion. According to ANSI rules, therefore, the statement

```
y = sqrt( 5 );
```

would expand to

```
y = ( (5 < 0 ? sqrt(-5) : sqrt(5) );
```

As a result, the *sqrt()* function would be called with 5 as the argument. Note that using a macro name in its own body makes sense only if there is a function with the same name.

10.1.3 Macros vs. Functions

Macros and functions are similar in that they both enable a set of operations to be represented by a single name. Sometimes it is difficult to decide whether to implement an operation as a macro or as a function. The following lists summarize the advantages and disadvantages of macros compared to functions.

Advantages

1. Macros are usually faster than functions since they avoid the function call overhead.

2. The number of macro arguments is checked to match the definition. (The C compiler also does this for functions if you use the new ANSI prototyping syntax. However, this feature may not be available on your compiler.)

3. No type restriction is placed on arguments so that one macro may serve for several data types.

Disadvantages

1. Macro arguments are reevaluated at each mention in the macro body, which can lead to unexpected behavior if an argument contains side effects (see Box 10-6).

2. Function bodies are compiled once so that multiple calls to the same function can share the same code without repeating it each time. Macros, on the other hand, are expanded each time they appear in a program. As a result, a program with many large macros may be longer than a program that uses functions in place of the macros.

3. Though macros check the number of arguments, they don't check the argument types. ANSI function prototypes check both the number of arguments and the argument types.

4. It is more difficult to debug programs that contain macros because the source code goes through an additional layer of translation, making the object code even further removed from the source code.

Box 10-6: Bug Alert — Side Effects in Macro Arguments

A potential hazard of macros involves side effect operators in argument expressions. Suppose, for instance, that we invoke the *min* macro as follows:

```
a = min( b++, c );
```

The preprocessor translates this into

```
a = ((b++) < (c) ? (b++) : c);
```

If *b* is less than *c*, it gets incremented twice, obviously not what is intended. To be on the safe side, you should never use a side effect operator in a macro invocation. Side effect operators include the increment and decrement operators, the assignment operators, and function invocations.

Box 10-7: Bug Alert — Binding of Macro Arguments

A potential problem with macros is that argument expressions that are not carefully parenthesized can produce erroneous results due to operator precedence and binding. Consider the following macro:

```
#define square( a ) a * a
```

square has the advantage that it will work regardless of the argument data types. However, watch what happens when we pass it an arithmetic expression:

```
j = 2 * square( 3 + 4 );
```

expands to

```
j = 2 * 3 + 4 * 3 + 4;
```

Because of operator precedence, the compiler interprets this expression as

```
j = (2 * 3) + (4 * 3) + 4;
```

which assigns the value of 22 to *j*, instead of 98. To avoid this problem, you should always enclose the macro body and macro arguments in parentheses:

```
#define square( a ) ((a) * (a))
```

Now, the macro invocation expands to

```
j = 2 * ((3 + 4) * (3 + 4));
```

which produces the correct result.

10.1.4 Built-In Macros

The ANSI Standard defines five macro names that are built into the preprocessor. Each name begins and ends with *two* underscore characters. You may not redefine or **#undef** these macros. (These macros may not be supported by older compilers.)

__LINE__   Expands to the source file line number on which it is invoked.

__FILE__   Expands to the name of the file in which it is invoked.

__TIME__   Expands to the time of program compilation.

__DATE__   Expands to the date of program compilation.

__STDC__   Expands to the constant 1 if the compiler conforms to
                      the ANSI Standard.

The *__LINE__* and *__FILE__* macros are available in most older compilers. The
__TIME__, *__DATE__*, and *__STDC__* macros are more recent ANSI additions
to the C preprocessor.

The *__LINE__* and *__FILE__* macros are valuable diagnostic tools. Suppose,
for example, that you want a check facility that compares two expressions for
equality and, if they are unequal, calls an error reporting function with the source
filename and the line number of the check failure.

```
#define CHECK( a, b ) \
    if ((a) != (b)) \
      fail( a, b, __FILE__, __LINE__ )

void fail( a, b, p, line )
int a, b, line;
char *p;
{
  printf( "Check failed in file %s at line %d:\
received %d, expected %d\n", p, line, a, b );
}
```

At various points in a program, you can check to make sure that a variable *x*
equals zero by including the following diagnostic:

```
CHECK(x, 0);
```

The *__DATE__* and *__TIME__* macros are useful for recording the date and time
a file was last compiled. For instance,

```
void print_version(()
{
  printf( "This utility compiled on %s at %s\n",
          __DATE__, __TIME__ );
}
```

The *__STDC__* macro, if it expands to 1, signifies that the compiler conforms to
the ANSI Standard. If it expands to any other value, or if it is not defined, you
should assume that the compiler does not conform to the ANSI Standard.
Section 10.2 illustrates a common use of this macro.

Box 10-8: ANSI Feature — String Producer

One of the limitations of the preprocessor described in the K&R standard is that there is no way to treat a series of characters as both a string and an expression. With an ANSI-conforming compiler, you can obtain this behavior by using the preprocessor token #, which forces the preprocessor to surround the next replacement argument with double quotes. For example,

```
#define str( s ) #s
```

The statement

```
printf( str( This is a string ) );
```

expands to

```
printf( "This is a string" );
```

Consider the following *ASSERT* macro, which treats its argument as both an expression and a string:

```
#define ASSERT( b ) if (!b) \
                    {\
                        printf("The following \
condition failed: %s\n", #b);\
                        exit( 1 );\
                    }
```

Now you can invoke ASSERT as follows:

```
ASSERT( array_ptr < array_start + array_size );
```

If the expression is false (that is, if *array_ptr* points to an address beyond the array), the program will print the following message and then exit:

```
The following condition failed:
array_ptr < array_start + array_size
```

Note that since preprocessor commands are terminated by newlines, we use backslashes to continue the definition of *ASSERT* onto more than one line.

Box 10-9: ANSI Feature — Token Pasting

The ANSI Standard defines a new preprocessor operator (##) that pastes two tokens. For example,

```
#define FILENAME( extension ) test_ ## extension
```

The sequence

```
FILENAME( bak )
```

expands to

```
test_bak
```

Note that you cannot obtain this behavior without using the paste operator. For example,

```
#define FILENAME( extension ) test_extension
```

does not work because *test_extension* is considered to be a single identifier and macro expansion does not occur within identifiers.

Here's another example using the token pasting operator:

```
#define READ( type ) ( file_##type == NULL ? \
  open_##type##_file(), read__##type() : \
  read_##type() )
```

This macro is useful for reading elements from files. If the file is not already opened (i.e., *file__##type == NULL*), the macro will open and then invoke the *read_##type()* function; otherwise it invokes *read_##type* without opening the file. For example,

```
s = READ( player );
```

expands to

```
s = ( file_player == NULL ? open_file_player(),
      read_player() : read_player() );
```

This is equivalent to

```
if (file_player == NULL)
{
  open_file_player();
  s = read_player;
}
else
  s = read_player;
```

10.2 Conditional Compilation

The preprocessor enables you to screen out portions of source code that you
don't want compiled. This is done through a set of preprocessor directives that
are similar to the **if** and **else** statements in the C language. The preprocessor
versions are **#if**, **#else**, **#elif**, and **#endif**. The syntax for using these directives is
shown in Figure 10-2.

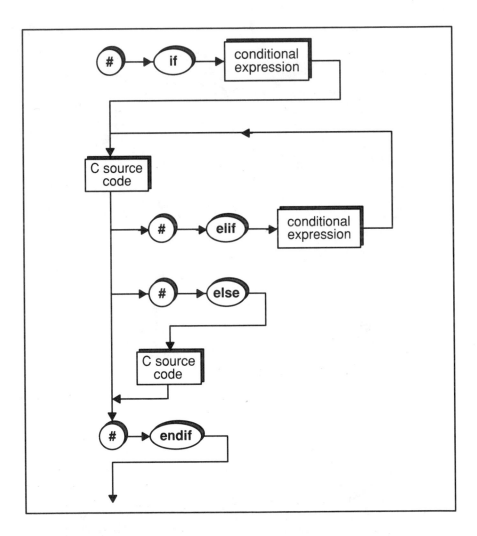

Figure 10-2. Syntax of Conditional Compilation Directives.

For example,

```
#if x == 1
  #undef x
  #define x 0
#elif x == 2
  #undef x
  #define x 3
#else
  #define y 4
#endif
```

The conditional expression in an **#if** or **#elif** directive must be a constant expression, so *x* must be a macro. If it expands to 1, it is redefined to expand to zero. If it expands to 2, it is redefined to expand to 3. Otherwise, *x* remains unchanged, but a new macro named *y* is defined. This example illustrates a number of differences between the preprocessor conditional statements and the C language conditional statements:

- The conditional expression in an **#if** or **#elif** statement need not be enclosed in parentheses. (Parentheses may optionally be included.)

- The **#elif** directive, which is not supported by K&R, is analogous to the C language **else if** construct.

- Blocks of statements under the control of a conditional preprocessor directive are not enclosed in braces. Instead, they are bounded by an **#elif**, **#else**, or **#endif** statement.

- Every **#if** block may contain any number of **#elif** blocks, but no more than one **#else** block, which should be the last one.

- Every **#if** block must end with an **#endif** directive.

In addition to these differences, there are other rules governing conditional preprocessor directives that are not apparent from our example:

- The conditional expression following an **#if** or **#elif** statement must be a constant expression. Normal arithmetic conversions take place. (According to the ANSI Standard, all constants in a conditional expression are converted to **long int**. In most previous versions of C, constants in conditional expressions obey the same type rules as other constants.)

- Any macros in the conditional expression are expanded before the expression is evaluated.

- If a conditional expression contains a name that has not been defined, it is replaced by the constant zero. For example, the sequence

```
#undef x
#if x
```

expands to

```
#if 0
```

(This is how undefined names are handled in the ANSI Standard. Some compilers, however, report an error if you use an undefined name.)

- Conditional preprocessor directives may be nested with the same semantics as nested **if** statements.

In our examples so far, the statements within the conditional blocks are themselves preprocessor statements, but this is not a restriction. They could just as easily be C language statements. In fact, conditional compilation is particularly useful during the debugging stage of program development since you can turn sections of code on or off by changing the value of a macro. The following snippet is from the C interpreter program that we develop in Chapter 12:

```
#if DEBUG
    if (exp_debug)
    {
      printf( "lhs = " );
      print_value( result );
      printf( " rhs = " );
      print_value( &rvalue );
      printf( "\n" );
    }
#endif
```

If the macro *DEBUG* is a nonzero value, the **if** statement and *printf()* calls will be compiled. If *DEBUG* is zero, these statements will be ignored as if they were a comment. If *DEBUG* is not defined, it is the same as if it were defined to expand to zero.

Most compilers have a command line option that lets you define macros before compilation begins. Most C compilers that run under UNIX and MS-DOS, for example, contain a **–D** option for defining macros. To receive debug information, you would define the macro *DEBUG* to be some nonzero value:

```
cc -DDEBUG=1 test
```

Note that the **#if** and **#endif** directives control whether the enclosed C statements are compiled, not necessarily whether they are executed. In the above example, the *printf()* calls are executed only if the *exp_debug* variable has a nonzero value. This double-layer approach enables you to include the diagnostic statements in the executable program but still decide each time you run the program whether you want them executed. If for the final version you need to reduce the size of the executable program, you can compile it with *DEBUG* set to zero.

Another common use of the conditional compilation mechanism is to choose between the old function declaration syntax and the new ANSI prototyping syntax:

```
#if ( __STDC__ == 1)
   extern int foo( char a, float b );
   extern *char goo( char *string );
#else
   extern int foo();
   extern *char goo();
#endif
```

If the compiler conforms to the ANSI standard (*__STDC__* equals 1), we use the prototyping syntax to declare the types of each argument. Otherwise, we use the old function declaration syntax.

10.2.1 Testing Macro Existence

The **#if** and **#elif** directives enable you to compile code conditionally based on the value of an arithmetic expression. You can also specify conditional compilation based on the existence or nonexistence of a macro using **#ifdef**, **#ifndef**, and **#endif**. For example,

```
#ifdef TEST
   printf( "This is a test.\n" );
#else
   printf( "This is not a test.\n" );
#endif
```

If the macro *TEST* is defined, the first *printf()* call will be compiled. If *TEST* is not a defined macro, the second *printf()* call is compiled. Note that it doesn't matter what *TEST* expands to, only whether it exists or not. As with **#if** and **#elif**, an **#ifdef** and **#ifndef** block must be terminated by an **#endif** statement.

Another way to write the previous example is to use the preprocessor **defined** operator (an ANSI extension):

```
#if defined TEST
```

or

```
#if defined( TEST )
```

The parentheses around the macro name are optional. By definition,

```
#if defined macro_name
```

is equivalent to

```
#ifdef macro_name
```

And the directive

```
#if !defined macro_name
```

is equivalent to

```
#ifndef macro_name
```

In most instances, you can use **#if** instead of **#ifdef** and **#ifndef**, since the macro name expands to zero if it is not defined. The one exception where you need to use **#ifdef** or **#ifndef** is when the macro is defined to zero. For example, you may want to define the macro *FALSE* to expand to zero. If you use an **#if** directive to test whether FALSE is defined, *FALSE* will be redefined even if it is already defined to expand to zero. More important, it won't be redefined if it is defined to something other than zero.

```
#if !FALSE
#   define FALSE 0
#endif
```

You can avoid both of these problems by using **#ifndef.**

```
#ifndef FALSE
#   define FALSE 0
#elif FALSE
#   undef FALSE
#   define FALSE 0
#endif
```

10.3 Include Facility

You have already been introduced to the **#include** directive as a means for inserting source code into a file. This section describes **#include** in more detail.

The **#include** command has two forms:

```
#include <filename>
```

or

```
#include "filename"
```

If the filename is surrounded by angle brackets, the preprocessor looks in a list of implementation-defined places for the file. (In UNIX systems, standard include files are often located in the directory */usr/include*.) If the file name is surrounded by double quotes, the preprocessor looks for the file according to the file specification rules of the operating system. If the preprocessor can't find the file there, it searches for the file as if it had been enclosed in angle brackets.

The **#include** command enables you to create common definition files, called *header files*, to be shared by several source files. Header files traditionally have a *.h* extension and contain data structure definitions, macro definitions, and any global data necessary for modules to communicate with each other. You should use header files to place common information in one place instead of duplicating it in each source module. This greatly simplifies the initial programming as well as the subsequent maintenance and modification. It also ensures that programmers working on different parts of a project do not use the same name in conflicting ways.

The C **extern** declaration is tailored to this sharing of a common definition file since you can redeclare the same **extern** variable any number of times, so long as the data type remains the same. Note, however, that most compilers do not allow you to initialize a global variable more than once. As a result, **extern** declarations that appear in an include file should not contain an initializer. Instead, you should choose a single file in which to enter the initialization. It is a good idea to enter a comment in the header file stating where the global variable is initialized and what the initial value is. For example, the header file might contain the declaration

```
/* Initialized to 1 in start.c */
extern int page_num;
```

In the source file start.c, you would write

```
int page_num = 1;
```

Operating systems such as UNIX supply many header files that describe structures internal to the operating system. The C runtime library also includes a
number of header files that must be included in order to invoke associated
functions. See Appendix A for more information about runtime library header
files.

10.4 Line Control

The ANSI Standard defines a preprocessor directive called **#line** that allows you
to change the compiler's knowledge of the current line number of the source file
and the name of the source file.

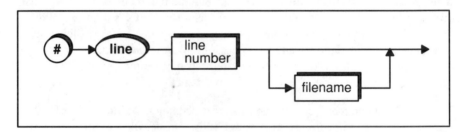

*Figure 10-3. Syntax of the **#line** Directive.*

The syntax for **#line** is shown in Figure 10-3. The line number that you enter
represents the line number of the next line in the source file. Most compilers use
this number when they report an error and source-level debuggers make use of
line numbers. The following example illustrates the behavior of **#line**.

```
/*  Example of the #line preprocessor directive
 */

main()
{
  printf( "Current line: %d\nFilename: %s\n\n",
          __LINE__, __FILE__ );
#line 100
  printf( "Current line: %d\nFilename: %s\n\n",
          __LINE__, __FILE__ );
#line 200 "new_name"
  printf( "Current line: %d\nFilename: %s\n\n",
          __LINE__, __FILE__ );
  exit(0);
}
```

Assuming that the source file for this program is called *line_example.c*, execution produces

```
Current line: 7
Filename: line_example.c

Current line: 101
Filename: line_example.c

Current line: 201
Filename: new_name
```

The preprocessor evaluates __LINE__ before deleting comments. However, if an **#include** directive appears before an occurrence of __LINE__, the preprocessor inserts the include file before computing the value of __LINE__.

The **#line** feature is particularly useful for programs that produce C source text. For instance, *yacc* (which stands for Yet Another Compiler Compiler) is a UNIX utility that facilitates building compilers. *yacc* reads files written in the *yacc* language and produces a file written in the C language, which can then be compiled by a C compiler. A problem arises, however, if the C compiler encounters an error in the *yacc*-produced C file. You want to know which line in the original *yacc* file is causing the error, but the C compiler will report the error-producing line in the C text file. To solve this problem, *yacc* writes **#line** directives in the C source file so that the compiler is fooled into reporting errors based on the *yacc* line numbers rather than the C line numbers.

Box 10-10: ANSI Feature — The *#error* Directive

The ANSI **#error** directive enables you to report errors during the preprocessing stage of compilation. Whatever text follow the **#error** command will be sent to the standard error device (usually your terminal). Typically, it is used to check for illegal conditional compilation values. For example,

```
#if INTSIZE < 16
#  error INTSIZE too small
#endif
```

If you attempt to compile a file with

```
cc -DINTSIZE=8 test.c
```

you will receive the error message

```
INTSIZE too small
```

Box 10-11: ANSI Feature — The *#pragma* Directive

The ANSI **#pragma** directive performs implementation-specific tasks. Every compiler is free to support special names that have implementation-defined behavior when preceded by **#pragma**. For instance, a compiler might support the names *NO_SIDE_EFFECTS* and *END_NO_SIDE_EFFECTS*, which inform the compiler whether it needs to worry about side effects for a certain block of statements. This information can help the compiler generate better-optimized machine code. In the following snippet, for instance, the compiler is free to assign 2 to **p before* the call to *fn()* because the programmer has guaranteed that *fn()* will not produce side effects that might affect **p*:

```
#pragma NO_SIDE_EFFECTS
    a = fn( x, 2 );
    *p = 2;
#pragma END_NO_SIDE_EFFECTS
```

Check the documentation for your compiler to see if it supports any special **#pragma** directives.

Exercises

1. Give the translation of the following macros:

    a) ```
        #define BUFFSIZE 1024
        int buf[BUFFSIZE+1];
        ```

    b)  ```
        #define a(b) b+1
        a(1) + 1
        ```

    c) ```
        #define a (b) b+1
        a(1) + 1
        ```

    d)  ```
        #define cos(x) *cos(x)
        cos(x) + cos(cos(y)+1)
        ```

    e) ```
        #define min(x,y) ((x)>=(y)?x:y)
        min(1,min(a,b))
        ```

    f)  ```
        #define DO_BIG_BUFFERS
        #define IO_FLAGS 0x5C
        #define IO_NO_ODD_BOUND 4
        #define DO_BIG_BUFFERS
        #if defined( BIG_BUFFERS ) && (IO_FLAGS & \
                        IO_NO_ODD_BOUND)
          input_stream = big_buf_init();
          stream_align( input_stream );
        #else
          input_stream = small_buff_init();
        #endif
        ```

2. Write macros to do the following:

    a) Set the *n*th bit of char array *buf* to *val*:

        SET_BIT(buf, n, val)

    b) Get the value of the *n*th bit of char array buf:

        GET_BIT(buf, n)

3.   Write a macro called MYGETC(*fd*), where *fd* is type *FILE_DESCRIP-TOR (see below)*. The macro will read a character from a buffer. If the buffer is empty, the macro must use

```
read( int fileChannel, char *buf, int len )
```

to fill the buffer.

You can assume that

1. *open()* has been called on *fd*
2. *fd–>fileChannel* is valid
3. *fd–>currentBufPointer == 0*.

Use the definitions in the following header file.

```
/* myio.h */
#define FILE_BUF_LEN (512)

typedef struct
{
   int fileChannel;
   char *buf;
   char *currentBufPointer;
} FILE_DESCRIPTOR;
```

4.   Write a macro called *MYPUTC(fd, c)* to write to the buffer in file descriptor *fd*. If the buffer is full, use

```
write( int fileChanel, char buf, int len )
```

to write it. Use *"myio.h"* above and the same assumptions about *fd* as in Exercise 3.

5.   Write a macro *ABS(x)* that expands to the absolute value of its argument *x*. Why might it be more efficient than a function call? Why might it be less efficient?

Chapter 11

Input and Output

In good writing, words become one with things. —
Emerson, Journals

File I/O is one of the trickiest aspects of any programming language because it is integrated so closely with the operating system. Operating systems vary greatly in the way they allow access to data in files and devices. This variation makes it extremely difficult to design I/O capabilities that are portable from one implementation of a programming language to another.

The C language performs I/O through a large set of runtime routines. Many of these functions were first described in the K&R standard. Others are derived from the UNIX I/O library. Historically, there has always been some overlap between these two libraries, although the "C library" deals mostly with buffered I/O while the UNIX library performs unbuffered I/O.

The ANSI Committee blended these two libraries, preserving some functions, deleting some functions, and modifying others. The most significant change is the elimination of unbuffered I/O functions. In the ANSI library, all I/O functions are buffered, although you have the capability to change the buffer size. In addition, the ANSI I/O functions make a distinction between accessing files in binary mode and accessing them in text mode. In UNIX environments, this distinction is moot because the UNIX operating system treats binary and text files the same. In some other operating systems, the distinction is extremely important.

The Standard C Library contains nearly forty functions that perform I/O operations. They can be divided into several groups, as shown in Tables 11-3 through 11-5. Appendix A describes each function detail. The remainder of this chapter provides more general information. We use the ANSI Standard as the basis of our discussion.

11.1 Streams

C makes no distinction between devices such as a terminal or tape drive and logical files located on a disk. In all cases, I/O is performed through *streams* that are associated with the files or devices. A stream consists of an ordered series of bytes. You can think of it as a one-dimensional array of characters, as shown in Figure 11-1. Reading and writing to a file or device involves reading data from the stream or writing data onto the stream.

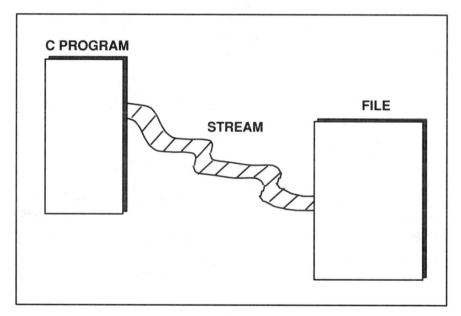

Figure 11-1.   Streams. C Programs access data on files through
                one-dimensional arrays of characters called streams.

To perform I/O operations, you must associate a stream with a file or device. You do this by declaring a pointer to a structure type called *FILE*. The *FILE* structure, which is defined in the *stdio.h* header file, contains several fields to hold such information as the file's name, its access mode, and a pointer to the next character in the stream. These fields are assigned values when you open the stream and access it, but they are implementation dependent, so they vary from one system to another.

The *FILE* structures provide the operating system with bookkeeping information, but your only means of access to the stream is the pointer to the *FILE* structure (called a *file pointer*). The file pointer, which you must declare in your program, holds the stream identifier returned by the *fopen()* function. You use the file pointer to read from, write to, or close the stream. A program may have more than one stream open simultaneously, although each implementation imposes a limit on the number of concurrent streams.

One of the fields in each *FILE* structure is a *file position indicator* that points to the byte where the next character will be read from or written to. As you read from and write to the file, the operating system adjusts the file position indicator to point to the next byte. Although you can't directly access the file position indicator (at least not in a portable fashion), you can fetch and change its value through library functions, thus enabling you to access a stream in nonserial order.

Do not confuse the file pointer with the file position indicator. The file pointer identifies an open stream connected to a file or device. The file position indicator refers to a specific byte position within a stream.

11.1.1 Standard Streams

There are three streams that are automatically opened for every program. Their names are *stdin*, *stdout*, and *stderr*. Usually, these streams point to your terminal, but many operating systems permit you to redirect them. For example, you might want error messages written to a file instead of the terminal.

The I/O functions already introduced, *printf()* and *scanf()* for example, use these default streams. *printf()* writes to *stdout*, and *scanf()* reads from *stdin*. You could use these functions to perform I/O to files by making *stdin* and *stdout* point to files (with the *freopen()* function). An easier method, however, is to use the equivalent functions, *fprintf()* and *fscanf()*, which enable you to specify a particular stream.

11.1.2 Text and Binary Formats

Data can be accessed in one of two formats: *text* or *binary*. (Implementations may support additional formats, but they are not required by the ANSI Standard to do so.) A *text stream* consists of a series of lines, where each line is terminated by a newline character. However, operating systems may have other ways of storing lines on disks and tapes, so each line in a text file does not necessarily end in a newline character. Many IBM systems, for instance, keep track of text lines through an index of pointers to the beginnings of each line. In this scheme, the files stored on disk or tape may not contain newline characters even though they are logically composed of lines. When these lines are read into memory in text mode, however, the runtime functions automatically insert newlines into the text stream. Likewise, when lines are written from a text stream to a mass storage device, the I/O functions may replace newlines in the stream with implementation-defined characters that get written to the I/O device. In this way, C text streams have a consistent appearance from one environment to another, even though the format of the data on the mass storage devices may vary.

Despite these rules, which promote portability to some extent, you should be extremely careful when performing textual I/O. Programs that work on one system may not work exactly the same way on another. In particular, the rules described above hold true only for printable characters (including tabs, form feeds, and newlines.) If control characters appear in a text stream, they are interpreted in an implementation-defined manner.

In binary format, the compiler performs no interpretation of bytes. It simply reads and writes bits exactly as they appear. Binary streams are used primarily for nontextual data, where there is no line structure and it is important to preserve the exact contents of the file. If you are more interested in preserving the line structure of a file, you should use a text stream. The three standard streams, for example, are all opened in text mode.

As we mentioned earlier, in UNIX environments the distinction between text and binary modes is moot since UNIX treats all data as binary data. However, even if you are programming in a UNIX environment, you should be thinking about potential difficulties in porting your program to other systems.

11.2 Buffering

Compared to memory, secondary storage devices such as disk drives and tape drives are extremely slow. For most programs that involve I/O, the time taken to access these devices overshadows the time the CPU takes to perform operations. It is extremely important, therefore, to reduce the number of physical read and write operations as much as possible. Buffering is the simplest way to do this.

A *buffer* is an area where data is temporarily stored before being sent to its ultimate destination. Buffering provides more efficient data transfer because it enables the operating system to minimize accesses to I/O devices.

All operating systems use buffers to read from and write to I/O devices. That is, the operating system accesses I/O devices only in fixed-size chunks, called *blocks*. Typically, a block is 512 or 1024 bytes. This means that even if you want to read only one character from a file, the operating system reads the entire block on which the character is located. For a single read operation, this isn't very efficient, but suppose you want to read 1000 characters from a file. If I/O were unbuffered, the system would perform 1000 disk seek and read operations. With buffered I/O, on the other hand, the system reads an entire block into memory and then fetches each character from memory when necessary. This saves 999 I/O operations.

The C runtime library contains an additional layer of buffering, which comes in two forms: *line buffering* and *block buffering*.

In line buffering, the system stores characters until a newline character is encountered, or until the buffer is filled, and then sends the entire line to the operating system to be processed. This is what happens, for example, when you read data from the terminal. The data is saved in a buffer until you enter a newline character. At that point, the entire line is sent to the program.

In block buffering, the system stores characters until a block is filled and then passes the entire block to the operating system. The size of a block is defined by the operating system but is typically 512 or 1024 bytes. By default, all I/O streams that point to a file are block buffered. Streams that point to your terminal (*stdin* and *stdout*) are either line buffered or unbuffered, depending on the implementation.

The C library standard I/O package includes a *buffer manager* that keeps buffers in memory as long as possible. So if you access the same portion of a stream more than once, there is a good chance that the system can avoid accessing the I/O device multiple times. Note, however, that this can create problems if the file is being shared by more than one process. For interprocess synchronization, you need to write your own assembly language functions or use system functions supplied with the operating system.

In both line buffering and block buffering, you can explicitly direct the system to flush the buffer at any time (with the *fflush()* function), sending whatever data is in the buffer to its destination.

Although line buffering and block buffering are more efficient than processing each character individually, they are unsatisfactory if you want each character to be processed as soon as it is input or output. For example, you may want to process characters as they are typed rather than waiting for a newline to be entered. C allows you to tune the buffering mechanism by changing the default size of the buffer. In most systems, you can set the size to zero to turn buffering off entirely. Section 11.8 describes unbuffered I/O in greater detail.

11.3 The *<stdio.h>* Header File

To use any of the I/O functions, you must include the *stdio.h* header file. This file contains:

- Prototype declarations for all the I/O functions.

- Declaration of the *FILE* structure.

- Several useful macro constants, including *stdin*, *stdout*, and *stderr*.

Another important macro is *EOF*, which is the value returned by many functions when the system reaches the end-of-file marker. Historically, *stdio.h* is also where *NULL*, the name for a null pointer, is defined. The ANSI Committee, however, moved the definition of *NULL* to a new header file called *stddef.h*. To use *NULL*, therefore, you must either include *stddef.h* or define *NULL* yourself:

```
#ifndef NULL
   #define NULL (void *) 0
#endif
```

11.4 Error Handling

Each I/O function returns a special value if an error occurs. The error value, however, varies from one function to another. Some functions return zero for an error, others return a nonzero value, and some return *EOF*. Read the function description in Appendix A to see what value it returns for an error.

There are also two members of the *FILE* structure that record whether an error or end-of-file has occurred for each open stream. End-of-file conditions are represented differently on different systems. Some systems have a special character that denotes the end of a file, while others use some method of counting characters to determine when the end of a file has been reached. In either case, an attempt to read data past the end-of-file marker will cause an end-of-file condition. A stream's end-of-file and error flags can be checked via the *feof()* and *ferror()* functions, respectively. In a few instances, an I/O function returns the same value for an end-of-file condition as it does for an error condition. In these cases, you need to check one of the flags to see which event actually occurred.

The following function checks the error and end-of-file flags for a specified stream and returns one of four values based on the results. The *clearerr()* function sets both flags equal to zero. You must explicitly reset the flags with *clearerr()*—they are not automatically reset when you read them, nor are they automatically reset to zero by the next I/O call. They are initialized to zero when the stream is opened, but the only way to reset them to zero is with *clearerr()*.

```
/*  If neither flag is set, stat will equal zero.
 *  If error is set, but not eof, stat equals 1.
 *  If eof is set, but not error, stat equals 2.
 *  If both flags are set, stat equals 3.
 */

#include <stdio.h>
#define EOF_FLAG 1
#define ERR_FLAG 2

char stream_stat( fp )
  FILE *fp;
{
  char stat = 0;

  if (ferror( fp ))
    stat |= ERR_FLAG;
  if (feof( fp ))
    stat |= EOF_FLAG;
  clearerr();
  return stat;
}
```

11.4.1 The *errno* Variable

In addition to the end-of-file and error flags, there is a global variable called *errno* that is used by a few of the I/O functions to record errors. A UNIX hand-me-down, *errno* is an integer variable declared in the *errno.h* header file. The *errno* variable is primarily used for math functions; very few of the I/O functions make use of *errno*. For more information about *errno*, see Appendix A.

11.5 Opening and Closing a File

Before you can read from or write to a file, you must open it with the *fopen()* function. *fopen()* takes two arguments—the first is the file name and the second is the access mode. There are two sets of access modes—one for text streams and one for binary streams. The text stream modes are shown in Table 11-1. The binary modes are exactly the same, except that they have a **b** appended to the mode name. To open a binary file with read access, for example, you would use **"rb"**.

"r"	Open an existing text file for reading. Reading occurs at the beginning of the file.
"w"	Create a new text file for writing. If the file already exists, it will be truncated to zero length. The file position indicator is initially set to the beginning of the file.
"a"	Open an existing text file in append mode. You can write only at the end-of-file position. Even if you explicitly move the file position indicator, writing still occurs at the end-of-file.
"r+"	Open an existing text file for reading and writing. The file position indicator is initially set to the beginning of the file.
"w+"	Create a new text file for reading and writing. If the file already exists, it will be truncated to zero length.
"a+"	Open an existing file or create a new one in append mode. You can read data anywhere in the file, but you can write data only at the end-of-file marker.

Table 11-1. fopen() *Text Modes.*

Table 11-2 summarizes the properties of the *fopen()* modes.

	r	w	a	r+	w+	a+
File must exist before open	✱			✱		
Old file truncated to zero length		✱			✱	
Stream can be read	✱			✱	✱	✱
Stream can be written		✱	✱	✱	✱	✱
Stream can be written only at end			✱			✱

Table 11-2. File and Stream Properties of fopen() *Modes.*

fopen() returns a file pointer that you can use to access the file later in the program. The following function opens a text file called *test* with read access.

```
#include <stddef.h>
#include <stdio.h>

FILE *open_test();   /* Returns a pointer to FILE */
{                    /* struct */
  FILE *fp;

  fp = fopen( "test", "r" );
  if (fp == NULL)
    fprintf( stderr, "Error opening file test\n" );
  return fp;
}
```

Note how the file pointer *fp* is declared as a pointer to *FILE*. The *fopen()* function returns a null pointer (*NULL*) if an error occurs. If successful, *fopen()* returns a nonzero file pointer. The *fprintf()* function is exactly like *printf()*, except that it takes an extra argument indicating which stream the output should be sent to. In this case, we send the message to the standard I/O stream *stderr*. By default, this stream usually points to your terminal.

The *open_test()* function is written somewhat more verbosely than is usual. Typically, the error test is combined with the file pointer assignment:

```
    if ((fp = fopen( "test","r" )) == NULL)
      fprintf( stderr, "Error opening file test\n" );
```

Box 11-1: Bug Alert — Opening a File

In the statement

```
if ((fp = fopen( "test","r" )) == NULL)
    fprintf( stderr, "Error opening file test\n"
);
```

the parentheses around

```
fp = fopen( "test", "r" )
```

are necessary because == has higher precedence than =. Without the parentheses, *fp* gets assigned zero or one, depending on whether the result of *fopen( )* is a null pointer or a valid pointer. This is a common programming mistake.

The *open_test()* function is a little too specific to be useful since it can only open one file, called `test`, and only with read-only access. A more useful function, shown below, can open any file with any mode.

```
#include <stddef.h>
#include <stdio.h>

FILE *open_file( file_name, access_mode )
  char *file_name, *access_mode;
{
  FILE *fp;
  if ((fp = fopen( file_name, access_mode )) == NULL)
    fprintf( stderr, "Error opening file %s with access\
mode %s\n", file_name, access_mode );
  return fp;
}
```

Our *open_file()* function is essentially the same as *fopen()*, except that it prints an error message if the file cannot be opened.

To open `test` from *main()*, you could write

```
#include <stddef.h>
#include <stdio.h>

main()
{
  extern FILE *open_file();

  if ((open_file("test", "r")) == NULL)
    exit(1);
      .
      .
      .
}
```

Note that the header files are included in both routines. You can include them in any number of different source files without causing conflicts.

11.5.1 Closing a File

To close a file, you need to use the *fclose()* function:

```
fclose( fp );
```

Closing a file frees up the *FILE* structure that *fp* points to so that the operating system can use the structure for a different file. It also flushes any buffers associated with the stream. Most operating systems have a limit on the number of streams that can be open at once, so it's a good idea to close files when you're done with them. In any event, all open streams are automatically closed when the program terminates normally. Most operating systems will close open files even when a program aborts abnormally, but you can't depend on this behavior. Moreover, networked systems tend to have a high overhead for closing streams that you have explicitly opened if you neglect to close them yourself.

11.6 Reading and Writing Data

Once you have opened a file, you use the file pointer to perform read and write operations. There are three degrees of I/O *granularity*. That is, you can perform I/O operations on three different sizes of objects. The three degrees of granularity are as follows:

- One character at a time

- One line at a time

- One block at a time

Each of these methods has some pros and cons. In the following sections, we show three ways to write a simple function that copies the contents of one file to another. Each uses a different degree of granularity.

One rule that applies to all levels of I/O is that you cannot read from a stream and then write to it without an intervening call to *fseek()*, *rewind()*, or *fflush()*. The same rule holds for switching from write mode to read mode. These three functions are the only I/O functions that flush the buffers.

11.6.1 One Character at a Time

There are four functions that read and write one character to a stream:

getc()	A macro that reads one character from a stream.
fgetc()	Same as *getc()*, but implemented as a function.
putc()	A macro that writes one character to a stream.
fputc()	Same as *putc()*, but implemented as a function.

Note that *getc()* and *putc()* are usually implemented as macros whereas *fgetc()* and *fputc()* are guaranteed to be functions. Because they are implemented as macros, *putc()* and *getc()* usually run much faster. In fact, on our machine, they are almost twice as fast as *fgetc()* and *fputc()*. Because they are macros, however, they are susceptible to side effect problems (see Box 10-6). For example, the following is a dangerous call that may not work as expected:

```
putc( 'x', fp[j++] );
```

If an argument contains side effect operators, you should use *fgetc()* or *fputc()*, which are guaranteed to be implemented as functions. Note that *getc()* and *putc()* are the only library calls for which this caveat applies. For the rest of the library, the ANSI Standard states that if a function is implemented as a macro, its argument(s) may appear only once in the macro body. This restriction removes side effect problems.

The following example uses *getc( )* and *putc( )* to copy one file to another.

```c
#include <stddef.h>
#include <stdio.h>
#define FAIL 0
#define SUCCESS 1

int copyfile( infile, outfile )
  char *infile, *outfile;
{
  FILE *fp1, *fp2;

  if ((fp1 = fopen( infile, "rb" )) == NULL)
    return FAIL;
  if ((fp2=fopen( outfile, "wb" )) == NULL)
  {
    fclose( fp1 );
    return FAIL;
  }

  while (!feof( fp1 ))
    putc( getc( fp1 ), fp2 );

  fclose( fp1 );
  fclose( fp2 );
  return SUCCESS;
}
```

We open both files in binary mode because we are reading each individual character and are not concerned with the file's line structure. This function will work for all files, regardless of the type of data stored in the file.

The *getc()* function gets the next character from the specified stream and then moves the file position indicator one position. Successive calls to *getc()* read each character in a stream. When the end-of-file is encountered, the *feof()* function returns a nonzero value. Note that we cannot use the return value of *getc()* to test for an end-of-file because the file is opened in binary mode. For example, if we write

```c
int c;
while ((c = getc( fp1 )) != EOF)
```

the loop will exit whenever the character read has the same value as *EOF*. This may or may not be a true end-of-file condition. The *feof()* function, on the other hand, is unambiguous.

11.6.2 One Line at a Time

Another way to write this function is to read and write lines instead of characters. There are two line-oriented I/O functions—*fgets()* and *fputs()*. The prototype for *fgets()* is

```
char *fgets( char *s, int n, FILE stream );
```

The three arguments have the following meanings:

s   A pointer to the first element of an array to
                            which characters are written.

n   An integer representing the maximum number of
                            characters to read.

stream   The stream from which to read.

fgets() reads characters until it reaches a newline, an end-of-file, or the maximum number of characters specified. *fgets()* automatically inserts a null character after the last character written to the array. This is why, in the following *copyfile()* function, we specify the maximum to be one less than the array size. *fgets()* returns *NULL* when it reaches the end-of-file. Otherwise, it returns the first argument. The *fputs()* function writes the array identified by the first argument to the stream identified by the second argument.

One point worth mentioning is the difference between *fgets()* and *gets()* (the function that reads lines from *stdin*.) Both functions append a null character after the last character written. However, *gets()* does not write the terminating newline character to the input array. *fgets()* does include the terminating newline character. Also, *fgets()* allows you to specify a maximum number of characters to read, whereas *gets()* reads characters indefinitely until it encounters a newline or end-of-file.

The following function illustrates how you might implement *copyfile* using the line-oriented functions. Note that we open the files in text mode because we want to access the data line by line. If we open the files in binary mode, the *fgets()* function might not work correctly because it would look explicitly for a newline character. The file itself may or may not include newline characters. If the file was written in text mode, it will contain newline characters only if that is how the operating system denotes new lines. In text mode, *fgets()* uses the implementation's definition of a newline.

```
#include <stddef.h>
#include <stdio.h>

#define FAIL 0
#define SUCCESS 1
#define LINESIZE 100

int copyfile( infile, outfile )
  char *infile, *outfile;
{
  FILE *fp1, *fp2;
  char line[LINESIZE];

  if ((fp1 = fopen( infile, "r" )) == NULL)
    return FAIL;
  if ((fp2 = fopen( outfile, "w" )) == NULL)
  {
    fclose( fp1 );
    return FAIL;
  }
  while (fgets( line, LINESIZE-1, fp1 ) != NULL)
    fputs( line, fp2 );
  fclose( fp1 );
  fclose( fp2 );
  return SUCCESS;
}
```

You might think that the *copyfile()* version that reads and writes lines would be faster than the version that reads and writes characters because it requires fewer function calls. Actually, though, the version using *getc()* and *putc()* is significantly faster. This is because most compilers implement *fgets()* and *fputs()* using *fputc()* and *fgetc()*. Since these are functions rather than macros, they tend to run more slowly.

11.6.3 One Block at a Time

In addition to character and line granularity, you can also access data in lumps called *blocks*. You can think of a block as an array. When you read or write a block, you need to specify the number of elements in the block and the size of each element. The two block I/O functions are *fread()* and *fwrite()*. The prototype for *fread()* is

```
size_t fread( void *ptr, size_t size, size_t nmemb,
              FILE *stream );
```

where *size_t* is an integral type defined in *stdio.h*.

The arguments represent the following data:

ptr	A pointer to an array in which to store the data.
size	The size of each element in the array.
nmemb	The number of elements to read.
stream	The file pointer.

fread() returns the number of elements actually read. This should be the same as the third argument unless an error occurs or an end-of-file condition is encountered.

The *fwrite()* function is the mirror image of *fread()*. It takes the same arguments, but instead of reading elements from the stream to the array, it writes elements from the array to the stream.

The following function shows how you might implement *copyfile()* using the block I/O functions. Note that we test for an end-of-file condition by comparing the actual number of elements read (the value returned from *fread()*) with the number specified in the argument list. If they are different, it means that either an end-of-file or an error condition occurred. We use the *ferror()* function to find out which of the two possible events happened. If an error occurred, we print an error message and return an error code. Otherwise we return a success code. For the final *fwrite()* function we use the value of *num_read* as the number of elements to write, since it is less than *BLOCKSIZE*.

Note that we took extra care to write the function so that it would be easy to modify. If we want to change the size of each element in the array, we need only change the **typedef** statement at the top of the function. If we want to change the number of elements read, we need only redefine *BLOCKSIZE*.

```c
#include <stddef.h>
#include <stdio.h>
#define FAIL 0
#define SUCCESS 1
#define BLOCKSIZE 512
typedef char DATA;

int copyfile( infile, outfile )
  char *infile, *outfile;
{
  FILE *fp1,*fp2;
  DATA block[BLOCKSIZE];
  int num_read;


  if ((fp1 = fopen( infile, "rb" )) == NULL)
  {
    printf( "Error opening file %s for input.\n",
            infile );
    return FAIL;
  }

  if ((fp2 = fopen( outfile, "wb" )) == NULL)
  {
    printf( "Error opening file %s for output.\n",
            outfile );
    fclose( fp1 );
    return FAIL;
  }

  while ((num_read = fread( block, sizeof(DATA),
          BLOCKSIZE, fp1 )) == BLOCKSIZE)
    fwrite( block, sizeof(DATA), num_read, fp2 );

  fwrite( block, sizeof(DATA), num_read, fp2 );
  fclose( fp1 );
  fclose( fp2 );

  if (ferror( fp1 ))
  {
    printf( "Error reading file %s\n", infile );
    return FAIL;
  }
  return SUCCESS;
}
```

Like *fputs()* and *fgets()*, the block I/O functions are usually implemented using *fputc()* and *fgetc()* functions, so they are not as efficient as the macros *putc()* and *getc()*. Note also that these block sizes are independent of the blocks used for buffering. The buffer size, for instance, might be 1024 bytes. If the block size specified in a read operation is only 512 bytes, the operating system will still fetch 1024 bytes from the disk and store them in memory. Only the first 512 bytes, however, will be made available to the *fread()* function. On the next *fread()* call, the operating system will fetch the remaining 512 bytes from memory rather than performing another disk access. The block sizes in *fread()* and *fwrite()* functions, therefore, do not affect the number of device I/O operations performed.

11.7 Selecting an I/O Method

As we have shown with the different versions of *copyfile()*, there are usually multiple ways to perform an I/O task. Choosing the best method is a matter of weighing pros and cons, paying special attention to simplicity, efficiency, and portability.

From an efficiency standpoint, the macros *putc()* and *getc()* are usually fastest. However, most operating systems have a means for performing very fast block I/O operations that can be even faster than *putc()* and *getc()*. These capabilities, however, are often not available through the C runtime library. You may need to write assembly code or call operating system services. UNIX systems, for example, provide routines called *read()* and *write()*, which perform efficient block I/O transfers. If you think you may want to use system block I/O operations in the future, it is probably a good idea to write the original C routines using *fread()* and *fwrite()* since it will be easier to adapt these routines if they are already block oriented.

Though efficiency is important, particularly with regard to I/O, it is not the only consideration. Sometimes the choice of an I/O method boils down to a question of simplicity. For example, *fgets()* and *fputs()* are relatively slow functions, but it may be worth sacrificing some speed if you need to process entire lines.

Consider a function that counts the number of lines in a file. Using *fgets()* and *fputs()*, the function can be written very simply:

```c
#include <stdio.h>
#include <stddef.h>
#define MAX_LINE_SIZE 120

int lines_in_file( fp )
  FILE *fp;
{
  char buf[MAX_LINE_SIZE];
  int line_num = 0;

  rewind(fp);   /* Moves the file position indicator
                 * to the beginning of the file.
                 */
  while (fgets( fp, MAX_LINE_SIZE, buf ) != NULL)
    line_num++;

  return line_num;
}
```

You could also write this function using character or block I/O, but the function would be more complex. If execution speed is not important, therefore, the version above is the best.

The last, but certainly not the least, consideration in choosing an I/O method is portability. In terms of deciding between character, line, or block I/O, portability doesn't really play a role. Portability is a major concern, however, in choosing between text mode and binary mode. If the file contains textual data, such as source code files and documents, you should open it in text mode and access it line by line. This will help you avoid many pitfalls if you port the program to a different machine. On the other hand, if the data is numeric and does not have a clear line structure, it is best to open it in binary mode and access it either character by character or block by block.

11.8 Unbuffered I/O

Although the C runtime library provides the means to change the buffer size, you should use the capability with care. In most cases, the compiler developers have chosen a default buffer size that is optimal for the operating system under which the program will be run. If you change it, you may experience a loss of I/O speed.

The one time when you need to tamper with the buffer size is when you want to turn off buffering altogether. Typically, this occasion arises when you want user input to be processed immediately. Normally, the *stdin* stream is line-buffered, requiring the user to enter a newline character before the input is sent to the program. For many interactive applications, this is unsatisfactory.

Consider, for example, a text editor program. The user may type characters as part of the text or enter commands. For instance, the user could press an up-arrow key to move the cursor to another line. The I/O functions must be capable of processing each character as it is input, without waiting for a terminating newline character.

To turn buffering off, you can use either the *setbuf()* function or the *setvbuf()* function. The *setbuf()* function takes two arguments: the first is a file pointer, and the second is a pointer to a character array which is to serve as the new buffer. If the array pointer is a null pointer, buffering is turned off, as in

```
setbuf( stdin, NULL );
```

The *setbuf()* function does not return a value.

The *setvbuf()* function is similar to *setbuf()*, but it is a bit more elaborate. It takes two additional arguments that enable you to specify the type of buffering (line, block, or no buffering) and the size of the array to be used as the buffer. The buffer type should be one of three symbols (defined in *stdio.h*):

_IOFBF	block buffering
_IOLBF	line buffering
_IONBF	no buffering

To turn buffering off, therefore, you would write

```
stat = setvbuf( stdin, NULL, _IONBF, 0 );
```

The *setvbuf()* function returns a nonzero value if it is successful. If, for some reason, it cannot honor the request, it returns zero. Consult Appendix A for more information about these two functions.

11.9 Random Access

The previous examples accessed files sequentially, beginning with the first byte and accessing each successive byte in order. For a function such as *copyfile()*, this is reasonable since you need to read and write each byte anyway. It's just as fast to access them sequentially as any other way.

For many applications, however, you need to access particular bytes in the middle of the file. In these cases, it is more efficient to use C's two random access functions—*fseek()* and *ftell()*.

The *fseek()* function moves the file position indicator to a specified character in a stream. The prototype for *fseek()* is

```
int fseek( FILE *stream, long int offset,
           int whence );
```

The three arguments are

> *stream*   A file pointer.
>
> *offset*   An offset measured in characters (can be positive or negative).
>
> *whence*   The starting position from which to count the offset.

There are three choices for the *whence* argument, all of which are designated by names defined in *stdio.h*:

> *SEEK_SET*   The beginning of the file.
>
> *SEEK_CUR*   The current position of the file position indicator.
>
> *SEEK_END*   The end-of-file position.

For example, the statement

```
stat = fseek(fp, 10, SEEK_SET)
```

moves the file position indicator to character 10 of the stream. This will be the next character read or written. Note that streams, like arrays, start at the zero position, so character 10 is actually the 11th character in the stream.

The value returned by *fseek()* is zero if the request is legal. If the request is illegal, *fseek()* returns a nonzero value. This can happen for a variety of reasons. For example, the following is illegal if *fp* is opened for read-only access because it attempts to move the file position indicator beyond the end-of-file position:

```
stat = fseek(fp, 1, SEEK_END)
```

Obviously, if *SEEK_END* is used with read-only files, the offset value must be less than or equal to zero. Likewise, if SEEK_SET is used, the offset value must be greater than or equal to zero.

For binary streams, the offset argument can be any positive or negative integer value that does not push the file position indicator out of the file. For text streams, the offset argument must be either zero or a value returned by *ftell( )*.

The *ftell( )* function takes just one argument, which is a file pointer, and returns the current position of the file position indicator. *ftell( )* is used primarily to return to a specified file position after performing one or more I/O operations. For example, in most text editor programs, there is a command that allows the user to search for a specified character string. If the search fails, the cursor (and file position indicator) should return to its position prior to the search. This might be implemented as follows:

```
cur_pos = ftell(fp);
if (search(string) == FAIL)
   fseek(fp, cur_pos, SEEK_SET);
```

Note that the position returned by *ftell( )* is measured from the beginning of the file. For binary streams, the value returned by *ftell( )* represents the actual number of characters from the beginning of the file. For text streams, the value returned by *ftell( )* represents an implementation-defined value that has meaning only when used as an offset to an *fseek( )* call.

The example in the next section illustrates random access, as well as some of the other I/O topics discussed in this chapter.

11.9.1 Printing a File in Sorted Order

Suppose you have a large data file composed of records. Let's assume that the file contains one thousand records, where each record is a *VITALSTAT* structure, as declared below:

```
#define NAME_LEN 19
typedef char NAME[NAME_LEN];
typedef struct date {
   unsigned day :   5,
            month : 5,
            year : 11;
} DATE;
typedef struct vitalstat
{
    NAME vs_name;
    char vs_ssnum[11];
    DATE vs_date;
    char vs_jersey;
} VITALSTAT;
```

Suppose further that the records are arranged randomly, but you want to print them alphabetically by the *name* field. First, you need to sort the records.

There are two ways to sort records in a file. One is to actually rearrange the records in alphabetical order. However, there are several drawbacks to this method. One drawback is that you need to read the entire file into memory, sort the records, and then write the file back to the storage device. This requires a great deal of I/O power. It also requires a great deal of memory since the entire file must be in memory at once. (There are ways to sort a file in parts, but they are complex and require even more I/O processing.) Another drawback is that if you add records in the future, you need to repeat the entire process.

The other sorting solution is to read only the part of the record that you want to sort (called the *key*) and pair each key with a file pointer (called an *index*) that points to the entire record in the file. Sorting the key elements involves less data than sorting the entire records. This is called an *index sort*.

Suppose that the first five records have the following values.

```
Jordan, Larry      043-12-7895      5-11-1954
Bird, Michael      012-45-4721      3-24-1952
Erving, Isiah      065-23-5553      11-01-1960
Thomas, Earvin     041-92-1298      1-21-1949
Johnson, Julius    012-22-3365      7-15-1957
```

The key/index pairs would be

```
index      key
0          Jordan, Larry
1          Bird, Michael
2          Erving, Isiah
3          Thomas, Earvin
4          Johnson, Julius
```

Instead of physically sorting the entire records, we can sort the key/index pairs by index value:

```
1          Bird, Michael
2          Erving, Isiah
4          Johnson, Julius
0          Jordan, Larry
3          Thomas, Earvin
```

The beauty of the indexing sort method is that you don't need to rearrange the actual records themselves. You need only sort the index, which is usually a smaller task (in our example, the records are so short that there isn't much difference between sorting the records themselves and sorting the entries in the index file). To figure out the alphabetical order, though, you do need to read in the *name* field of each record.

The following function reads the key field of every record and stores them in an array of structures that contain just two fields—the record id (index) and the key.

We assume that the data file has already been opened, so that the function is passed a file pointer. The include file *recs.h* contains the following:

```
#include "vitalstat.h"
#include <stdio.h>
#include <stddef.h>
#define MAX_REC_NUM 1000
#define NAME_LEN 19
typedef struct {
   int index;
   char key[NAME_LEN];
} INDEX;
```

The function reads the first *NAME_LEN* characters of each record using *fgets( )* and stores them in the array *names_index*, then moves the file position indicator to the beginning of the next record with *fseek( )*. In this way, we avoid reading extraneous parts of the record. In reality, of course, the I/O buffering mechanism fetches blocks of 512 or 1024 characters, so the entire records are read anyway. Within each buffer, however, we need only access the first field in each record. This saves us memory-to-memory data copying time, even though we don't save any device-to-memory processing time. For large records, which span blocks, this approach could also save you device-to-memory processing time.

We include some error checking to ensure that the *fseek( )* request is legitimate. If *fseek( )* returns an error that is not an end-of-file condition, we exit the program with an error code. Otherwise, when an end-of-file condition exists, we return the number of records read, which is also the number of index fields stored in the array.

```
/*  Reads up to max_rec_num records from a file and
 *  stores the key field of each record
 *  in an index array.  Returns
 *  the number of key fields stored.
 */

#include "recs.h"

int get_records( data_file, names_index,
max_rec_num)
    FILE *data_file;
    INDEX names_index[];
    int max_rec_num;
{
    int offset = 0, counter = 0;

    for (k = 0; !feof( data_file ) &&
         counter < max_rec_num; k++)
    {
     fgets(names_index[k].key, NAME_LEN, data_file);
      offset += sizeof(VITALSTAT);
      if (fseek( data_file, offset, SEEK_SET ) &&
          (!feof( data_file )))
          exit( 1 );
      counter++;
    }
    return counter;
}
```

Note that the *offset* value is computed by taking the size of the *VITALSTAT* structure. By using the **sizeof** operator, we make the function more portable, since the size of **short**s may vary from one machine to another. In addition, the structure may contain gaps due to alignment restrictions.

The next task is to sort the array of *NAMES INDEX* structures. This function, which makes use of the library function *qsort()*, is shown on the following page. The return value is a pointer to an ordered array of *NAMES_INDEX* structures.

```
/*  Sort an array of NAMES_INDEX structures by the
 *  name field.  There are index_count elements to
 *  be sorted.  Returns a pointer to the sorted
 *  array.
 */

#include <stdlib.h>  /* Header file for qsort() */
#include "recs.h"

void sort_index( names_index, index_count)
   INDEX names_index[];
   int index_count;
{
   int j;
   static int compare_func(); /*  Defined in this
                               *   file.
                               */
/*  Assign values to the index field of each
 *   structure.
 */
   for (j = 0; j < index_count; j++)
     names_index[j].index = j;

   qsort( names_index, index_count,
          sizeof(INDEX), compare_func );

   return names_index;
}


static int compare_func( p, q )
   NAMES_INDEX *p, *q;
{
   return strcmp( p->name, q->name );
}
```

The next step is to print out the records in their sorted order. We definitely need to use *fseek()* for this function because we need to jump around the file. We can compute the starting point of each record by multiplying the index value with the size of the *VITALSTAT* structure. If each *VITALSTAT* structure is 40 characters long, for example, record 50 will start at character 2000. After positioning the file position indicator with *fseek()*, we use *fread()* to read each record. Finally, we print each record with a *printf()* call.

```
/*  Print the records in a file in the order
 *  indicated by the index array.
 */

#include recs.h

void print_indexed_records( data_file, index,
                              index_count )
  FILE *data_file;
  INDEX index[];
  int index_count;
{
  VITALSTAT vs;
  int j;

  for (j = 0; j <= index_count; j++)
  {
    if (fseek( data_file,
            sizeof(VITALSTAT) * index[j].index,
            SEEK_SET ))
        exit( 1 );
    fread( &vs, 1, sizeof(VITALSTAT), data_file );
    printf( "%20s, %hd, %hd, %hd, %12s", vs.name,
            vs.bdate.day, vs.bdate.month,
            vs.bdate.year, vs.ssnum );
  }
}
```

To make this program complete, we need a *main()* function that calls these other functions. We have written *main()* so the filename can be passed as an argument.

```
#include "recs.h"

main( argc, argv )
  int argc;
  char *argv[];
{
  extern int get_records();
  extern void sort_index();
  extern int print_indexed_records();

  FILE *data_file;
  static INDEX index[MAX_REC_NUM];

  int num_recs_read;

  if (argc != 2)
  {
    printf( "Error: must enter filename\n" );
    printf( "Filename: " );
    scanf( "%s", filename );
  }
  else
    filename = argv[1];

  if ((data_file = fopen( filename, "r" )) == NULL)
  {
    printf( "Error opening file %s.\n", filename );
    exit( 1 );
  }

  num_recs_read = get_index( data_file, index,
                            MAX_REC_NUM );
  sort_index( index, num_recs_read );
  print_indexed_records( data_file, index,
                         num_recs_read );
  exit( 0 );
}
```

getchar()	Reads the next character from the standard input stream. *getchar()* is identical to *getc(stdin)*.
gets()	Reads characters from *stdin* until a newline or end-of-file is encountered.
printf()	Outputs one or more values according to user-defined formatting rules.
putchar()	Outputs a single character to the standard output stream. *putchar()* is identical to *putc(stdout)*.
puts()	Outputs a string of characters to *stdout*, appending a newline character to the end of the string.
scanf()	Reads one or more values from *stdin*, interpreting each according to user-defined formatting rules.

Table 11-3. I/O to stdin *and* stdout.

fclose()	Closes a stream.
fflush()	Flushes a buffer by writing out everything currently in the buffer. The stream remains open.
fgetc()	Same as *getc()*, but it is implemented as a function rather than a macro.
fgets()	Reads a string from a specified input stream. Unlike *gets()*, *fgets()* enables you to specify a maximum number of characters to read.

Table 11-4. I/O to files (continued on next page)

fopen()	Opens and possibly creates a file and associates a stream with it. *fopen()* takes two arguments: a character string identifying the file and a mode specification that determines what types of operations may be performed on the file.
fprintf()	Exactly like *printf()*, except that output is to a specified file.
fputc()	Writes a character to a stream. This is the same as *putc()*, but it is implemented as a function rather than a macro.
fputs()	Writes a string to a stream. This is like *puts()*, except that it does not append a newline to the stream.
fread()	Reads a block of binary data from a stream. The arguments specify the size of the block and where it should be stored.
freopen()	Closes a stream and then reopens it for a new file. This is useful for recycling a stream, particularly *stdin*, *stdout*, and *stderr*.
fscanf()	Same as *scanf()*, except that data is read from a specified file.
fseek()	Positions a file position indicator, enabling you to perform random access on a file.
ftell()	Returns the position of a file position indicator.
fwrite()	Writes a block of data from a buffer to a stream.
getc()	Reads a character from a stream.
putc()	Writes a character to a specified stream.
ungetc()	Pushes a character onto a stream. The next call to *getc()* returns this character.

Table 11-4. I/O to files. (continued from preceding page)

clearerr()	Resets the error and end-of-file indicators for the specified stream.
feof()	Checks whether an end-of-file was encountered during a previous read operation.
ferror()	Returns an integer error code (the value of *errno*) if an error occurred while reading from or writing to a stream.

Table 11-5. Error-Handling Functions.

remove()	Deletes a file.
rename()	Renames a file.
tmpfile()	Creates a temporary binary file.
tmpnam()	Generates a string that can be used as the name of a temporary file.

Table 11-6. File Management Functions.

Exercises

1. Write a program that implements the **#include** preprocessor command.

2. Write a function called *compress()* that removes all extraneous white space from a C source file. (Warning: don't remove white space from character and string constants.)

3. Write a program to check for proper pairing of braces and parentheses in a C source file.

4. Write a program that counts the number of characters, words, and lines in a file.

5. Write a program that copies all files on the command line (see *argv*) to *stdout*.

6. Write a program that enables you to enter data into a file containing *VITALSTAT* structures.

7. Write a program that reads characters from standard input and copies them to standard output, translating each '\r' '\n' sequence into '\n'.

8. Write a program similar to Exercise 7 except that it takes two command line options:

   > –from *srcstr*
   > –to *deststr*

   Each occurrence of *srcstr* on input is converted to *deststr* on output.

9. Write a program that opens a file specified on the command line and prints it out backward.

10. Write a program to read any file specified on the command line (even a binary file) and print out only those sequences of two or more printable characters ('a'–'z', 'A'–'Z', '_', '0'–'9').

    Use your executable program as input. Explain what comes out.

Chapter 12

Software Engineering

"For 'tis the sport to have the engineer
Hoist with his own petar." — Shakespeare, Hamlet

Though the cost of computer hardware—the silicon chips containing the thousands of transistors that form the instruction set and memories—has shown a consistent trend downward in cost over the years, the cost of software has not followed suit. The high cost of software is due largely (and paradoxically) to the ease and flexibility with which it can be shaped. The ease with which software can be created and changed can also lead to unworkably complex systems.

Unlike the physical limitations imposed on hardware (such as the number of gates you can fit on a chip, the speed of electrons in the medium, and the amount of heat that can be dissipated), software is limited mainly by the imagination of the software engineer. While flexibility is an important aspect of software, *unrestrained* use of this flexibility is a siren song that all responsible software engineers must resist.

As John Shore points out in his book *The Sacher Tort Algorithm*, the curse of flexibility is both deceptive and seductive. Without the discipline of software engineering, unsuspecting programmers soon find themselves deeply mired in the tar pits of complexity. Using the techniques of software engineering, it takes a little longer to be caught in those pits.

In this chapter we cover the basic elements of software engineering. One aspect of software engineering that we have discussed throughout this book is good *programming style*. Programming style consists of three important qualities:

Readability	Write the source code so that it is readable to you and others. This includes aesthetic formatting, meaningful variable names, and consistency within and across source files.
Portability	Write the code so that it is easy to port to other machines. If possible, avoid nonstandard features, and use the standard library runtime routines rather than writing your own.
Maintainability	As you write the code, think about how you might want to change or extend it in the future. Put data structure definitions in header files where changes will be automatically broadcast to all source files that include the header file. Use **#define** to create constant names for parameters that appear more than once.

Table 12-1 summarizes some of the stylistic issues that we addressed earlier. Though style is important, there are other aspects of software engineering that are every bit as critical. These include:

- Product Specification

- Software Design

- Project Planning and Cost Estimation

- Software Tools for Software Production

- Debugging Techniques

- Testing

- Performance Analysis

- Documentation

- Source Control and Organization

To illustrate these principles, we are going to show the steps we performed to develop an *interpreter* for the C language. Unlike compilers, interpreters enable you to execute source code immediately after you write it, without going through the compilation and linking stages. On the downside, however, interpreted programs usually take longer to execute than compiled programs. For this reason, interpreters are often used in the development stage, where execution speed is less important than compilation time. When the program has been written and debugged, it is compiled to produce efficient executable code. Interpreters are also useful learning tools because of their interactive nature.

The interpreter we develop in this chapter is only a subset of a complete C interpreter. The techniques we use in its development illustrate principles that hold true for all large projects. See Appendix F for the complete listings of all modules described in this chapter.

Poor Programming Style	Good Programming Style
Putting **extern** declarations source files.	Putting **extern** declarations in .c in .h header files.
Sharing data among functions by making the data global.	Sharing data by passing arguments.
Giving data global scope when file scope would suffice.	Using **static** to give data and functions file scope.
Creating numerous special-purpose functions.	Creating fewer, more general primitives.
Using non-mnemonic names.	Using names that connote usage.
Using numeric constants.	Using named constants.
Using **goto**.	Using structured control flow statements.
Writing redundant code sequences.	Using functions for code sequences that are used repeatedly.

Table 12-1. Summary of Programming Style Issues.

12.1 Product Specification

To produce a quality software product, it is important that the product be well understood before the work starts. To ensure that everyone involved has the same idea about what the product is supposed to do, it is important to develop a detailed specification that describes exactly how the product is expected to behave. A *product specification* does not detail how the product is to be implemented (this is covered in a project plan). Instead, it describes how the final product will appear to users.

A product specification is useful to both users and project members. Users can tell early on whether the product will meet their needs. Project members will know just what their software is supposed to do. It is the responsibility of the product designers to make sure that no unreasonable expectations are set. Vague language such as "fast response" or "easy to use" should be avoided. "Fast" may mean ten minutes, a second, or less than a microsecond. How easy something is to use can be just as relative.

The two cardinal rules for product specifications are *consistency* and *simplicity*. To attain these goals, it is best if the specification is driven by one person. Committees are good for review but poor for design. This well-known truism is memorialized in the old joke that a camel is a horse designed by committee.

A specification of a software product can get complicated fast, so you should always be alert to signs of needless complexity. One indication of unnecessary complexity is the existence of several ways to perform the same operation. For instance, some software products have two commands—"date" and "time"—that perform the same operation. This may not create a programming problem, but it makes the user interface messy. It is confusing to users, who naturally assume that every command has a unique purpose.

Another sign of needless complexity is verbosity. This is especially true of interactive software products. For example, suppose your program needs a way to return the current date and set the date. Rather than create two commands to perform these operations, it is better to have one command, "date," that returns the date if there is no argument or sets the date if an argument is present:

```
$ date
1/29/87
$ date 1/30/87
$ date
1/30/87
```

Note that this is superior only for interactive products where readability is less important than succinctness and typing ease. For batch programs (programs that run without human interaction), readability is more important than succinctness. For a batch program, therefore, it would be better to define two commands, "getdate" and "setdate."

The ideal specification consists of a few primitive operations out of which all the user requirements can be met.

You shouldn't spend too much time on the initial specification. Typically, a specification receives feedback from the software design phase. As the product gets built, system limitations usually force the designers to rewrite the specification. When the product reaches the state where it can be run, experimentation usually results in changes to both the software design and the product specification.

Because of this feedback process, we advocate an evolutionary approach in which an executable prototype is developed as soon as the basic features of the specification and design are fairly firm. The prototype can then undergo enhancements in parallel with the addition of new features in the design specification. This method results in fewer surprises during the course of development because progress can be tracked by adding new levels of functionality. Each level is called a *milestone*.

Sometimes it is not clear what the set of primitives should be, especially when designing interactive programs. Parts of the product that drive the user interface, such as the assignment of edit functions to keys on the keyboard, should be designed with enough abstraction so that they can adapt to changes in the specification. There are even screen-design tools available that enable you to experiment with different user interfaces. This can make the product specification process much easier.

The product specification is usually the base document from which the final user documentation is created. As such, it is important that this be kept accurate and current.

A good outline for a specification is as follows:

1. Abstract of project.

2. Command line interface.

3. Input file syntax.

4. Screen design.

5. Output file format descriptions.

6. Interactive command language (if any).

7. Error messages.

8. Future extensions.

The specification for our C interpreter is shown below. This is a short specification. It benefits from pointing at specifications in other documents. Large projects, without benefit of prior specifications, may require hundreds, or even thousands, of pages to define product behavior.

1. Abstract

The intent of this project is to create an interpreter that supports a subset of the C language. It will support

- C scalar data types.

- Most C expressions.

- Some control-flow constructs.

A typical session with the interpreter might look like the session shown in Figure 12-1.

The goal is to write this interpreter in a way that illustrates the concepts of software engineering that would be used in projects many times larger than this one.

2. Command Line Interface

Unless a command line argument starts with the dash (–) character, it is treated as a source file. This file will be read and preparsed before the user receives a prompt. Any functions defined in the source files will be available to the user.

If a command line argument is prefixed with a dash character, it is parsed as an option flag to the interpreter. The valid option flags are:

–dlex	Enables debugging information for the lexical analyzer.
–dexp	Enables debugging information for the expression parser.
–dstmt	Enables debugging information for the statement parser.
–run	Runs the program as soon as it is read and exits when finished.

3. Input File Syntax

The input file format is a subset of the C language as specified by the ANSI Standard. The following subsections describe the supported subset.

3.1 Data Types

The interpreter supports the following scalar types: **char**, **short**, **int**, **long**, **float**, **double**, **void**, and pointers. Arrays of the scalar type are also supported.

The following are *not* supported: **typedef**s, structures, unions, and **enum**s.

3.2 Expressions

Precedence rules and conversion rules are as described by the ANSI Standard.

3.2.1 Constants

Fixed and floating-point constants are allowed as specified by the ANSI Standard. Double-quoted strings and single-quoted characters are allowed.

Long and unsigned constants are *not* supported.

3.2.2 Variables

Variables of up to 31 characters are supported with standard C naming conventions.

3.2.3 Operators

For the type **double**, the following C expression operators are supported: **sizeof**, =, +, – (unary), – (binary), *, /, <, >, <= ,> =, ==, !=, !, function call, and array reference.

For the type **int**, the following C expression operators are supported: **sizeof**, =, +, – (unary), – (binary), *, /, %, |, & (binary), ^, <, >, <=, >=, ==, !=, !, ++, —, >>, <<, ~, function call, and array reference.

The following operators are *not* supported: ?:, casts, ->, &&, ||, and . .

3.3 Statements

The following statement constructs are supported: expressions, **for**, **while**, **if**, **break**, **return**, and compound statements.

The following statement constructs are *not* supported: **switch**, **continue**, **goto**, **do...while**, and statement labels.

3.4 Preprocessor Directives

No preprocessor directives are supported.

3.5 Library Functions

The following runtime library functions are available: *printf()*, *scanf()*, *exit()*, *sin()*, *cos()*, *tan()*, *sqrt()*, *pow()*, *exp()*, *malloc()*, *free()*, *date()*, *ctime()*, *strcpy()*, *strcmp()*, *strcat()*.

4. Output File Specification

None.

5. Interactive Command Language

The interpreter supports a command language, as described in the following subsections.

5.1 Prompt

The prompt consists of the string "cint> ".

5.2 run Command

The **run** command starts execution of the procedure *main()*.

5.3 list Command

The **list** command displays the entire entered program to standard output.

5.4 Editing Capability

None.

5.5 Command Set

The complete C subset as described in Section 3 can be typed in from the console after all command-line files have been read in.

Additionally, any expression that does not parse as a declaration, or one of the extensions in Section 3.6, will be parsed as a C expression.

6. Errors

The interpreter supports the following diagnostic error messages. Italicized words represent parameters that are replaced by variable names or character strings.

1	Expected symbol *token*
2	Missing ']' in array declaration
3	Error in arg list. Wanted a symbol, not a *string*
4	Bad argument syntax
5	Can't have nested functions
6	Expected '{'
7	Missing '(' after function name
8	Missing ')' in function call
9	Missing ']'
10	Noninteger operand to '!'
11	Noninteger operand to '~'
12	Bad operand to '++'
13	Bad operand to '—'
14	Unmatched parentheses
15	Unexpected token in expression: *string*
16	Bad operand to '++'
17	Bad operand to '—'
18	Bad subscript expression
19	Missing ']' in array subscript

20	Illegal LHS to assign op
21	Unexpected token in expression: *'string'*
22	End of file before end of comment
23	No main function
24	Missing semicolon
25	Missing '(' after if
26	Missing ')' after if
27	Missing '(' after while
28	Missing ')' after while
29	Missing '(' after for
30	Missing ')' after for
31	Internal error in cint, premature token list end
32	Missing '}'
33	Bad function name *string*

12.2 Software Design

Once the product is specified, a plan of attack must be formulated. This involves deciding on the various phases of processing and the major data structures.

First, you should consult the library. There is a wealth of literature about data structures and algorithms for many different software disciplines. For instance, compiler technology has evolved to the point where it is well understood [see Aho & Ullman, *Principles of Compiler Design*]. Graphics software includes a rich set of common algorithms and data structures [see Foley & Van Dam, *Fundamentals of Interactive Graphics*]. Operating system design is well laid out in A. Tannenbaum's *Operating System Design*. Algorithms for database systems can be found in C. J. Date's *Database Design*. Other software disciplines are also documented to varying degrees. So to begin high level-design of a software product, you should first gain a good understanding of the problem and past solutions.

A common design method that we have found effective is called *stepwise refinement*, which was first enunciated by Niklaus Wirth in his 1971 CACM paper, *Program Development by Stepwise Refinement*. In this method, you carve up the problem at a high level of abstraction and then address each subproblem, dividing it into smaller, less abstract parts until each part can be easily implemented. The highest level of division is typically a program, though it may be a set of programs; at the next level, the program consists of cohesive sets of functions, called *modules*. A module consists of locally scoped (via the **static** keyword) support routines and globally visible interface routines. You should have one source file (which optionally includes header files) per module.

There are three basic phases to software design:

1. Identify major divisions of functionality (i.e., define what goes into each module).

2. Identify the major data structures that are shared by modules identified in Step 1.

3. Create an additional module for each data structure identified in Step 2.

Applying the first step in the design of our interpreter, we arrive at the modules shown in Table 12-2.

Module Name	Purpose
main.c	Read the command line and provide the starting point for the program.
lex.c	"Tokenize" the input (i.e., divide the input into meaningful C language tokens).
decl.c	Parse declarations.
expr.c	Parse and evaluate expressions.
sym.c	Manipulate symbols.
stmt.c	Parse and execute statements.

Table 12-2. List of Modules in the C Interpreter.

The goal in dividing a program into modules is to find clearly demarcated and cohesive sections that are not strongly interrelated with other sections. Once the modules are set forth, the same divide and conquer method that we used for determining modules can be used to decide upon the functions within a module. For example, *sym.c* includes functions to

*   Enter a symbol.

*   Find a symbol.

*   Get the type of a symbol.

*   Set the type of a symbol.

- Get the value of a symbol.

- Set the value of a symbol.

The fewer intermodule dependencies that exist, the easier the program is to read and maintain. Some of the modules we defined for our interpreter are similar to the chapters we chose for the book. This is not surprising since the same goals of clarity and cohesion guided our organization of this book.

In Steps 2 and 3 of the design process, we identified the major data structures required by each module and created additional modules to manage access to these structures:

token_st.c	Manage the data structure for the tokenized input stream.
sym.c	Manage the symbol table.
memory.c	Control access to program memory.

In addition to these modules, we created several header files that contain declarations and definitions used across modules.

Header Files

cint.h	Used by all modules.
sym.h	Defines values and data structures used by *sym*.
lex.h	Defines values and data structures used by *lex*.
token_st.h	Defines values and data structures used by *token_st*.

12.2.1 Choosing Efficient Data Structures and Algorithms

An important part of the design stage involves selecting appropriate data structures and efficient algorithms for accessing the data structures. There a number of factors to consider when designing data structures and algorithms. How fast is the algorithm in processing typical data? How much memory will the structure require? Will it be easy to change if we want to add new capabilities? In this section, we give a taste of what's involved in resolving these issues by discussing the symbol table in *cint*.

The *symbol table* is the data structure which holds information about each variable that is declared in a program. We need to know the variable's name, its data type, its storage class, and its location in memory. All of this information is stored in a structure named *SYM*.

Given N number of symbols declared in a program, we need a way of organizing the *SYM* structures so that they can be easily accessed. The most obvious organization scheme is a linked list. Each time a new symbol is declared, we add an element to the list. Unfortunately, searching through a linked list for a particular element is relatively inefficient. In the best case, the element we want will be the first element in the list. But in the worst case, it will be the last element, which means we will have to look at N elements before we find the right one. On average, the number of look-ups to find a particular element is $N/2$, which is not very good.

A better way to organize the symbol elements is in the form of a binary tree. In Chapter 5, we introduced binary trees as a way to parse expressions, but binary trees are also widely used to store symbol tables. In this method, each symbol has two branches coming off it—a left branch and a right branch. The left points to all symbols that are alphabetically before the node and right branch points to all symbols that are alphabetically after the node.

Table 12-1 shows a binary tree for 15 symbols. In the case of a binary tree, the maximum number of look-ups is the same as the number of levels in the tree. To find x, for instance, we need to go through *pf*, *sub_s*, and *var*. Note that the number of symbols on each level is 2 to the m power, where m is the level number. If the number of symbols is N, therefore, the maximum number of levels (and hence look-ups) is $log_2 N$. This is considerably better than N, which is the maximum number of look-ups for the linked-list method.

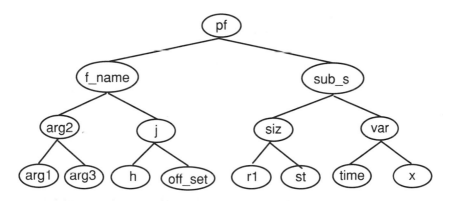

Figure 12-1.   Balanced Binary Tree Implementation of a Symbol Table.

Note, however, that the number of levels is $log^2 N$ only if the tree is *balanced*—that is, if each node has the same number of nodes below it on the left as on the right. If the tree is unbalanced, as in Figure 12-2, the maximum number of look-ups approaches N again. In fact, a tree that is completely unbalanced is identical to a simple linked list. It is a difficult task to keep a tree balanced as you add symbols to it. (We leave it as an exercise to the reader to design an algorithm that turns an unbalanced tree into a balanced tree.)

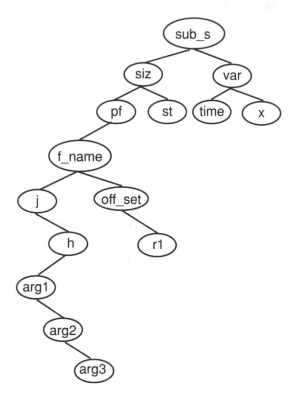

Figure 12-2.   Unbalanced Binary Tree Implementation of a Symbol Table.

Because it is hard keep a binary tree balanced, it is often better to use an alternative method called a *hash table*. A hash table is an array of pointers, each of which typically points to the beginning of a linked list. Each symbol is assigned to one of the linked lists. To determine which linked list a symbol is assigned to, you need to convert the symbol name into an integer that serves as the subscript to the array. For example, the symbol name *var* might be converted to the integer value 5, which would then be used as the subscript for the array of pointers. *var* would be stored somewhere in the linked list pointed to by element 5 of the array.

Ideally, each linked list should be short so that once the array subscript is determined, the number of look-ups is minimal. In a very sparse hash table, for example, each linked list contains only one or two elements, so the maximum number of look-ups is two. Note, however, that you must allocate space for the entire array at the start of the program. It is sometimes impractical, therefore, to create an array large enough to ensure that the hash table will always be sparse. Also, it is important to convert the symbol names into integers in such a way that the resulting integer values are spread evenly across the range of subscript values. The following function is a good hash function that returns a number between 0 and *HASHSIZE* based on the values of all the characters in the symbol name. Experience has shown that this function produces a uniform distribution.

```
#define HASHSIZE 211   /* The size of the table
                        * should be a prime number.
                        */
int hash_function( p )
  char *p;
{
  int hash_val = 0;

  for (; *p; p++)
    hash_val = hash_val * 65599 + *p;
  hash_val %= HASHSIZE
  return hash_val;
}
```

Assuming that symbols are evenly distributed throughout the hash table, the maximum number of look-ups is simply N/h, where h is the size of the table. For example, if there are 400 symbols and 200 linked lists, each linked list will contain two entries, so the maximum number of look-ups will be two. In practice, the symbols are never distributed this evenly, but the number of look-ups is still likely to be smaller than in a binary tree model. Note, however, that there is a random element to hash tables that makes it impossible to predict in a deterministic way exactly how efficient it will be. It takes some trial–and– error testing to arrive at the ideal size for the table and the best algorithm for producing a uniform distribution of symbols.

This discussion barely touches the surface of searching algorithms, but it does show that you need to devote considerable thought and research to choosing efficient algorithms at the design stage. For more information about this subject, we recommend the third volume ("Searching and Sorting Algorithms") of *The Art of Computer Programming*, by Donald E. Knuth. Another good book on this subject is *Design and Analysis of Computer Algorithms* by Aho, Hopcroft, and Ullman.

Regardless of what algorithm you select, you should implement the data struc-ture so that it can be easily modified for different algorithms. In our version of *cint*, for example, we use a simple and inefficient linked-list organization for the symbol table. But the symbol table is a well-abstracted module in that it hides its implementation from the other parts of the product. Given this abstract interface, it is relatively easy to modify the program to use a more efficient searching algorithm. We pose this enhancement as an exercise for the reader.

12.2.2 Information Hiding

To control software complexity, it is often useful to limit the amount of information that each module can "see." Each module "owns" certain data objects on which it operates. The ability to operate on an object implies an understanding of the object's internal structure. A module should give other modules enough information to properly declare common objects, but not so much information that the other modules can also operate on the objects. Developing mechanisms to isolate objects from external modules is a software engineering technique known as *information hiding*. Information hiding makes it easier to modify a data structure because only one module is dependent on the internal organization of the object.

There are a number of ways to implement information hiding. We have borrowed a notion called *private types* from the Ada programming language. Private types expose enough information about data structures so that other modules can declare them properly for type-checking purposes but cannot access the data structures.

In C, we implement private types by conditionally compiling two declarations of the symbol data structure in *sym.h*. The detailed declaration is compiled for the *sym.c* module, while a deliberately vague declaration is compiled for other modules. The detailed declaration is compiled only if the macro *SYM_OWNER* is defined to expand to a nonzero value (it is defined in *sym.c*, but not in the other modules):

```
struct _private_type_sym
{
  char *sym_name;
  VALUE sym_value;
};

#if SYM_OWNER
  typedef struct _private_type_sym SYM;
#else
  typedef struct {
   char _x[sizeof struct _private_sym];
  } SYM;
#endif
```

If *SYM_OWNER* is defined, *SYM* is declared as a structure with two members, *sym_name* and *sym_value*. If *SYM_OWNER* is not defined, *SYM* is declared as a structure with an array of char. In either case, the size of *SYM* is the same, so there won't be conflicts. External modules, however, will not be able to access the module through the member names.

12.3 Project Management and Cost Estimation

Like any construction endeavor, creation of software requires management of the necessary people and resources. Management will be effective only if there is, at the outset, a good understanding of the costs in terms of people, time, and computing power. In this section, we discuss techniques for estimating these costs and providing effective management.

A seminal work on the software engineering process is *The Mythical Man-Month* by Dr. Fredrick P. Brooks. Dr. Brooks describes the pitfalls and obstacles he experienced in the development of IBM's OS/360, a large operating system that runs on IBM's 360 series of mainframes. Despite the fact that it was written 15 years ago, and despite the many advances made in software production since that time, many of Brooks' observations are still valid today.

Unlike other engineering disciplines, software is pure abstraction. As Dr. Brooks points out, a programmer "builds his castles in the air, from air, creating by exertion of the imagination." The civil engineer at least knows the distance his bridge has to span. From that he has a rough estimate of the bricks or steel beams required to make his bridge. With software there are no physical parameters to measure against. The only guides are previous attempts at solving similar problems.

Brooks recommends that you plan to throw away the first attempt, since it's likely to be worthless. Fortunately, there is more literature available today on various software efforts than there was in 1972 when Brooks wrote of his experiences, so the first attempt is often salvageable. Still, there is no substitute for having done it before.

Brooks, based on his experience as IBM's O/S 360 project manager, claims that most software product schedules can be broken down as follows:

1/3 product specification and scheduling personnel

1/6 coding

1/4 component testing and early system testing

1/4 complete system integration and testing

Our experience in the production of compilers, editors, and debuggers supports this contention. If the schedule does not allow for 50% debugging and testing time, you will be faced with the choice of shipping a poor-quality product or delaying shipment in order to properly test and debug the system.

When scheduling the development of a large product, you need to have a good understanding of all the major parts of the product. One of the arts in explaining difficult concepts is in finding the right way to split the concept into smaller, more easily digested parts. It is exactly this partitioning that a project manager must perform. Ideally, the parts should be well-defined tasks, with little need for communication with the rest of the product. Additionally, each task should require no more than one person. When people have to spend time disputing large, ill-defined interfaces between sections, a lot of time and energy is wasted. If the parts are not well selected and time has to be spent later in the project to repartition and hire and train more personnel, the project is likely to run way past its target date.

The phenomenon of losing time due to the overhead of training more people and choosing bad partitions gives rise to Brooks' law:

Adding more people to a late software project makes it later.

Partitioning allows each engineer to concentrate on his or her particular section of the product. It is important to keep the amount of interaction between one partition and other partitions to a minimum so that development of different partitions can occur simultaneously. This is the notion of *modularity*. While modularity may result in redundant code across modules, it allows everyone to get on with their end of the effort without wasting time in endless design meetings.

Tracking a project's progress can be a bit tricky. Initial progress is generally quite fast. As complexity builds, however, progress slows down. Our experience has shown that most products follow the development curve shown in Figure 12-3. In fact, as the curve suggests, by the time 90% of the functionality is in place, you are still only halfway to a shippable product.

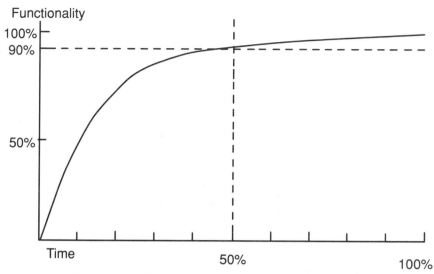

Figure 12-3. Typical Software Development Curve.

12.3.1 Project Planning

For scheduling purposes a project plan should be created that explains how the project is to be fulfilled. The project plan breaks down the task into manageable subtasks and gives time estimates for each subtask. Dependencies and milestones are mentioned as well. The granularity of such a schedule is usually a staff-week. There are various software products available to help with just this sort of scheduling.

A common pitfall of software design is known as the *NIH* (Not Invented Here) syndrome. This refers to a tendency among some engineers to feel that if a product or subsystem was not invented by members of the design team, it can't be any good. There are many high-quality software companies that will sell sources for all kinds of software products. A part of a responsible software design plan should include the option of buying part or all of the system from another source.

A good outline for a project plan is as follows:

1. Abstract

2. Itemization of subtasks and time estimates

3. Time lines and milestones (pert chart)

4. Resource requirements (people, computers, disk storage, special hardware)

5. Other projects this project depends on

6. Other projects that depend on this project working

As an illustration, the following shows our project plan for the C interpreter.

1. Abstract

This document details a plan for implementing the product specification for the "Cint" C subset interpreter.

2. Itemization of subtasks and time estimates

The following modules need to be written:

Module	Time Estimate
memory manager	0.5 weeks
lexical analyzer	2.0 weeks
symbol table handler	2.0 weeks
main (reads command line and handles file open/close)	1.0 weeks
expression handler	4.0 weeks
token stream manager	2.0 weeks
declaration parser	1.0 weeks
statement parser	1.0 weeks
debug & test	13.0 weeks
total time	26.5 weeks

3. Time lines and milestones (pert chart)

The overlap of some of the modules in Figure 12-4 indicates that some modules can be developed simultaneously. The overall time for project completion, therefore, can be decreased by adding staff. It is clear from the figure that an additional programmer would cut our development time in half.

4.   **Resources required**

Machine: Any system that supports a C compiler and *make* utility (for example, any UNIX system or MS/DOS system)
Software: A C compiler and *make* utility.
Programmers: 1
Disk storage: 10 megabytes of hard-disk storage

5.   **Other projects this project depends on**

None.

6.   **Other projects that depend on this project**

Publication of this book *Software Engineering in C* depends on the successful completion of this project.

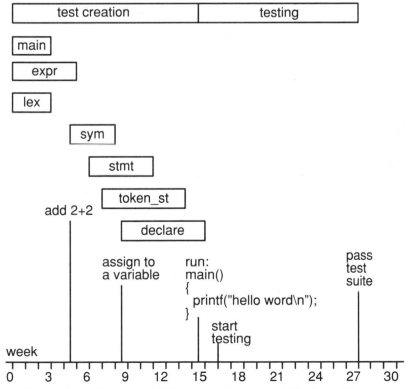

Figure 12-4.   *Time Lines and Milestones for the* cint *Project. The lines coming up from the horizontal time line indicate major milestones.*

12.3.2 Source Management

For a large software product with many subsystems and modules and more than one programmer, it is important to organize the source files so that people don't get in each other's way. A good organization scheme is to create a directory for each subsystem and a directory for subsystem include files. For instance, if our interpreter included an editor and debugger as subsystems, its source-file directory structure would look like Figure 12-5.

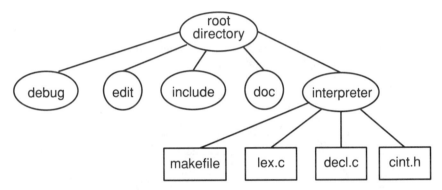

*Figure 12-5.   Directory Structure for C Interpreter Project Containing
Debug and Edit Subsystems.*

During development of the product, a version of the source tree is stored in a publicly accessible place. To work on particular files, an individual makes copies of the files, edits the private copies, and generates a private copy of the product using the public object files combined with the newly modified private object files. After testing the private version to make sure that the changes are correct, the modified source files are copied back into the public source tree, replacing the older files.

A source-control system can be extremely useful in managing the source tree. A source-control utility maintains a log of changes to a source file and a status of the file. For example, it keeps track of whether the file is logged out for editing and who logged it out. That way, two people can't accidentally edit the same file at the same time and enter incompatible changes. The change history is useful for removing ill-conceived features or discovering what change has caused the latest bug. Under UNIX, *sccs* is a popular source-control utility.

It is common for bugs to be introduced into a product by programmers who change one part of the program without realizing how the change will affect other parts of the product. For this reason, it is important that you record changes to source files. When new bugs crop up, the first place to look is in recently changed files.

12.4   Software Tools for Software Production

A C compiler, as we have discussed in the prior 11 chapters, is a software tool for software production, as are editors and debuggers. A full C interpreter is also a valuable software tool for debugging because it shortens the compile-edit-debug cycle. There are a number of other tools that are helpful for efficient software production. In fact, there is an entire industry, called Computer-Aided Software Engineering (CASE), that develops utilities to facilitate software production. The UNIX operating system includes the following utilities:

flow	Analyzes the function call tree.
grep	Finds every occurrence of a name in a set of files and prints out the file name and line containing the match.
lint	Examines C source files to detect potential bugs and nonportable constructs.
prof	Pinpoints CPU-expensive parts of a program.

Most computer systems sold today also have source-code control and automatic product-build software tools available. These tools are indispensable for building large software systems. A well-known source code control system under the UNIX system is *sccs*. An even more famous UNIX software build utility is known as *make*. A good book on using and building software tools is *Software Tools* by Kernighan and Plauger.

12.4.1 Automatic Product Building

The idea behind automatic product building is that a single file describes how the parts of a product combine to make the final set of programs. For example, it lists the object files that need to be built, lists the header files that each object file depends on, and describes how the object files are to be linked together to create an executable image. More important, the build file lists dependencies for each object file. When any file is out of date with respect to the final product, only the parts of the product that need to be rebuilt are processed.

The instructions for building a product are stored in a file called a *build file*. The build file serves two purposes: first, it specifies the minimum amount of work required to build a product; and second, it acts as a design document, detailing the dependencies and build rules for a product.

An automatic build utility also helps prevent *version skew*, a problem that occurs when an object file compiled with obsolete header files is linked with more current modules.

The UNIX *make* utility gets its instructions for building programs from a build file named *makefile*. The *makefile* for *cint* follows:

```
#  makefile for cint - a subset C interpreter
OBJECTS = expr.o lex.o sym.o main.o token_st.o \
          stmt.o declare.o memory.o
CFLAGS = -DDEBUG=1
cint:  $(OBJECTS)
            cc -o cint $(OBJECTS)
$(OBJECTS): cint.h lex.h sym.h token_st.h
# end of makefile
```

The first line is a comment describing the makefile (the pound sign (#) signifies a comment). The second line is a macro definition that associates the name *OBJECTS* with the names of the files to the right of the equal sign. In this case, the files are the objects required to build *cint*. The fourth line is another macro definition. *CFLAGS* holds the command line flags that are to be used when the make utility produces a C compile command line. In this case, the *–DDE-BUG=1* option tells the C compiler to compile as if the line

```
#define DEBUG 1
```

were inserted as the first line of the program.

The lines with colons in them are called *dependency lines*. The filenames on the left-hand side of the colon depend on the filenames on the right-hand side. For example, the line

```
cint: $(OBJECTS)
```

means that the executable file *cint* depends on all of the object files. The notation

```
$(OBJECTS)
```

expands the macro *OBJECTS*. If the line following a dependency starts with a tab, it is treated as a command to be issued by *make* whenever any of the objects on the right-hand side of a dependency line are newer than the object on the left-hand side. The command line in our example is

```
cc -o cint $(OBJECTS)
```

If there is no command line present, *make* uses default rules for issuing commands that create files of one suffix type from files of another suffix type. For instance, when make detects that a *.c* file is newer than a *.o* file, it invokes its default rule for building *.o* files from *.c* files:

```
cc -c changed-file.c
```

which creates *changed–file.o.*

To see how *make* works, assume you just edited *sym.c* to fix a bug. When you type "make," *make* reads *makefile* and notices that *cint* is dependent on a number of files, including *sym.o.* Because *sym.o* does not occur on the left-hand side of a ':' in the makefile,, *make* uses its built-in default dependency rules to determine that *sym.o* must be dependent on *sym.c.* When it checks the *file modified dates,* *make* discovers that *sym.c* is newer than *sym.o.* Make then uses its default build rule for turning *.c* files into *.o* files and issues the command

```
cc -c -DDEBUG sym.c
```

Now *make* determines that *cint* is older than *sym.o,* and since, from the makefile, cint depends on sym.o, it issues the command given in the makefile to build cint:

```
cc -o cint expr.o lex.o sym.o main.o token_st.o\
        stmt.o declare.o
```

which creates *cint* out of the latest versions of all the objects.

12.5 Debugging

Not even the best, most experienced programmers write bug-free code on their first try. A large part of programming, therefore, consists of finding and fixing *bugs.* The original computer "bug" was a moth caught in the electromechanical switches of the Mark II computer and discovered there by Lieutenant Grace Hopper in 1945. The term bug has come to mean any erroneous behavior of a computer system. Nowadays though, most bugs are caused by problems in software, not hardware. The process of finding and fixing bugs is known as *debugging.*

Once the development phase of a project is under way, the edit-compile-debug cycle becomes the norm. Most products, if they become successful, eventually fall into a *maintenance mode,* where they spend most of their useful life.

There are three laws of debugging:

1. *All complex software has bugs.*

2. *The bug is probably caused by the last thing you touched.*

3. *If the bug isn't where you are looking, it's somewhere else.*

The first law reflects the insidious nature of algorithms to grow exponentially more complex as they gain added functionality. The second law reflects the opposing natures of computers and human beings—computers require painful attention to detail; humans are prone to err. The third law is inspired by the human tendency to stick to first impressions. For instance, you may be convinced that your bug is caused by the second law, but after an exhaustive search you still can't find it. Obviously, you need to look elsewhere. Although this is obvious to the dispassionate reader, it is often not so clear to the frustrated programmer.

Debugging is an art that requires patience and ingenuity, but most of all, experience. The first step in fixing a bug is to isolate the erroneous behavior. Frequently, news of a bug comes from a user in the form: "It doesn't work." This general comment needs to be pinpointed to something like: "After I type *run*, it prints the first variable and then hangs."

The important point is that you, the programmer doing the debugging, must be able to reproduce the bug at your console. If at all practical, this means using exactly the same input as the person who reported the bug.

When it isn't obvious from examination of the user input why a product fails, you should rely on internal product debug information. This is usually available through a command line option that is not divulged to the general public. Our C interpreter, for example, contains three such debug options. If the answer still eludes you, an interactive debugger is the answer.

12.5.1 Software Maintenance and Entropy

Maintenance of physical objects, like bridges and cars, refers to periodic replacement of worn-out parts. This tendency of mechanisms to wear out and work less well over time is an example of a general principle known as *entropy*. Entropy embodies the second law of thermodynamics, which can be paraphrased: *all systems tend to become less ordered over time.*

Though software does not "wear out" like physical objects, it is equally susceptible to the effects of entropy. Software products often suffer the effects of fast employee turnover or rapid expansion. As new engineers join a project, they need to become familiar with the product before they can make substantial contributions. It is not unusual for bugs to be created by engineers who have only a partial understanding of the product. Obviously, this problem can be mitigated by readable code and good documentation.

Another entropic phenomenon that affects software is the tendency to add too many bells and whistles to a product. As a software product becomes more popular, its user community grows, and so also grows the number of suggestions for new features. There is a great temptation to add as many of these features as possible, but you need to consider how the new features will affect the overall program. Adding new features usually means that the program will run slower and will require more system resources. In addition, new features can make a product more difficult to learn, use, and maintain. You should carefully consider these potential drawbacks before adding new features to a stable product.

Bugs aside, the *completeness* or *orderedness* of a software product can only be measured relative to the environment in which it operates. That is, does it run on the right hardware, does it have sufficient speed and power, is it easy to use, is it cost-competitive? By itself, a software product might be bug free, and if it were not touched it could remain bug free till doomsday. But the environment in which it operates is constantly changing, and the product must change with it. Maintenance of software products, therefore, is a constant struggle to keep up with an ever-changing industry.

12.5.2 Debuggers

Debugging tools are available at various levels, from assembler to high-level source language. Most compilers sold today come with a full debugging system. Source-level debuggers are the easiest to use. They allow you to put breakpoints on source lines and set and examine local and global variables when program execution reaches a breakpoint. Some allow you to step through a program one source line at a time, examining variable values as you go. However, this mode of attack is often too slow to be truly useful. The art of debugging is knowing what is useful information and what isn't.

12.6 Testing

A product is only as good as its test system. In fact, the process of testing and validating software systems is a discipline in its own right. Throughout development, testing is done to ensure that each module performs as expected. The tests themselves may consist of ANSI-sanctioned validation suites, customer benchmarks, commercial test suites, tests developed by the development team, and a set of tests that probe for the existence of prior bugs that are claimed to have been fixed. Commercially available suites consist of input data and a convenient control and analysis system that automates the test and summarizes results. Such test systems may take days to complete.

There are two major test phases of the complete product before it is ready to ship to users: *alpha test* and *beta test.*

The alpha test consists of testing performed by the development team and others within the organization for the express purpose of turning up any bugs in the final product. Once a product has entered alpha test, the code for that version of the product should be frozen. The only changes to the software should be bug fixes. Source-code control systems are a big help in maintaining version integrity.

The beta test refers to a phase of testing that allows select customers to try out the new product before it is made available to the general public. These customers should be people who understand that in return for newer and better products, they are accepting a bit of risk that the product still contains significant bugs. The beta-test phase begins when the alpha test is complete, or far enough along to guarantee a large measure of reliability.

The point of a beta test is to make sure that the product will function properly in "real life." For instance, most test systems only test that the system behaves properly when fed correct input. Proper diagnosis and treatment of erroneous input can be essential to a usable product.

12.6.1 Test Engineering

Most software engineering organizations have a group dedicated to testing that is responsible for final acceptance of products. This group creates, maintains, and runs test suites and has the power to delay shipping a product if it decides the product is not dependable.

Test engineering is a challenging part of software engineering. It is not enough to write tests that cover every aspect of a product. The tests must be sophisticated enough to pinpoint problem areas when a failure occurs. Though the tests themselves are not shipped with a product, the quality of the test system is directly reflected in the quality of the final product.

12.7 Performance Analysis

Since the main thrust of a development effort is toward modularity and correctness, it is possible that execution speed may suffer. To some degree, this is to be expected, although even in the design stages you should be careful to choose efficient high-level algorithms. No amount of trickery can compensate for an algorithm that is fundamentally slow. However, it is much easier to pinpoint bottlenecks (places where the program spends much of its time) after the program is working than to predict in advance where the bottlenecks will lie. It is unwise, therefore, to devote much of the initial design to low-level efficiency.

A common feature of C compilers is an option known as *profiling*. This refers to the ability to count each function call made and keep track of the amount of time spent in each function. The program is compiled with the profiling option and run with some typical input. The profiler then generates a data file that contains the call frequency and duration. A profile display program reads the data file and prints out a formatted analysis. This analysis shows immediately the functions in which the program spends most of its time. This allows you to focus your tuning efforts on the trouble spots.

Some systems support a more fine-grained analysis that works across arbitrary code segments. This allows you to pinpoint CPU-hungry lines within functions.

Common bottlenecks in programs that use heap storage are *malloc()* and *free()*. If extensive use is made of *malloc()* and *free()*, the internal list of free blocks can contain large amounts of fragmented sized data. Most programs use only a handful of different-sized data types. It is often possible, therefore, to gain a significant increase in speed by writing a program that keeps its own free list array, with a list for each commonly used type.

12.8 Documentation

Up to now, we have focused on internal documentation. Equally important to the success of the project, however, is the documentation that goes to the end user. Typically, end-user documentation is written by one or more professional technical writers. A good technical writer combines a rare talent for clear writing with a grasp of computer technology and is indispensable in any software endeavor.

The technical writer should become involved in the project at an early date and may actually help write the product and design specifications. It is in the interest of both the technical writer and the developers to produce specifications that are well written and accurate. The technical writer uses them as base documents from which to write more polished end-user documentation.

If the technical writer cannot find the answer to a question in one the specifications, he or she has two options:

1. Test the product itself, if it's available.

2. Ask the developers for the information.

Both approaches have advantages and disadvantages. The advantage of the first approach is that the writer actually tests the product. This testing may turn up unexpected behavior unknown to the developers, including bugs. Moreover, it ensures that the writer will be familiar with the product and will document exactly what the user will see. The disadvantage of this approach is that it is time-consuming. Also, a reliable version of the product may not be available until it's too late.

The main advantage of the second approach is that it is fast. Also, by asking the developer for information, the writer implies that the information is not available in the specs. This may be an oversight that the developers should address. There are two disadvantages to this approach. First, the developer may give the technical writer erroneous information. Second, time taken to answer questions is time not spent programming. Usually, these disadvantages go hand in hand since a busy programmer may give offhand and incorrect answers just to mollify an inquisitive tech writer.

One documentation technique that we have found effective is for the technical writer to write a rough draft of the manual(s), inserting notes and question marks where there is confusion. The developers can then review this draft at their leisure rather than being periodically interrupted with isolated questions. The more draft versions a document undergoes, the better the final version will be.

An alternative strategy is for the programmer to write the initial draft and have the tech writer edit it. Our own experience has proven that this technique is effective only if the programmer is a talented writer and is motivated to write a high-quality initial draft.

To produce quality documentation, a tech writer should make use of all the resources available—specifications, versions of the product itself, and developers. For their part, the developers must understand that the quality of the documentation will affect the ultimate success or failure of the product. Tech writers cannot perform their jobs without the developers' cooperation.

Exercises

1. Find five bugs in the sample C interpreter, *cint* (listed in Appendix F), and fix them. Be sure to include test programs that detect the presence of the bug.

2. Add the "op=" operators to *exp.c* in *cint*.

3. Write a specification and project plan for one of the following projects:

   a) Add preprocessor directives to lex.c in *cint*.

   b) Give the list command an optional file name so that the listing can be sent to the file.

   c) Add unsigned data types.

   d) Add switch statements and the **?:** operator to *cint*.

   e) Add casts to *cint*.

   f) Add structures and unions to *cint*.

   g) Write a screen-oriented editor front-end to *cint*, so that you can edit the token stream directly.

   h) Create a breakpoint facility that allows you to stop at any source line and examine and set the values of local and global variables.

4. Profile *cint* or some other program to which you have the source, identify the bottlenecks, and suggest ways of speeding up the program.

5. Write a specification for and develop a library of graphics calls that can draw lines, squares, triangles, and circles of arbitrary size. Be sure to use a consistent naming convention and argument placement. Use the library to make a pretty picture.

6. Write a program to solve the three queens problem. (How do you put three queens on a chess board such that no piece threatens another?)

7. Implement the symbol table (modules *sym.c* and *sym.h* of *cint*) as a binary tree.

8. Implement the symbol table as a hash tree.

9. Assuming that a binary tree holds a list of symbols arranged alphabeti-
    cally (as in the examples on pages 385 and 386), write a function that
    prints all of the symbols in alphabetic order. Hint: Use recursion.

10. Write a function that balances an unbalanced binary tree. The function
    should accept one argument, which is a pointer to the top of the binary
    tree. How efficient is your algorithm?

11. Write a program to solve the following problem, called the *traveling
    salesman problem*. A salesman wants to travel to five cities in such an
    order that the total number of miles traveled is minimized. Using the
    5×5 multidimensional array shown below, which represents distances
    between the five cities, write a program that finds the shortest route.

```
int distances[5][5] = {
/* NY */            {   0, 300, 150,  400, 500},
/* Boston */        {300,   0, 150,  700, 800 },
/* Hartford */      {150, 150,   0,  500, 700 },
/* DC */            {400, 700, 500,    0, 450 },
/* Cleveland */     {500, 800, 700,  450,   0 }
            }; /*    NY, Bos, Hart, DC, Cleve.
*/
```

12. If *N* represents the number of cities in the traveling salesman problem,
    how efficient is your algorithm in terms of operations per *N*? Note that
    there is no known efficient solution for this problem. Problems such as
    these are known as *NP-complete*.

Appendix A

The ANSI Runtime Library

Until recently, each compiler manufacturer delivered its own unique library of runtime routines and there was little effort toward standardization. This state of affairs wreaked havoc on programmers trying to write portable code. There was no guarantee that a program using library functions from one compiler manufacturer would still run when ported to another machine. With ratification of the ANSI Standard, this situation should improve.

The task of deriving a single set of routines, however, was no simple matter. The ANSI Committee was faced with literally dozens of existing functions, many with the same names but with different effects. One of the committee's main goals was to break as little existing code as possible. The result was a somewhat larger and less consistent library than anyone really desired. Nevertheless, once you learn some of its subtleties and quirks, the ANSI C library becomes a remarkably powerful tool.

The main source for the routines in the ANSI library is the UNIX operating system. Many of the functions supported by ANSI are exactly the same as those supported by System V and BSD4.2, while others are very similar. As of this writing, AT&T, in conjunction with the UNIX Standard IEEE Committee, appears committed to bringing its library into accord with the ANSI Standard.

A.1 Function Names

All library function names are reserved as external identifiers. Therefore, you cannot define a name that matches a library name, even if you are defining a function that performs the same operation. Likewise, all identifiers beginning with an underscore are reserved for behind-the-scenes macros. Appendix C provides a complete list of reserved names.

A.2 Header Files

In addition to the functions themselves, the C runtime library comes with a set of include files called *header files*. Every function is associated with one or more header files that must be included wherever the function is invoked. These files contain the declarations for any related functions, macros, or data types needed to execute a set of library functions. Table A-1 lists the standard header files. Note that some of these header files may not be available with your compiler if it is not ANSI-conforming.

The ANSI Standard guarantees that the header files are *idempotent*. This means that multiple inclusions of the same header file will not have adverse effects and you can include header files in any order.

A.3 Synopses

The form of each function and the header file it requires are provided in a format called a *synopsis*. The synopsis format is taken from UNIX documentation and has the following form:

```
#include header_file
function_prototype
```

For example, the following is the synopsis for the function *gets()*, which reads a string from standard input:

```
#include <stdio.h>
char *gets(char *s);
```

Header File	Associated Functions
<assert.h>	Diagnostic functions (currently just the *assert()* macro).
<ctype.h>	Character testing and mapping functions.
<errno.h>	Defines several macros related to error reporting: *EDOM*, *ERANGE*, and *errno*.
<float.h>	Defines a number of macros that describe the characteristics of floating-point objects in the environment (see Appendix D).
<limits.h>	Contains parameter values that describe the execution environment (see Appendix D).
<locale.h>	The *setlocale()* function, which enables you to set locale parameters.
<math.h>	Double-precision mathematics functions.
<setjmp.h>	The *setjmp()* and *longjmp()* functions, which enable you to bypass the normal function call and return discipline.
<signal.h>	Functions that handle signals.
<stdarg.h>	Functions and macros for implementing functions that accept a variable number of arguments.
<stddef.h>	This is a new header file that contains definitions of five macros: *ptrdiff_t*, *size_t*, *NULL*, *wchar_t*, *offsetof*, and *errno*. These macros are also defined in any header file declaring functions that use them.
<stdio.h>	I/O functions.
<stdlib.h>	General utility functions.
<string.h>	String manipulation functions.
<time.h>	Time manipulation functions.

Table A-1. Header Files for the Runtime Library.

This tells you that you must include the header file *<stdio.h>* and that *gets()* takes one argument that is a pointer to a **char** and returns a pointer to a **char**. To use *gets()* in a program, you would include the line

```
#include <stdio.h>
```

in your source file. You do not need to declare *gets()* since any necessary declarations are performed in the header file. The angle brackets enclosing the filename inform the compiler to search for the header file in a system-defined location. So long as your C compiler is installed as directed by the vendor, you should not need to worry about the real location of the header files.

It is also possible to declare a library function explicitly without referring to a header file. To declare *gets()*, for instance, you could write

```
extern char *gets( char * );
```

However, this can be a dangerous practice for a couple of reasons. First, the function you declare may refer to other functions or macros that are defined in the header file. If you don't include the header file, the function may not work. Second, the library function may have a macro implementation that runs faster than the real function. By declaring it as a function, you force the system to use the function version, which makes your program less efficient. For these reasons, we recommend that you always include whatever header files are indicated in the synopsis.

A.4 Functions vs. Macros

As described in Chapter 9, it is often possible to implement a function more efficiently as a macro. Most C compiler developers take advantage of this capability by implementing many of the library functions as macros. However, since this introduces some potential side effect problems, the ANSI Standard enforces some restrictions to protect you. First, the ANSI Standard ensures that in any macro implementation, an argument is expanded once and only once. This avoids the pitfalls associated with side effect operators in the argument expression (see Box 10-6). Second, the ANSI Standard guarantees that there is an actual function for each library function listed. This enables you to take the address of any library function. (*getc()* and *putc()* are exceptions to both these rules.)

In many cases, there exist both a function and a macro that perform the same operation. By default, the macro gets executed since it is usually faster. If you want to execute the function instead, you can explicitly **#undef** the macro. The following examples illustrate this principle.

**Example 1 — Using the function as defined in the header file (it
may be a macro or it may be a function)**

```
#include <stdio.h>
        .
        .
s = gets(s);
        .
        .
```

Example 2 — Forcing use of a function instead of a macro

```
#include <stdio.h>
#undef gets
        .
        .
s = gets(s);
        .
        .
```

A.5 Error Handling

Most library functions return a special value when an error occurs. The error
value differs from routine to routine and is listed in the description of each
individual function. The special macro *NULL* is often returned as an error value
for functions that return pointers. It is an implementation-defined null pointer
constant. *NULL* is defined in all header files that require it.

In some cases, in addition to returning an error value, a function also assigns a
special error code to a global variable (or macro) called *errno*. *errno* is declared
in the *<errno.h>* header file and has type **int**. For most implementations of C,
each possible *errno* value is associated with an error message that you can output
with the *perror()* function. You can also assign the error message to a string with
the *strerror()* function.

A.6 Diagnostics

The C runtime library contains one header file and one macro for outputting diagnostics. In addition, there are several preprocessor symbols and commands that can be utilized to print diagnostic information (see Chapter 11). The header file is called *<assert.h>*. It defines a macro called *assert* and refers to another macro called *NDEBUG*. *NDEBUG*, however, is not defined by *<assert.h>*. In fact, if *NDEBUG* is defined when *<assert.h>* is included, then all subsequent calls to *assert()* will have no effect. Hence, *NDEBUG* provides a useful mechanism for turning off diagnostics, as illustrated in the following example.

```
#define NDEBUG
#include <assert.h>

/* calls to assert() will have no effect */
                 .
                 .
```

A.6.1 The *assert()* Function

```
#include <assert.h>
void assert( int expression );
```

According to the ANSI Standard, *assert()* must be implemented as a macro. The *assert()* macro tests the value of *expression*. If it is nonzero, no action is taken, and zero is returned. If *expression* equals zero, *assert()* writes information about the program's current status to *stderr* and then calls *abort()*. The diagnostic information contains the value of the expression, the current source file name, and the current line number. The latter two values are taken from the preprocessor symbols *__FILE__* and *__LINE__*. The *assert()* macro is used most frequently to test the status of a function call. For instance,

```
/*  If fopen() returns zero, send status
 * information to stderr, and abort.
 */
  assert( fp = fopen( "file","r" ) );
```

Note, however, that *fopen()* will not even be invoked if *NDEBUG* is defined.

A.7 Character Handling

There are two groups of character-handling functions, which are usually implemented as macros. The first group, called *character-testing functions*, checks to see whether the argument is a member of a particular set of characters. The second group, called *case-mapping functions*, changes a letter from uppercase to lowercase, or vice versa. These functions are *not* ASCII-biased. They should work with any existing character code, including EBCDIC and European codes. Note, however, that there is some variation concerning how these functions operate, depending on what character set is being used. In these cases, a minimum operation is defined for programs operating in a *C locale* (see Section A.8 for more information about locales).

A.7.1 Character-Testing Functions

All of the character-testing functions have a similar format. They accept an **int** as the argument and return a nonzero value if the argument is a member of a specified set of characters. Otherwise they return zero. If the value of the argument cannot be represented in an **unsigned char**, the results are undefined. The generic synopsis is

```
#include <ctype.h>
int func_name( int c );
```

Table A-2 lists all of the character-testing functions and the set of characters for which they test membership.

A.7.2 Character Case-Mapping Functions

There are two case-mapping functions, one that changes a letter from uppercase to lowercase and another that changes a letter from lowercase to uppercase. Both functions take an **int** argument and return an **int**. If the argument is not relevant (i.e., it is not a letter or it is already the case to which it is being converted), it is returned unchanged. The synopses for the two functions are

```
#include <ctype.h>
int tolower( int c );
```

and

```
#include <ctype.h>
int toupper( int c );
```

Function	Membership Set
isalnum()	Alphabetic and digit characters (any character for which *isalpha()* or *isdigit()* is true).
isalpha()	Alphabetic characters (any character for which *isupper()* or *islower()* is true, or any implementation-defined set of characters for which *iscntrl()*, *isdigit()*, *ispunct()*, and *isspace()* are false. In the C locale, *isalpha()* is true only if *islower()* or *isupper()* is true).
iscntrl()	Control characters.
isdigit()	Decimal digit characters.
isgraph()	All printable characters except space characters.
islower()	Lowercase letters or any implementation-defined subset of characters for which *iscntrl()*, *isdigit()*, *ispunct()*, and *isspace()* are false.
isprint()	All printing characters, including space.
ispunct()	All printing characters except a space and characters for which *isalnum()* is true.
isspace()	A space(' '), form feed ('\f'), newline ('\n'), carriage return ('\r'), horizontal tab ('\t'), or vertical tab ('\v').
isupper()	Uppercase letter or any implementation-defined subset of characters for which *iscntrl()*, *isdigit()*, *ispunct()*, and *isspace()* are false.
isxdigit()	Hexadecimal digits.

Table A-2. Character-Testing Functions.

A.8 Setting Locale Parameters

Though ANSI is a U.S. organization, the C Standards Committee took pains to make the C language as universal as possible. Among the problems it confronted were

- Different alphabets and hence different character sets.

- Different collating sequences in the character set (the numeric codes for alphabetic characters are not always ordered as they are in ASCII or EBCDIC).

- Different methods of representing decimal points (a period in the U.S., but a comma in many European countries).

- Different ways of displaying times and dates.

A large part of the problem was solved by putting locale-defined behavior into library functions rather than the language itself. For example, the *isalpha()* function can return different results depending on what character set is being used. This flexibility, however, raised another problem. If a library function has different interpretations based on locale, how can you force one particular interpretation? Also, how can you find out dynamically, while a program is running, which locale-specific behavior the program will exhibit?

The ANSI Committee solved both of these problems by inventing a function called *setlocale()*, which enables you to select a specific locale setting or to discover the current locale setting. By changing the locale setting, you can immediately change the action of all relevant functions. Note that these changes occur at runtime, not at compile time.

The header file associated with *setlocale()* is *<locale.h>*. This file contains definitions of at least six macros that enable you to select a particular part of the C language that you want to affect with the new locale setting:

LC_ALL	The entire language
LC_COLLATE	The *strcoll()* function
LC_CTYPE	All of the character-handling functions
LC_MONETARY	The monetary formatting information returned by the *locale_conv()* function
LC_NUMERIC	The decimal point character for the formatted I/O and string conversion functions
LC_TIME	The *strftime()* function

Implementations may define additional macros that begin with *LC_*. In addition to the macros, the *locale.h* header file also defines a structure type named *lconv*. The elements of this structure are described in Section A.8.2.

A.8.1 The *setlocale()* Function

```
#include <locale.h>
char *setlocale( int category, const char *locale );
```

The *setlocale()* function sets or queries locale-specific behavior for the part of the C language specified by *category*. *category* should be one of the macros defined in *locale.h*.

If *locale* is a null pointer, the function is interpreted as a query. It returns a string that represents the current locale setting for the specified category. The only ANSI-defined locale is "C," which represents the minimal environment for C translation. Implementations are free to define other locale strings.

You can find out what the implementation-defined locale is by entering a null string as the second parameter. In this case, *setlocale()* returns a pointer to the string associated with the specified category. The program's current locale is not changed.

If *locale* is not a null pointer, the function is interpreted as a request to change the locale setting for the specified category. If the request can be honored, *setlocale()* returns the *locale* argument. If the request cannot be honored, *setlocale()* returns a null pointer.

At program start-up, the equivalent of

```
setlocale( LC_ALL, "C" );
```

is executed.

A.8.2 The *localeconv()* **Function**

```
#include <locale.h>
struct lconv *localeconv( void );
```

The *localeconv()* function returns a pointer to a structure of type *lconv* that contains appropriate values for formatting numbers and monetary values under the current locale. The *lconv* structure contains the members shown below. Any member with type **char *** (except *decimal_point*) can point to a null string indicating that the locale does not define a format for this object. Likewise, any member with type **char** can have the value *CHAR_MAX* to indicate that there is no locale-defined value for that member.

char *decimal_point
The decimal-point character used to format nonmonetary values.

char *thousands_sep
The character used to separate groups of digits (to the left of the decimal point) for nonmonetary values.

char *grouping   A string whose elements indicate the size of each group of digits in a nonmonetary value. The string can contain characters with the following values:

integer value	The number of digits that comprise the group.
0	Use the previous element to determine the number of digits to use for the current group.
CHAR_MAX	No further grouping is to be performed.

char *int_curr_symbol

The international currency symbol used by the current locale. The first three characters indicate the currency symbol as specified by ISO 4217. The fourth character defines the character used to separate the currency symbol from the monetary unit.

char *currency_symbol

The local currency symbol used by the current locale.

char *mon_decimal_point

The decimal point used to format monetary values.

char *mon_thousands_sep

The character used to separate groups of digits (to the left of the decimal point) for monetary values.

char *mon_grouping

A string whose elements indicate the size of each group of digits in a monetary value (see the description of grouping).

char *negative sign   The string used to indicate a negative monetary value.

char int_frac_digits

The number of fractional digits (to the right of the decimal point) that are displayed in an internationally formatted monetary value.

char frac_digits   The number of fractional digits (to the right of the decimal point) that are displayed in a monetary value.

char p_cs_precedes Set to 1 if the currency symbol precedes the monetary value when the value is positive, or to 0 if the symbol follows the monetary value.

char p_sep_by_space

Set to 1 if a space separates the currency symbol from a positive monetary value, or to 0 if there is no space.

char n_cs_precedes Set to 1 if the currency symbol precedes the monetary value when the value is negative, or to 0 if the symbol follows the monetary value.

char n_sep_by_space

Set to 1 if a space separates the currency symbol from a negative monetary value, or to 0 if there is no space.

char p_sign_posn Indicates where the positive sign is positioned for monetary values.

char n_sign_posn Indicates where the negative sign is positioned for monetary values. *p_sign_posn* and *n_sign_posn* can have the following values:

0	Parentheses surround the value and the currency symbol to indicate the sign.
1	The sign symbol precedes the value and currency symbol.
2	The sign symbol follows the value and currency symbol.
3	The sign symbol immediately precedes the currency symbol.
4	The sign symbol immediately follows the currency symbol.

A.9 Mathematics

All the math functions require inclusion of the header file *<math.h>*. This file contains a definition of the *HUGE_VAL* macro, which defines the value returned by all functions when the true result is too large to be represented.

There are two types of errors that can occur: *domain errors* and *range errors*. A *domain error* occurs when an input argument to the function is outside the legal domain for argument values. For example, it is a domain error to pass a negative number to the *sqrt( )* function. In this case, the function returns an implementation-defined value and sets *errno* equal to the value of *EDOM*, which is an implementation-defined nonzero integer.

A *range error* occurs when the result of the function cannot be represented in a **double**. In this case, *errno* receives the value of the macro *ERANGE*, which again is an implementation-defined nonzero value. If a range error occurs because of an underflow (the value is too small), the function returns zero. If an overflow occurs, then the function returns the value of the macro *HUGE_VAL*. Generally, *HUGE_VAL* is the largest value that can be stored in a **double**.

Note that *EDOM* and *ERANGE* are defined in *<errno.h>*, which must be included if you want to check these values.

The math functions are divided into several groups:

- Trigonometric and Hyperbolic Functions

- Exponential and Logarithmic Functions

- Miscellaneous Math Functions

All of the math functions operate on **double** values. However, the ANSI Committee plans to add equivalent functions for **float**s and **long double**s some time in the future. The names of these new functions will be the same as the current names with an **f** or **l** appended. Therefore, you should consider these future names as reserved to avoid conflicts at a later date.

The functions *ecvt( )*, *fcvt( )*, and *gcvt( )*, which are available on many systems, were not included in the ANSI Standard because the same functionality can be obtained through *sprintf( )*.

A.9.1 Trigonometric and Hyperbolic Functions

With one exception (*atan2()*), all of the trigonometric and hyperbolic functions take a **double** argument and return a **double** result. The general synopsis is

```
#include <math.h>
double func_name( double x );
```

These functions are described in Table A-3 (the *atan2()* function is listed separately). The trigonometric functions use radians, not degrees.

A.9.1.1 The *atan2()* Function

```
#include <math.h>
double atan2( double y, double x );
```

The *atan2()* function returns the principal value of the arc tangent of y/x, using the signs of both arguments to determine the quadrant of the return value. Viewed in terms of a Cartesian coordinate system, the result is the angle between the positive x-axis and a line drawn from the origin through the point (x,y). The result is in radians and lies between –p and p. A domain error occurs if both arguments equal zero.

A.9.2 Exponential and Logarithmic Functions

The following library routines perform exponential and logarithmic functions. Each of these functions returns a **double**.

A.9.2.1 The *exp()* Function

```
#include <math.h>
double exp( double x );
```

The *exp()* function returns the exponential function of x. If the magnitude of x is too large, a range error occurs.

Function	Operation
acos()	Returns the principal value of the arc cosine of *x*. The result lies in the range 0 through p. A domain error occurs if *x* is less than –1 or greater than 1.
asin()	Returns the principal value of the arc sine of *x*. The result is in the range –p/2 through p/2. A domain error occurs if *x* is less than –1 or greater than 1.
atan()	Returns the principal value of the arc tangent of *x*. The result is in the range –p/2 through p/2.
cos()	Returns the cosine of *x*, where *x* is measured in radians. If *x* is very large, the result may not be meaningful.
cosh()	Returns the hyperbolic cosine of *x*. A range error occurs if the magnitude of *x* is too large.
sin()	Returns the sine of *x*, where *x* is measured in radians. If *x* is very large, the result may not be meaningful.
sinh()	Returns the hyperbolic sine of *x*. A range error occurs if the magnitude of *x* is too large.
tan()	Returns the tangent of *x*, measured in radians. If *x* is very large, the result may not be meaningful.
tanh()	Returns the hyperbolic tangent of *x*. A range error occurs if the magnitude of *x* is too large.

Table A-3. Trigonometric and Hyperbolic Functions.

A.9.2.2 The *frexp()* **Function**

```
#include <math.h>
double frexp( double value, int *exp );
```

The *frexp()* function converts *value* into a fraction multiplied by a power of 2. The fractional part, which is between 0.5 and 1.0, is returned by the function and the exponential value is stored in the object pointed to by *exp*. If the original value of *value* is zero, then both *value* and the object pointed to by *exp* are assigned the value zero.

A.9.2.3 The *ldexp()* **Function**

```
#include <math.h>
double ldexp( double x, int exp );
```

The *ldexp()* function multiplies the value *x* by 2 to the power of *exp* and returns the result. If the resulting value is too large to fit in a **double**, a range error may occur.

A.9.2.4 The *log()* **Function**

```
#include <math.h>
double log( double x );
```

The *log()* function returns the natural logarithm of *x*. If *x* is negative, a domain error occurs. If *x* is zero, a range error may occur.

A.9.2.5 The *log10()* **Function**

```
#include <math.h>
double log10( double x );
```

The *log10()* function returns the base-ten logarithm of *x*. If *x* is negative, a domain error occurs. If *x* is zero, a range error may occur.

A.9.2.6 The *modf()* **Function**

```
#include <math.h>
double modf( double value, double *iptr );
```

The *modf()* function divides *value* into its integral and fractional parts, each of which has the same sign as *value*. The fractional part is returned and the integral part is stored in the object pointed to by *iptr*.

A.9.2.7 The *pow()* **Function**

```
#include <math.h>
double pow( double x, double y );
```

The *pow()* function returns the value of *x* raised to the power of *y*. A domain error occurs if *x* is zero and *y* is less than or equal to zero, or if *x* is negative and *y* is not an integer. If *x* is zero and *y* is positive, the result is zero. If *x* is nonzero and *y* is zero, the result is approximately 1.0. If *x* is negative and *y* is an integer, then

```
pow( x, y )
```

is computed as

```
pow( -x, y )
```

if *y* is even, and as

```
-pow( -x, y )
```

if *y* is odd. If the result cannot be stored in a **double**, a range error may occur.

A.9.2.8 The *sqrt()* **Function**

```
#include <math.h>
double sqrt( double x );
```

The *sqrt()* function returns the nonnegative square root of *x*. If *x* is negative, a domain error occurs.

A.9.3 Miscellaneous Math Functions

A.9.3.1 The *ceil()* Function

```
#include <math.h>
double ceil( double x );
```

The *ceil()* function returns the smallest integer not less than *x*. That is, it rounds toward positive infinity.

A.9.3.2 The *fabs()* Function

```
#include <math.h>
double fabs( double x );
```

The *fabs()* function returns the absolute value of *x*.

A.9.3.3 The *floor()* Function

```
#include <math.h>
double floor( double x );
```

The *floor()* function returns the largest integer not greater than *x*. That is, it rounds toward negative infinity.

A.9.3.4 The *fmod()* Function

```
#include <math.h>
double fmod( double x, double y );
```

The *fmod()* function returns the floating-point remainder of *x* divided by *y*. The result has the same sign as *x*. (Note that technically *fmod()* returns the *remainder*, not the *modulus*, since the sign agrees with *x*, not with *y*.) If the quotient of *x*/*y* cannot be represented, the behavior is undefined. If *y* is zero, the function returns *x*.

A.10 Nonlocal Jumps

The C library contains two functions—*setjmp()* and *longjmp()*—that enable you
to bypass the normal functional call and return procedures. This is particularly
useful for dealing with unusual conditions in low-level functions.

The header file for these functions is *<setjmp.h>*, which defines a data type
called *jmp_buf*. *jmp_buf* is an array capable of holding the information needed
to restore a calling environment.

setjmp() is called once to initialize a *jmp_buf* variable with the current values of
the machine's state (e.g., the values of the stack pointer and frame pointer and
the registers). When *longjmp()* is called, the machine is reset to the state
contained in the *jmp_buf* array. This causes *longjmp()* to return to the place
where *setjmp()* was last called with the same *jmp_buf* variable.

A.10.1 The *setjmp()* Function

```
#include <setjmp.h>
int setjmp( jmp_buf env );
```

The *setjmp()* function saves the current environment in its *jmp_buf* argument for
later use by the *longjmp()* function. When *setjmp()* returns from an initialization
call, it returns zero. When *setjmp()* returns from a *longjmp()* call, it returns a
nonzero value.

In some implementations, a *setjmp()* call can appear only in a comparison expression, where the returned value is compared to an integral constant
expression.

A.10.2 The *longjmp()* Function

```
#include <setjmp.h>
void longjmp( jmp_buf env, int val );
```

The *longjmp()* function restores the environment saved by the most recent call to
setjmp() with the same *env* argument. If there has been no such call, or if the
function containing the call to *setjmp()* has terminated (i.e., through a return
statement), the behavior is undefined.

After a successful *longjmp()* call, all accessible objects have the same value they
had immediately prior to the *longjmp()* call. The only exceptions are dynamic
variables that are not **volatile** and have been changed between the calls to
setjmp() and *longjmp()*. The values of these objects are indeterminate.

If *longjmp()* is invoked from a nested signal handler (that is, from a function
invoked as a result of a signal raised during the handling of another signal), the

behavior is undefined.   In all other interrupt and signal handling situations, *longjmp()* should execute correctly.

A.10.3 Example

setjmp() and *longjmp()* are typically used to recover from an error deep in the program structure by returning to an earlier state where the program was functioning properly.   In the following example, we initialize *main_loop* at the beginning of the program.   Then, whenever *error()* is invoked, the program returns to this initial state.

```
#include <setjmp.h>

jmp_buf main_loop;

main()
{
  if (setjmp( main_loop ))
    printf( "Restarting.\n" );
  for (;;)
  {
    printf( "cint> ");
          .
          .       /* loop body */
          .
  }
}

error( s )
char *s;
{
  printf(" Error %s\n", s );
  longjmp( main_loop ),
}
```

Note that the "Restarting" line is not printed the first time *setjmp()* is called because *setjmp()* returns zero when it is explicitly invoked.   When *setjmp()* returns via a *longjmp()* call, however, it returns a nonzero value.

A.11 Signal Handling

The C runtime library contains two functions for handling various conditions that may arise during program execution. These functions are a subset of those available in the UNIX library. Both functions make use of a number of macros declared in the header file *<signal.h>*. The macros and their meanings are listed in Table A-4. There is no guarantee, however, that an implementation will use any of these signals (except as the result of explicit calls to *raise()*). In addition to the listed names, the ANSI Committee has also reserved all names that begin with *SIG* for possible future use.

A.11.1 The *signal()* Function

```
#include <signal.h>
void ( *signal (int sig, void (*func)(int))) ( int );
```

The *func* argument to *signal()* selects one of three methods for subsequent handling of signal number *sig*. If the argument is *SIG_DFL*, then the signal is handled in the default manner. If the argument is *SIG_IGN*, the signal will be ignored. Otherwise, *func* should point to a function that is invoked when the signal occurs.

Even if *func* points to a signal-handling function, the system will still execute the equivalent of

```
signal( sig, SIG_DFL );
```

before invoking

```
(*func) ( sig );
```

The function *func* may terminate in several ways, including calls to *abort()*, *exit()*, or *longjmp()*. If it returns through a **return** statement, and the return value is *SIGFPE* or any other implementation-defined value that corresponds to an exception, the behavior is undefined. Otherwise, the program resumes execution at the point it was interrupted. If the requested change can be honored, *signal()* returns the value of *func*. Otherwise, it returns *SIG_ERR* and sets *errno* to indicate an error.

Since the functions in the C runtime library are not guaranteed to be reentrant, they may not be used reliably with a signal handler that returns.

Macro	Meaning
SIGABRT	Abort Signal — Expands to a positive integral constant expression that is the signal number corresponding to an abnormal termination, such as that indicated by the *abort()* function.
SIG_DFL	Same as *SIG_IGN*, except that it specifies that the signal is to be handled in an implementation-defined manner.
SIG_ERR	Same as *SIG_IGN* except that it specifies that the call to *signal()* is erroneous.
SIGFPE	Floating-Point Exception Signal — Expands to a positive integral constant expression that is the signal number corresponding to an erroneous arithmetic operation, such as zero divide, or an operation resulting in overflow.
SIG_IGN	Expands to a constant expression of type "pointer to function returning void." It is used as an argument to the *signal()* function, in place of a function address, to specify that a given signal should be ignored.
SIGILL	Illegal Instruction Signal — Expands to a positive integral constant expression that is the signal number corresponding to detection of an invalid function image.
SIGINT	Interrupt Signal — Expands to a positive integral constant expression that is the signal number corresponding to receipt of an interactive attention signal.
SIGSEGV	Segment Violation Signal — Expands to a positive integral constant expression that is the signal number corresponding to an invalid access to storage.
SIGTERM	Termination Signal — Expands to a positive integral constant expression that is the signal number corresponding to a termination request sent to the program.

Table A-4. Signal-Handling Macros.

At program start-up, the equivalent of

```
signal( sig, SIG_IGN )
```

may be executed for some signals in an implementation-defined manner.

For all other signals the equivalent of

```
signal( sig, SIG_DFL );
```

is executed.

A.11.2 The *raise()* Function

```
#include <signal.h>
int raise( int sig );
```

The *raise()* function sends the signal *sig* to the executing program. If successful, *raise()* returns zero; if it is unsuccessful, it returns a nonzero value.

A.12 Variable Argument Lists

The C Library contains several tools for writing functions that can accept a variable number of arguments in a portable fashion. Without using these tools, you need to know the stack implementation of a particular compiler to write a variable argument function. The macros and function discussed in this section enable you to avoid the compiler internals.

To declare a function capable of accepting a variable number of arguments, use the "..." prototype syntax. For example, the following defines a function *f1()* that will always be passed at least two arguments, but might be passed more.

```
void f1( arg1, arg2, ... )
int arg1, arg2;
{
          .
          .
```

Within *f1()*, you would use the variable argument macros and functions to process all of the arguments to *f1()*. Wherever *f1()* is invoked, there must be a function allusion of the form

```
void f1( int, int, ... );
```

The *<stdarg.h>* file contains definitions of two macros, one function, and one data type. The macros are *va_start, va_arg*, the function is *va_end*, and the type is *va_list*. *va_list* defines an array type suitable for holding information needed by *va_arg* and *va_macro*. In the following discussion, the name of the array with this type is *ap*.

A.12.1 The *va_start* Macro

```
#include <stdarg.h>
void va_start( va_list ap, parmN );
```

The *va_start* macro initializes the array *ap* for subsequent use by *va_arg* and *va_end*. It should be invoked before any arguments are processed. The *parmN* argument should be the name of the rightmost argument before the three dots. Continuing our example of *f1()*, the *va_start* invocation would be

```
va_start( ap, arg2 );
```

A.12.2 The *va_arg* Macro

```
#include <stdarg.h>
type va_arg( va_list ap, type );
```

The *va_arg* macro expands to an expression that has the type and value of the next argument. It should be invoked once for each argument. The argument *ap* should be the same argument initialized by the *va_start* macro. The parameter *type* should be the type of the argument (after default conversions to **int**, **unsigned int**, or **double**). For example, if all the arguments to *f1()* are integers, you would write

```
va_arg( ap, int )
```

to get the value of each argument. If the type specified in *va_arg* does not match the actual argument type, the behavior is undefined.

A.12.3 The *va_end()* Function

```
#include <stdarg.h>
void va_end( va_list ap );
```

The *va_end()* function should be invoked after all of the arguments have been processed to facilitate a normal return from the function. If it is not invoked, the behavior is undefined.

A.12.4 Example

The following function accepts from 1 to 20 integer arguments, which it processes and stores in elements of the array *args[]*. The first argument specifies the total number of arguments in the call.

```
#include <stdarg.h>
#define MAX_ARGS 20

void f1( arg_num, ... )
int arg_num;
{
  va_list ap;
  int args[MAX_ARGS];
  int array_element = 1;

  va_start( ap, arg_num );
  while (arg_num--)
    arg[array_element++] = va_arg( ap, int );
  va_end( ap );
}
```

A.13 I/O Functions

This section describes each standard I/O function in detail. See Chapter 11 for more general information about how to perform I/O using the C library.

A.13.1 The *clearerr()* Function

```
#include <stdio.h>
void clearerr( FILE *stream );
```

The *clearerr()* function clears the end-of-file and error indicators associated with the specified stream. Use *ferror()* and *feof()* to see whether these indicators are set. The only other time these indicators are cleared is when the file is opened or when a *rewind()* function is executed. The *clearerr()* function does not return a value.

A.13.2 The *fclose()* Function

```
#include <stdio.h>
int fflush( FILE *stream );
```

The *fclose()* function closes the file associated with the specified stream and disassociates the stream from the file. Before closing the file, *fclose()* flushes the associated buffers. If the buffers had been automatically allocated, they are deallocated. Whenever the *exit()* function is invoked, it calls *fclose()* for any open streams.

The *fclose()* function returns zero if it successfully closes the stream, or nonzero if an error occurs. If the stream is already closed, *fclose()* returns nonzero.

On some operating systems, it is impossible to create a file without writing something to it. Programs that rely on a file being created, therefore, should write something to the associated stream before closing it.

A.13.3 The *feof()* Function

```
#include <stdio.h>
int feof( FILE *stream );
```

The *feof()* function tests the end-of-file indicator for the specified stream to see whether an end-of-file was encountered in a previous read or write operation. If the indicator is set, *feof()* returns a nonzero value; otherwise it returns zero. Note that *feof()* does not reset the error indicator so that repeated calls to *feof()* will report the same condition over and over. To reset the error indicator, use *clearerr()*.

A.13.4 The *ferror()* Function

```
#include <stdio.h>
int ferror( FILE *stream );
```

The *ferror()* function tests the error indicator for the specified file to see whether an error has occurred on a previous read or write operation. If the indicator is set, *ferror()* returns a nonzero value; otherwise it returns zero. Note that *ferror()* does not reset the error indicator so that repeated calls to *ferror()* will report the same error over and over. To reset the error indicator, use *clearerr()*.

A.13.5 The *fflush()* Function

```
#include <stdio.h>
int fflush( FILE *stream );
```

The *fflush()* function empties the buffer associated with the specified stream, causing any data in the buffer to be written to the destination file or device. The stream remains open. If the call is successful, *fflush()* returns zero; otherwise it returns a nonzero value.

A.13.6 The *fgetc()* Function

```
#include <stdio.h>
int fgetc( FILE *stream );
```

The *fgetc()* function fetches the next character from the specified stream, returns the value after converting it to an **int**, and advances the associated file position indicator. Successive calls to *fgetc()* return successive characters from the stream. If an end-of-file is encountered, or if an error occurs, *fgetc()* returns *EOF*. Use *feof()* or *ferror()* to determine whether an error or end-of-file occurred.

A.13.7 The *fgetpos()* Function

```
#include <stdio.h>
int fgetpos( FILE *stream, fpos_t *pos );
```

The *fgetpos()* function stores the current file position indicator in the object pointed to by *pos*. It is similar to *ftell()*, except that the file position indicator value is stored in an object of type *fpos_t*, rather than being returned as a **long int**. The value stored contains implementation-defined information that can only be used by *fsetpos()* to reposition the file position indicator to its position at the time of the *fgetpos()* call. See the description of *fsetpos()* for more information.

If successful, *fgetpos()* returns zero. On a failure, *fgetpos()* returns a nonzero value and sets *errno* to an implementation-defined value.

A.13.8 The *fgets()* Function

```
#include <stdio.h>
char *fgets( char *s, int n, FILE *stream );
```

The *fgets()* function reads characters from the specified stream and assigns them to the array identified by *s*. The stream must be open with read access. Characters are read until a newline or end-of-file is encountered, or until *n − 1* characters have been fetched, whichever comes first. Unlike the *gets()* function, *fgets()* includes the terminating newline in the array. *fgets()* then appends a null character after the last character assigned, so that the maximum number of array elements used is *n*.

If successful, *fgets()* returns the pointer *s*. If an end-of-file is encountered before any characters are read, *fgets()* leaves the array untouched and returns a null pointer. If an error occurs, a null pointer is returned, but the contents of the array are unpredictable.

A.13.9 The *fopen()* Function

```
#include <stdio.h>
FILE *fopen( const char *filename,
             const char *mode);
```

The *fopen()* function opens a file identified by *filename* and associates a stream with the file. The second argument is a pointer to a character string that identifies the file access type. Table A-5 shows the legal values for the argument *mode*.

Many of these access types were invented by the ANSI Committee, so they may not be implemented on older compilers. The traditional access types, documented in K&R, are **"r"**, **"w"**, and **"a"**. The corresponding *update modes*, **"r+"**, **"w+"**, and **"a+"**, have also been in existence for some time. The types for accessing binary data (those with a **b** in them) are new and reflect ANSI's efforts to develop a consistent library of functions. Formerly, I/O to binary files was performed through a set of UNIX derived functions that paralleled the standard text I/O functions. Now they are merged into one group.

The **"ab"**, **"ab+"**, and **"a+b"** access modes may initially position the file position indicator beyond the last data written, due to null padding. The Standard also leaves it open for compilers to support additional access modes beyond the ones listed here.

Mode	Meaning
"r"	Open an existing text file for reading.
"w"	Create a new text file for writing or truncate an existing file.
"a"	Open a text file in append mode; writing to the file occurs at end-of-file marker.
"rb"	Open a binary file for reading.
"wb"	Create a new binary file for writing or truncate an existing binary file.
"ab"	Open or create a binary file in append mode; writing occurs at end-of-file marker.
"r+"	Open an existing text file for reading and writing.
"w+"	Create a new text file for reading and writing or truncate an existing file.
"a+"	Open an existing file or create a new one in append mode; writing occurs at end-of-file.
"r+b" *or* "rb+"	Open a binary file for reading and writing.
"w+b" *or* "wb+"	Create a new binary file for writing or truncate an existing binary file.
"a+b" *or* "ab+"	Open an existing binary file or create a new one for reading and writing in append mode; writing occurs at end-of-file.

Table A-5. The fopen() *Modes.*

Opening a file with one of the append modes ("a", "a+", "ab", or "a+b") forces all subsequent writes to occur at the current end-of-file, regardless of previous calls to *fseek()*. After each write operation, the file position indicator is repositioned to the end of the file and the buffer is flushed.

Opening a file in read mode (where **r** is the first character of the mode argument) fails if the file does not exist or cannot be read.

One peculiarity of the update modes (which stems from the fact that I/O is buffered) is that you cannot write to a file and then read from it, or vice versa, without an intervening *fseek()*, *fsetpos()*, *rewind()*, or *fflush()* call (unless the read or write operation encounters an end-of-file).

The *fopen()* function returns a pointer to a structure of type *FILE*. This pointer, called a *file pointer*, is then used to access the file in subsequent I/O operations. If an error occurs while opening the file, *fopen()* returns a null pointer.

A.13.10 The *fprintf()* Function

```
#include <stdio.h>
int fprintf( FILE *stream, const char *format, ...
);
```

The *fprintf()* function enables you to send formatted output to a file. This function is equivalent to *printf()*, except that it takes one additional argument, *stream*, which lets you specify a stream (the *printf()* function automatically writes to the standard output stream *stdout*). See the description of *printf()* for more information.

A.13.11 The *fputc()* Function

```
#include <stdio.h>
int fputc( int c, FILE *stream );
```

The *fputc()* function writes a single character to the specified stream and advances the associated file position indicator. Note that the character is passed as an **int**, but *fputc()* converts it to an **unsigned char** before outputting it. *fputc()* returns *EOF* if an error occurs; otherwise it returns the character written.

The ANSI Standard guarantees that *fputc()* will not be implemented as a macro. *putc()* is an equivalent function that may be implemented as a macro. See Chapter 11 for more information about *putc()* and *fputc()*.

A.13.12 The *fputs()* Function

```
#include <stdio.h>
int fputs( const char *s, FILE *stream )
```

The *fputs()* function writes the array identified by the pointer *s* to the specified stream. Characters from the array are written up to, but not including, the terminating null character. Note that *fputs()* does not insert a newline as *puts()* does. Also note that the string must have a terminating null character or *fputs()* will output successive bytes from memory indefinitely. If successful, *fputs()* returns zero; otherwise it returns a nonzero value.

A.13.13 The *fread()* Function

```
#include <stdio.h>
int fread( void *ptr, size_t size, int nelem,
           FILE *stream );
```

The *fread()* function is used to read a block of binary or text data into an array. The array is identified by *ptr*. The argument *nelem* specifies the number of elements to read, and *size* specifies the size of each element in bytes. Normally, the size is computed by using the **sizeof** operator. For example,

```
fread( arr, sizeof(*arr), 100, fp );
```

reads 100 elements from the stream identified by *fp* and stores the results in an array called *arr*. It is your responsibility to ensure that the array is large enough to hold the data.

The *fread()* function concludes when it reads in the specified number of bytes, it encounters an end-of-file, or a read error occurs. In all three cases, *fread()* returns the number of elements read. If the returned value is less than the number of bytes specified in the call, you must use *ferror()* or *feof()* to determine why *fread()* ended prematurely. After a *fread()* call, the file position indicator is positioned just after the last byte read. You can reposition it with an *fseek()* or *rewind()* call.

A.13.14 The *freopen()* **Function**

```
#include <stdio.h>
FILE *freopen(const char *filename,
              const char *mode, FILE *stream );
```

The *freopen()* function is used to associate an existing stream with a different file. Normally it is used to redirect the standard streams, *stdin*, *stdout*, and *stderr*. First, *freopen()* closes the file associated with the stream; then it opens the file identified by *filename* and associates the stream to it. The *mode* argument serves the same role as in an *fopen()* function. If *freopen()* encounters an error, it returns a null pointer; otherwise it returns the value of the file pointer (the third argument).

A.13.15 The *fscanf()* **Function**

```
#include <stdio.h>
int fscanf(FILE *stream, const char *format, ... );
```

The *fscanf()* function enables you to read formatted data into variables. It is equivalent to *scanf()*, except that it takes one additional argument, *stream*, which lets you specify an input stream (the *scanf()* function automatically reads from *stdin*). See the description of *scanf()* for more information.

A.13.16 The *fsetpos()* **Function**

```
#include <stdio.h>
int fsetpos( FILE *stream, const fpos_t *pos );
```

The *fsetpos()* function is designed to be used in conjunction with *fgetpos()* to move the file position indicator to the spot specified by the object pointed to by *pos*. *pos* must be a value returned by an earlier call to *fgetpos()*. The *fgetpos()* and *fsetpos()* functions should be used instead of *ftell()* and *fseek()* when the file position indicator value is too large to fit in a **long int**. The *fpos_t* data type should be defined by each implementation to be large enough to hold the largest possible file position indicator value.

The *fsetpos()* function clears the end-of-file flag for the specified stream and undoes the effects of any previous calls to *ungetc()* on the same stream. After an *fsetpos()* call, the next operation on the stream can be either input or output.

If successful, *fsetpos()* returns zero. If it fails, *fsetpos()* returns a nonzero value and sets *errno* to an implementation-defined nonzero value.

A.13.17 The *fseek()* Function

```
#include <stdio.h>
int fseek( FILE *stream, long offset, int ptrname );
```

The *fseek()* function enables you to move the file position indicator in order to perform random access on a file. The offset refers to the number of bytes from a fixed position specified by *ptrname*. *ptrname* can have one of three values represented by macros defined in *<stdio.h>*:

SEEK_SET	Offset from the beginning of the file.
SEEK_CUR	Offset from the current value of the file position indicator.
SEEK_END	Offset from the end of the file.

Note that the offset can be negative. However, if you attempt to move the file position indicator before the beginning of the file, the results are unpredictable.

The *fseek()* function has somewhat different semantics depending on whether the stream is open in binary or text mode. For binary streams, the name *SEEK_END* may not have meaning. For text streams, *ptrname* must be *SEEK_SET* and the offset must be either zero or a value returned by a previous call to *ftell()*.

The *fseek()* function undoes the effects of an *ungetc()* function. It also resets the end-of-file flag. *fseek()* returns zero if it is successful; if unsuccessful, it returns a nonzero value.

A.13.18 The *ftell()* Function

```
#include <stdio.h>
long ftell( FILE *stream );
```

The *ftell()* function returns the current value of the file position indicator. For binary streams, this is the number of bytes from the beginning of the file. For text streams, *ftell()* returns an implementation-defined value that is suitable for use as an offset value in an *fseek()* function. Using the value in an *fseek()* call repositions the file position indicator to its position at the time of the *ftell()* call.

The *ftell()* function can fail for at least two reasons:

- The stream is associated with a terminal, or other file type, for which the concept of a file position indicator is meaningless.

- The current value of the file position indicator cannot be represented in a **long int** (see the description of *fsetpos()*).

If either of these failures occurs, *ftell()* returns –*1L* and sets *errno* to an implementation-defined nonzero value.

A.13.19 The *fwrite()* Function

```
#include <stdio.h>
int fwrite( const void *ptr, size_t size,
            size_t nmemb, FILE *stream );
```

The *fwrite()* function writes the array pointed to by *ptr* to the specified stream. It writes *nmemb* elements, where each element is *size* bytes long. Normally, *size* is computed by using the **sizeof** operator. For example,

```
fwrite( arr, sizeof(*arr), 100, s );
```

writes 100 elements from array *arr* to stream *s*. Note that *fwrite()* continues fetching elements from the array until *nelem* elements have been read, even if this means going past the end of the array. It is your responsibility to ensure that the size of the array is at least as long as *nelem* times *size*. After the *fwrite()* call has completed, the file position indicator is positioned just after the last character written. *fwrite()* does not modify the array in any way.

fwrite() returns the number of elements written. Assuming no error occurs, this will be the same as *nmemb*.

A.13.20 The *getc()* Function

```
#include <stdio.h>
int getc( FILE *stream );
```

The *getc()* function reads the next character from the specified stream and returns it as an **int**. *getc()* is equivalent to *fgetc()* except that it may be implemented as a macro instead of a function. If the next character in the stream is an end-of-file, or if an error occurs during the read operation, *getc()* returns *EOF*. Use *ferror()* or *feof()* to determine whether an end-of-file or error occurred.

A.13.21 The *getchar()* **Function**

```
#include <stdio.h>
int getchar( void );
```

The *getchar()* function is equivalent to

```
getc( stdin )
```

which is, in fact, how it is implemented by most compilers. It returns the next character from the standard input stream, or *EOF* if an end-of-file or error occurs. Use *ferror()* or *feof()* to determine whether an error or end-of-file occurred.

A.13.22 The *gets()* **Function**

```
#include <stdio.h>
char *gets( char *s );
```

The *gets()* function reads characters from the standard input stream (*stdin*) and assigns them to the character array identified by *s*. Characters are read and assigned until a newline or end-of-file is encountered. *gets()* is similar to

```
fgets( s, n , stdin )
```

where *n* is a large number. Note, however, that unlike *fgets()*, *gets()* does not allow you to specify a maximum number of characters to read. *gets()* and *fgets()* also differ in the way they handle newlines. If *gets()* ends by reading a newline, it absorbs the newline (i.e., positions the file position indicator after the newline) but does not assign the newline to the array. In contrast, *fgets()* includes the newline in the array. Both *gets()* and *fgets()* append a null character after the last character assigned to the array.

If an end-of-file is encountered before any characters are read, *gets()* returns a null pointer and leaves the array untouched. If an error occurs during the read operation, a null pointer is returned and the contents of the array are unpredictable. Otherwise, if *gets()* concludes successfully, it returns *s*.

A.13.23 The *perror()* Function

```
#include <stdio.h>
char *perror( const char *s );
```

The *perror()* function returns an error message corresponding to the value of *errno*. If *s* is not a null pointer, *perror()* writes the string pointed to by *s* to *stderr*, then writes a colon, and then the error message that matches the current value of *errno*. If *s* is a null pointer, *perror()* returns a pointer to the error message string but performs no output. Note that *perror()* does not reset *errno*, so you should explicitly reset *errno* to zero after each *perror()* call.

A.13.24 The *printf()* Function

```
#include <stdio.h>
int printf( const char *format, ... );
```

The *printf()* function writes formatted data to the standard output stream (*stdout*). The first argument is a character string that may contain text and format control expressions called *conversion specifiers*. The remaining arguments represent the actual data to be written. For each data argument, there should be one, and only one, conversion specifier in the format string which defines how the data is to be output. Conversion specifiers and arguments are associated in the order in which they occur. If there are more data arguments than conversion specifiers, the remaining data expressions are evaluated and then ignored. If there are more format specifiers than data arguments, the behavior is implementation-defined.

The *printf()* function is closely related to the *fprintf()*, *sprintf()*, *vfprintf()*, and *vprintf()* functions. They all obey the same formatting rules. The only difference is that *printf()* always writes to *stdin*, whereas *fprintf()* and *sprintf()* allow you to specify an output stream or internal buffer, respectively. *vprintf()* and *vfprintf()* are identical to *printf()* and *fprintf()* except that the argument list is replaced by a predeclared argument array. All of these functions return the number of bytes written, or a negative number if an error occurs.

Each conversion specifier starts with a percent sign (%) and is followed by optional *format modifiers* and a *conversion character*. The conversion character specifies the type of data (integer, floating-point, or character). The corresponding data argument must match this type. The format modifiers control such things as field width, left and right justification, and the padding character. The following example shows a simple *printf()* call.

```
int j = 5;
printf( "The value of j is: %d\nThe value of j\
squared is: %6d", j, j*j );
```

The output is

```
The value of j is: 5
The value of j squared is:     25
```

Note that there is no explicit separator between text and conversion specifiers. The *printf()* function knows it has reached the end of a conversion specifier when it reads a conversion character. In the example, the conversion character is **d**, which directs *printf()* to write an integer in decimal format. The conversion specifier **%d** is associated with argument *j*, and **%6d** is associated with *j*j*. The **6** following the percent sign is a field width. Note in the output that the value is right-justified by default and padded with spaces on the left.

The legal conversion characters are shown in Table A-6.

Conversion Character	Effect
d, i, o, u, x, X	Used to format integer output. **d** and **i** output the data item in decimal form; **o** prints the data in octal form; **u** prints the unsigned value of the data item; **x** and **X** print the value in hexadecimal format. **x** uses the lowercase letters abcdef, while **X** uses ABCDEF. These formats output as many digits as are required to represent the number. Just before one of these conversion characters, you may enter an **h**, **l**, or **L**. The **h** signifies that the corresponding data item is a **short int** or **unsigned short int**, and the **l** and **L** signify that the data item is a **long int** or **unsigned long int.**
f	Prints floating-point values in decimal notation (i.e., 35.734). The precision designates the number of digits to appear after the decimal point. The default precision is 6. If the precision equals zero, the decimal point is not printed. So long as there is a decimal point, however, there must be at least one digit to the left of it, even if the value is less than one (i.e., 0.3411).
e, E	Outputs a floating-point value using scientific notation (i.e., 3.67e+08). There is always one digit to the left of the decimal point. The number of digits to the right of the decimal point is determined by the precision. The default precision is 6. If the precision is zero, the decimal point is not printed. The exponent value contains at least two digits and as many digits thereafter as are needed to represent the datum. The letter separating the decimal value from the exponent is either **e** or **E** depending on which conversion character you use.

Table A-6. printf() *Conversion Characters. (continued on next page)*

Conversion Character	Effect
g, G	Uses either **f** or **e** (**E** if **G** is specified), depending on the value of the datum. If the value would require an exponent less than –4 or greater than the precision, then **e** (or **E**) is used. Otherwise **f** is used. The precision specifier has the same effect it has for the **f**, **e**, and **E** conversions. Trailing zeros are removed from the result, and a decimal point is printed only if it is followed by a digit.
c	Prints a character. Since the data argument is passed as an **int**, *printf( )* prints the least significant byte.
s	Prints a string of characters. The data argument should be a pointer to a null-terminated array. For this conversion format, the precision is interpreted as the maximum number of characters to output. Any additional characters in the string are ignored. If you do not specify a precision, all characters up to, but not including, the terminating null character are printed.
p	The corresponding data argument should be a pointer to an object of type **void**. The value of the pointer is converted into a sequence of characters in an implementation-defined manner.
n	Records the number of data items written so far. The corresponding data argument should be a pointer to an **int**. *printf( )* fills the **int** with the number of objects printed so far.
%	The sequence % % outputs a percent sign.

Table A-6. printf() *Conversion Characters.*
(continued from preceding page)

The following program illustrates the default format for each conversion character. The next sections describe how to change the default by specifying a
minimum field width, a precision, left justification, and zero as the pad character.

```
main ()
{
  printf ( "%%d\t%%u\t\t\t%%o\t%%x\n" );
  printf ( "%d\t%u\t%o\t%x\n\n", -25, -25, 25, 25 );

  printf ( "%%c\t%%s\n" );
  printf ( "%c\t%s\n\n", 'A', "String" );

  printf ( "%%f\t\t\t%%e\t\t\t\t%%g\n" );
  printf ( "%f\t%e\t%g\n", 234.5678, 234.5678,
                           234.5678 );
  exit ( 0 );
}
```

The output is

%d	%u	%o	%x
-25	4294967271	31	19

%c	%s
A	String

%f	%e	%g
234.567800	0.234568e+03	234.568

Flag Characters — There are a number of optional format modifiers that may come before the conversion character. The first, called a *flag character,* can be any of the characters shown in Table A-7.

Flag Character	Meaning
−	Specifies left justification.
+	Causes all numeric data to be prefixed with a plus or minus sign. The default, which this character overrides, is to print a minus sign for negative numbers but no plus sign for positive numbers.
space	Causes negative numbers to be prefixed with a minus sign and positive numbers to be prefixed with a space. (The default is no space for positive numbers.)
#	This modifier has various meanings depending on what conversion character is specified. For **c**, **d**, **i**, **s**, and **u**, this flag has no effect. For **o** conversions, the # flag causes the value to be prefixed with a zero (the precision is widened if necessary). For **x** and **X** conversions, the value is prefixed with **0x** or **0X**. For **e**, **E**, **f**, **g**, and **G** conversions, the # causes the result to contain a decimal point, even if the precision is zero. For **g** and **G** conversions, trailing zeros will not be removed from the result, as they are normally.

Table A-7. printf() *Flag Characters.*

The following program shows the effects of the flag characters in various situations.

```
main()
{
    printf( "%%5d\t%5d\n", 25 );
    printf( "%%-5d\t%-5d\n", 25 );
    printf( "%%+5d\t%+5d\n\n", 25 );
    printf( "%%o\t%o\n", 25 );
    printf( "%%#o\t%#o\n", 25 );
    printf( "%%x\t%x\n", 25 );
    printf( "%%#x\t%#x\n\n", 25 );
    printf( "%%5.0f\t%5.0f\n", 25.0 );
    printf( "%%#5.0f\t%#5.0f\n\n",25.0 );
    printf( "%%+-5d\t%+-5d\n", 25 );
    printf( "%%+#5.0f\t+#5.0f\n\n", 25.0 );
    exit( 0 );
}
```

The output is

```
%5d            25
%-5d     25
%+5d           +25

%o       31
%#o      031
%x       19
%#x      0x19

%5.0f    25
%#5.0f   25.

%+-5d    +25
%+#5.0f  +25.
```

Note that the flags are not mutually exclusive. You can combine them, as shown in the last two *printf()* calls.

Minimum Field Width — The next optional format component is an optional *minimum field width*. This is a decimal constant that represents the minimum number of characters to output. If the data item requires fewer characters, it is padded on either the left or the right until the minimum width is reached. (The default is to pad on the left, but you can specify right padding with the *left adjustment flag.*) The default pad character is a space, but you can make it a zero by making the first digit of the minimum field width a zero. If the value requires

more characters than the minimum field width, the field is expanded to accommodate the data. The value is never truncated.

Another way to express the minimum field width is through a dynamic variable.
In this case, you enter an asterisk (*), which informs the *printf()* function to use
the next data argument as the field width. The following examples show the
effects of several minimum field width specifications.

```
main ()
{
   printf( "%%10d\t%10d\n", 25 );
   printf( "%%010d\t%010d\n", 25 );
   printf( "%%1d\t%1d\n", 25 );
   printf( "%%*f\t%*f\n", 5, 33.87 );
   printf( "%%7f\t%7f\n", 33.87 );
   exit( 0 );
}
```

The output is

```
%10d                25
%010d      0000000025
%1d        25
%*f        33.87000
%7f        33.8700000
```

Note that the 5 in the fourth *printf()* call corresponds to the asterisk in the format
specifier and represents the minimum field width for the next data item.

Precision Specifier — The next optional component is a *precision specifier*,
which is designated by a period followed by a decimal constant. For floating-point values, the precision determines the number of digits to appear after
the decimal point. For integer values, the precision specifier has the same
meaning as the minimum field width specifier and overrides that specifier. For
strings, the precision specifier denotes the maximum number of characters to
print.

The program below illustrates the effects of several precision specifications.

```
main()
{
    printf( "%%5d\t%5d\n", 25 );
    printf( "%%5.3d\t%5.3d\n", 25 );
    printf( "%%.3d\t%.3d\n", 25 );
    printf( "%%4.3f\t%4.3f\n", 23.45 );
    printf( "%%4.3f\t%4.3f\n", 23.456789 );
    printf( "%%4.3e\t%4.3e\n", 23.456789 );
    printf( "%%.10s\t%.10s\n", "Print only the first\
ten characters." );
    exit( 0 );
}
```

The output is

```
%5d            25
%5.3d          025
%.3d       025
%4.3f      23.450
%4.3f      23.457
%4.3e      0.235e+02
%.10s      Print only
```

Note that for integer conversions, the field is padded with zeros on the left until the precision length is reached. For floating-point values, if the true value cannot be expressed in the number of digits reserved by the precision, it is rounded. Rounding can occur either up or down, depending on the implementation.

Short and Long Specifiers — Just before the conversion character, you may enter an **h**, **l**, or **L**. The **h** signifies that the corresponding data item is a **short int** or **unsigned short int**, and the **l** signifies that the data item is a **long int** or **unsigned long int.** These prefixes may only be used for integer specifiers. An **L** signifies that the corresponding argument is a **long double.** Since integral arguments are converted to **int** and floating-point arguments are converted to **double** when they are passed to *printf()*, these prefixes ensure that arguments are cast back to their original type. If used for incompatible types, these flags are are ignored.

A.13.25 The *putc()* Function

```
#include <stdio.h>
int putc( int c, FILE *stream );
```

The *putc()* function writes a character to the specified stream. It is equivalent to *fputc()* except that it may be implemented as a macro instead of a function. *putc()* returns *EOF* if an error occurs; otherwise, it returns the character written. Note that both the argument and the returned value are **int**s. *putc()* outputs the least significant byte of the argument.

A.13.26 The *putchar()* Function

```
#include <stdio.h>
int putchar( int c );
```

The *putchar()* function writes its argument to the standard output stream (*stdout*) and returns the character written. If an error occurs, *putchar()* returns *EOF*.

The expression

```
putchar( c )
```

is equivalent to

```
putc( c, stdout )
```

A.13.27 The *puts()* Function

```
#include <stdio.h>
int puts( const char *s );
```

The *puts()* function writes the string pointed to by *s* to the standard output stream (*stdout*) and appends a newline character to the output. The terminating null character in the array is not written. The call

```
puts( s )
```

is equivalent to

```
fputs( s, stdin )
```

except that *fputs()* does not append a newline character. If *puts()* is successful, it returns zero; if an error occurs, it returns a nonzero value.

A.13.28 The *remove()* **Function**

```
#include <stdio.h>
int remove( const char *filename );
```

The *remove()* function is used to delete the file identified by *filename*. If you try to delete a file that is open, the results are implementation-defined. *remove()* returns zero if successful or a nonzero value in the event of a failure. This is a new function that is not included in older C and UNIX libraries.

A.13.29 The *rename()* **Function**

```
#include <stdio.h>
int rename( const char *old, const char *new );
```

The *rename()* function enables you to change the name of a file from the name pointed to by *old* to the name pointed to by *new*. After execution, the name identified by the pointer *old* no longer exists. If the file identified by the pointer *old* is open, the effect is implementation-defined. Likewise, if the name pointed to by *new* already exists, the results are implementation-defined. *rename()* returns zero when it succeeds and a nonzero value when it fails.

A.13.30 The *rewind()* **Function**

```
#include <stdio.h>
void rewind( FILE *stream );
```

The *rewind()* function moves the file position indicator for *stream* to the beginning of the file. The file identified by *stream* should be open on a *rewind()* call. The function call

```
rewind( s )
```

is equivalent to

```
(void)fseek( s, 0L, SET_SEEK )
```

except that the *rewind()* function clears the end-of-file and error indicators for the stream and does not return a value.

A.13.31 The *scanf()* Function

```
#include <stdio.h>
int scanf( FILE *stream, const char *format, ... );
```

The *scanf()* function reads data from *stdin* in a form specified by a format string. The syntax and semantics of *scanf()* are, to a large extent, the reverse of the *printf()* function. However, there are enough differences that you should not assume that conversion specifiers behave identically in both functions.

As with the *printf()* function, the first argument to *scanf()* is a format string. There can be any number of data arguments following the format string. Each one should be the address of a variable where the data is to be stored. The data type of each pointer argument must match the type specified by the corresponding conversion character.

The format string consists of literal characters interspersed with conversion specifiers. A conversion specifier begins with a percent sign followed by optional conversion modifiers and a required conversion character. It designates how many characters to read and how to interpret them. Characters other than a conversion string, a space, a newline, or a vertical tab must match characters in the input stream. A space, horizontal tab, or newline character occurring in the format string causes *scanf()* to skip over characters up to the next nonspace character. For example, the statement

```
scanf( " Value: %d", &n );
```

directs *scanf()* to skip over leading spaces, to read the literal "Value:", and then to read a decimal constant and store it in the object pointed to by *n*. If the first nonspace characters are not "Value:", the function will fail and the results are unpredictable.

The legal conversion characters and their meanings are shown in Table A-8.

Conversion Character	Effect
d	Reads a decimal integer. The corresponding data argument should be a pointer to an integer.
i	Reads a decimal integer, possibly with a prefix and/or suffix. Legal prefixes are a minus sign (–), a plus sign (+), **0x** or **0X** to denote a hexadecimal constant, and **0** to denote an octal constant. Legal suffixes are **u** or **U** to denote an **unsigned** integer and **l** or **L** to denote a **long** integer. The corresponding data argument should be the address of a variable with the appropriate type.
o	Reads an octal constant. Even if the constant does not begin with a **0**, it is treated as an octal value. The corresponding argument should be the address of an integer variable.
u	Reads an unsigned decimal constant. The corresponding data argument should be the address of an integer variable.
x, X	Reads a hexadecimal constant. The corresponding data argument should be the address of an integer variable.
e, E, f, g, G	Reads a floating-point constant. The corresponding data argument should be a pointer to a **float**. (Use an **l** prefix to indicate that the corresponding argument is a pointer to a **double** and an **L** prefix to indicate that the corresponding argument is a pointer to a **long double**.) The floating-point constant may appear in either decimal or scientific form. These format characters may be used interchangeably.

Table A-8. scanf() *Conversion Characters. (continued on next page)*

Conversion Character	Effect
s	Reads a character string. Characters are read until a space, horizontal tab, or newline is encountered. The corresponding argument should be a pointer to an array of **char**s. Each character in the string is loaded into the subsequent array element up to, but not including, the terminating null character. The *scanf()* function automatically adds a null character as the last character of the string. Since there is no bounds checking in C, it is your responsibility to ensure that the character array is long enough to hold the input string.
c	Reads the next character in the stream. It does not skip over spaces, null characters, or tabs. To read the next nonspace character, use **%1s**. If the **c** conversion character is preceded by a field width, then the specified number of characters are read and the corresponding data argument should be a pointer to an array of **char**s. Otherwise, the data argument can be a pointer to a single **char**.
p	Reads a pointer. The actual representation of the pointer value in the input field is implementation-defined, but it should be the same as that produced by the **%p** conversion of *printf()*. The corresponding data argument must be a pointer to a pointer to **void**.
n	Records the number of characters read thus far by this *scanf()* call. No characters are read for this conversion character. The corresponding data argument should be a pointer to an integer.

Table A-8. scanf() *Conversion Characters. (continued on next page)*

Conversion Character	Effect
[*scan list*]	Reads a character string. If the first character in the *scan list* (a list of characters) is not a circumflex (^), then characters are read from the input stream until a character is read that is *not* a member of the *scan list*. If the first character is a circumflex, then the *scan list* serves as a terminating set—*scanf( )* reads characters from the input stream until it encounters one of the characters in the list. The corresponding data argument should be a pointer to an array of **char**s. The array is loaded with the characters read. *scanf( )* automatically appends a null character after the last character.
%	Reads a percent sign. No assignment occurs.

Table A-8. scanf() *Conversion Characters.*
(continued from preceding pages)

Any conversion character may be preceded by a *maximum field width* or an *assignment suppression flag*. The field width is written in the form of a decimal digit and directs the *scanf( )* function not to read any more than the specified number of characters for that particular item. The assignment suppression flag is an asterisk (*), which causes *scanf( )* to read the data item but not to assign it to a variable. Consequently, you should not enter a corresponding data pointer for a conversion specification with an asterisk.

The *scanf( )* function continues reading characters from the input stream until the format string is exhausted, or an end-of-file is encountered, or a conflict occurs. A conflict can occur whenever the next character in the stream does not match the conversion specifier. For example, the next character might be a letter, whereas the conversion specifier indicates a numeric value. A conflict also occurs if the format string contains a string literal that is not matched by the next character in the input stream. Regardless of whether a conflict occurs or whether *scanf( )* completes successfully, it returns the number of data items assigned. However, if an end-of-file is encountered before a conversion or conflict takes place, *scanf( )* returns *EOF*.

The following examples show several ways to read an input stream using *scanf()*. Assume that the input stream for all three examples is

```
The value of pi to 7 digits is 3.1415978
```

Example 1:

```
int digits;
float pi;
scanf( "The value of pi to %d decimal digits is %f",
        &digits, &pi );
```

The value 7 is loaded into *digits* and 3.1415978 is assigned to *pi*. The string literals are matched and ignored. They serve only to move the file position indicator so that the numeric data can be read.

Example 2:

```
short digits;
double pi;
char str[80];
scanf( "%19c %hd %*19c %5lf", str, &digits, &pi );
```

In this example, the number of digits and the value of *pi* are assigned to **short** and **double** variables, respectively. The field width designation in **%5lf** causes *scanf()* to read only the first 5 characters of *pi* (3.1415). The first part of the text is assigned to the array *str[]*; the second part has assignment suppressed by the asterisk. Note that there are only three data arguments even though there are four conversion specifiers because one of them is suppressed. Also note that the data argument for the text string is simply *str*, since an array name by itself is automatically converted to a pointer to the initial element of the array.

Example 3:

```
long digits;
long double pi;
str[80];
scanf( "%*s %*s %*s %*s %*s %ld %*s %*s %*s %Lf",
        &digits, &pi );
```

The number of digits and the value of *pi* are assigned to a **long** and **long double**, respectively. Each word in the input text is read by a **%s** conversion specifier, but assignment is suppressed.

A.13.32 The *setbuf()* Function

```
#include <stdio.h>
void setbuf( FILE *stream, char *buf );
```

The *setbuf()* function is used to change the buffering properties of a stream. Normally, input and output are stored in blocks until the block is filled, and then the entire block is sent to its destination. The size of a block is implementation defined, but is typically 512 or 1024 bytes. This function enables you to make the stream unbuffered. When a stream is unbuffered, characters are sent to their destination immediately. Use *setvbuf()* to change the size of the buffer.

The *setbuf()* function should be called only after a stream has been opened and before it has been read from or written to. Once you have performed an I/O operation on a stream, you cannot change its buffer properties.

To change the default size of a block, you must allocate your own buffer by declaring an array of **char**s of the desired block size. Then pass a pointer to this array as the second argument. Note that this array must exist at least as long as the stream is open. If it has automatic duration, therefore, make sure that its scope is wide enough so that it is not deallocated before the stream is closed. To make a stream unbuffered, pass a null pointer.

The maximum size of a buffer is implementation-defined and is recorded in the constant *BUFSIZ*.

The standard output stream *stdout* is automatically buffered only if the stream does not point to a terminal.

The standard diagnostic stream *stderr* is unbuffered by default.

Except that it returns no value, the *setbuf()* function is equivalent to *setvbuf()* invoked with the values of *_IOFBF* for *mode* and *BUFSIZ* for *size* or (if *buf* is a null pointer) with the value *_IONBF* for *mode*.

A.13.33 The *setvbuf()* Function

```
#include <stdio.h>
int setvbuf( FILE *stream, char *buf, int mode,
             size_t size );
```

The *setvbuf()* function enables you to change the default buffering parameters for a stream. Use *setvbuf()* after you have opened a stream but before you have read from or written to it.

There are three choices for the argument *mode*, each of which is a macro defined in *stdio.h*:

    _IOFBF   forces I/O to be fully buffered.

    _IOLBF   causes output to be line buffered.

    _IONBF   causes I/O to be unbuffered.

If *buf* is not a null pointer, the array it points to may be used as the buffer instead of an array automatically allocated by the runtime system. Note, however, that the array pointed to by *buf* must have at least as long a lifetime as the stream to which it is associated.

The argument *size* specifies the size of the array pointed to by *buf*. The contents of this array at any time are indeterminate.

The *setvbuf( )* function returns zero if it is successful. It returns a nonzero value if the arguments are invalid or if the request cannot be honored for some other reason.

A.13.34 The *sprintf()* Function

```
#include <stdio.h>
int sprintf( char *s, const char *format, ... );
```

The *sprintf( )* function behaves exactly like *fprintf( )*, except that the data is written to a character array instead of an output stream. *sprintf( )* appends a null character after the last character written. It returns the number of characters assigned, not including the terminating null. See the description of *printf( )* for more information.

The *sprintf( )* function subsumes the older *ecvt( )*, *fcvt( )*, and *gcvt( )* functions.

A.13.35 The *sscanf()* Function

```
#include <stdio.h>
int sscanf( char *s, const char *format, ... );
```

The *sscanf( )* function is the same as *fscanf( )*, except that the first argument identifies an array rather than a stream from which to read input. See the description of *scanf( )* for more information.

A.13.36 The *tmpfile()* Function

```
#include <stdio.h>
FILE *tmpfile( void );
```

The *tmpfile()* function creates a temporary binary file. The file is opened with update status in binary mode (**wb+**). It is automatically deleted when it is closed, whether explicitly or implicitly. *tmpfile()* returns a pointer to the stream of the new file. If for some reason the file cannot be created, *tmpfile()* returns a null pointer.

A.13.37 The *tmpnam()* Function

```
#include <stdio.h>
char *tmpnam( char *s );
```

Like the *tmpfile()* function, *tmpnam()* is used to create a temporary file. However, *tmpnam()* is more flexible than *tmpfile()*. The *tmpnam()* function enables you to open a file in either binary or text mode, and the file is not automatically deleted.

tmpnam() generates a filename that is guaranteed not to conflict with other filenames. If you pass a null pointer, *tmpnam()* generates a file name but leaves it in an internal static object and returns a pointer to that object. Subsequent calls to *tmpnam()* can modify the file name. If you pass a pointer with a nonzero value, however, *tmpnam()* assumes that you have allocated enough storage for the new name so it generates a name, stores it at the passed address, and returns the pointer argument as the result. The maximum file name length is stored in *L_tmpnam*, which is defined in *<limits.h>*.

The *tmpnam()* function is guaranteed to generate at least 25 unique names before it begins duplicating itself. The actual implementation-defined number of unique names is represented by the constant *TMP_MAX*. The file that is created has the same properties as other files created within the C context. You can open and close it with calls to *fopen()* and *fclose()*. To delete it, you must explicitly *remove()* it.

A.13.38 The *vfprintf()* Function

```
#include <stdarg.h>
#include <stdio.h>
int vfprintf( FILE *stream, const char *format,
              va_list arg );
```

The *vfprintf()* function can be used in conjunction with the variable argument macros to perform the same operation as *fprintf()*. The difference is that the variable argument list is replaced by the array *arg*, which must be initialized by the *va_start* macro. See Section A.12 on variable argument macros for more information.

A.13.39 The *vprintf()* Function

```
#include <stdarg.h>
#include <stdio.h>
int vprintf( const char *format, va_list arg );
```

The *vprintf()* function can be used in conjunction with the variable argument macros to perform the same operation as *printf()*. The difference is that the variable argument list is replaced by the array *arg*, which must be initialized by the *va_start* macro. See Section A.12 on variable argument macros for more information.

A.13.40 The *vsprintf()* Function

```
#include <stdarg.h>
#include <stdio.h>
int vsprintf( FILE *stream, const char *format,
              va_list arg );
```

The *vsprintf()* function can be used in conjunction with the variable argument macros to perform the same operation as *sprintf()*. The difference is that the variable argument list is replaced by the array *arg*, which must be initialized by the *va_start* macro. See Section A.12 on variable argument macros for more information.

A.13.41 The *ungetc()* Function

```
#include <stdio.h>
int ungetc( int c, FILE *stream );
```

The *ungetc()* function pushes a character (specified by *c*) back onto the specified input stream. The pushed character will be the next character read assuming there is no intervening *fseek()*. Note that *ungetc()* affects the buffer, but not the file or device associated with the stream. Moreover, *ungetc()* affects the file position indicator in undefined ways, so it is not wise to mix calls to *ungetc()* with calls to *fseek()* that use the *SEEK_CUR* mode.

If *ungetc()* cannot push the character onto a stream, it returns *EOF*. Otherwise, it returns *c*.

A.14 General Utilities

The *<stdlib.h>* header file declares four types and a number of functions that fall under the category of "general utilities." This group of functions can be further divided into the following subgroups:

- String Conversion Functions

- Pseudo-Random Number Generation Functions

- Memory Management Functions

- Environment Functions

- Searching and Sorting Functions

- Integer Arithmetic Functions

The types defined in *<stdlib.h>* are

div_t	A structure returned by the *div()* function.
ldiv_t	A structure returned by the *ldiv()* function.
size_t	The data type that results from a **sizeof** expression.
wchar_t	An integral type whose range can represent all characters in the largest character set supported by the compiler.

The *<stdlib.h>* header file also defines several macros:

EXIT_FAILURE	An integral expression that can be returned by the *exit()* function to indicate unsuccessful termination.
EXIT_SUCCESS	An integral expression that can be returned by the *exit()* function to indicate successful termination.
MB_CUR_MAX	A positive integer expression that represents the greatest number of bytes that can be used to represent a multibyte character in the current locale.
RAND_MAX	Expands to an integral constant expression whose value represents the maximum value returned by the *rand()* function.

A.14.1 String Conversion Functions

The following functions convert a string of characters into a numeric value. For example,

```
atoi( "1234" )
```

returns the integer value 1234.

A.14.1.1 The *atof()* Function

```
#include <stdlib.h>
double atof( const char *nptr );
```

The *atof()* function converts the string pointed to by *nptr* into a **double** value. It is equivalent to the *strtod()* function except that it does not have the same error-reporting facilities.

A.14.1.2 The *atoi()* Function

```
#include <stdlib.h>
int atoi( const char *nptr );
```

The *atoi()* function converts the string pointed to by *nptr* into its **int** representation.

A.14.1.3 The *atol()* Function

```
#include <stdlib.h>
long atol( const char *nptr );
```

The *atol()* function converts the string pointed to by *nptr* into its **long int** representation. It is equivalent to the *strtol()* function except that it does not include the same error-reporting facilities.

A.14.1.4 The *strtod()* Function

```
#include <stdlib.h>
double strtod( const char *nptr, char **endptr );
```

The *strtod()* function interprets the string pointed to by *nptr* as a floating-point value and returns its **double** representation. The string may contain leading spaces, which are ignored, followed by an optional plus or minus sign, followed by the floating-point number in either regular or scientific notation. If the string represents an integer value (i.e., there is no decimal point), the *strtod()* function assumes a decimal point following the last digit. If an inappropriate character appears before the first digit following an **e** or **E**, the exponent is assumed to be zero.

The function continues reading and processing characters in the string until it reaches a character that cannot be part of the floating-point value. At this point, the function concludes and assigns a pointer to the unrecognized character to *endptr* (if *endptr* is a null pointer, however, no assignment takes place).

Assuming successful completion, the *strtod()* function returns the **double** value of the string. If the function cannot decipher a floating-point value, it returns zero and sets *errno* to *EDOM*. It also assigns the value of *nptr* to the object pointed to by *endptr*, assuming *endptr* is not a null pointer.

If *strtod()* successfully interprets the floating-point value, but the value is too large to fit in a **double**, the function returns *HUGE_VAL* (or negative *HUGE_VAL* if the floating-point value is negative) and sets *errno* to *ERANGE*. If the floating-point value is too small to be represented in a **double**, the function returns zero and sets *errno* to *ERANGE*.

A.14.1.5 The *strtol()* Function

```
#include <stdlib.h>
long strtol( const char *nptr, char **endptr,
             int base );
```

The *strtol()* function converts the string pointed to by *nptr* into its **long int** representation in any base from 2 through 36. Leading white space is ignored and an optional plus or minus sign is allowed.

If the *base* value is zero, then the string is interpreted as a decimal integer constant, possibly preceded by a plus or minus sign but not including an integer suffix. Otherwise, the value of base should be between 2 and 36 to indicate the base to be used for conversion. Bases greater than 10 use alphabetic letters from **a** (valued at 10) to **z** (valued at 35). If the value of *base* is 16, the integer may include a **0X** or **0x** prefix to indicate a hexadecimal constant.

The *strtol()* function continues reading characters until it reaches a character that cannot be part of the number. A pointer to this character is assigned to *endptr*. (If *endptr* is a null pointer, however, no assignment takes place.)

Upon successful completion, *strtol( )* returns the converted value. If it cannot decipher an integer from the string, it returns zero and sets *errno* to *EDOM*. It also assigns the value of *nptr* to the object pointed to by *endptr*, assuming *endptr* is not a null pointer.

If *strtol( )* successfully interprets the integer value but it is too large to fit in a **long int**, the function returns *LONG_MAX* or *LONG_MIN*, depending on the sign of the value, and sets *errno* to *ERANGE*.

A.14.1.6 The *strtoul()* Function

```
#include <stdlib.h>
unsigned long int strtoul( const char *nptr,
                           char **endptr, int base );
```

The *strtoul( )* function converts the string pointed to by *nptr* into its **unsigned long int** representation in any base from 2 through 36. Leading white space is ignored. An optional plus or minus sign is *not* allowed.

If the *base* value is zero, then the string is interpreted as a decimal integer constant, not including an integer suffix. Otherwise, the value of base should be between 2 and 36 to indicate the base to be used for conversion. Bases greater than 10 use alphabetic letters from **a** (valued at 10) to **z** (valued at 35). If the value of *base* is 16, the integer may include a **0X** or **0x** prefix to indicate a hexadecimal constant.

The *strtol( )* function continues reading characters until it reaches a character that cannot be part of the number. A pointer to this character is assigned to *endptr*. (If *endptr* is a null pointer, however, no assignment takes place.)

Upon successful completion, *strtol( )* returns the converted value. If it cannot decipher an integer from the string, it returns zero and sets *errno* to *EDOM*. It also assigns the value of *nptr* to the object pointed to by *endptr*, assuming *endptr* is not a null pointer.

If *strtol( )* successfully interprets the integer value but it is too large to fit in an **unsigned long int**, the function returns *ULONG_MAX* and sets *errno* to *ERANGE*.

A.14.2   Pseudo-Random Number Generator Functions

The *rand()* and *srand()* functions enable you to generate pseudo-random numbers.

A.14.2.1 The *rand()* Function

```
#include <stdlib.h>
int rand( void );
```

The *rand()* function returns an integer in the range 0 through RAND_MAX. Successive calls to *rand()* should produce different integers. However, the sequence of random numbers could be the same for each program execution unless you use a different seed value via the *srand()* function.

A.14.2.2 The *srand()* Function

```
#include <stdlib.h>
void srand( unsigned int seed );
```

The *srand()* function uses the argument as a seed for a new sequence of pseudo-random numbers to be returned by subsequent calls to *rand()*. If *srand()* is invoked with the same seed value, the sequence of generated numbers will be the same. The default seed value is 1.

A.14.3 Memory Management Functions

The memory management functions enable you to allocate and deallocate memory dynamically. See Chapter 7 for more information about these functions.

A.14.3.1 The *calloc()* Function

```
#include <stdlib.h>
void *calloc( size_t nmemb, size_t size );
```

The *calloc()* function allocates contiguous space for *nmemb* objects, each of which has a length in bytes specified by *size*. All bits in the allocated space are initialized to zero. *calloc()* returns a pointer to the first byte of the allocated space. If the space cannot be allocated, or if *nelem* or *size* is zero, *calloc()* returns a null pointer.

A.14.3.2 The *free()* Function

```
#include <stdlib.h>
void free( void *ptr );
```

The *free()* function deallocates the space pointed to by *ptr,* which should hold an address returned by a previous call to *calloc()*, *malloc()*, or *realloc()*. If *ptr* is a null pointer, *free()* takes no action. If *ptr* points to an area that was not previously allocated by one of the memory-management functions, or to an area that has already been deallocated, the behavior is undefined. Once a memory area has been freed, you should assume that its contents have been destroyed. You should not attempt to use the area again. The operating system may recycle the area for future use, but this is beyond your control.

Note that the ANSI Standard does not support *cfree()*, which in many implementations is used to free space allocated by *calloc()*.

A.14.3.3 The *malloc()* Function

```
#include <stdlib.h>
void malloc( size_t size );
```

The *malloc()* function allocates space for an object whose length is specified by *size*. *malloc()* returns a pointer to the first byte of the allocated space. If the space cannot be allocated, or if *size* is zero, *malloc()* returns a null pointer. The space allocated by *malloc()* is not initialized to any special value.

A.14.3.4 The *realloc()* Function

```
#include <stdlib.h>
void realloc( void *ptr, size_t size );
```

The *realloc()* function changes the size of a previously allocated space. The *ptr* argument should hold the address of an area previously allocated by *malloc()*, *calloc()*, or *realloc()*. The *size* argument specifies the new size. If the new size is smaller than the old size, the unused portion at the end is discarded. If the new size is larger than the old size, then all of the old contents are preserved and new memory is tacked on to the end. The new space is not initialized.

realloc() returns a pointer to the first byte of the new object. If the space cannot be allocated, *realloc()* returns a null pointer but leaves the memory area unchanged. If *ptr* is a null pointer, *realloc()* behaves just like a *malloc()* function. If *size* equals zero, *realloc()* returns a null pointer and frees up the space pointed to by *ptr*. If *ptr* does not point to a previously allocated area, the behavior is undefined.

A.14.4 Environment Functions

The C library contains several functions for communicating with the computer environment, usually through the operating system. These functions enable you to exit prematurely from a program, to specify behavior after program termination, and to execute operating system commands.

A.14.4.1 The *abort()* Function

```
#include <stdlib.h>
void abort( void );
```

The *abort()* function causes abnormal termination of a program. There is no guarantee that buffers will be flushed, that open streams will be closed, or that temporary files will be deleted. The *abort()* function can be turned off by catching the *SIGABRT* signal with the *signal()* function. If the *SIGABRT* signal is not caught, the *abort()* function causes an unsuccessful termination status to be returned to the host environment by means of the function call

```
raise( SIGABRT )
```

If the *SIGABRT* signal is being ignored, *abort()* returns no value. Otherwise, *abort()* causes program termination, so it cannot return to its caller.

A.14.4.2 The *atexit()* Function

```
#include <stdlib.h>
int atexit( void (*func)( void ) );
```

The *atexit()* function provides a program with a convenient way to clean up an environment before the program exits. The *atexit()* function takes a pointer to a function as an argument and registers that function to be called at program termination. You can register at least 32 functions that will be invoked in the reverse order from which they are registered. The registered functions may not themselves take arguments. When the registered functions are executed, the program environment is the same as when the *main()* function is called at program start-up. Therefore, these functions should not use variables declared in other modules, even if they have fixed duration.

If it succeeds, *atexit()* returns zero. Otherwise, it returns a nonzero value.

A.14.4.3 The *exit()* Function

```
#include <stdlib.h>
void exit( int status );
```

The *exit()* function produces normal program termination. First, all functions registered by the *atexit()* function are called, in reverse order of their registration. Next, all open output streams are flushed, all open streams are closed, and all files created by the *tmpfile()* function are deleted. Finally, control is returned to the host environment. If the value of *status* is zero or *EXIT_SUCCESS*, the status returned is *successful termination*. If the returned value is *EXIT_FAIL-URE,* an implementation-defined meaning of *unsuccessful termination* is indicated. Otherwise the returned status is *unsuccessful termination*. Invoking *exit()* is the same as returning from *main()*, with the exception that the *exit()* call causes all functions registered by *atexit()* to be invoked.

A.14.4.4 The *getenv()* Function

```
#include <stdlib.h>
char *getenv( const char *name );
```

Each environment has an implementation-defined *environment list*, of which each entry has the form *name == value*. The *getenv()* function matches the argument string to one of the names in the list and returns the corresponding *value*. If the argument does not match any names in the list, a null pointer is returned.

A.14.4.5 The *system()* Function

```
#include <stdlib.h>
int system( const char *string );
```

The *system()* function passes the string pointed to by *string* to the host environment to be executed. The string should be a command meaningful to the command processor in the host environment. Before calling *system()*, you should close all open files since the operating system may access them in unexpected ways.

If *string* is a null pointer, the function call is interpreted as a request to see whether a command processor exists. *system()* returns zero if there is no command processor or a nonzero value to indicate that a command processor exists. If the argument is not a null pointer, *system()* returns an implementation-defined value.

A.14.5 Searching and Sorting Functions

These functions are efficient routines that enable you to search for an object in an array and to sort an array. Although they are general-purpose routines, they have usually been finely tuned to run efficiently.

A.14.5.1 The *bsearch()* Function

```
#include <stdlib.h>
void bsearch( const void *key, const void *base,
    size_t nel, size_t *keysize,
    int (*compar) ( const void *, const void * ) );
```

The *bsearch()* function searches an array for an element that matches the object pointed to by *key*. The array itself is identified by the *base* argument, which points to the array's initial element. The *nel* argument specifies the number of array elements to search through, and *keysize* represents the size of each element.

The array must have been previously sorted in ascending order according to a comparison function pointed to by *compar*. The comparison function, which you must supply, takes two arguments and returns a negative number if the object pointed to by the first argument is less than the object pointed to by the second, zero if the two arguments are equal, or a positive number if the first argument is greater than the second. The runtime library supplies a standard comparison function called *memcmp()*.

bsearch() returns a pointer to the matching object in the array or a null pointer if no match is found. If two members compare as equal, a pointer to either one may be returned, depending on the implementation.

A.14.5.2 The *qsort()* Function

```
#include <stdlib.h>
void qsort( void *base, size_t nel, size_t keysize,
    int (*compar)( const void *, const void * ) );
```

The *qsort()* function sorts an array of *nel* objects in ascending order. The initial element of the array is pointed to by *base*, and *keysize* specifies the length of each object. The array is sorted according to a comparison function pointed to by *compar*.

The comparison function, which you must supply, takes two arguments and returns a negative number if the first argument is less than the second, zero if the two arguments are equal, or a positive number if the first argument is greater than the second. The runtime library supplies a standard comparison function called *memcmp()*. If two elements in the array are equal, their order is unspecified. *qsort()* does not return a value.

A.14.6 Integer Arithmetic Functions

The following functions take integer arguments.

A.14.6.1 The *abs()* Function

```
#include <stdlib.h>
int abs( int i );
```

The *abs()* function returns the absolute value of *i*. If the result cannot be represented by an **int**, the behavior is undefined. For example, in two's complement notation, the absolute value of the largest negative number cannot be represented.

A.14.6.2 The *div()* Function

```
#include <stdlib.h>
div_t idiv( int numer, int denom );
```

The *div()* function divides *denom* into *numer* and returns a structure containing the quotient and remainder. The structure contains the following members:

```
int quot;     /* quotient */
int rem;      /* remainder */
```

If the result cannot be represented, the behavior is undefined.

A.14.6.3 The *labs()* Function

```
#include <stdlib.h>
long int labs( long int j );
```

The *labs()* function is equivalent to the *abs()* function, except that the argument and return value have type **long int**.

A.14.6.4 The *ldiv()* Function

```
#include <stdlib.h>
ldiv_t ldiv( long numer, long denom );
```

The *ldiv()* function is identical to *idiv()*, except that the arguments and results are **long int**s instead of **int**s.

A.15 String-Handling Functions

The C library contains a number of useful functions for manipulating character strings. All of these functions require that the header file *<string.h>* be included. These functions fall into three general categories:

- Functions that begin with *str* operate on null-terminated strings.

- Functions that begin with *strn* operate on strings with a specified maximum length.

- Functions that begin with *mem* operate on arrays of data objects of specified length.

The type *size_t* used by many of these functions is a type defined in *string.h*, which is the type returned by a **sizeof** expression.

A.15.1 The *memchr()* Function

```
#include <string.h>
void *memchr( const void *s, int c, size_t n );
```

The *memchr()* function locates the first occurrence of *c* (converted to an **unsigned char**) in the array pointed to by *s*. If it finds the value, *memchr()* returns a pointer to it; otherwise, *memchr()* returns a null pointer.

A.15.2 The *memcmp()* Function

```
#include <string.h>
int memcmp( const void *s1, const void *s2,
          size_t n );
```

The *memcmp()* function compares the first *n* characters of *s1* with *s2*. Each element in *s1* is compared in turn to the corresponding element in *s2*. As soon as they differ, *memcmp()* determines which is numerically greater. If *s1* is greater, *memcmp()* returns a positive value; if *s2* is greater, a negative value is returned; if the two are equal up to *n* elements, *memcmp()* returns zero. If there are fewer than *n* elements in either array, the results are undefined.

Although the arguments to this function are defined as **void ***, the function was really intended to compare character strings. It may not work as expected for other types of objects. This is especially true for structures that contain holes and objects that have the high-order bit set. See the description of *strcmp()* for contrast.

A.15.3 The *memcpy()* Function

```
#include <string.h>
void *memcpy( void *s1, const void *s2, size_t n );
```

The *memcpy()* function copies *n* characters from string *s2* to string *s1*. If the strings overlap, the behavior is undefined. *memcpy()* returns the value of *s1*.

A.15.4 The *memmove()* Function

```
#include <string.h>
void memmove( void *s1, const void *s2, size_t n );
```

The *memmove()* function copies *n* characters from object *s2* to object *s1*. It is essentially the same as the *memcpy()* function except that it works even when the two objects (*s1* and *s2*) overlap. The *memmove()* function acts as if the *s2* object were first copied to a temporary array and then copied from the temporary holding area to *s1*.

A.15.5 The *memset()* Function

```
#include <string.h>
void *memset( void *s, int c, size_t n );
```

The *memset()* function provides a means for initializing an array to a particular value. It copies the value *c* (converted to an **unsigned char**) into the first *n* elements of array *s*. The *memset()* function returns the value *s*.

A.15.6 The *strcpy()* Function

```
#include <string.h>
char *strcpy( char *s1, const char *s2 );
```

The *strcpy()* function copies the contents of string *s2* into the array pointed to by *s1*. The string identified by *s2* must have a terminating null character, which is also copied. If the string and the array overlap, the results are undefined. *strcpy()* returns the value of *s1*. See the descriptions of *memcpy()* and *strncpy()* for contrast.

A.15.7 The *strncpy()* Function

```
#include <string.h>
char *strncpy( char *s1, const char *s2, size_t n );
```

The *strncpy()* function copies up to *n* characters from the string *s2* into the array pointed to by *s1*. If the string to be copied is shorter than *n* characters, null characters are appended to the array as padding until *n* characters have been written. Note that if the string to be copied is longer than *n* characters, the array that gets the copy will not be null-terminated. If the string and the array overlap, the results are undefined. *strcpy()* returns the value of *s1*. See the descriptions of *memcpy()* and *strcpy()* for contrast.

A.15.8 The *strcoll()* Function

```
#include <string.h>
size_t strcoll( char *to, size_t maxsize,
                const char *from );
```

The *strcoll()* function transforms the string pointed to by *from* so that it is suitable as an argument to *memcmp()* or *strcmp()*. This is particularly applicable to implementations where the local language forces text to be stored in an inconsistent manner. For example, some languages contain so many characters that they cannot all be stored in a **char**. The *strcoll()* function makes it possible for two strings in such an implementation to be compared to one another.

The transformed string is placed in the array pointed at by *to*. The resulting string will never be more than twice the length of the original string (plus room for the terminating null character). You can ensure that even fewer characters are stored in the *to* array with the *maxsize* argument. *maxsize* represents the maximum number of characters to be placed in the resulting string, including the terminating null character.

If the resulting string contains no more than *maxsize* characters, *strcoll()* returns the number of characters placed in the string. Otherwise, it returns zero and the contents of the *to* array are indeterminate.

A.15.9 The *strcat()* Function

```
#include <string.h>
char *strcat( char *s1, const char *s2 );
```

The *strcat()* function appends a copy of string *s2* to string *s1*. The terminating null character in *s1* is overwritten by the initial character in *s2*. Characters are copied from *s2* until a terminating null character is reached (the null character is also copied). The results are undefined if the two strings overlap. In particular, you cannot necessarily double a string by using the same string as both arguments. *strcat()* returns the value of *s1*.

A.15.10 The *strncat()* Function

```
#include <string.h>
char *strncat( char *s1, const char *s2, size_t n );
```

The *strncat()* function appends up to *n* characters from string *s2* to the end of string *s1*. The terminating null character in *s1* is overwritten by the initial character in *s2*. If the terminating null character in *s2* is reached before *n* characters have been written, the null character is copied, but no other characters are written. If *n* characters are written before a terminating null is encountered, the *strncat()* function appends its own terminating null character to *s1*, so that *n+1* characters are written. The results are undefined if the two strings overlap in memory. *strncat()* returns *s1*.

A.15.11 The *strcmp()* Function

```
#include <string.h>
int strcmp( const char *s1, const char *s2 );
```

The *strcmp()* function compares string *s1* with string *s2*. If *s1* is less than *s2*, *strcmp()* returns an integer greater than zero; if *s1* is less than *s2*, a negative integer is returned; and if the two strings are equal, *strcmp()* returns zero. See the description of *memcmp()* for contrast.

A.15.12 The *strerror()* Function

```
#include <string.h>
char *strerror( int errnum );
```

The *strerror()* function returns a pointer to an error message represented by *errnum*. The array which holds the message cannot be modified, but it can be overwritten by subsequent calls to *strerror()*.

A.15.13 The *strlen()* **function**

```
#include <string.h>
size_t strlen( const char *s );
```

The *strlen()* function returns the length of the string (number of bytes) pointed to by *s*. The terminating null character is not included in the length.

A.15.14 The *strncmp()* **Function**

```
#include <string.h>
int strncmp( const char *s1, const char *s2,
             size_t n );
```

The *strncmp()* function is the same as *strcmp()* except that it does not compare more than *n* characters. If *s1* is greater than *s2*, *strncmp()* returns an integer greater than zero; if *s1* is less than *s2*, a negative integer is returned; and if the two strings are equal, *strncmp()* returns zero.

A.15.15 The *strchr()* **Function**

```
#include <string.h>
char *strchr( const char *s, int c );
```

The *strchr()* function locates the first occurrence of *c* (converted to a **char**) in the string *s*. The terminating null character is considered part of the string. If the character is located, *strchr()* returns a pointer to it. Otherwise, it returns a null pointer.

A.15.16 The *strcspn()* **Function**

```
#include <string.h>
size_t strcspn( const char *s1, const char *s2 );
```

Starting from the beginning of *s1*, the *strcspn()* function counts characters that are not present in *s2*. As soon as it matches a character in the two strings, or it reaches the end of *s1*, it returns the number of characters read. The terminating null character is not considered part of *s2*.

A.15.17 The *strpbrk()* function

```
#include <string.h>
char *strpbrk( const char *s1, const char *s2 );
```

The *strpbrk()* function is the inverse of the *strcspn()* function. It locates the first character in *s*1 that is also present in *s2*. It returns a pointer to this character, or a null character if no match occurs. The terminating null characters are not included.

A.15.18 The *strrchr()* Function

```
#include <string.h>
char *strrchr( const char *s, int c );
```

The *strrchr()* function locates the last occurrence of *c* (converted to a **char**) in string *s*. It returns a pointer to this character, or a null pointer if the character is not present in the string.

A.15.19 The *strspn()* Function

```
#include <string.h>
size_t strspn( const char *s1, const char *s2 );
```

The *strspn()* function counts characters in *s1*, starting from the beginning of the string, until it reaches a character that is not present in *s2*. It returns the number of characters counted.

A.15.20 The *strstr()* Function

```
#include <string.h>
char *strstr( const char *s1, const char *s2 );
```

The *strstr()* function locates the first occurrence of string *s2* (not including the terminating null character) in the string *s1*. It returns a pointer to the located string in *s1*, or a null pointer if no match occurs.

A.15.21 The *strtok()* **Function**

```
#include <string.h>
char *strtok( char *s1, const char *s2 );
```

The *strtok()* function divides a string into a number of tokens. The semantics of *strtok()* are somewhat complex. The string *s1* is the string to be tokenized, while *s2* contains the separator characters. The *strtok()* function is designed to be called multiple times to fully tokenize *s1*. Its behavior on the first call is somewhat different from its behavior on subsequent calls. The first call to *strtok()* operates as follows:

1. *strtok()* locates the first character in *s1* that is *not* contained in *s2*. If no such character is found, *strtok()* returns a null pointer. If such a character is found, it represents the beginning of the first token. Ultimately a pointer to this character is returned, but first *strtok()* finds the end of the token as described in Step 2.

2. Assuming it finds the beginning of a token, *strtok()* then looks for a character that *is* contained in *s2*. If it cannot find such a character, then the token extends to the end of *s1*, and subsequent searches for a token will fail. If it does find such a character, it overwrites it with a null character which terminates the token. The *strtok()* function then saves a pointer to the next character in *s1* for use in subsequent calls.

After the first call, all subsequent calls to *strtok()* should have *NULL* as the first argument. They begin tokenizing where the last *strtok()* function left off and behave as described in Step 2. The following example illustrates the behavior of the *strtok()* function.

```
#include <stddef.h>
#include <string.h>

main()
{
  static char s[] = "+a+b*(c-d)/e"
  char *token;

  token = strtok( s, "+" ); /* token points to
                                "a" */
  printf( "%s\n", token );

/* token points to "b*" */
  token = strtok( NULL, "(" );
  printf( "%s\n", token );

/*token points to "c-d" */
  token = strtok( NULL, "+*/)" );
  printf( "%s\n", token );

/* token points to "/e" */
  token = strtok( NULL, "+" );
  printf( "%s\n", token );

/* token is a null pointer */
  token = strtok( NULL, "+" );
  exit( 0 );
}
```

The output is

```
a
b*
c-d
/e
```

The *strxfrm()* **Function**

```
#include <string.h>
size_t strxfrm( char *s1, const char *s2, size_t n );
```

The *strxfrm()* function transforms a string (*s2*) in some implementation-defined manner so that it is suitable as an argument to the *strcmp()* function. The resulting string is placed in the array pointed to by *s1*. *n* specifies the maximum length of the transformed string (including the terminating null character).

The only requirement on the transformation is that any two strings transformed by *strxfrm()* and compared with *strcmp()* must return the same result as would occur if they were compared with *strcoll()* prior to the transformation. In other words, the transformation may change certain character codes, but the collating sequence must remain the same.

strxfrm() returns the length of the transformed string, not including the terminating null character.

A.16 Multibyte Character Functions

The ANSI standard defines several runtime routines to assist programmers working with extended character sets that utilize multibyte characters. Whether or not
multibyte characters are in use and the interpretation of each multibyte character are determined by the value of the *LC_TYPE* macro and the current locale
setting (see Section A.8).

A.16.1 Character Functions

Multibyte characters can have different *shift states* which determine how each
multibyte character is interpreted. A programmer can change shift states by forcing the system to read special multibyte characters. If a call to one of these
functions changes the shift state, the shift state will remain changed until a subsequent call changes it again. Passing a null pointer to any of the following
functions returns the multibyte character system to its initial shift state.

A.16.1.1 The *mblen()* Function

```
#include <stdlib.h>
int mblen( const char *s, size_t n );
```

If *s* is not a null pointer, *mblen()* returns the number of characters composing the
multibyte character pointed to by *s*. If s points to a null character, *mblen()* returns 0. If *s* does not point to a valid multibyte character, *mblen()* returns −1.

If *s* is a null pointer, *mblen()* sets the multibyte character system to its initial shift
state. The function returns 0 if there is only one shift state and a nonzero value if
there exists more than one shift state.

A.16.1.2 The *mbtowc()* Function

```
#include <stdlib.h>
int mbtowc( wchar_t *pwc, const char *s, size_t n );
```

If *s* is not a null pointer, the *mbtowc()* function converts a multibyte character into an integer code and stores the code at the address pointed to by *pwc*. The *mbtowc()* function will attempt to determine how many bytes compose each multibyte character and will read that many bytes. At no time, however, will it read more than *n* bytes or the number of bytes specified by the *MB_CUR_MAX* macro, whichever is less. The value returned by *mbtowc()* is zero if *s* points to a null character, or the number of bytes comprising the multibyte character if *mbtowc()* successfully converts it.

If *s* is a null pointer, *mbtowc()* sets the multibyte character system to its initial shift state. The function returns 0 if there is only one shift state and a nonzero value if there exists more than one shift state.

A.16.1.3 The *wctomb()* Function

```
#include <stdlib.h>
int wctomb( char *s, wchar_t wchar );
```

If *s* is not a null pointer, *wctomb()* converts a character code into into its multibyte representation and stores the multibyte character in the array pointed to by *s*. *wctomb()* returns the number of characters in the multibyte character. If *wchar* does not correspond to a valid multibyte character, *wctomb()* returns −1.

If *s* is a null pointer, *wctomb()* sets the multibyte character system to its initial shift state. The function returns 0 if there is only one shift state and a nonzero value if there exists more than one shift state.

A.16.2 Multibyte String Functions

A.16.2.1 The *mbstowcs()* Function

```
#include <stdlib.h>
size_t mbstowcs( wchar_t *pwcs, const char *s,
                 size_t n );
```

The *mbstowcs()* function converts a multibyte character string pointed to by *s* into an array of integer codes that correspond to each character. The codes are placed in the array pointed to by *pwcs*. *mbstowcs()* stops reading multibyte characters as soon as it encounters a null character or it reads *n* multibyte characters, whichever comes first.

Each *mbstowcs()* call begins in the initial shift state. Characters that are read may change the shift state for the duration of the function call, but they have no effect on subsequent calls to any other function.

mbstowcs() returns the number of converted characters, not including the null character, if there is one. If *mbstowcs()* encounters an invalid multibyte character, it returns −1.

A.16.2.2 The *wcstombs()* Function

```
#include <stdlib.h>
size_t wcstombs( char *s, const wchar_t *pwcs,
                 size_t n );
```

The *wcstombs()* function converts an array of codes pointed to by *pwcs* into an array of multibyte characters and stores the characters in the array pointed to by *s*. *wcstombs()* stops converting characters as soon as it encounters a null character or after it has filled *n* bytes in the string pointed to by *s*, whichever comes first.

Each *wcstombs()* call begins in the initial shift state. Characters that are read may change the shift state for the duration of the function call, but they have no effect on subsequent calls to any other function.

wcstombs() returns the number of bytes written to *s*, not including the terminating null character, if there is one. If *wcstombs()* encounters an invalid multibyte code, it returns −1.

A.17 Date and Time Functions

The date and time functions enable you to access the system clock and calendar in a variety of ways. All of these functions require inclusion of the header file *<time.h>*. There are three types of time that these functions return:

- *calendar time* represents the current date and time according to the Gregorian calendar;

- *local time* is the calendar time expressed for a specific time zone;

- *daylight savings time* reflects a temporary change in the local time due to daylight savings regulations.

The header file defines one macro and declares three type definitions. The macro is

CLOCKS_PER_SEC
> Represents the number per second of the value returned by the *clock()* function.

The type definitions are

clock_t   Arithmetic type capable of representing time.

time_t   Arithmetic type capable of representing time.

tm   Structure that holds the components of a calendar time (see below).

The *tm* structure contains the following components at least (it may contain additional components):

```
int tm_sec; /* seconds after the minute -- [0, 59] */
int tm_min; /* minutes after the hour   -- [0, 59] */
int tm_hour; /* hours since midnight     -- [0, 23] */
int tm_mday; /* day of the month         -- [1, 31] */
int tm_mon; /* months since January     -- [0, 11] */
int tm_year; /* years since 1900         -- [    ] */
int tm_wday; /* days since Sunday        -- [0, 6 ] */
int tm_yday; /* days since January 1     --[0, 365] */
int tm_isdst; /* daylight savings time flag        */
```

The value of *tm_isdt* is positive if daylight savings time is in effect, zero if daylight savings time is not in effect, and negative if the information is not available.

A.17.1 The *clock()* Function

```
#include <time.h>
clock_t clock( void );
```

The *clock()* function returns the amount of processor time used by the program. To get the value in terms of seconds, divide the returned value by the macro *CLOCKS_PER_SEC*. The behavior of the *clock()* function is largely implementation defined. There is no precise definition for determining when the clock should start counting, and an implementation only needs to give its best approximation. If the processor time is not available, the *clock()* function returns −1 cast to the *clock_t* type.

A.17.2 The *time()* Function

```
#include <time.h>
time_t time( time_t *timer );
```

The *time()* function returns the implementation's best approximation of the calendar time. The encoding of the value is unspecified. If *timer* is not a null pointer, the calendar time is also assigned to the object that it points to. If the calendar time is unavailable, *time()* returns −1.

A.17.3 The *mktime()* Function

```
#include <time.h>
time_t mktime( struct tm *timeptr );
```

The *mktime()* function converts a broken-down time in a *tm* structure into a calendar time of the same form returned by the *time()* function. The values of *tm_wday* and *tm_yday* are ignored, and the values of the other fields are not restricted to the values shown in the earlier description of *tm*. In addition to returning a calendar time, *mktime()* also sets the fields in the structure pointed to by *timeptr* to appropriate values. This means that if the original values are out of range, *mktime()* forces them into the ranges listed above. *mktime()* also assigns appropriate values to *tm_wday* and *tm_yday*.

If *mktime()* cannot calculate a returnable calendar time, it returns *(time_t)–1*.

The following example shows how you might use the *mktime()* function to write a function that performs some loop for a specified number of minutes.

```
#include <time.h>

void do_for_x_minutes( x_minutes )
int x_minutes;
{
   struct tm when;
   time_t now, deadline;

   time( now );
   when = *localtime( now );
   when.tm_min += x_minutes;
   deadline = mktime( when );

/* Do foo() for x_minutes */
   while (difftime( time( 0 ), deadline ) > 0)
      foo();
}
```

Note that the *mktime()* function will work even if the expression

```
when.tm_min += x_minutes
```

is greater than 59.

A.17.4 The *asctime()* Function

```
#include <time.h>
char *asctime( const struct tm *timeptr );
```

The *asctime()* function converts the time represented by the structure pointed to by *timeptr* into a character string with the following form:

```
Sun Sep 16 01:03:52 1973\n\0
```

asctime() returns a pointer to the generated string. Subsequent calls to *asctime()* or *ctime()* may overwrite this string.

A.17.5 The *ctime()* Function

```
#include <time.h>
char *ctime( const time_t *timer );
```

The *ctime()* function converts the calendar time pointed to by *timer* to local time in the form of a character string. It is equivalent to

```
asctime( localtime( timer ) )
```

A.17.6 The *difftime()* Function

```
#include <time.h>
double difftime( time_t time1, time_t time0 );
```

The *difftime()* function returns the difference *time1 – time0*, expressed in seconds.

A.17.7 The *gmtime()* Function

```
#include <time.h>
struct tm *gmtime( const time_t *timer );
```

The *gmtime()* function converts the calendar time pointed to by *timer* into a broken-down time, expressed as Greenwich Mean Time (GMT). The *gmtime()* function returns a pointer to a structure containing the time components. If the GMT is not available, *gmtime()* returns a null pointer. Subsequent calls to *gmtime()* or *localtime()* may point to the same static structure *tm*, which is overwritten by each call.

A.17.8 The *localtime()* Function

```
#include <time.h>
struct tm *localtime( const time_t *timer );
```

The *localtime()* function converts the calendar time pointed to by *timer* into a broken-down time, expressed as local time. The *localtime()* function returns a pointer to a structure containing the time components. Subsequent calls to *gmtime()* or *localtime()* may point to the same static structure *tm*, which is overwritten by each call.

A.17.9 The *strftime()* Function

```
#include <time.h>
size_t strftime( char *s, size_t maxsize,
                 const char *format,
                 const struct tm *timeptr );
```

The *strftime()* function enables you to construct a string containing information from the structure pointed to by *timeptr*. The format of *strftime()* is similar to *printf()*, where the first argument is a format string that can contain text as well as format specifiers. In this case, however, the format specifiers are replaced with particular data from the *timeptr* structure. No more than *max_size* characters will be placed in the resulting string pointed to by *s*.

The format specifiers and what they are replaced by are listed in Table A-9. The exact value and format of each specifier depend on the particular implementation and the values stored in the structure pointed to by *timeptr*.

Format Specifier	Meaning
%a	The abbreviated weekday name.
%A	The full weekday name.
%b	The abbreviated month name.
%B	The full month name.
%c	An appropriate date and time representation.
%d	The day of month as a decimal number (01 – 31).
%H	The hour (24–hour clock) as a decimal number (00 – 23).
%I	The hour (12–hour clock) as a decimal number (01 – 12).
%j	The day of the year as a decimal number (001 – 386).
%m	The month as a decimal number (01 – 12).
%M	The minute as a decimal number (00 – 59).
%p	Either AM or PM (or the equivalent in the local language).
%S	The second as a decimal number (00 – 59).

Table A-9. Format Specifiers for the ctime() *Function.*
(continued on next page)

If the total number of characters resulting from replacements is not more than *maxsize*, *strftime( )* returns the number of characters written to the array pointed to by *s* (not including the terminating null character). Otherwise, *strftime( )* returns zero and the contents of the *s* array are indeterminate.

Format Specifier	Meaning
%U	The week number of the year (Sunday being the first day of the week) as a decimal number (00 – 52).
%w	The weekday as a decimal number (0 – 6) — Sunday is 0.
%W	The week number of the year (where Monday is the first day of the week) as a decimal number (00 – 52).
%x	An appropriate date representation.
%X	An appropriate time representation.
%y	The year (last two digits only) as a decimal number (00 – 99).
%Y	The year (all four digits) as a decimal number.
%Z	The time zone name, or no characters if no time zone exists.
%%	%

Table A-9. Format Specifiers for ctime() *Function.*
(continued from preceding page)

Appendix B

Syntax of ANSI C

file:

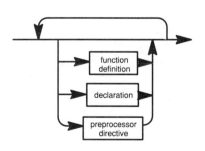

function definition:

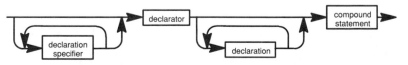

declaration specifier:

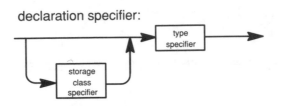

declarator:

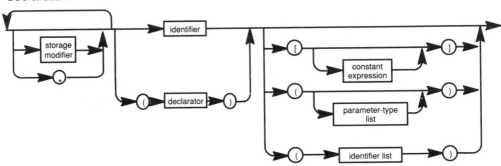

declaration:

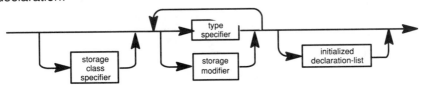

storage class specifier:

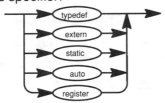

type specifier:

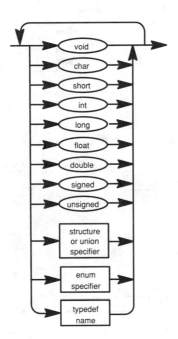

storage modifier:

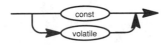

structure or union specifier:

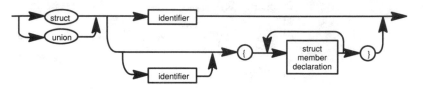

struct member declaration:

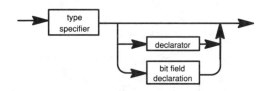

bit field declaration:

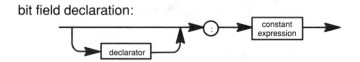

enum specifier:

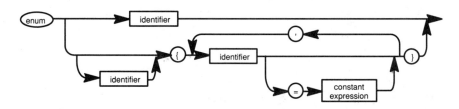

parameter type list:

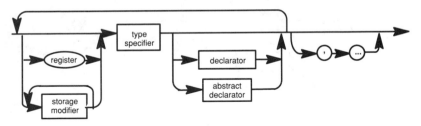

abstract declarator:

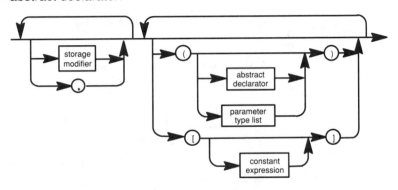

initialized declaration list:

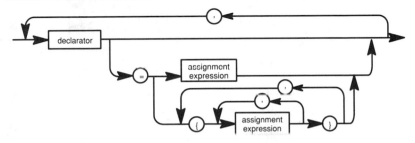

identifier:

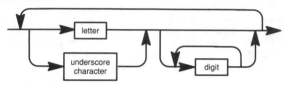

constant:

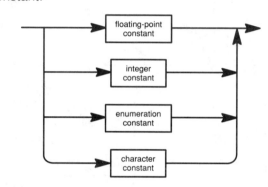

floating-point constant:

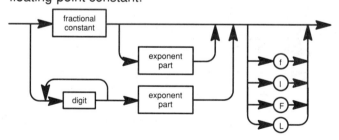

fractional constant:

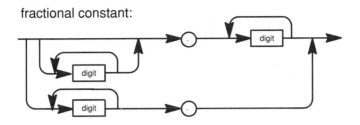

exponent part:

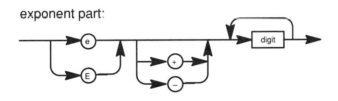

integer constant:

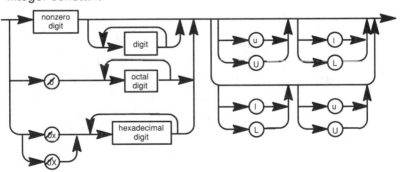

character constant:

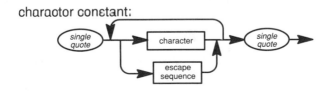

escape sequence:

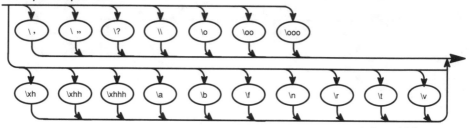

note: 0 = octal digit
h = hexadecimal digit

string literal:

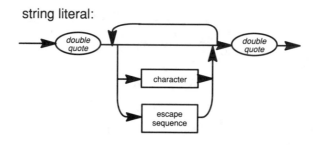

expression:

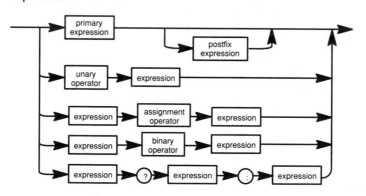

primary expression:

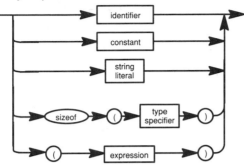

postfix expression:

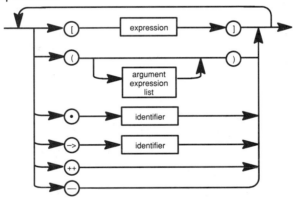

argument expression list:

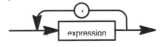

unary operator:

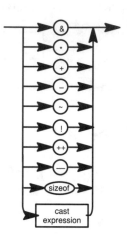

cast expression:

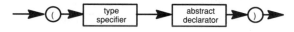

binary operator:
(in order of decreasing precedence)

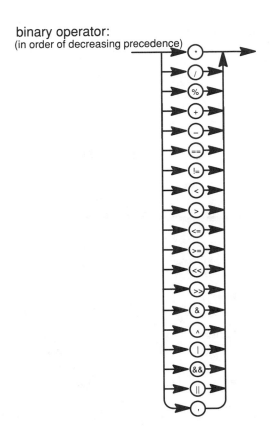

assignment operator:

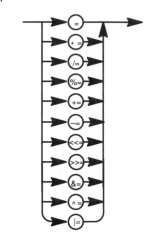

statement:

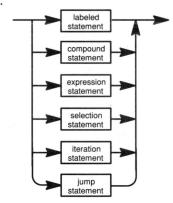

labeled statement:

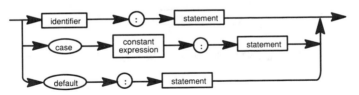

compound statement:

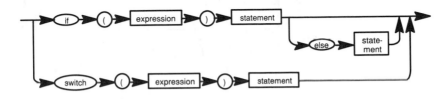

expression statement:

selection statement:

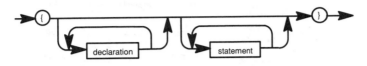

iteration statement:

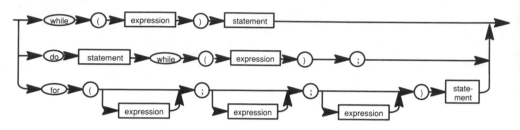

jump statement:

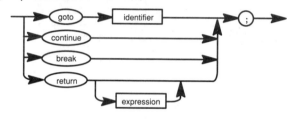

preprocessor directive:

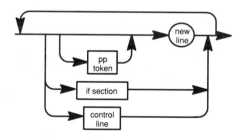

if section:

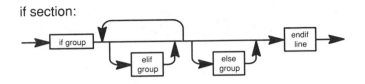

if group:

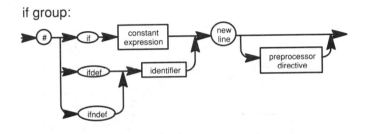

elif group:

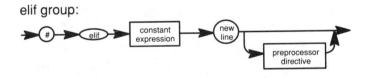

else group:

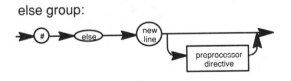

endif line:

control line:

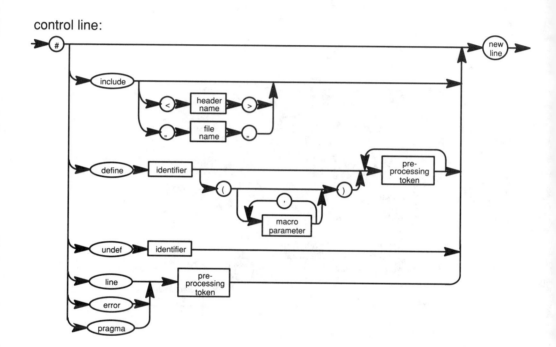

preprocessing token:

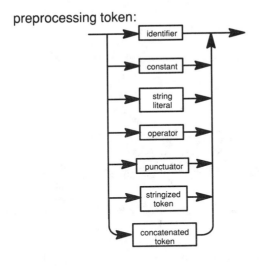

stringized token:

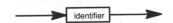

macro parameter:

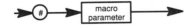

concatenated token:

Appendix C

Implementation Limits

Every C compiler imposes certain limitations upon the types of programs it will compile, such as the maximum length of variable names and the maximum length of lines in source files. These constraints are called *translation limits* because they concern how the compiler translates source text. There are also *numerical limits*, which concern the minimum and maximum values that can be represented by variously typed objects. For both types of limits, the ANSI Standard defines minimum values. An ANSI-conforming C compiler must support at least these minimum values but is free to exceed these limitations. In fact, ANSI recommends that implementations avoid imposing any limits wherever possible. Your compiler documentation should list all limits.

C.1 Translation Limits

An ANSI-conforming compiler must at least support the following:

- 15 nesting levels of compound statements, iteration control structures, and selection control structures

- 6 nesting levels in conditional compilation

- 12 pointer, array, and function declarators modifying a basic type in a declaration

- 32 expressions nested by parentheses

- 31 significant initial characters in an internal identifier or macro name

- 6 significant initial characters in an external identifier

- 511 external identifiers in one source file

- 127 identifiers with block scope in one block

- 1024 macro names simultaneously defined in one source file

- 31 parameters in one function definition or call

- 31 parameters in one macro definition or invocation

- 509 characters in a source line

- 509 characters in a string literal (after concatenation)

- 32767 bytes in an array or structure

- 8 nesting levels for **#include**d files

- 257 **case** labels in a **switch** statement

- 127 members in a single structure or union

- 127 enumeration constants in a single enumeration

- 15 levels of nested structure or union definitions in a declaration

C.2 Numerical Limits

The ANSI Standard defines the mimimum range of values that each scalar type of object must be able to represent. For integral objects, the low end and high end of these ranges are recorded in macro constants that are defined in the *limits.h* header file. Implementations may, of course, support larger ranges.

For floating-point types, the ANSI Standard defines a number of macros that describe an implementation's floating-point representation. These macros are defined in the *float.h* header file.

C.2.1 Sizes of Integral Types

The following page lists the macro names defined in *limits.h*, their meanings, and their minimum value for ANSI-conforming implementations:

Macro Name	Value	Meaning
CHAR_BIT	8	minimum number of bits for smallest object that is not a bit field (i.e., a byte)
SCHAR_MIN	−127	minimum value for an object of type **signed char**
SCHAR_MAX	+127	maximum value for an object of type **signed char**
UCHAR_MAX	255	maximum value for an object of type **unsigned char**
CHAR_MIN	*	minimum value for an object of type **char**
CHAR_MAX	*	maximum value for an object of type **char**
SHRT_MIN	−32767	minimum value for an object of type **short int**
SHRT_MAX	+32767	maximum value for an object of type **short int**
USHRT_MAX	65535	maximum value for an object of type **unsigned short int**
INT_MIN	−32767	minimum value for an object of type **int**
INT_MAX	+32767	maximum value for an object of type **int**
UINT_MAX	65535	maximum value for an object of type **unsigned int**
LONG_MIN	−2147483647	minimum value for an object of type **long int**
LONG_MAX	+2147483647	maximum value for an object of type **long int**
ULONG_MAX	4294967295	maximum value for an object of type **unsigned long int**

* If chars are signed by default, the value of *CHAR_MIN* should be the same as that of *SCHAR_MIN* and the value of *CHAR_MAX* should be the same as that of *SCHAR_MAX*. If chars are unsigned by default, the value of *CHAR_MIN* should be zero, and the value of *CHAR_MAX* should be the same as that of *UCHAR_MAX*.

C.2.2 Characteristics of Floating-Point Types

The ANSI Standard defines the characteristics of floating-point types in terms of a model that describes a representation of floating-point numbers and values that provide information about an implementation's floating-point arithmetic. We recommend that you read the ANSI Standard for a detailed discussion of this model. In this section, we present information about the limits for floating-point objects.

For any floating-point object, there are four limits:

max	The largest positive value that can be represented.
min	The largest negative value that can be represented.
epsilon	The minimum positive number, x, such that $1.0 + x \mathrel{!=} 1.0$
precision	The number of decimal digits of precision.

Each ANSI-conforming compiler provides values for these four limits in names. These names, however, need not be constants — they can also represent expressions evaluated at runtime. The names for each of the floating-point types and the minimum values that an ANSI-conforming compiler must support are shown below. Compilers are free to support values greater in magnitude (absolute value) to those shown, with the same size.

Maximum Value

float	*FLT_MAX*	1e+37
double	*DBL_MAX*	1e+37
long double	*LDBL_MAX*	1e+37

Minimum Value

float	*FLT_MIN*	1e−37
double	*DBL_MIN*	1e−37
long double	*LDBL_MIN*	1e−37

Epsilon

float	*FLT_EPSILON*	1e−5
double	*DBL_EPSILON*	1e−9
long double	*LDBL_EPSILON*	1e−9

Precision

float	*FLT_DIG*	6
double	*DBL_DIG*	10
long double	*LDBL_DIG*	10

Appendix D

Differences Between the ANSI and K&R Standards

This appendix summarizes the differences between the K&R standard and the ANSI Standard. The references listed in each section point to other parts of this book where you can find more information about the topic.

D.1 Source Translation Differences

The differences listed in this section relate to the lexical analysis stage of compilation.

D.1.1 Name Length

ANSI: Compilers must support internal names of at least 31 characters and external names of at least 6 characters.

K&R: Compilers must support internal names of at least 8 characters; external names may be shorter.

Reference: Section 2.3.2 Names; Section 7.3 Global Variables

D.1.2 Continuation Character

ANSI: The continuation character may be used to carry names as well as string literals to the next line.

K&R: The continuation character may be used only to continue string literals.

Reference: Section 2.6.1 Continuation Character

D.1.3 String Concatenation

ANSI: Supports this new feature that causes the compiler to concatenate adjacent string literals into a single string.

K&R: Does not support this feature.

Reference: Box 6-3: String Concatenation

D.1.4 Trigraph Sequences

ANSI: Supports trigraph sequences for entering characters not available on some keyboards.

K&R: Does not support trigraph sequences.

Reference: Box 3-4: Trigraph Sequences

D.1.5 Alert and Vertical Tab Escape Sequences

ANSI: Requires compilers to support \a (alert) and \v (vertical tab) escape sequences.

K&R: Does not require compilers to support \a and \v.

Reference: Section 3.3.1 Escape Character Sequences

D.1.6 Hexadecimal Escape Sequences

ANSI: Supports escape sequences of the form:

\xhhh

where the *h*'s are hexadecimal digits.

K&R: Does not support hexadecimal escape sequences.

Reference: Section 3.3.1 Escape Character Sequences

D.2 Data Type Differences

The entries in this section cover differences in data types.

D.2.1 *signed* Type Specifier

ANSI: Supports the new keyword **signed**, which explicitly makes an
                   integral type signed.

K&R: Does not support the **signed** keyword.

Reference: Box 3-1: signed *Qualifier*

D.2.2 *long double* Type

ANSI: Supports **long double** type.

K&R: Does not support **long double** type.

Reference: Box 3-5: long double *Type; Section 3.9.4 Mixing Floating-Point
                   Values*

D.2.3 *unsigned short*, *unsigned long*, **and** *unsign
        char* **Types**

ANSI: Explicitly requires C compilers to support these types.

K&R: Implies that these types are not legal.

Reference: Section 3.2.1 Unsigned Integers; Section 3.10 Typedefs

D.2.4 The *void* Type

ANSI: Included as a new type, an object of which cannot be used. Pointers to **void** may be converted to pointers of any other type object.

K&R: Not supported at all in the original version.

Reference: Section 3.9 The void *Type; Box 7-6: Generic Pointers*

D.2.5 Enumeration Types

ANSI: Supported as integer type.

K&R: Not supported in the original document, though added in a later draft.

Reference: Section 3.8 Enumeration Types

D.2.6 Byte Length

ANSI: A byte must be at least 8 bits long.

K&R: Bytes have unspecified size.

Reference: Section 3.2 Different Types of Integers

D.2.7 Minimum Ranges for Integral Types

ANSI: Imposes ranges that must be met for each type.

K&R: Does not impose ranges but lists typical sizes.

Reference: Section 3.2 Different Types of Integers; Appendix D—"Implementation Limits"

D.2.8 Unsigned Constants

ANSI: Allows you to append a **u** or **U** to an integral constant to make it unsigned.

K&R: Does not support unsigned constants.

Reference: Box 3-3: unsigned Constants

D.2.9 "8" and "9" Not Allowed in Octal Constants

ANSI: Does not allow the digits 8 and 9 to be used in an octal constant.

K&R: Allows the use of 8 and 9 (which have octal values 10 and 11).

Reference: Section 3.3 Different Kinds of Integer Constants

D.2.10 float and long double Constants

ANSI: Allows you to append an **f** or **F** to a floating-point constant to give it type **float**, or an **l** or **L** to give it type **long double**.

K&R: Does not support **float** and **long double** constants.

Reference: Box 3-6: float *and* long double *Constants*

D.2.11 Type of Integer Constants

ANSI: Has defined rules for determining type.

K&R: Rules for type determination are vague.

Reference: Section 3.3 Different Kinds of Integer Constants

D.2.12 Conversion Rules for Mixing signed and unsigned Types

ANSI: Uses value-preserving rules.

K&R: Uses sign-preserving rules.

Reference: Box 3-7: Unsigned Conversions

D.3 Statement Differences

There is only one significant difference concerning control flow statements.

D.3.1 Controlling Expression of a *switch* Statement

ANSI: Allows the controlling expression of a switch statement to have any integral type.

K&R: States that the controlling expression must have type **int**.

Reference: Section 4.2.1 Syntax of a switch *Statement*

D.4 Expression Differences

This section lists several differences involving the way expressions are evaluated.

D.4.1 Unsigned Conversions

ANSI: Uses value-preserving rules.

K&R: Uses sign-preserving rules.

Reference: Box 3-7 Unsigned Conversions

D.4.2 Unary Plus Operator

ANSI: Supports a unary plus operator.

K&R: Does not support a unary plus operator.

Reference: Section 5.2 Unary Plus and Minus Operators

D.4.3 Float Expressions

ANSI: Does not require the compiler to convert all **float** operands to **double**.

K&R: Requires conversion of all **float** operands to **double**.

Reference: Section 3.9.4 Mixing Floating-Point Values

D.4.4 Shifting by a *long int* **and** *unsigned int*

ANSI: States that the type of the shift count does not affect the type of the left-hand operand.

K&R: Implies that shifting by a **long int** or **unsigned int** forces the compiler to convert the left operand to a **long int** or **unsigned int**, respectively.

Reference: Section 5.9.1 Shift Operators

D.4.5 Structure Assignment

ANSI: Allows a structure to be assigned to a structure variable, provided that the two operands share the same structure type.

K&R: Does not support structure assignment.

Reference: Section 8.1.10 Assigning Structures

D.4.6 Passing Structures as Arguments

ANSI: Supports passing structures as function arguments.

K&R: Does not allow structures to be passed as function arguments.

Reference: Section 8.1.8 Passing Structures

D.4.7 Pointers to Functions

ANSI: Allows you to omit the dereferencing operator when invoking a function through a pointer to a function. If pf is a function, then

```
pf();
```

is the same as

```
(*pf)()
```

K&R: Implies that the dereferencing operator is required.

Reference: Section 9.3.3 Calling a Function Using Pointers

D.5 Storage Class and Initialization Differences

The ANSI Standard includes several extensions to storage classes and initializations.

D.5.1 Function Prototypes

ANSI: Supports a new feature that allows you to declare the number and type of arguments to a function defined elsewhere. Prototyping enables the compiler to perform argument type-checking.

K&R: Not supported.

Reference: Box 9-1: Function Prototypes

D.5.2 The *const* Storage-Class Modifier

ANSI: Supports **const**, which indicates that the object's value may not be changed.

K&R: Does not support **const**.

Reference: Box 7-4: The const *Storage-Class Modifier*

D.5.3 The *volatile* Storage-Class Modifier

ANSI: Supports **volatile**, which indicates that the object's value can change in ways that the compiler cannot predict.

K&R: Does not support **volatile**.

Reference: Box 7-5: The volatile *Storage-Class Modifier*

D.5.4 Definitions vs. Allusions

ANSI: Uses the presence or absence of an initializer to determine whether a declaration is a definition or an allusion.

K&R: Uses the presence or absence of the **extern** specifier to determine whether a declaration is a definition or an allusion.

Reference: Section 7.3.1 Definitions and Allusions; Box 7-3 Non-ANSI Strategies for Declaring Global Variables

D.5.5 Initializing Automatic Arrays and Structures

ANSI: Permitted.

K&R: Not permitted.

Reference: Section 6.3 Initializing Arrays; Box 6-1 Initialization of Arrays; Section 8.1.1 Initializing Structures

D.5.6 Scope of Function Arguments

ANSI: Arguments declared as function parameters have the same scope as objects declared in the function's top-level block.

K&R: Function arguments may be hidden by declarations of the same name in the top-level block.

Reference: Box 7-1: Scope of Function Arguments

D.5.7 *struct* **and** *union* **Name Spaces**

ANSI: Each structure and union has its own name space, which means that fields in different structures or unions can have the same name without conflict.

K&R: Places all structure and union fields in the same name space.

Reference: Box 8-1: struct *and* union *Name Spaces*

D.5.8 Initialization of Union Members

ANSI: Supported — initializes the first member of the union.

K&R: Not supported.

Reference: Box 8-3: Initializing Unions

D.6 Preprocessor Differences

The preprocessor defined by the ANSI Standard differs substantially from the preprocessor described by K&R.

D.6.1 Formatting Preprocessor Lines

ANSI: Requires the pound sign to be the first *nonspace* character on a line.

K&R: Requires the pound sign to be the first character on a line.

Reference: Box 10-1: Flexible Formatting of Preprocessor Lines

D.6.2 Recursive Macro Definitions

ANSI: Prevents infinite recursion of a macro by inhibiting the expansion of a macro name in its own definition.

K&R: Provides no mechanism to avoid infinite recursion of a macro.

Reference: Box 10-5: Using a Macro Name in Its Own Definition

D.6.3 Redefining Macro Names

ANSI: Requires an intervening **#undef** of the macro name if the redefinition is different from the current definition.

K&R: Does not require an intervening **#undef**.

Reference: Section 10.1.2 Removing a Macro Definition

D.6.4 String Producer

ANSI: Supports a new preprocessor operator (#) that surrounds its argument with quotes when it expands.

K&R: Does not support the string-producing operator.

Reference: Box 10-8: String Producer

D.6.5 Built-In Macros

ANSI: Requires implementations to define five built-in macros: __LINE__, __FILE__, __TIME__, __DATE__, __STDC__.

K&R: Does not require implementations to define any built-in macros (nor does it prohibit them from doing so).

Reference: Section 10.1.4 Built-In Macros

D.6.6 Token Pasting

ANSI: Supports a new preprocessor operator (##) that pastes two preprocessor tokens.

K&R: Does not support the paste operator.

Reference: Box 10-9: Token Pasting

D.6.7 The *#elif* Directive

ANSI: Supports **#elif**.

K&R: Does not support **#elif**.

Reference: Section 10.2 Conditional Compilation

D.6.8 The *defined* **Operator**

ANSI: Supports the **defined** preprocessor operator.

K&R: Does not support **defined**.

Reference: Section 10.2.1 Testing Macro Existence

D.6.9 The *#error* **Directive**

ANSI: Supports **#error**, which enables you to output error messages during the preprocessing stage of compilation.

K&R: Does not support **#error**.

Reference: Box 10-10: The **#error** *Directive*

D.6.10 The *#pragma* **Directive**

ANSI: Supports **#pragma**, which allows implementations to add their own preprocessing directives.

K&R: Does not support **#pragma**.

Reference: Box 10-11: The **#pragma** *Directive*

Appendix E

Reserved Names

The C language, as defined by the ANSI Standard, contains a number of reserved words and names that you should not use as private variable names. The reserved words fall into several categories:

- **Keywords** — You may not use keywords for names of objects.

- **Runtime Function Names** — You should avoid using function names, except when you want to write your own version of a standard function or macro.

- **Macro Names** — The runtime library header files contain definitions for many constant names. You should avoid using these names for variables.

- **Type Names** — Some of the header files define types (with typedefs) that are applied to the arguments or the function return type.

- **Preprocessor Command Names** — In general, the preprocessor names do not create conflicts because they must be preceded by a pound sign, which makes their meaning unambiguous. However, you cannot write something like

```
#define define
```

Table E-1 lists all of these reserved names. For macros and functions, the table also shows where they are defined. Although it is possible to avoid naming conflicts by not including the header file in which a reserved name is defined, this is a dangerous practice because you may need to include the header file at a later date. We recommend that you avoid using these names for private variables.

In addition to the names listed in Table E-1, you should also consider all names beginning with an underscore to be reserved for system use. Finally, ANSI has reserved all names beginning with two underscores, or an underscore followed by an uppercase letter, for future use.

__DATE__	macro defined by the implementation
__FILE__	macro defined by the implementation
__IOFBF	macro defined by the implementation
__IOLBF	macro defined by the implementation
__IONBF	macro defined by the implementation
__LINE__	macro defined by the implementation
__STDC__	macro defined by the implementation
__TIME__	macro defined by the implementation
abort	function defined in *assert.h*
abs	function defined in *stdlib.h*
acos	function defined in *math.h*
asctime	function defined in *time.h*
asin	function defined in *math.h*
assert	macro defined in *assert.h*
atan	function defined in *math.h*
atan2	function defined in *math.h*
atexit	function defined in *stdlib.h*
atof	function defined in *stdlib.h*
atoi	function defined in *stdlib.h*
atol	function defined in *stdlib.h*
auto	keyword (storage class specifier)
break	keyword (statement)
bsearch	function defined in *stdlib.h*
BUFSIZ	macro defined in *stdio.h*
calloc	function defined in *stdlib.h*
case	keyword (label)
ceil	function defined in *math.h*
CHAR_BIT	macro defined in *limits.h*
CHAR_MAX	macro defined in *limits.h*
CHAR_MIN	macro defined in *limits.h*
clearerr	function defined in *stdio.h*
clock	function defined in *time.h*
clock_t	type defined in *time.h*
CLOCKS_PER_SEC	macro defined in *time.h*
const	keyword (storage class modifier)
continue	keyword (statement)
cos	function defined in *math.h*
cosh	function defined in *math.h*
ctime	function defined in *time.h*
DBL_MANT_DIG	macro defined in *float.h*

Table E-1. Reserved Names.

DBL_DIG	macro defined in *float.h*
DBL_EPSILON	macro defined in *float.h*
DBL_MIN_EXP	macro defined in *float.h*
DBL_MIN	macro defined in *float.h*
DBL_MIN_10_EXP	macro defined in *float.h*
DBL_MAX_EXP	macro defined in *float.h*
DBL_MAX	macro defined in *float.h*
DBL_MAX_10_EXP	macro defined in *float.h*
default	keyword (label)
defined	preprocessing operator
difftime	function defined in *time.h*
div_t	type defined in *stdlib.h*
do	keyword (statement)
double	keyword (type specifier)
EDOM	macro defined in *float.h*
else	keyword (statement)
enum	keyword (type specifier)
EOF	macro defined in *stdio.h*
ERANGE	macro defined in *float.h*
errno	macro defined in *stddef.h*
exit	function defined in *stdlib.h*
exp	function defined in *math.h*
extern	keyword (storage class specifier)
fabs	function defined in *math.h*
fclose	function defined in *stdio.h*
feof	function defined in *stdio.h*
ferror	function defined in *stdio.h*
fflush	function defined in *stdio.h*
fgetc	function defined in *stdio.h*
fgetpos	function defined in *stdio.h*
fgets	function defined in *stdio.h*
FILE	type defined in *stdio.h*
float	keyword (type specifier)
floor	function defined in *math.h*
FLT_EPSILON	macro defined in *float.h*
FLT_DIG	macro defined in *float.h*
FLT_MANT_DIG	macro defined in *float.h*
FLT_MAX	macro defined in *float.h*
FLT_MAX_EXP	macro defined in *float.h*
FLT_MAX_10_EXP	macro defined in *float.h*
FLT_MIN	macro defined in *float.h*
FLT_MIN_EXP	macro defined in *float.h*
FLT_MIN_10_EXP	macro defined in *float.h*
FLT_RADIX	macro defined in *float.h*
FLT_ROUNDS	macro defined in *float.h*

Table E-1. Reserved Names.

fmod	function defined in *math.h*
fopen	function defined in *stdio.h*
for	keyword (statement)
fpos_t	type defined in *stdio.h*
fprintf	function defined in *stdio.h*
fputc	function defined in *stdio.h*
fputs	function defined in *stdio.h*
fread	function defined in *stdio.h*
free	function defined in *stdlib.h*
freopen	function defined in *stdio.h*
frexp	function defined in *math.h*
fscanf	function defined in *stdio.h*
fseek	function defined in *stdio.h*
fsetpos	function defined in *stdio.h*
ftell	function defined in *stdio.h*
fwrite	function defined in *stdio.h*
getc	function defined in *stdio.h*
getchar	function defined in *stdio.h*
getenv	function defined in *stdlib.h*
gets	function defined in *stdio.h*
gmtime	function defined in *stdlib.h*
goto	keyword (statement)
HUGE_VAL	macro defined in *math.h*
if	keyword (statement)
int	keyword (type specifier)
INT_MAX	macro defined in *limits.h*
INT_MIN	macro defined in *limits.h*
isalnum	function defined in *ctype.h*
isalpha	function defined in *ctype.h*
iscntrl	function defined in *ctype.h*
isdigit	function defined in *ctype.h*
isgraph	function defined in *ctype.h*
islower	function defined in *ctype.h*
isprint	function defined in *ctype.h*
ispunct	function defined in *ctype.h*
isspace	function defined in *ctype.h*
Isupper	function defined in *ctype.h*
isxdigit	function defined in *ctype.h*
jmp_buf	type defined in *setjmp.h*
L_tmpnam	macro defined in *stdio.h*
labs	function defined in *math.h*
LDBL_DIG	macro defined in *float.h*
LDBL_EPSILON	macro defined in *float.h*
LDBL_MANT_DIG	macro defined in *float.h*
LDBL_MAX	macro defined in *float.h*

Table E-1. Reserved Names.

LDBL_MAX_EXP	macro defined in *float.h*
LDBL_MAX_10_EXP	macro defined in *float.h*
LDBL_MIN	macro defined in *float.h*
LDBL_MIN_EXP	macro defined in *float.h*
LDBL_MIN_10_EXP	macro defined in *float.h*
ldexp	function defined in *math.h*
ldiv	function defined in *stdlib.h*
ldiv_t	type defined in *stdlib.h*
localtime	function defined in *time.h*
log	function defined in *math.h*
log10	function defined in *math.h*
long	keyword (type specifier)
longjmp	function defined in *setjmp.h*
LONG_MAX	macro defined in *limits.h*
LONG_MIN	macro defined in *limits.h*
main	function defined by the implementation
malloc	function defined in *stdlib.h*
memchr	function defined in *string.h*
memcmp	function defined in *string.h*
memcpy	function defined in *string.h*
memmove	function defined in *string.h*
memset	function defined in *string.h*
mktime	function defined in *time.h*
modf	function defined in *math.h*
NDEBUG	macro defined in *assert.h*
NULL	macro defined in *stddef.h*
offsetof	macro defined in *stddef.h*
OPEN_MAX	macro defined in *stdio.h*
perror	function defined in *stdio.h*
pow	function defined in *math.h*
printf	function defined in *stdio.h*
ptrdiff_t	type defined in *stddef.h*
putc	function defined in *stdio.h*
putchar	function defined in *stdio.h*
puts	function defined in *stdio.h*
qsort	function defined in *stdlib.h*
raise	function defined in *signal.h*
rand	function defined in *stdlib.h*
RAND_MAX	macro defined in *stdlib.h*
realloc	function defined in *stdlib.h*
register	keyword (storage class specifier)
remove	function defined in *stdio.h*
rename	function defined in *stdio.h*
return	keyword (statement)
rewind	function defined in *stdio.h*

Table E-1. Reserved Names.

SCHAR_MAX	macro defined in *limits.h*
SCHAR_MIN	macro defined in *limits.h*
SEEK_CUR	macro defined in *stdio.h*
SEEK_END	macro defined in *stdio.h*
SEEK_SET	macro defined in *stdio.h*
setbuf	function defined in *stdio.h*
setjmp	function defined in *setjmp.h*
setlocale	function defined in *locale.h*
setvbuf	function defined in *stdio.h*
short	keyword (type specifier)
SHRT_MAX	macro defined in *limits.h*
SHRT_MIN	macro defined in *limits.h*
sig_atomic_t	type defined in *signal.h*
SIG_DFL	macro defined in *signal.h*
SIG_ERR	macro defined in *signal.h*
SIG_IGN	macro defined in *signal.h*
SIGABRT	macro defined in *signal.h*
SIGFPE	macro defined in *signal.h*
SIGILL	macro defined in *signal.h*
SIGINT	macro defined in *signal.h*
signal	function defined in *signal.h*
signed	keyword (type specifier)
SIGSEGV	macro defined in *signal.h*
SIGTERM	macro defined in *signal.h*
sin	function defined in *math.h*
sinh	function defined in *math.h*
size_t	type defined in *stddef.h*
sizeof	keyword (operator)
sprintf	function defined in *stdio.h*
sqrt	function defined in *math.h*
srand	function defined in *stdlib.h*
sscanf	function defined in *stdio.h*
static	keyword (storage class specifier)
stderr	file pointer defined by the implementation
stdin	file pointer defined by the implementation
stdout	file pointer defined by the implementation
strcat	function defined in *string.h*
strchr	function defined in *string.h*
strcmp	function defined in *string.h*
strcoll	function defined in *string.h*
strcpy	function defined in *string.h*
strcspn	function defined in *string.h*
strerror	function defined in *string.h*
strftime	function defined in *time.h*
strlen	function defined in *string.h*

Table E-1. Reserved Names.

strncat	function defined in *string.h*
strncmp	function defined in *string.h*
strncpy	function defined in *string.h*
strpbrk	function defined in *string.h*
strrchr	function defined in *string.h*
strspn	function defined in *string.h*
strstr	function defined in *string.h*
strtod	function defined in *string.h*
strtok	function defined in *string.h*
strtol	function defined in *string.h*
strtoul	function defined in *string.h*
switch	keyword (statement)
system	function defined in *stdlib.h*
tan	function defined in *math.h*
tanh	function defined in *math.h*
time	function defined in *time.h*
time_t	type defined in *time.h*
tm	type defined in *time.h*
TMP_MAX	macro defined in *stdio.h*
tmpfile	function defined in *stdio.h*
tmpnam	function defined in *stdio.h*
tolower	function defined in *ctype.h*
toupper	function defined in *ctype.h*
typedef	keyword (type specifier)
UCHAR_MAX	macro defined in *limits.h*
UINT_MAX	macro defined in *limits.h*
ULONG_MAX	macro defined in *limits.h*
ungetc	function defined in *stdio.h*
unsigned	keyword (type specifier)
USHRT_MAX	macro defined in *limits.h*
va_arg	macro defined in *stdarg.h*
va_end	function defined in *stdarg.h*
va_list	type defined in *stdarg.h*
va_start	macro defined in *stdarg.h*
vfprintf	function defined in *stdio.h*
void	keyword (type specifier)
volatile	keyword (storage class modifier)
vprintf	function defined in *stdio.h*
vsprintf	function defined in *stdio.h*
wchar_t	macro defined in *stddef.h*
while	keyword (statement)

Table E-1. Reserved Names.

Appendix F

C Interpreter Listing

This appendix contains the listing for the C interpreter that we described in Chapter 12. It is written with good software engineering features and can be built using *make*. Use the source order form at the end of this book if you would like to order a floppy containing the source.

Index of Cint Functions

```
/* lex.h */
typedef enum lex_vals {
 LEX_NULL, SYMBOL, CONSTANT, BUILTIN_FUNCTION,
 RETURN, IF, ELSE, FOR, SWITCH, WHILE='a', STATIC, EXTERN,
 VOID, CHAR, SHORT, INT, LONG, DOUBLE, FLOAT, SIGNED, UNSIGNED,
 LSHIFT, RSHIFT, EQ, NEQ, GEQ, LEQ, INCREMENT, DECREMENT,
 SIZEOF, BREAK, CONTINUE, LIST, RUN, LAST_TOKEN
} LEX_TOKEN;


#if __STDC__
extern LEX_TOKEN lex( struct value* );
extern LEX_TOKEN lex0( struct value* );
extern LEX_TOKEN current_token();
#else
extern LEX_TOKEN lex();
extern LEX_TOKEN lex0();
extern LEX_TOKEN current_token();
#endif
```

```
/* sym.h
 * Author:  P Darnell
 * 10/86 Created
 * Purpose: declare global types and variables used in Cint
 * and manipulated by sym.c
 */

typedef enum storage { STACK, GLOBAL } STORAGE;

typedef enum {
    T_UNKNOWN, T_DOUBLE, T_INT, T_PTR, T_ARRAY, T_STRUCT, T_UNION,
    T_FUNC_PTR, T_FUNC, T_VOID, T_CHAR, T_SHORT, T_LONG, T_FLOAT
} VALUE_TYPE;


typedef struct _private_type_desc {
    struct _private_type_desc *next;     /* Pointer to next type descriptor */
    VALUE_TYPE         type;             /* Type of sym */
    int               size;             /* Size of arrays */
} _PRIVATE_TYPE_DESC;

typedef struct _private_sym {
    STORAGE         sym_storage;    /* storage class of sym */
    _PRIVATE_TYPE_DESC sym_type;    /* type of sym */
    int             sym_offset;     /* memory offset of symbol */
    char            *sym_name;      /* pointer to text name of sym */
    /* pointer to next sym at same scope level */
    struct _private_sym   *sym_next;
      struct {
        VALUE_TYPE    func_type;  /* return type of function */
        struct token *func_start; /* pointer to start of function body */
        /* pointer to locally scoped symbols */
        struct _private_sym **func_sym_list;
      } func_descriptor;
} _PRIVATE_SYM;

#ifdef SYM_OWNER
    typedef _PRIVATE_SYM SYM;
    typedef _PRIVATE_TYPE_DESC TYPE_DESC;
#else
    typedef struct { char _x[sizeof (struct _private_sym)];} SYM;
    typedef struct { char _x[sizeof (struct _private_type_desc)];} TYPE_DESC;
#endif

#if __STDC__
extern SYM          *sym_enter( char* );
extern int          sym_find( char*, SYM**);
extern   void       sym_declaring( int );
extern void         sym_list();
extern void         print_sym( SYM *, int );
extern void         init_param( SYM *);
extern void         add_param( SYM *, SYM *);
extern SYM          *next_param( );
extern SYM          *first_param( SYM *);
extern void         add_sym_type( SYM*, VALUE_TYPE );
extern TYPE_DESC    *get_sym_type_desc( SYM* );
extern TYPE_DESC    *get_type_desc_next( TYPE_DESC* );
extern VALUE_TYPE   get_type_desc_type( TYPE_DESC* );
extern VALUE_TYPE   get_sym_type( SYM* );
extern void         set_sym_type( SYM *, VALUE_TYPE);
```

```
extern void         set_sym_frame_offset( SYM *, int );
extern int          get_sym_frame_offset( SYM * );
extern void         set_sym_storage( SYM *, STORAGE );
extern STORAGE      get_sym_storage( SYM * );
extern void         set_func_start( SYM *, struct token *);
extern struct token *get_func_start( SYM * );
extern void         set_func_type( SYM *, VALUE_TYPE);
extern VALUE_TYPE   get_func_type( SYM * );
#else
extern SYM          *sym_enter();
extern int          sym_find();
extern  void        sym_declaring();
extern void         sym_list();
extern void         print_sym();
extern void         init_param();
extern void         add_param();
extern SYM          *next_param();
extern SYM          *first_param();
extern void         add_sym_type();
extern TYPE_DESC    *get_sym_type_desc();
extern TYPE_DESC    *get_type_desc_next();
extern VALUE_TYPE   get_type_desc_type();
extern VALUE_TYPE   get_sym_type();
extern void         set_sym_type();
extern void         set_sym_frame_offset();
extern int          get_sym_frame_offset();
extern void         set_sym_storage();
extern STORAGE      get_sym_storage();
extern void         set_func_start();
extern struct token *get_func_start();
extern void         set_func_type();
extern VALUE_TYPE   get_func_type();
#endif
```

```c
/* cint.h
 * Author:  P Darnell
 * 10/86 Created
 * Purpose: declare global types and variables used in Cint
 */

typedef char MEMORY;
typedef int BUILTIN_PTR;
typedef int (*FUNC_PTR) ();

typedef struct value {
  VALUE_TYPE type;         /* Type of this value */
  union {                  /* Value of this value */
    int i[sizeof(double) / sizeof(int)];
    int fix;
    double flt;
    MEMORY *mptr;
    SYM *sym;
    struct value *ptr;
    BUILTIN_PTR builtin_ptr;
    struct {
      struct token *loop_test;
      struct token *loop_body;
      struct token *loop_increment;
      struct token *loop_exit;
    } loop_descriptor;
    struct {
      struct token *if_exit;
      struct token *if_else;
    } if_descriptor;
  } value;
} VALUE;

struct {
  char executing;                 /* True if executing program */
  char using_token_stream;        /* True if using internal token stream */
  char saving_token_stream;       /* True if saving tokens to stream */
  char returning;                 /* True if return stmt executed */
  char calc_mode;                 /* True if new line is expression terminator */
  char prompting;                 /* True if we want a statement prompt */
} state;

int lex_debug; /* Set to true to get lex debug info */
int exp_debug; /* Set to true to get expression debug info */
int stmt_debug; /* Set to true to get statement debug info */


#define TRUE    1
#define FALSE   0

#ifndef NULL
#  define NULL 0
#endif


#if __STDC__
void            assign_memory_to_value( VALUE *, MEMORY *, VALUE_TYPE);
void            assign_value_to_memory( VALUE *, MEMORY *, VALUE_TYPE);
MEMORY          *memory( SYM *);
void            err( char*, );
```

```
void            warn( char*, );
char            *get_builtin_func_name( BUILTIN_PTR );
FUNC_PTR        get_builtin_func_ptr( BUILTIN_PTR );
struct token    *get_loop_test(        struct token * );
struct token    *get_loop_body(        struct token * );
struct token    *get_loop_increment(   struct token * );
struct token    *get_loop_exit(        struct token * );
void            set_loop_test(         struct token *, struct token *);
void            set_loop_body(         struct token *, struct token * );
void            set_loop_increment(    struct token *, struct token * );
void            set_loop_exit(         struct token *, struct token * );
#else
void            err();
void            warn();
char            *get_builtin_func_name( );
FUNC_PTR        get_builtin_func_ptr( );
struct token    *get_loop_test();
struct token    *get_loop_body();
struct token    *get_loop_increment();
struct token    *get_loop_exit();
void            set_loop_test();
void            set_loop_body();
void            set_loop_increment();
void            set_loop_exit();
MEMORY          *memory();
#endif
```

```
#ifdef TOKEN_OWNER
typedef struct token {
  struct token *tk_next;           /* Pointer to next token */
  LEX_TOKEN      tk_token;         /* Enumerated type of token */
  struct value  tk_value;          /* value of token */
  short          tk_line;          /* Source line of token definition */
} TOKEN;

#else
  typedef struct token { char filler; } TOKEN;
#endif

TOKEN *get_token_pc();
#if __STDC__
void print_value( struct value * );
void print_token_list( TOKEN * );
#endif
```

```
/* declare.c
 * Author: P. Darnell
 * 9/86  Initial coding.
 * 11/86 Added arrays.
 * Purpose: To parse declarations, set the types of variables in the
 * symbol table, and allocate space for the variables in memory.
 */

#include "lex.h"
#include "token_st.h"
#include "sym.h"
#include "cint.h"

/*==================================================================
 * Function: pointer_decl(base_type)
 * Purpose: parse and modify symbol table entry for pointer declarations.
 * Algorithm:
 *    Recursively calls itself for each '*' prefix to symbol.
 *    Symbol entry is only modified if we are not in execution mode.
 * Inputs:
 *    base_type - type that the pointer points at.
 * Result: pointer to sym_entry for declared variable.
 *==================================================================*/
/* Note use of static storage class modifier to pointer_decl to
 * restrict this function name to file scope.
 */
static SYM *pointer_decl(base_type)
  VALUE_TYPE base_type;
{
  VALUE v;
  SYM *sym = NULL;
  LEX_TOKEN token;

  token = lex(&v);
  /*
   * Note use of cast (int) to suppress possible mismatch between int type of
   * the char constant '*' and enum type of token
   */
  if ((int) token == '*')
  {
    /* Note use of recursion */
    sym = pointer_decl(base_type);
    if (!state.executing)
      add_sym_type(sym, T_PTR);
  }
  else if (token == SYMBOL)
  {
    sym = v.value.sym;
    if (!state.executing)
      set_sym_type(sym, base_type);
  }
  return sym;
}
```

```
/*====================================================================
 * Function: array_decl(sym)
 * Purpose: parse array declaration and modify type entry for sym
 * Algorithm:
 *   Recursively look for trailing []'s.
 *   if array modifiers are found, modify sym type appropriately.
 * Inputs:
 *   sym - pointer to sym entry to be modified by []'s
 * Result:
 *   First token to follow ']', or original token if no '[' found
 *====================================================================*/
static LEX_TOKEN array_decl(sym)
  SYM *sym;
{
  LEX_TOKEN token;
  VALUE v;

  token = lex(&v);
  if ((int) token == '[')         /* Array declaration */
  {
    /* Parse dimension size */
    expression(0, &v, 0);

    if ((int) current_token() != ']')
      err("Missing ']' in array declaration\n");

    /* Recursively look for more array modifiers */
    token = array_decl(sym);

    if (!state.executing)
    {
      if (v.type != T_INT)
        err("Non integral array size expression\n");
      add_sym_type(sym, T_ARRAY, v.value.fix);
    }
  }
  return token;
}

/*====================================================================
 * Function: declare(token, pvalue)
 * Purpose: external entry for declaration parsing
 * Algorithm:
 *   Recursive descent. Enter symbols and modify type information if
 *   we are not in execution mode. Otherwise just parse and do nothing.
 * Note: a speed up of execution could be seen if functions had two
 *       token lists, one for executable code and one for declarations. That
 *       way declarations would not slow down execution.
 * Inputs:
 *   token - enum of last unparsed token.
 *   pvalue - pointer to VALUE struct of last unparsed token.
 * Result: TRUE if declaration is found, FALSE if not.
 * Bug: Parens in declarations are not handled properly
 *====================================================================*/
int declare(token, pvalue)
  LEX_TOKEN token;
  VALUE *pvalue;
{
  VALUE_TYPE typo = T_INT;
```

```
VALUE val, *value();
SYM *sym, *first_arg;

switch (token)
{
case EXTERN:
case STATIC:
  break;
case CHAR:
  type = T_CHAR;
  break;
case SHORT:
  type = T_SHORT;
  break;
case LONG:
  type = T_LONG;
  break;
case INT:
  type = T_INT;
  break;
case FLOAT:
  type = T_FLOAT;
  break;
case DOUBLE:
  type = T_DOUBLE;
  break;
case VOID:
  type = T_VOID;
  break;

default:
  sym_declaring(FALSE);
  return FALSE;
}

sym_declaring(TRUE);

/* Note use of do-while */
do
{
  /* Parse symbol with any pointer prefix modifiers */
  sym = pointer_decl(type);
  if (sym == NULL)
  {
    err("Expected symbol\n", token);
    continue;
  }

  token = array_decl(sym, NULL);

  if (!state.executing)
    sym_allocate(sym);

  if ((int) token == '=')        /* Initialization */
  {
    sym_declaring(FALSE);
    expression(0, &val, 0);
    sym_declaring(TRUE);
    if (scope_level() == 0 || state.executing)
      assign_value_to_memory(&val, memory(sym),
                          get_type_desc_type(get_sym_type_desc(sym)));
    token = (LEX_TOKEN) current_token();
```

```
     }
} while ((int) token == ',');


if ((int) token == '(')          /* function declaration */
{
   set_func_type(sym, get_sym_type(sym));
   set_sym_type(sym, T_FUNC);
   set_sym_storage(sym, GLOBAL);
   set_func_sym(sym);              /* register this sym as function symbol */
   enter_scope();                  /* put arg declarations in new scope */
   first_arg = NULL;

   for (token = lex(&val); (int) token != ')'; token = lex(&val))
   {
     if (token != SYMBOL)
     {
       err("Syntax error in arg list. Wanted a symbol, not a %s\n",
           token_name(token));
       break;
     }
     if (first_arg == NULL)
       first_arg = val.value.sym;
     set_sym_type(val.value.sym, T_INT);
     token = lex(&val);
     if ((int) token != ',')
       break;
   }
   if ((int) token != ')')
     err("Bad argument syntax\n");

   token = lex(&val);

   /* Note acceptable use of goto to exit this block */
   if ((int) token == ';')
     goto exit_declare;

   if (scope_level() > 1)
   {
     err("Can't have nested functions\n");
   }

   /* parse all parameter declarations. */
   while (declare(token, &val))
     token = lex(&val);

   sym_arg_allocate(first_arg);

   if ((int) current_token() != '{')
     err("Expected '{'\n");

   set_func_start(sym, get_token_pc());

   /* Parse function body */
   statement('{', &val);
   sym_declaring(TRUE);
   set_sym_frame_offset(sym, get_frame_size());
   leave_scope();
}
else if ((int) token != ';')
   err("Missing ';' in declaration\n");
```

```
exit_declare:
  sym_declaring(FALSE);
  return TRUE;
}
/*================================================================
 * expr.c
 * Author P. Darnell
 * 9/86:  Initial coding
 * 11/86: Added pointer and array reference
 * Purpose:
 *        To parse and compute values for C expressions. User functions and
 *        C runtime calls are handled here as well as the usual unary
 *        and binary operators
 * Algorithm:
 *        Uses recursive descent to parse expressions.
 *        Assignments and calls are not done unless state.executing is true.
 * Bugs: Missing struct reference, ?:, and cast operators.
 *================================================================*/

#include <stdio.h>
#include "lex.h"
#include "token_st.h"
#include "sym.h"
#include "cint.h"

/* Note internal function allusions */
#if __STDC__
static MEMORY *primary(LEX_TOKEN *, VALUE *, TYPE_DESC **);
static MEMORY *unary_expression(LEX_TOKEN *, VALUE *, TYPE_DESC **);
static MEMORY *post_op(LEX_TOKEN *, VALUE *, MEMORY *, TYPE_DESC **);
#else
static MEMORY *primary();
static MEMORY *unary_expression();
static MEMORY *post_op();
#endif

#define ARG_MAX 32
static int arg_stack[ARG_MAX];
static int arg_stack_pointer;

/*================================================================
 * Function: arg_list
 * Purpose: Gather an arg list for a call to an external, compiled function.
 * Algorithm:
 *        Create an array of argument expressions until a closing ')' is seen.
 *        Array of argument expressions until a closing ')' is seen.
 *        Array is filled in lexical order, and EXTERNAL_ARG_MAX elements will
 *        be passed to the called function.
 *================================================================*/
static void arg_list()
{
  VALUE arg;
  int *ap = arg_stack;
  LEX_TOKEN token;

  token = lex(&arg);
  if ((int)token == ')')
    return;

  while ((int) current_token() != ')')
  {
    expression(token, &arg, 0);
```

```
      token = LEX_NULL;
      if (arg.type == T_DOUBLE)
      {
        *(double *) &arg_stack[arg_stack_pointer] = arg.value.flt;
        arg_stack_pointer += sizeof(double) / sizeof(int);
      }
      else
        arg_stack[arg_stack_pointer++] = arg.value.fix;
      if ((int)current_token() != ',')
        break;
   }
   if ((int)current_token() != ')')
     err("Missing ')' in function call");
}


/*=================================================================
 * Function: push_args
 * Purpose:  Push argument expressions for an internal call.
 * Algorithm: Keep pushing until a closing ')' is seen.
 *        Calls itself recursively to push args in opposite order from
 *        their lexical appearance. This way, after all pushes are done,
 *        the first arg is closest to the stack pointer,
 *        second arg is second closest, etc.
 *=================================================================*/
static void push_args(formal_param, check_args)
  SYM *formal_param;
  int check_args;
{
  VALUE arg;
  LEX_TOKEN token;

  token = lex(&arg);
  if ((int) token == ')')
    return;

  expression(token, &arg, 0);
  if (!state.executing && check_args)
  {
    if (!formal_param)
      warn("Too many args for call\n");
    else if (get_sym_type(formal_param) != arg.type)
      warn("Arg type mismatch\n");
  }

/* Recursive call to push_arg here causes args to be pushed in reverse order.
 * This puts first arg at -1 off the frame poiner, 2nd arg at -2, etc.
 */
  if ((int)current_token() == ',')
    push_args(next_param(), check_args);

  /* copy actual arg to stack */
  if (state.executing)
    push_value(&arg);
}
```

```
/*=================================================================
 * Function:  user_arg_list(fn)
 * Purpose: Process arg list to internal function call.
 * =============================================================*/
static void user_arg_list(fn)
  SYM *fn;
{
  VALUE arg;

  push_args(first_param(fn), fn != NULL);
  if ((int)current_token() != ')')
    err("Missing ')' in function call");
}

#define I_MEAN_DEC 1
#define POST_INC_DEC 2

/*=================================================================
 * Function: inc_value( v, m, td, flags)
 * Purpose: Handle pre/post auto inc/dec (++.--) operations.
 * Args: pointer to VALUE struct with contents of memory location to be inc'ed
 *        pointer to memory location to inc
 *        pointer to type descriptor of memory location to inc
 *        flags word: I_MEAN_DEC = decrement, POST_INC_DEC = postfix ++/--
 * Result: inc'ed memory and inc'ed value struct (if not post inc/dec)
 *=============================================================*/
static void inc_value(v, m, td, flags)
  VALUE *v;
  MEMORY *m;
  TYPE_DESC *td;
  int flags;
{
  int inc;
  VALUE_TYPE type;

  if (exp_debug)
  {
    printf("inc_value: m=%x, ", m);
    print_type(NULL, td);
    print_value(v);
  }
  if (!state.executing)
  {
    if (!td)
      err("Bad operand to '%s'\n", flags & I_MEAN_DEC ? "--" : "++");
    return;
  }
  type = get_type_desc_type(td);
  inc = (type == T_PTR) ? type_desc_size(get_type_desc_next(td)) : 1;

  if (flags & I_MEAN_DEC)
    inc = -inc;

  assign_memory_to_value(v, m, type);

  if (type == T_DOUBLE)
    v->value.flt += inc;
  else
    v->value.fix += inc;
```

```
    assign_value_to_memory(v, m, type);

    if (flags & POST_INC_DEC)
    {
      if (type == T_DOUBLE)
        v->value.flt -= inc;
      else
        v->value.fix -= inc;
    }
}


/*=================================================================
 * Function:  precedence( token )
 * Purpose: return precedence of an operator.
 *===============================================================*/
static int precedence(token)
  LEX_TOKEN token;
{
  switch (token)
  {
  case '[':
  case '(':
    return 15;
  case '!':
  case '~':
    return 14;
  case '*':
  case '/':
  case '%':
    return 13;
  case '+':
  case '-':
    return 12;
  case RSHIFT:
  case LSHIFT:
    return 11;
  case GEQ:
  case LEQ:
  case '>':
  case '<':
    return 10;
  case EQ:
  case NEQ:
    return 9;
  case '&':
    return 8;
  case '^':
    return 7;
  case '|':
    return 6;
  case '=':
    return 7;
  }
  return 0;
```

```c
/*==================================================================
 * Function: unary_expression( ptoken, result, pp_type_desc)
 * Purpose: Parse any legal unary expression
 * Inputs: token - currently unparsed token, Null if none.
 *          result - pointer to value of expression result.
 *          ptoken - pointer to current token.
 *          pp_type_desc - pointer to pointer to the type descriptor of the
 *                  variable specified by the lhs expression.
 * Returns:
 *          a pointer to the address of the unary expression.
 *          ptoken - points to first token AFTER unary expression.
 *==================================================================*/
static MEMORY *unary_expression(ptoken, result, pp_type_desc)
  LEX_TOKEN *ptoken;
  VALUE *result;
  TYPE_DESC **pp_type_desc;
{
  MEMORY *lhs;
  VALUE v;
  LEX_TOKEN token;

  if (exp_debug)
    printf("In unary_expression: 1st token = '%s'\n", token_name(*ptoken));

  switch (*ptoken)
  {

  case SYMBOL:
    return primary(ptoken, result, pp_type_desc);

  case CONSTANT:
    return primary(ptoken, result, pp_type_desc);
    break;

  case BUILTIN_FUNCTION:
    return primary(ptoken, result, pp_type_desc);

  case '*':
    *ptoken = lex(result);
    lhs = unary_expression(ptoken, result, pp_type_desc);
    *pp_type_desc = get_type_desc_next(*pp_type_desc);
    if (exp_debug)
      printf("pointer ref (%x)\n", lhs, result->value.fix);
    lhs = result->value.mptr;
    assign_memory_to_value(result, lhs, get_type_desc_type(*pp_type_desc));
    return lhs;

  case '&':
    *ptoken = lex(result);
    lhs = unary_expression(ptoken, result, pp_type_desc);
    result->value.mptr = lhs;
    result->type = T_PTR;
    return NULL;

  case SIZEOF:
    *ptoken = lex(result);
    unary_expression(ptoken, result, pp_type_desc);
    result->type = T_INT;
    result->value.fix = type_desc_size(*pp_type_desc);
    return NULL;
```

```
case '+':
  *ptoken = lex(result);
  return unary_expression(ptoken, result, pp_type_desc);

case '!':
  *ptoken = lex(result);
  unary_expression(ptoken, result, pp_type_desc);
  if (result->type == T_INT)
    result->value.fix = !result->value.fix;
  else
    err("Non integral operand to '!'\n");
  return NULL;

case '~':
  *ptoken = lex(result);
  unary_expression(ptoken, result, pp_type_desc);
  if (result->type == T_INT)
    result->value.fix = ~result->value.fix;
  else
    err("Non integer operand to '~'\n");
  return NULL;

case '-':
  *ptoken = lex(result);
  unary_expression(ptoken, result, pp_type_desc);
  if (result->type == T_INT)
    result->value.fix = -result->value.fix;
  else
    result->value.flt = -result->value.flt;
  return NULL;


case INCREMENT:                    /* prefix ++ */
  *ptoken = lex(result);
  lhs = primary(ptoken, result, pp_type_desc);
  inc_value(result, lhs, *pp_type_desc, 0);
  return lhs;

case DECREMENT:                    /* prefix -- */
  *ptoken = lex(result);
  lhs = primary(ptoken, result, pp_type_desc);
  inc_value(result, lhs, *pp_type_desc, I_MEAN_DEC);
  return lhs;

case ')':
  return lhs;

case '(':
  expression(0, result, 0);
  if ((int)current_token() != ')')
    err("Unmatched paren's\n");
  break;

default:
  return NULL;
}

*ptoken = lex(&v);
return lhs;
}
```

```
/*==================================================================
 * Function:post_op( ptoken, value, address, ptype)
 * Purpose: Handle post fix operators like "[]", "()", "++", "--"
 * Args: ptoken - pointer to current token,
 *        value - pointer to result  value
 *        address - pointer to user memory
 *        ptype - pointer to type pointer
 * Result: memory address of expression result
 *================================================================*/
static MEMORY *post_op(ptoken, value, address, ptype)
 LEX_TOKEN *ptoken;
 VALUE *value;
 MEMORY *address;
 TYPE_DESC **ptype;
{
 int old_arg_stack_pointer;
 SYM *psym;
 VALUE v;
 VALUE_TYPE type;

 if (exp_debug)
   printf("In post_op: ");
 for (;; *ptoken = lex(&v))
 {
   if (exp_debug)
     printf("post_op looks at: '%s'\n", token_name(*ptoken));
   switch (*ptoken)
   {
   case INCREMENT:                /* post-fix ++ */
     inc_value(value, address, *ptype, POST_INC_DEC);
     continue;

   case DECREMENT:                /* post-fix -- */
     inc_value(value, address, *ptype, POST_INC_DEC | I_MEAN_DEC);
     continue;

   case '(':                      /* function call */
     old_arg_stack_pointer = get_stack_pointer();
     if (value->type != T_FUNC && value->type != T_FUNC_PTR)
       { err("Illegal function call\n");
         return;
       }
     psym = value->value.sym;
     user_arg_list(psym);
     value->type = get_sym_type(psym);
     if (state.executing)
       user_call(psym, value);
     if (exp_debug)
     {
       printf("fn return val is:");
       print_value(value);
     }
     set_stack_pointer(old_arg_stack_pointer);
     continue;

   case '[':                      /* array reference */
     type = get_type_desc_type(*ptype);
     /* Need extra memory dereference for subscripted pointers */
     if (type == T_PTR)
     {
```

```
              assign_memory_to_value(value, address, T_PTR);
              address = value->value.mptr;
            }
          else if (type != T_ARRAY)
            err("Need pointer or array base for subscript expression.\n");

          expression(0, value, 0);
          if (value->type != T_INT)
            err("Non-integral subscript expression\n");
          if ((int)current_token() != ']')
            err("Missing ']'");
          *ptype = get_type_desc_next(*ptype);
          type = get_type_desc_type(*ptype);
          if (exp_debug)
            printf("array ref (%x)[%d]\n", address, value->value.fix);
          address += value->value.fix * type_desc_size(*ptype);
          assign_memory_to_value(value, address, type);
          continue;

      default:
        if (exp_debug)
          printf("leaving post_op\n");
        return address;
      }
  }
}

/*==================================================================
 * Function: primary( ptoken, result, pp_type_desc)
 * Purpose: Parse primary syntactic tokens, symbols and constants for now.
 * Inputs:
 *          result - pointer to value of expression result.
 *          ptoken - pointer to first token AFTER primary expression.
 *          pp_type_desc - pointer to the data type descriptor of the
 *                   variable specified by the lhs expression.
 * Returns: a pointer to the memory location represented by the
 *          expression.
 *================================================================*/
static MEMORY *primary(ptoken, result, pp_type_desc)
  LEX_TOKEN *ptoken;
  VALUE *result;
  TYPE_DESC **pp_type_desc;
{
  MEMORY *address;
  VALUE_TYPE type;
  int old_arg_stack_pointer;
  int *ap;
  BUILTIN_PTR pbuiltin;
  FUNC_PTR pfunc;

  if (exp_debug)
    printf("In primary: 1st token = '%s'\n", token_name(*ptoken));

  switch (*ptoken)
  {
  case BUILTIN_FUNCTION:
    pbuiltin = result->value.builtin_ptr;
    if ((int) lex(result) != '(')
      break;
    /* Allow for nested calls by using current stack base */
    ap = &arg_stack[arg_stack_pointer];
    old_arg_stack_pointer = arg_stack_pointer;
```

```
    arg_list();
    if (exp_debug)
    {
      int a;

      printf("Calling %s(",
             get_builtin_func_name(pbuiltin));
      for (a = arg_stack_pointer - old_arg_stack_pointer; a; a--)
        printf("%x,", ap[a]);
      printf(")\n");
    }
    arg_stack_pointer = old_arg_stack_pointer;
    if (!state.executing)
      break;
    pfunc = get_builtin_func_ptr(pbuiltin);
    if (result->type == T_DOUBLE)
      result->value.flt = (*(double (*) ()) pfunc) (
                  ap[0], ap[1], ap[2], ap[3], ap[4], ap[5], ap[6], ap[7],
                                ap[8], ap[9], ap[10], ap[11], ap[12]);
    else
      result->value.fix = (*(int (*) ()) pfunc) (
                  ap[0], ap[1], ap[2], ap[3], ap[4], ap[5], ap[6], ap[7],
                                ap[8], ap[9], ap[10], ap[11], ap[12]);
    break;

  case SYMBOL:
    *pp_type_desc = get_sym_type_desc(result->value.sym);
    type = get_type_desc_type(*pp_type_desc);
    if (type == T_FUNC)
      result->type = T_FUNC;
    else
      {
        address = memory(result->value.sym);
        assign_memory_to_value(result, address, type);
      }
    break;

  case CONSTANT:
    break;

  default:
    return NULL;
  }

  *ptoken = lex(result);
  address = post_op(ptoken, result, address, pp_type_desc);
  if (exp_debug)
    printf("leaving primary\n ");
  return address;
}


/*=================================================================
 * Function: expression(token, result, last_precedence)
 * Purpose: Parse legal C expressions.
 * Algorithm:
 *      If precedence of current operator is greater or equal to
 *      last_precedence parse current operation and return.
 *      Otherwise recursively call expression to look for more operations
 *      at this precedence.
 * Inputs:
 *      token - current token value (nil means get a new token)
```

```
 *       result - pointer to value struct of expression result
 *       last_precedence - value of precedence of last operator seen
 * Result: TRUE if legal expression, FALSE if not
 *================================================================*/
int expression(token, result, last_precedence)
  LEX_TOKEN token;
  VALUE *result;
{
  VALUE rvalue;
  MEMORY *address = NULL;
  TYPE_DESC *p_type_desc = NULL;
  int old_arg_stack_pointer;
  int a;
  int this_precedence;

  if (token == LEX_NULL)
    token = lex(result);
  address = unary_expression(&token, result, &p_type_desc);
  if (exp_debug)
    printf("In expression (prec %d): ", last_precedence);

  for (;; token = current_token())
  {
    if (exp_debug)
      printf(" exp looks at %s\n ", token_name(token));
    this_precedence = precedence(token);
    switch (token)
    {

    case '+':
    case '-':
    case '*':
    case '/':
    case '&':
    case '|':
    case '^':
    case '>':
    case '<':
    case RSHIFT:
    case LSHIFT:
    case EQ:
    case LEQ:
    case GEQ:
    case NEQ:
      if (last_precedence >= this_precedence)
        return;
      else
        expression(0, &rvalue, this_precedence);
#if DEBUG
      if (exp_debug)
      {
        printf(" operator is %s: ", token_name(token));
        printf("address = ");
        print_value(result);
        printf(" rhs = ");
        print_value(&rvalue);
        printf("\n");
      }
#endif
      /* If types don't agree, we must convert int side to double */
      if (rvalue.type != result->type)
      {
```

```c
    if (result->type != T_DOUBLE)
    {
      result->value.flt = result->value.fix;
      result->type = T_DOUBLE;
    }
    else
    {
      rvalue.value.flt = rvalue.value.fix;
    }
  }

  if (result->type == T_DOUBLE)
    switch (token)
    {
    case '+':
      result->value.flt += rvalue.value.flt;
      continue;
    case '-':
      result->value.flt -= rvalue.value.flt;
      continue;
    case '*':
      result->value.flt *= rvalue.value.flt;
      continue;
    case '/':
      result->value.flt /= rvalue.value.flt;
      continue;
    case EQ:
      result->value.fix = result->value.flt == rvalue.value.flt;
      continue;
    case NEQ:
      result->value.fix = result->value.flt != rvalue.value.flt;
      continue;
    case GEQ:
      result->value.fix = result->value.flt >= rvalue.value.flt;
      continue;
    case LEQ:
      result->value.fix = result->value.flt <= rvalue.value.flt;
      continue;
    case '>':
      result->value.fix = result->value.flt > rvalue.value.flt;
      continue;
    case '<':
      result->value.fix = result->value.flt < rvalue.value.flt;
      continue;
    }
  else if (result->type == T_INT)
    switch (token)
    {
    case '+':
      result->value.fix += rvalue.value.fix;
      continue;
    case '-':
      result->value.fix -= rvalue.value.fix;
      continue;
    case '*':
      result->value.fix *= rvalue.value.fix;
      continue;
    case '/':
      result->value.fix /= rvalue.value.fix;
      continue;
    case '|':
      result->value.fix |= rvalue.value.fix;
```

```
            continue;
        case '&':
            result->value.fix &= rvalue.value.fix;
            continue;
        case '^':
            result->value.fix ^= rvalue.value.fix;
            continue;
        case LSHIFT:
            result->value.fix <<= rvalue.value.fix;
            continue;
        case RSHIFT:
            result->value.fix >>= rvalue.value.fix;
            continue;
        case EQ:
            result->value.fix = result->value.fix == rvalue.value.fix;
            continue;
        case NEQ:
            result->value.fix = result->value.fix != rvalue.value.fix;
            continue;
        case GEQ:
            result->value.fix = result->value.fix >= rvalue.value.fix;
            continue;
        case LEQ:
            result->value.fix = result->value.fix <= rvalue.value.fix;
            continue;
        case '>':
            result->value.fix = result->value.fix > rvalue.value.fix;
            continue;
        case '<':
            result->value.fix = result->value.fix < rvalue.value.fix;
            continue;
        }

        return;

    case '=':
        expression(0, result, this_precedence);   /* Parse RHS */
        if (!p_type_desc)
            err("Illegal Left Hand Side to assign op\n");
        else if (state.executing)
            assign_value_to_memory(result, address,
                                   get_type_desc_type(p_type_desc));
        return;

    case ')':
    case '(':
    case ']':
    case ',':
    case '\r':
    case ';':
    case '\n':
        return;

    default:
        err("Unexpected token in expression: '%s'\n", token_name(token));
        return;
    }
}
    return;
}
```

```
/*===============================================================
 * lex.c
 * Author: P. Darnell
 * Initial coding: 10/86
 * Purpose:
 *    This module reads the input stream and identifies tokens.
 *    Contiguous digits are recognized as numbers and contiguous
 *    letters are recognized as symbols.
 *    The token code is returned as an int, and related data, if any, is stored
 *    into the VALUE structure pointed at by the pvalue parameter to lex.
 *    If EOF is detected and the input stream is not stdin, it is set to stdin.
 *    if EOF is detected and the input stream is already stdin,
 *    the program exits.
/*===============================================================

#include <math.h>
#include <ctype.h>
#include <stdio.h>
#include "token_st.h"
#include "lex.h"
#include "sym.h"
#include "cint.h"

#define MAX_SYM 128
#define MAX_STR 256

extern FILE *input_stream;

static char str_buf[MAX_STR];

typedef struct
{
  char *key_name;
  LEX_TOKEN key_value;
} KEY_TABLE;

static KEY_TABLE key_table[] = {
  {"break", BREAK},
  {"char", CHAR},
  {"continue", CONTINUE},
  {"double", DOUBLE},
  {"int", INT},
  {"else", ELSE},
  {"extern", EXTERN},
  {"float", FLOAT},
  {"for", FOR},
  {"if", IF},
  {"list", LIST},
  {"return", RETURN},
  {"run", RUN},
  {"short", SHORT},
  {"signed", SIGNED},
  {"sizeof", SIZEOF},
  {"static", STATIC},
  {"switch", SWITCH},
  {"unsigned", UNSIGNED},
  {"void", VOID},
  {"while", WHILE},
  {"LEX_NULL", LEX_NULL},
  {">>", RSHIFT},
  {"<<", LSHIFT},
```

```
      {"==", EQ},
      {"!=", NEQ},
      {">=", GEQ},
      {"<=", LEQ},
      {"++", INCREMENT},
      {"--", DECREMENT},
      {"Symbol", SYMBOL},
      {"Constant", CONSTANT},
      {"Builtin_function", BUILTIN_FUNCTION},
      {NULL, (LEX_TOKEN) 0},
};


/*==================================================================
 * Function: token_name(token)
 * Purpose: return pointer to string corresponding to token.
 * Algorithm:  Look up token in keyword spelling table. If not found,
 *    assume that token is single letter and make into string by putting
 *    char in buffer and following with a null.
 *    Note subsequent calls to this routine overwrite the single letter buffer.
 * Inputs: token to convert to string
 * Result: pointer to char
 *=================================================================*/
char *token_name(token)
  LEX_TOKEN token;
{
  KEY_TABLE *pkeytab;
  static char token_buf[2];

  for (pkeytab = key_table; pkeytab->key_name; pkeytab++)
    if (pkeytab->key_value == token)
      return pkeytab->key_name;

  token_buf[0] = (char) token;
  token_buf[1] = 0;
  return token_buf;
}

/*==================================================================
 * Function: keyword()
 * Purpose: return LEX enum of keyword or LEX_NULL if not keyword.
 * Algorithm: simple linear search of keyword list.
 * Inputs: name - spelling of candidate keyword
 * Result:
 *=================================================================*/
static LEX_TOKEN keyword(name)
  char *name;
{
  KEY_TABLE *pkeytab;
  for (pkeytab = key_table; pkeytab->key_value; pkeytab++)
    if (!strcmp(name, pkeytab->key_name))
      return pkeytab->key_value;
  return LEX_NULL;
}
```

```
typedef struct
{
  VALUE_TYPE type;
  char *func_name;
  FUNC_PTR func_ptr;
} FUNC_TABLE;

extern printf(), rand(), exit(), strcpy(), strcmp(), strcat();
extern double log(), log10(), cos(), sin(), tan(), sqrt(), pow(), exp();
extern int user_malloc(), user_free(), scanf(), time(), ctime();

/* Table of external function names from C library.
 * These could be external user routines as well
 */
static FUNC_TABLE func_table[] = {
    {T_DOUBLE, "cos", (FUNC_PTR) cos},
    {T_INT, "ctime", (FUNC_PTR) ctime},
    {T_INT, "exit", (FUNC_PTR) exit},
    {T_DOUBLE, "exp", (FUNC_PTR) exp},
    {T_INT, "free", (FUNC_PTR) user_free},
    {T_DOUBLE, "log", (FUNC_PTR) log},
    {T_DOUBLE, "log10", (FUNC_PTR) log10},
    {T_INT, "malloc", (FUNC_PTR) user_malloc},
    {T_DOUBLE, "pow", (FUNC_PTR) pow},
    {T_INT, "printf", (FUNC_PTR) printf},
    {T_INT, "rand", (FUNC_PTR) rand},
    {T_INT, "scanf", (FUNC_PTR) scanf},
    {T_INT, "strcat", (FUNC_PTR) strcat},
    {T_INT, "strcmp", (FUNC_PTR) strcmp},
    {T_INT, "strcpy", (FUNC_PTR) strcpy},
    {T_DOUBLE, "sin", (FUNC_PTR) sin},
    {T_DOUBLE, "sqrt", (FUNC_PTR) sqrt},
    {T_DOUBLE, "tan", (FUNC_PTR) tan},
    {T_INT, "time", (FUNC_PTR) time},
    {T_UNKNOWN, 0}
};

/*=================================================================
 * Function: builtin_function(name, pvalue)
 * Purpose: see if name is a builtin function
 * Algorithm: simple linear search of function table
 *    Put the array index of the matched function into the value node.
 * Inputs:
 *   name - spelling of candidate builtin function
 *   pvalue - pointer to VALUE struct that gets assigned if builtin is found
 * Result: TRUE if name is builtin, FALSE if not.
 *=================================================================*/
static BUILTIN_PTR builtin_function(name, pvalue)
  char *name;
  VALUE *pvalue;
{
  int a = 0;

  FUNC_TABLE *pfunctab;
  for (pfunctab = func_table; pfunctab->func_ptr; pfunctab++, a++)
    if (!strcmp(name, pfunctab->func_name))
      {
        pvalue->type = pfunctab->type;
        pvalue->value.builtin_ptr = a;
        return TRUE;
```

```
    }
  return FALSE;
}

/* Return spelling of builtin name given index into function table */
char *get_builtin_func_name(bp)
  BUILTIN_PTR bp;
{
  return func_table[bp].func_name;
}

/*
 * Return function pointer of builtin given index into function table */
 */
FUNC_PTR get_builtin_func_ptr(bp)
  BUILTIN_PTR bp;
{
  return func_table[bp].func_ptr;
}

/*
 * local wrappers to getc/ungetc
 */

static char lex_get()
{
  return getc(input_stream);
}

static void lex_unget(c)
  int c;
{
  ungetc(c, input_stream);
}

/*================================================================
 * Function: string_char(c)
 * Purpose: return value of single quoted char constant
 * Algorithm: check for backslash and return proper
 * Inputs: first character of char constant
 * Result: int value of char constant
 * Bug:  Doesn't handle backslashed octal constants
 *===============================================================*/
static int string_char(c)
{
  if (c == '\\')
    switch (lex_get())
      {
      case 'n':return '\n';
      case 't':
        return '\t';
      case 'r':
        return '\r';
      case 'b':
        return '\b';
      case 'f':
        return '\f';
      case 'v':
        return '\v';
      case 'a':
        return '\a';
      }
```

```
    return c;
}

static char sym_buf[MAX_SYM];

/*====================================================================
 * Function: lex0()
 * Purpose:  Read input stream, and break into tokens of the C lexicon.
 * Algorithm:
 *    Ignore extra whitespace.
 *    Detect numeric constants, string constants, keywords, builtin functions
 *    and symbols. Store the associated value or pointer in the VALUE struct
 *    pointed at by pvalue.
 *    The lex main entry is found in the module token_st.c, it is there because
 *    lex0 is called only on the initial parse. When executing, lex takes its
 *    tokens from a linked list of tokens that lex stored away
 *    on the initial parse.
 * Inputs:
 *    pvalue - pointer to VALUE struct to be initialized with
 *             relevant token data
 * Result: Enum of lex'ed token.
 *====================================================================*/

LEX_TOKEN lex0(pvalue)
  VALUE *pvalue;
{
  VALUE *sym_value;
  char *p;
  double value, scale;
  LEX_TOKEN kw;
  char c, c2;

next_char:
  c = lex_get();


  if (c == '.')
    goto leading_dot;

/* lex a numeric constant
 */
  if (isdigit(c))
    {
      int radix = 10;

/* We assume here that digits 0-9 are in consecutive ascending order.
 * (like ASCII or EBCDIC)
 */
      value = c - '0';
      if (value == 0)                 /* Hex or Octal */
        {
          if ((c = lex_get()) == 'x' || c == 'X')    /* 0x prefix means hex */
            {
              for (c = lex_get(); isxdigit(c); c = lex_get())
                {
                  value *= 16;
                  if (isdigit(c))
                    c -= '0';
                  else
                    {
                      c = toupper(c);
                      c = 10 + (c - 'A');
```

```
        }
        value += c;
      }
      goto return_int_constant;
    }
    else
    {
      radix = 8;
      lex_unget(c);
    }
  }
  for (c = lex_get(); isdigit(c); c = lex_get())
  {
    value *= radix;
    value += c - '0';
  }

  if (c != '.' && c != 'e' && c != 'E')
  {
return_int_constant:
    pvalue->value.fix = value;
    pvalue->type = T_INT;
    lex_unget(c);
    return CONSTANT;
  }

  if (c == '.')
  {
leading_dot:
    scale = 1;
    for (c = lex_get(); isdigit(c); c = lex_get())
    {
      double fract_digit;

      scale *=.1;
      fract_digit = c - '0';
      fract_digit *= scale;
      value += fract_digit;
    }
  }

  /* Deal with exponent: e/E[+/-]<digit>* */
  if (c == 'e' || c == 'E')
  {
    int neg_exp = FALSE;

    c = lex_get();
    switch (c)
    {
    case '-':
      neg_exp = TRUE;
    case '+':
      c = lex_get();
    case '0':
    case '1':
    case '2':
    case '3':
    case '4':
    case '5':
    case '6':
    case '7':
    case '8':
```

```
    case '9':
      for (scale = 0; isdigit(c); c = lex_get())
      {
        scale *= 10;
        scale += c - '0';
      }
      value *= pow(10.0, neg_exp ? -scale : scale);
      break;
    default:
      err("Badly formed float constant\n");
    }
  }
  pvalue->value.flt = value;
  pvalue->type = T_DOUBLE;
  lex_unget(c);

  return CONSTANT;
}
else if (isalpha(c) || c == '_')
{
  p = sym_buf;
  while (isalpha(c) || c == '_' || isdigit(c))
  {
    *p++ = c;
    c = lex_get();
  }
  lex_unget(c);
  *p = 0;
  if (kw = keyword(sym_buf))
    return kw;
  if (builtin_function(sym_buf, pvalue))
    return BUILTIN_FUNCTION;

  pvalue->type = T_PTR;
  if (!sym_find(sym_buf, &pvalue->value.sym))
  {
    pvalue->value.sym = sym_enter(sym_buf);
  }
  return SYMBOL;
}

switch (c)
{
case '/':
  c2 = lex_get();
  if (c2 == '*')                  /* process a comment */
  {
    while ((c2 = lex_get()) != EOF)
    {
      if (c == '*' && c2 == '/')
        goto next_char;           /* end of comment */
      c = c2;
      if (c2 == '\n')
        bump_line_count();
    }
    err("End of file before end of comment.");
  }
  else
    lex_unget(c2);
  break;

case '\n':
```

```
case '\r':
  bump_line_count();
  if (state.calc_mode)
    break;
case '\t':
case ' ':
  goto next_char;

case '\'':
  /* Process a char constant */
  pvalue->value.fix = string_char(lex_get());
  if (lex_get() != '\'')
    printf("Missing trailing ' in string constant\n");
  pvalue->type = T_INT;
  return CONSTANT;

case '"':
  /* Process a quoted string */
  c = lex_get();
  for (p = str_buf; c != '"' && c != EOF; c = lex_get())
    *p++ = string_char(c);
  *p = 0;
  pvalue->value.fix = user_malloc(strlen(str_buf) + 1);
  strcpy(pvalue->value.fix, str_buf);
  pvalue->type = T_PTR;
  return CONSTANT;

case '=':
  c2 = lex_get();
  if (c2 == '=')
    return EQ;
  else
    lex_unget(c2);
  break;

case '!':
  c2 = lex_get();
  if (c2 == '=')
    return NEQ;
  else
    lex_unget(c2);
  break;

case '>':
  c2 = lex_get();
  if (c2 == '=')
    return GEQ;
  else if (c2 == '>')
    return RSHIFT;
  else
    lex_unget(c2);
  break;

case '<':
  c2 = lex_get();
  if (c2 == '=')
    return LEQ;
  else if (c2 == '<')
    return LSHIFT;
  else
    lex_unget(c2);
  break;
```

```
      case '+':
        c2 = lex_get();
        if (c2 == '+')
          return INCREMENT;
        else
          lex_unget(c2);
        break;

      case '-':
        c2 = lex_get();
        if (c2 == '-')
          return DECREMENT;
        else
          lex_unget(c2);
        break;

      case ',':
      case ';':
      case '[':
      case ']':
      case '{':
      case '}':
      case '(':
      case ')':
      case '*':
      case '|':
      case '&':
      case '^':
        break;

      case EOF:
        /* exits if user types EOF */
        if (input_stream == stdin)
          exit(0);
        input_stream = next_file();
        goto next_char;
        break;

      default:
        printf(" Unknown character %d\n", c);
        break;
      }
      return (LEX_TOKEN) c;
}
```

```c
#include <stdio.h>
#include "lex.h"
#include "token_st.h"
#include "sym.h"
#include "cint.h"

FILE *input_stream = stdin;

/* Stashs away a file name for later retrieval by * next_file()
 */
#define MAX_USER_FILES 20
static char *user_file[MAX_USER_FILES];
static int file_count = 0;

static void stash_file(f)
  char *f;
{
  if (file_count > MAX_USER_FILES)
  {
    err("Too many files, sorry.\n");
    exit(1);
  }
  user_file[file_count++] = f;
}

static int auto_startup;            /* True if we should start at main
                                     * automatically */



/*==================================================================
 * Function: call_main()
 * Purpose: call user's main routine
 * Algorithm:
 *   Set global state, and call routine called "main"
 *==================================================================*/
void call_main()
{
  SYM *sym;
  VALUE value;

  if (!sym_find("main", &sym))
  {
    err("No main function\n");
    return;
  }
  state.saving_token_stream = FALSE;
  state.executing = TRUE;
  user_call(sym, &value);
  state.saving_token_stream = TRUE;
  state.executing = FALSE;
}
```

```
static void put_prompt()
{
    printf("Cint> ");
}



/*=================================================================
 * Function: next_file()
 * Purpose: Return the file pointer to the next input file.
 * Algorithm:
 *    Return the file pointer to the next file stashed away by stash_file()
 *    If no files are left, use stdin, and turn on prompts.
 *================================================================*/
FILE *next_file()
{
    FILE *fp;

    if (file_count == 0)
        if (auto_startup)
        {
            call_main();
            exit(0);
        }
        else
        {
            state.prompting = TRUE;
            put_prompt();
            return stdin;
        }

    fp = fopen(user_file[--file_count], "r");
    if (!fp)
    {
        printf("Can't open %s\n", user_file[file_count]);
        exit(1);
    }
    return fp;
}




/*=================================================================
 * Function: main(argc, argv)
 * Purpose: first routine to be called.
 * Algorithm:
 *    Parse command line for files and options.
 *    Then go into loop reading input from files (if any), then stdin.
 *    Look for LIST, and RUN commands, if neither, look for declaration.
 *     If not that either, assume that use is typeing in expression to
 *     be evaluated, parse it and print result.
 * Inputs:
 *        argc - count of command line args
 *        argv - pointer to list of null terminated strings representing
 *               command line args.
 *================================================================*/

main(argc, argv)
   int argc;
   char **argv;
{
```

```
VALUE value;
LEX_TOKEN token;
int expression();

for (argv++; argc-- > 1; argv++)
  if (**argv == '-')
  {
    if (!strcmp(*argv, "-dlex"))
      lex_debug = TRUE;
    else if (!strcmp(*argv, "-dexp"))
      exp_debug = TRUE;
    else if (!strcmp(*argv, "-dstmt"))
    {
      stmt_debug = TRUE;
      state.prompting = TRUE;
    }
    else if (!strcmp(*argv, "-run"))
      auto_startup = TRUE;
    else
      printf("Unknown option %s\n", *argv);
  }
  else
    stash_file(*argv);

input_stream = next_file();
state.saving_token_stream = TRUE;

for (;;)                          /* loop until user types exit() or EOF
                                   * character */
{
  if (state.prompting)
    put_prompt();
  token = lex(&value);
  switch (token)
  {
  case RUN:
    printf("Calling main...\n");
    call_main();
    continue;

  case LIST:
    sym_list();
    continue;
  }
  if (!declare(token, &value))
  {
    state.calc_mode = TRUE;
    state.executing = TRUE;
    state.saving_token_stream = FALSE;
    expression(token, &value, 0);
    state.executing = FALSE;
    state.saving_token_stream = TRUE;
    state.calc_mode = FALSE;
    if (value.type == T_DOUBLE)
      printf("%g\n", value.value.flt);
    else if (value.type != T_VOID)
      printf("%d\n", value.value.fix);
  }
 }
}
```

```
/*===============================================================
 * stmt.c
 * Author: P. Darnell
 * 10/86 Created
 * Purpose: Parse and execute C statements.
 *==============================================================*/
#include "token_st.h"
#include "sym.h"
#include "cint.h"
#include "lex.h"

/* Check for semicolon, report error if missing */
static void check_semicolon()
{
  VALUE val;

  if ((int) current_token() != ';')
  {
    err("Missing semicolon\n");
    lex(&val);
  }
}

static int statement_level;
static char break_seen;

/*===============================================================
 * Function: statement(token, pvalue)
 * Purpose: parse and execute C statements
 * Algorithm: Uses recursive descent
 *    When in execution mode, little syntax checking is performed, and pointers
 *    to things like statement_top and end_of_if tokens are assumed to have been
 *    successfully handled in the parse phase.
 * Inputs:
 *    token - enum of last lex'ed token
 *    pvalue - pointer value of last lex'ed token
 *==============================================================*/
void statement(token, pvalue)
  LEX_TOKEN token;
  VALUE *pvalue;
{
  TOKEN *statement_top;
  TOKEN *loop_exit;

  statement_level++;
  if (!state.executing && state.prompting)
    printf("slvl %d> ", statement_level);
  if (token == LEX_NULL)
    token = lex(pvalue);
  if (stmt_debug)
    printf("First token in stmt lvl %d: %s\n",
           statement_level, token_name(token));
  switch (token)
  {

  case '{':                      /* Compound statement */
    enter_scope();
    while (declare(lex(pvalue), pvalue));
    while ((int) current_token() != '}')
    {
      statement((int) current_token(), pvalue);
```

```
      if (state.returning || break_seen)
        break;
      if (stmt_debug)
        printf("tokens after stmt in block: %s,",
               token_name(current_token()));
      token = lex(pvalue);
      if (stmt_debug)
        printf("%s\n", token_name(token));
    }
    leave_scope();
    break;

  case IF:                          /* If statement */
    statement_top = get_token_pc();

    if (!state.executing)           /* initial parse */
    {
      set_if_else(statement_top, NULL);
      if ((int) lex(pvalue) != '(')
        err("Missing '(' after if\n");
      expression(0, pvalue, 0);
      if ((int) current_token() != ')')
        err("Missing ')' after if\n");
      statement(0, pvalue);
      if (lex(pvalue) == ELSE)
      {
        token = lex(pvalue);
        set_if_else(statement_top, get_token_pc());
        statement(token, pvalue);
      }
      else
      {
        set_if_else(statement_top, NULL);
        unlex();
      }

      set_if_exit(statement_top, get_token_pc());
    }
    else                            /* Running */
    {
      skip_token();                 /* '(' */
      expression(0, pvalue, 0);
      if (pvalue->value.fix != 0)
        statement(0, pvalue);
      else if (get_if_else(statement_top))
      {
        set_token_pc(get_if_else(statement_top));
        statement(0, pvalue);
      }

      set_token_pc(get_if_exit(statement_top));
    }
    break;

  case WHILE:                       /* While statement */
    statement_top = get_token_pc();
    if (!state.executing)           /* initial parse */
    {
      loop_exit = NULL;
      if ((int) lex(pvalue) != '(')
        err("Missing '(' after while\n");
      expression(0, pvalue, 0);
```

```
        if ((int) current_token() != ')')
          err("Missing ')' after while\n");
        statement(0, pvalue);
        /* Lex to next token to get token after WHILE stmt */
        lex(pvalue);
        set_loop_exit(statement_top, get_token_pc());
        unlex();
      }
      else                           /* Running */
      {
        loop_exit = get_loop_exit(statement_top);
        while (1)
        {
          skip_token();              /* '(' */
          expression(0, pvalue, 0);
          if (pvalue->value.fix == 0)
            break;
          statement(0, pvalue);
          if (break_seen)
            break;
          set_token_pc(statement_top);
          skip_token();              /* 'while' */
        }
        break_seen = FALSE;
        set_token_pc(loop_exit);
      }

      break;

    case FOR:                        /* For statement */
      statement_top = get_token_pc();
      if (!state.executing)          /* initial parse */
      {
        loop_exit = NULL;
        if ((int) lex(pvalue) != '(')
          err("Missing '(' after for\n");
        expression(0, pvalue, 0); /* init expression */
        check_semicolon();
        set_loop_test(statement_top, get_token_pc());
        expression(0, pvalue, 0); /* boolean expression */
        check_semicolon();
        set_loop_increment(statement_top, get_token_pc());
        expression(0, pvalue, 0); /* increment expression */
        if ((int) current_token() != ')')
          err("Missing ')' after for\n");
        set_loop_body(statement_top, get_token_pc());
        statement(0, pvalue);
        /* Lex to next token to get token after FOR stmt */
        lex(pvalue);
        set_loop_exit(statement_top, get_token_pc());
        unlex();
      }
      else                           /* Running */
      {
        loop_exit = get_loop_exit(statement_top);
        skip_token();                /* '(' */
        expression(0, pvalue, 0); /* init */
        while (1)
        {
          set_token_pc(get_loop_test(statement_top));
          skip_token();              /* ';' */
          expression(0, pvalue, 0);      /* boolean test */
```

```
              if (pvalue->value.fix == 0)
                break;
              set_token_pc(get_loop_body(statement_top));
              skip_token();              /* ')' */
              statement(0, pvalue);
              if (break_seen)
                break;
              set_token_pc(get_loop_increment(statement_top));
              skip_token();              /* ';' */
              expression(0, pvalue, 0);        /* increment */
          }
        break_seen = FALSE;
        set_token_pc(loop_exit);
      }

    break;
  case RETURN:                        /* Return statement */
    expression(0, pvalue, 0);
    check_semicolon();
    if (state.executing)
      state.returning = TRUE;
    break;

  case BREAK:                         /* Break statement */
    lex(pvalue);
    check_semicolon();
    if (state.executing)
      break_seen = TRUE;
    break;

  case LEX_NULL:                      /* Error in token list */
    err("Internal error in Cint, premature token list end");

  case ';':                           /* Null statement */
    break;

  default:                            /* Expression */
    expression((int) current_token(), pvalue, 0);
    check_semicolon();
    break;
  }
  if (stmt_debug)
    printf("Leaving stmt level %d\n", statement_level);

  statement_level--;

}
```

```
/*================================================================
 * sym.c
 * Author: P. Darnell
 * Initial coding: 8/86
 * Purpose: Handle symbol creation and access.
 *===============================================================*/

#define SYM_OWNER
#include "token_st.h"
#include "sym.h"
#include "cint.h"

/* maximum scope nesting depth */
#define MAX_SCOPE_LEVEL 32

static SYM *sym_head;
static SYM **local_scope_table;

static int Scope_level;
static int frame_offset;

int scope_level()
{
    return Scope_level;
}

/* Flag to tell sym_enter() if we are in a declaration section. */
static char Sym_declaring;

/*================================================================
 *   Set declaration state.
 *===============================================================*/
void sym_declaring(x)
  int x;
{
  Sym_declaring = x;
}


/*================================================================
 * Function: enter_scope()
 * Purpose: Increment Scope_level to reflect entered scope.
 *    Scope level 1 is for arguments, scope level 2 and on are function
 *    local symbols.
 * Result: Scope_level incremented, and frame_offset zeroed for
 *   entry to arg scope or function scope.
 *===============================================================*/
void enter_scope()
{
    Scope_level++;
  if (Scope_level == 1 || Scope_level == 2)
    frame_offset = 0;
}
```

```
typedef struct list
{
  struct list *l_next;
  SYM *l_object;
} LIST_ELEMENT;


LIST_ELEMENT *make_list(s)
  SYM *s;
{
  LIST_ELEMENT *p = (LIST_ELEMENT *) malloc(sizeof(LIST_ELEMENT));
  p->l_next = NULL;
  p->l_object = s;
  return p;
}

static SYM *func_sym;
void set_func_sym(sym)
  SYM *sym;
{
  func_sym = sym;
}

/*
 * Note that we are leaving a scope level. If we have returned to scope level
 * 0, that means that we just finished a function declaration. Store the
 * symbol table as a linked list off the function sym node.
 */
void leave_scope()
{
  int a;
  SYM *p;
  LIST_ELEMENT *plist;

  if (stmt_debug)
    printf("Leaving scope level %d\n", Scope_level);
  Scope_level--;

  /*
   * End of function declaration. Remember symbols scoped to this function.
   */
  if (Sym_declaring && Scope_level == 0)
  {
    func_sym->func_descriptor.func_sym_list = local_scope_table;
    local_scope_table = NULL;
  }
}

int get_frame_size()
{
    return frame_offset;
}
```

```
int type_desc_size(td)
  TYPE_DESC *td;
{
  if (td->type == T_ARRAY)
    return td->size * type_desc_size(td->next);
  return type_size(td->type);
}


/*================================================================
 * Function: sym_table(scope_level)
 * Purpose: * Return a pointer to the first symbol at scope_level.
 * Algorithm:
 *    If there is no local symbol table for the current function, make one.
 * Inputs: scope_level - current scope level
 * Result: pointer to sym table for current scope level.
 *================================================================*/
static SYM **sym_table(scope_level)
  int scope_level;
{
  if (local_scope_table == NULL)
  {
    local_scope_table = (SYM **) calloc(sizeof(SYM), MAX_SCOPE_LEVEL);
    if (local_scope_table == NULL)
    {
      err("Symbol table overflow\n");
      exit(1);
    }
  }
  if (scope_level > 0)
    return &local_scope_table[scope_level - 1];
  return &sym_head;
}


/*================================================================
 * Function: sym_allocate(sym)
 * Purpose: Allocate storage in memory for a symbol.
 * Algorithm:
 *    Keep a running count of the next available memory location in
 *    the static var "frame_offset" for args and frame locals.  Call
 *    static_alloc to assign memory to globals and statics.
 *    Note that args are positive offsets from the frame pointer,
 *    locals are negative. (We grow the stack downward in memory ) .
 * Inputs: sym - pointer to symbol to allocate
 * Result:
 *================================================================*/
void sym_allocate(sym)
  SYM *sym;
{
  if (exp_debug)
    print_sym(sym, 0);

  /* Actually alloc the space */
  switch (Scope_level)
  {
  case 0:                            /* Global sym */
    sym->sym_storage = GLOBAL;
    sym->sym_offset = static_alloc(type_desc_size(&sym->sym_type));
    break;
```

```
  case 1:                            /* Args */
    sym->sym_storage = STACK;
    sym->sym_offset = frame_offset;

    /* Array arguments are treated as pointers */
    if (sym->sym_type.type == T_ARRAY)
      sym->sym_type.type = T_PTR;

    frame_offset += type_desc_size(&sym->sym_type);
    break;

  default:                           /* Locals */
    sym->sym_storage = STACK;
    frame_offset -= type_desc_size(&sym->sym_type);
    sym->sym_offset = frame_offset;
    break;
  }
}

#define FIRST_ARG_OFFSET 0

/*
 * Allocate storage offsets for argument list, given the first arg in the
 * list.
 */
void sym_arg_allocate(first_arg)
  SYM *first_arg;
{
  SYM *p;

  frame_offset = FIRST_ARG_OFFSET;
  for (p = first_arg; p; p = p->sym_next)
    sym_allocate(p);
}


/*==================================================================
 * Function: sym_enter(name)
 * Purpose: Enter a symbol in the symbol table.
 * Algorithm:
 *    If we are sym_declaring, enter at
 *    current scope, if not declaring, assume we have a reference to an
 *    undeclared function that needs to be as scope level 0.  If we ever support
 *    goto label, the label needs to be at scope level 1.
 * Inputs: name - pointer to null terminated string of symbol name.
 * Result: pointer to symbol entry.
 *==================================================================*/
SYM *sym_enter(name)
  char *name;
{
  SYM *p, *q;
  SYM **ptable;
  int enter_level;

  if (stmt_debug)
    printf("sym_entering %s at scope_level %d\n", name, Scope_level);
  p = (SYM *) malloc(sizeof(SYM));

  p->sym_type.type = T_UNKNOWN;
  p->sym_type.next = NULL;
  enter_level = Sym_declaring ? Scope_level : 0;
```

```
  ptable = sym_table(enter_level);

  if (*ptable)
  {
    q = *ptable;
    while (q->sym_next)
      q = q->sym_next;
    q->sym_next = p;
  }
  else
    *ptable = p;

  p->sym_name = (char *) malloc(strlen(name) + 1);
  if (p->sym_name == NULL)
  {
    err("Symbol table overflow\n");
    exit(1);
  }
  strcpy(p->sym_name, name);
  p->sym_next = NULL;
  p->func_descriptor.func_sym_list = NULL;
  return p;
}


/*==================================================================
 * Function: sym_find(name, psym)
 * Purpose:  Try to find a symbol called "name" in the symbol table.
 * Algorithm:
 *    Use a an array of linked list. One linked list per scope. This coule
 *    Be sped up by using a hash table for a symbol table, at least for the
 *    file level scoping, but this is an exercise left for the student.
 *    If we are declaring symbols, only look for the name in the current scope.
 * Inputs: name - pointer to null terminated string of symbol name.
 *         psym - pointer to sym pointer to be filled in if name is found.
 * Result: TRUE if name is found, FALSE if it isn't.
 *==================================================================*/
int sym_find(name, psym)
  char *name;
  SYM **psym;
{
  SYM *p;
  int slvl;

  for (slvl = Scope_level; slvl >= 0; slvl--)
  {
    for (p = *sym_table(slvl); p; p = p->sym_next)
      if (!strcmp(p->sym_name, name))
      {
        *psym = p;
        return TRUE;
      }
    if (Sym_declaring)
      break;
  }
  *psym = (SYM *) NULL;
  return FALSE;
}
```

```c
/* Return C spelling of a type */
static char * type_name(type)
  VALUE_TYPE type;
{
  switch (type)
  {
  case T_ARRAY:
    return "[]";
  case T_PTR:
    return "*";
  case T_CHAR:
    return "char";
  case T_SHORT:
    return "short";
  case T_INT:
    return "int";
  case T_VOID:
    return "void";
  case T_FLOAT:
    return "float";
  case T_DOUBLE:
    return "double";
  }
  return "??";
}


/*==================================================================
 *  Sym printing support routines.
 *================================================================*/
static void print_pointer_type(td)
  TYPE_DESC *td;
{
  if (td->next)
    print_pointer_type(td->next);
  if (td->type != T_ARRAY)
    printf("%s", type_name(td->type));
}

static void print_array_type(td)
  TYPE_DESC *td;
{
  if (td->type == T_ARRAY)
    printf("[%d]", td->size);
  if (td->next)
    print_array_type(td->next);
}

void print_type(sym, td)
  SYM *sym;
  TYPE_DESC *td;
{
  print_pointer_type(td);
  if (sym)
    printf("\t%s", sym->sym_name);
  print_array_type(td);
}
```

```
/*================================================================
 * Function: print_sym(p, indent_level)
 * Purpose: print out information about a symbol.
 * Algorithm:
 * Inputs: p             - pointer to symbol entry
 *         indent_level - amount of indenting to print before symbol.
 *================================================================*/
void print_sym(p, indent_level)
  SYM *p;
  int indent_level;
{
  LIST_ELEMENT *plist;
  int a;
  SYM *param;
  VALUE_TYPE t, t2;
  TOKEN *func_body;

  if (p == NULL)
    return;

  for (a = 0; a < indent_level; a++)
    printf("  ");

  t = p->sym_type.type;

  if (t == T_FUNC)
  {
    printf("%s %s( ",
           type_name(p->func_descriptor.func_type), p->sym_name);
    for (param = first_param(p); param;)
    {
      printf("%s", param->sym_name);
      param = next_param();
      if (param != NULL)
        printf(", ");
    }
    printf(" )\n");
    for (param = first_param(p); param; param = next_param())
      print_sym(param, indent_level + 1);
    if (exp_debug)
      printf(" body %x, frame size %d\n"
             ,p->func_descriptor.func_start, p->sym_offset);
    func_body = p->func_descriptor.func_start;
    if (func_body != NULL)
    {
      if (!state.executing)
        print_token_list(func_body);
    }
    else
      printf(";\n");
  }
  else
  {
    print_type(p, &p->sym_type);
    if (exp_debug)
      printf("<%d+%d>", p->sym_storage, p->sym_offset);
    printf(";\n");
  }
}
```

```
/*=================================================================
 * Function: add_sym_type(sym, type, size)
 * Purpose:
 *    Add a type modifier (like pointer or array) to a symbol with an existing
 *    base type.
 * Inputs: sym  - pointer to sym entry to add type information to.
 *         type - type to be added
 *         size - size of array dimension if type is array
 *=================================================================*/
void add_sym_type(sym, type, size)
   SYM *sym;
   VALUE_TYPE type;
   int size;
{
   TYPE_DESC *p, *q;

   p = (TYPE_DESC *) malloc(sizeof(TYPE_DESC));
   q = &sym->sym_type;
   *p = *q;
   q->next = p;
   q->type = type;
   if (type == T_ARRAY)
   {
     if (size <= 0)
     {
       err("Bad size to array declaration.");
       return;
     }
     q->size = size;
   }
}

/*=================================================================
 * Function: sym_list()
 * Purpose: List all symbols in table
 *=================================================================*/
void sym_list()
{
   SYM *p;
   int s;

   for (s = MAX_SCOPE_LEVEL - 1; s >= 0; s--)
     for (p = *sym_table(s); p; p = p->sym next)
       print_sym(p, s);
}

/*
 * Define accessor functions for SYM fields.
 */

char *get_sym_name(p)
   SYM *p;
{
   return p->sym_name;
}
```

```
static SYM *param_ptr;

SYM *first_param(fn)
  SYM *fn;
{
  SYM **pt;
  pt = fn->func_descriptor.func_sym_list;
  if (pt != NULL)
    param_ptr = *pt;
  return param_ptr;
}

SYM *next_param()
{
  if (param_ptr == NULL)
    return NULL;
  return param_ptr = param_ptr->sym_next;
}


TYPE_DESC *get_sym_type_desc(p)
  SYM *p;
{
  return &p->sym_type;
}

TYPE_DESC *get_type_desc_next(p)
  TYPE_DESC *p;
{
  return p->next;
}

VALUE_TYPE get_type_desc_type(p)
  TYPE_DESC *p;
{
  return p->type;
}

VALUE_TYPE get_sym_type(p)
  SYM *p;
{
  return p->sym_type.type;
}

void set_sym_type(p, t)
  SYM *p;
  VALUE_TYPE t;
{
  p->sym_type.type = t;
}
```

```
void set_sym_frame_offset(sym, frame_offset)
  SYM *sym;
  int frame_offset;
{
  sym->sym_offset = frame_offset;
}

int get_sym_frame_offset(sym)
  SYM *sym;
{
  return sym->sym_offset;
}

void set_sym_storage(sym, storage)
  SYM *sym;
  STORAGE storage;
{
  sym->sym_storage = storage;
}

STORAGE get_sym_storage(sym)
  SYM *sym;
{
  return sym->sym_storage;
}

void set_func_start(sym, pc)
  SYM *sym;
  TOKEN *pc;
{
  sym->func_descriptor.func_start = pc;
}

TOKEN *get_func_start(sym)
  SYM *sym;
{
  return sym->func_descriptor.func_start;
}

void set_func_type(sym, type)
  SYM *sym;
  VALUE_TYPE type;
{
  sym->func_descriptor.func_type = type;
}

VALUE_TYPE get_func_type(sym)
  SYM *sym;
{
  return sym->func_descriptor.func_type;
}
```

```c
/*
 * token_st.c
 * Author: P. Darnell
 * Purpose: Manage the token stream. The token stream is a linked list of
 * tokens with lex'ed values.
 *
 */
#define TOKEN_OWNER
#include "lex.h"
#include "sym.h"
#include "cint.h"
#include "token_st.h"
#include <stdio.h>

char *token_name();

static TOKEN *token_head;
static TOKEN *token_PC;
static TOKEN *next_token_PC;
static TOKEN *last_token_PC;
static TOKEN *pushed_token_PC;

static LEX_TOKEN token;

static int line_count;
void bump_line_count()
{
    line_count++;
}

/*==================================================================
 * Function: err(str, arg1, arg2, arg3, arg4)
 * Purpose: print out error message
 * Inputs: str      - printf format string
 *         arg1..4 - 4 args to be printed by str control
 *==================================================================*/
void err(str, arg1, arg2, arg3, arg4)
  char *str;
  int arg1, arg2, arg3, arg4;
{
  printf("Error at line %d: ", line_count);
  printf(str, arg1, arg2, arg3, arg4);
}


/*==================================================================
 * Function: warn(str, arg1, arg2, arg3, arg4)
 * Purpose: print out warning message
 * Inputs: str      - printf format string
 *         arg1..4 - 4 args to be printed by str control
 *==================================================================*/
void warn(str, arg1, arg2, arg3, arg4)
  char *str;
  int arg1, arg2, arg3, arg4;
{
  printf("Warning at line %d: ", line_count);
  printf(str, arg1, arg2, arg3, arg4);
}
```

```
/*================================================================
 * Push current token back into lex stream, so next call to
 * lex will return it.
 *==============================================================*/
void unlex()
{
   pushed_token_PC = token_PC;
   token_PC = last_token_PC;
}



/*================================================================
 * Function: add_to_token_stream(token, pvalue)
 * Purpose: add a lexical token to the token stream.
 * Algorithm:
 *    Token stream is a linked list of C tokens. Each function has a pointer
 *    to a token stream that represents the function body. It is this stream
 *    that gets interpreted at execution time.
 * Inputs: token - the lexical token
 *         pvalue- pointer to the value node associated with the token.
 *==============================================================*/
void add_to_token_stream(token, pvalue)
   LEX_TOKEN token;
   VALUE *pvalue;
{
   TOKEN *p;

   last_token_PC = token_PC;
   if (token == RUN || token == LIST)
     return;
   p = (TOKEN *) malloc(sizeof(TOKEN));
   p->tk_line = line_count;
   p->tk_token = token;
   p->tk_value = *pvalue;
   p->tk_next = NULL;
   if (token_PC)
   {
     token_PC->tk_next = p;
     token_PC = p;
   }
   else
     token_PC = token_head = p;
}

/*================================================================
 * Function: skip_token()
 * Purpose: Skip over the current token. Used for execution mode to skip
 * over uninteresting tokens.
 *==============================================================*/
void skip_token()
{
   token_PC = next_token_PC;
   token = token_PC->tk_token;
   next_token_PC = token_PC->tk_next;
   if (lex_debug)
     printf("Skipping token %s\n", token_name(token));
}
```

```
/*================================================================
 * Function: next_token(pvalue)
 * Purpose: return the next token in the token stream.
 * Algorithm: next_token_PC holds the current pointer in the
 *   token list. The enumeration value of the token is always returned,
 *   and the VALUE struct is assigned to pvalue if necessary.
 * Inputs: pvalue - pointer to VALUE struct to receive value part of token.
 * Result: the next token in the stream, LEX_NULL if none.
 *================================================================*/
LEX_TOKEN next_token(pvalue)
  VALUE *pvalue;
{
  LEX_TOKEN token;
  if (next_token_PC == NULL)
  {
    err("Missing '}'\n");
    state.executing = FALSE;
    return LEX_NULL;
  }

  token_PC = next_token_PC;
  token = token_PC->tk_token;
  line_count = token_PC->tk_line;
/* see if we need to copy value part of token */
  switch (token)
  {
  case CONSTANT:
  case SYMBOL:
  case IF:
  case WHILE:
  case FOR:
  case BUILTIN_FUNCTION:
    *pvalue = token_PC->tk_value;
  }
  next_token_PC = token_PC->tk_next;
  return token;
}

/*================================================================
 * Return current token value
 *================================================================*/
LEX_TOKEN current_token()
{
    return token;
}

/*================================================================
 * Print a string the way it was typed in.
 *================================================================*/
static void print_string(s)
  char *s;
{
  char c;

  putchar('"');
  while (c = *s)
    switch (*s++)
    {
    case '\f':
```

```
        putchar('\\');
        putchar('f');
        break;

    case '\n':
        putchar('\\');
        putchar('n');
        break;

    case '\t':
        putchar('\\');
        putchar('t');
        break;

    case '\b':
        putchar('\\');
        putchar('b');
        break;

    default:
        putchar(c);
    }

  putchar('"');
}

/*================================================================
 * Print the value of a VALUE struct.
 *================================================================*/
void print_value(p)
  VALUE *p;
{
  if (p->type == T_INT)
    printf("%d ", p->value.fix);
  else if (p->type == T_PTR)
    print_string(p->value.ptr);
  else if (p->type == T_DOUBLE)
    printf("%#g ", p->value.flt);
  else if (p->type == T_FUNC)
    printf("func");
  else
    printf("??");
}

static void print_newline(indent_level)
{
  int a;
  printf("\n");
  for (a = 0; a < indent_level; a++)
    printf("  ");
}
```

```
/*================================================================
 * Function: print_token_list(p)
 * Purpose: print token list for LIST command.
 * Algorithm: Follow links in token list, printing each token
 *  in order.  Try to be clever about when to print new lines and
 *  how far to indent.  This needs some more smarts, especially
 * for "for" loops.
 * Inputs: p - pointer to token list head.
 *================================================================*/
void print_token_list(p)
  TOKEN *p;
{
  int indent_level = 0;
  int suppress_newline = 0;

  for (; p; p = p->tk_next)
    switch (p->tk_token)
      {
      case SYMBOL:
        printf("%s ", get_sym_name(p->tk_value.value.sym));
        break;

      case CONSTANT:
        print_value(&p->tk_value);
        break;

      case BUILTIN_FUNCTION:
        printf("%s ", get_builtin_func_name(p->tk_value.value.sym));
        break;

      case FOR:
        suppress_newline = 2;
      default:
        if ((int) p->tk_token == '{')
          {
            if (indent_level > 0)
              print_newline(indent_level);
            indent_level++;
          }
        printf("%s ", token_name(p->tk_token));
        if ((int) p->tk_token == ';')
          {
            if (suppress_newline)
              suppress_newline--;
            else
              {
                if ((int) p->tk_next->tk_token == '}')
                  indent_level--;
                print_newline(indent_level);
              }
          }
        else if (p->tk_token == (LEX_TOKEN) '}')
          {
            if (indent_level == 0)
              {
                printf("\n\n");
                return;
              }
            if (p->tk_next->tk_token == (LEX_TOKEN) '}')
```

```
            indent_level--;
          print_newline(indent_level);
        }

     }
}


/*================================================================
 * Define accessor functions for token stream objects.
 *==============================================================*/
void set_token_pc(new_pc)
  TOKEN *new_pc;
{
  next_token_PC = token_PC = new_pc;
  token = LEX_NULL;
}

TOKEN *get_token_pc()
{
    return token_PC;
}

TOKEN *get_next_token_pc()
{
    return next_token_PC;
}

TOKEN *token_list_head()
{
    return token_head;
}

/*================================================================
 * Debug routine to print current token */
 *==============================================================*/
void ptoken()
{
    printf("current token is %s\n", token_name(token_PC->tk_token));
}



/*================================================================
 * Function: lex(pvalue)
 * Purpose: return the next lexical token.
 * Algorithm:
 *    If there is a pushed token, return it and reset pushed_token_PC.
 *    If we are using the token stream, get the previously saved away token
 *       otherwise call lex0 to lexically analyse input files.
 *    If we are in saving token state, add the token to the saved token stream.
 *    from the token stream.
 * Inputs:
 *    pvalue - pointer to VALUE struct to be filled in by lex'ed item.
 * Result:
 *==============================================================*/
LEX_TOKEN lex(pvalue)
  VALUE *pvalue;
{
  if (pushed_token_PC)
  {
    token_PC = pushed_token_PC;
```

```
        token = pushed_token_PC->tk_token;
        pushed_token_PC = NULL;
      }
    else if (state.using_token_stream)
      token = next_token(pvalue);
    else
      {
        token = lex0(pvalue);
        if (state.saving_token_stream)
          add_to_token_stream(token, pvalue);
      }
#if DEBUG
    if (lex_debug)
      {
        printf("token %s ", token_name(token));
        if (token == SYMBOL && pvalue->value.sym)
          print_sym(pvalue->value.sym, 0);
        else if (token == CONSTANT)
          print_value(pvalue);
        printf("\n");
      }
#endif
    return token;
}

int frame_pointer = 0;


/*=================================================================
 * Function: user_call(fn, return_val)
 * Purpose: Call an internal interpreted function.
 * Algorithm:
 *    Save the current frame pointer, set the frame pointer to top of stack,
 *    allocate a new top of stack past local function variables.
 *    Start execution of function by setting the token stream pointer
 *    to the token stream stored away for this function.
 *    Assume that all args have been pushed.
 * Inputs:
 *    fn - pointer to symbol entry for the function.
 *    return_val - pointer to VALUE struct to receive function result
 *=================================================================*/
void user_call(fn, return_val)
  SYM *fn;
  VALUE *return_val;
{

  char save_return_state;
  TOKEN *save_token_pc;
  int old_frame_pointer;

  if (stmt_debug)
    {
      printf("calling %s\n", get_sym_name(fn));
      print_sym(fn, 0);
    }
  if (!fn || (get_sym_type(fn) != T_FUNC
              && (state.executing || get_sym_type(fn) != T_UNKNOWN)))
    {
      err("Bad function name '%s'\n", get_sym_name(fn));
      return;
    }
  if (!state.executing)
```

```
      return;
   if (state.using_token_stream == FALSE)
     save_token_pc = NULL;
   else
     save_token_pc = next_token_PC;
   state.using_token_stream = TRUE;
   save_return_state = state.returning;
   old_frame_pointer = frame_pointer;
   frame_pointer = get_stack_pointer();
   set_stack_pointer(frame_pointer + get_sym_frame_offset(fn));
   set_token_pc(get_func_start(fn));
   statement(0, return_val);
   if (stmt_debug)
     printf("returned from call\n");
   frame_pointer = old_frame_pointer;
   state.returning = save_return_state;
   if (save_token_pc == NULL)
     state.using_token_stream = FALSE;
   else
     set_token_pc(save_token_pc);
}

/*================================================================
 * Accessor functions for token stream related VALUE fields
 *==============================================================*/
TOKEN *get_loop_exit(p)
   TOKEN *p;
{
   return p->tk_value.value.loop_descriptor.loop_exit;
}

void set_loop_exit(p, q)
   TOKEN *p, *q;
{
   p->tk_value.value.loop_descriptor.loop_exit = q;
}

TOKEN *get_if_exit(p)
   TOKEN *p;
{
   return p->tk_value.value.if_descriptor.if_exit;
}

void set_if_exit(p, q)
   TOKEN *p, *q;
{
   p->tk_value.value.if_descriptor.if_exit = q;
}

TOKEN *get_if_else(p)
   TOKEN *p;
{
   return p->tk_value.value.if_descriptor.if_else;
}
```

```
void set_if_else(p, q)
  TOKEN *p, *q;
{
  p->tk_value.value.if_descriptor.if_else = q;
}

TOKEN *get_loop_test(p)
  TOKEN *p;
{
  return p->tk_value.value.loop_descriptor.loop_test;
}

TOKEN *get_loop_body(p)
  TOKEN *p;
{
  return p->tk_value.value.loop_descriptor.loop_body;
}

TOKEN *get_loop_increment(p)
  TOKEN *p;
{
  return p->tk_value.value.loop_descriptor.loop_increment;
}

void set_loop_body(p, q)
  TOKEN *p;
  TOKEN *q;
{
  p->tk_value.value.loop_descriptor.loop_body = q;
}

void set_loop_test(p, q)
  TOKEN *p;
  TOKEN *q;
{
  p->tk_value.value.loop_descriptor.loop_test = q;
}

void set_loop_increment(p, q)
  TOKEN *p;
  TOKEN *q;
{
  p->tk_value.value.loop_descriptor.loop_increment = q;
}
```

```c
/*
 * memory.c
 * Author: P. Darnell
 * Purpose: Manage access to variable storage space
 *
 */
#include "lex.h"
#include "sym.h"
#include "cint.h"
#include "token_st.h"
#include <stdio.h>


/* define number of memory bytes for stack and global variables */
#define MAX_MEMORY_ADDRESS 16383

static MEMORY Memory[MAX_MEMORY_ADDRESS];
extern int frame_pointer;        /* defined in token_st.c */
/* Stack starts at high memory and works down */
static int stack_pointer = MAX_MEMORY_ADDRESS;

/* Return a pointer to the memory location referenced by the symbol.
 * If we are not executing, then stack variables do not refer to a meaningful
 * place.
 */
MEMORY *memory(sym)
  SYM *sym;
{
  unsigned memory_index;
  if (get_sym_storage(sym) == STACK)
    memory_index = frame_pointer + get_sym_frame_offset(sym);
  else
    memory_index = get_sym_frame_offset(sym);

  if (exp_debug)
  {
    printf("var at %x: ", memory_index);
    print_sym(sym, 0);
  }

  if (memory_index > MAX_MEMORY_ADDRESS)
  {
    if (state.executing)
      err("Attempt to address past top of memory (0x%X)\n", memory_index);
    memory_index = 0;
  }

  return Memory + memory_index;
}

void assign_memory_to_value(v, m, type)
  VALUE *v;
  MEMORY *m;
  VALUE_TYPE type;
{
  if ((unsigned) (m - Memory) > MAX_MEMORY_ADDRESS && state.executing)
  {
    err("Memory address out of range (0x%X)\n", m - Memory);
    return;
  }
```

```
/*   m += (int) Memory; */
  if (type != T_DOUBLE && type != T_FLOAT)
  {
    switch (type)
    {
      /* Array type means use address of array, not contents */
    case T_ARRAY:
      v->value.mptr = m;
      break;

    case T_FUNC:
    case T_PTR:
      v->value.mptr = *(MEMORY **) m;
      break;
    case T_CHAR:
      v->value.fix = *(char *) m;
      break;
    case T_SHORT:
      v->value.fix = *(short *) m;
      break;
    case T_LONG:
      v->value.fix = *(long *) m;
      break;
    case T_INT:
      v->value.fix = *(int *) m;
      break;
    case T_FLOAT:
      v->value.fix = *(float *) m;
      break;
    case T_DOUBLE:
      v->value.fix = *(double *) m;
      break;
    default:
      err("Unknown type in assign m to v(%d)\n", type);
    }
    v->type = T_INT;
  }
  else
  {
    switch (type)
    {
    case T_CHAR:
      v->value.flt = *(char *) m;
      break;
    case T_SHORT:
      v->value.flt = *(short *) m;
      break;
    case T_LONG:
      v->value.flt = *(long *) m;
      break;
    case T_INT:
      v->value.flt = *(int *) m;
      break;
    case T_FLOAT:
      v->value.flt = *(float *) m;
      break;
    case T_DOUBLE:
      v->value.flt = *(double *) m;
      break;
    default:
      err("Unknown type in assign m to v(%d)\n", type);
    }
```

```
      v->type = T_DOUBLE;
   }

   if (exp_debug)
   {
     printf("asg mem (%x) type = %d to value:", m - Memory, type);
     print_value(v);
   }
}

/* Assign a value to memory pointed to by m, of type type. */
void assign_value_to_memory(v, m, type)
   VALUE *v;
   MEMORY *m;
   VALUE_TYPE type;
{
/* Following cast to unsigned causes negative values of (m-Memory)
 * to be > MAX_MEMORY_ADDRESS, thus capturing upper and lower bounds
 * check in one compare.
 */
   if ((unsigned) (m - Memory) > MAX_MEMORY_ADDRESS && state.executing)
   {
     err("Memory address out of range (0x%X)\n", m - Memory);
     return;
   }

/*   m += (int) Memory; */
   if (v->type != T_DOUBLE)
     switch (type)
     {
     case T_FUNC:
     case T_PTR:
       *(MEMORY **) m = v->value.mptr;
       break;
     case T_CHAR:
       *(char *) m = v->value.fix;
       break;
     case T_SHORT:
       *(short *) m = v->value.fix;
       break;
     case T_LONG:
       *(long *) m = v->value.fix;
       break;
     case T_INT:
       *(int *) m = v->value.fix;
       break;
     case T_FLOAT:
       *(float *) m = v->value.fix;
       break;
     case T_DOUBLE:
       *(double *) m = v->value.fix;
       break;
     default:
       err("Unknown type in assign v to m(%d)\n", type);
     }
   else
     switch (type)
     {
     case T_CHAR:
       *(char *) m = v->value.flt;
       break;
     case T_SHORT:
```

```
            *(short *) m = v->value.flt;
            break;
         case T_LONG:
            *(long *) m = v->value.flt;
            break;
         case T_INT:
            *(int *) m = v->value.flt;
            break;
         case T_FLOAT:
            *(float *) m = v->value.flt;
            break;
         case T_DOUBLE:
            *(double *) m = v->value.flt;
            break;
         default:
            err("Unknown type in assign v to m(%d)\n", type);
      }

   if (exp_debug)
   {
      printf("asg value to mem (%x) type = %d:", m - Memory, type);
      print_value(v);
   }
}

/* Return the size of a type */
int type_size(type)
   VALUE_TYPE type;
{
   switch (type)
   {
   case T_FUNC:
   case T_PTR:
      return sizeof(char *);
   case T_CHAR:
      return sizeof(char);
   case T_SHORT:
      return sizeof(short);
   case T_LONG:
      return sizeof(long);
   case T_INT:
      return sizeof(int);
   case T_FLOAT:
      return sizeof(float);
   case T_DOUBLE:
      return sizeof(double);
   case T_VOID:
      return 0;
   default:
      err("Unknown type (%d) in type_size\n", type);
   }
}
```

```
push_value(v)
  VALUE *v;
{
  stack_pointer -= type_size(v->type);
  if (exp_debug)
  {
    printf("pushing arg at mem address %x: ", stack_pointer);
    print_value(v);
  }
  assign_value_to_memory(v, Memory + stack_pointer, v->type);
}

int get_stack_pointer()
{
   return stack_pointer;
}

void set_stack_pointer(new_sp)
  int new_sp;
{
  stack_pointer = new_sp;
}

static int global_offset;
int static_alloc(size)
{
  int o;
  o = global_offset;
  global_offset += size;
  return o;
}

/* Very simple memory free algorithm */
void user_free(m)
  MEMORY *m;
{
}

/* Very simple  memory allocate algorithm */
MEMORY *user_malloc(size)
{
   return Memory + static_alloc(size);
}
```

Appendix G

ASCII Codes

oct	dec	hex	char		oct	dec	hex	char	
0	0	0	NUL	^@	31	25	19	EM	^Y
1	1	1	SOH	^A	32	26	1A	SUB	^Z
2	2	2	STX	^B	33	27	1B	ESC	^[
3	3	3	ETX	^C	34	28	1C	FS	^|
4	4	4	EQT	^D	35	29	1D	GS	^]
5	5	5	ENQ	^F	36	30	1E	RS	^^
6	6	6	ACK	^F	37	31	1F	US	^_
7	7	7	BEL	^G	40	32	20	SPACE	
10	8	8	BS	^H	41	33	21	!	
11	9	9	TAB	^I	42	34	22	"	
12	10	A	LF	^J	43	35	23	#	
13	11	B	VT	^K	44	36	24	$	
14	12	C	FF	^L	45	37	25	%	
15	13	D	VR	^M	46	38	26	&	
16	14	E	SO	^N	47	39	27	'	
17	15	F	SI	^O	50	40	28	(	
20	16	10	DLE	^P	51	41	29	)	
21	17	11	DC1	^Q	52	42	2A	*	
22	18	12	DC2	^R	53	43	2B	+	
23	19	13	DC3	^S	54	44	2C	,	
24	20	14	DC4	^T	55	45	2D	–	
25	21	15	NAK	^U	56	46	2E	.	
26	22	16	SYN	^V	57	47	2F	/	
27	23	17	ETB	^W	60	48	30	0	
30	24	18	CAN	^X	61	49	31	1	

oct	dec	hex	char		oct	dec	hex	char
62	50	32	2		131	89	59	Y
63	51	33	3		132	90	5A	Z
64	52	34	4		133	91	5B	[
65	53	35	5		134	92	5C	\
66	54	36	6		135	93	5D	]
67	55	37	7		136	94	5E	^
70	56	38	8		137	95	5F	_
71	57	39	9		140	96	60	'
72	58	3A	:		141	97	61	a
73	59	3B	;		142	98	62	b
74	60	3C	<		143	99	63	c
75	61	3D	=		144	100	64	d
76	62	3E	>		145	101	65	e
77	63	3F	?		146	102	66	f
100	64	40	@		147	103	67	g
101	65	41	A		150	104	68	h
102	66	42	B		151	105	69	i
103	67	43	C		152	106	6A	j
104	68	44	D		153	107	6B	k
105	69	45	E		154	108	6C	l
106	70	46	F		155	109	6D	m
107	71	47	G		156	110	6E	n
110	72	48	H		157	111	6F	o
111	73	49	I		160	112	70	p
112	74	4A	J		161	113	71	q
113	75	4B	K		162	114	72	r
114	76	4C	L		163	115	73	s
115	77	4D	M		164	116	74	t
116	78	4E	N		165	117	75	u
117	79	4F	O		166	118	76	v
120	80	50	P		167	119	77	w
121	81	51	Q		170	120	78	x
122	82	52	R		171	121	79	y
123	83	53	S		172	122	7A	z
124	84	54	T		173	123	7B	{
125	85	55	U		174	124	7C	|
126	86	56	V		175	125	7D	}
127	87	57	W		176	126	7E	~
130	88	58	X		177	127	7F	del

Index

Symbols

.
  decimal point, 52
  structure member operator, 155, 246

..., ellipsis, 295, 429

.c filename extension, 12

.h filename extension, 13, 335

.o filename extension, 12

!, logical negation operator, 139

!=, not equal to operator, 82, 138

?:, conditional operator, 154–155

,, comma operator, 136–137

; semicolon, 19
  misplaced, 106
  mistakenly used to end macro definitions, 318

:, bit fields, 255–260
  conditional expression operator, 154–155
  statement label, 113

", double quote, 31, 178, 328
  surrounding filenames, 335

', single quote, 45

()
  cast operator, 65, 151–152
  function call, 19, 29, 290
  macro call, 319
  parenthesized expression, 122–123

[], array subscript operator, 155

{}
  array initialization, 162
  function body, 19, 286
  initialization of arrays, 194
  initialization of nested structures, 252
  initialization of structures, 246

{} compound statement, 85–88
  missing braces, 87

&
  address of operator, 155, 297
    See also address-of operator
  illegal with bit fields, 255
  illegal with register variables, 229

  in *scanf( )* calls, 283
  bitwise AND operator, 143, 146

&&, logical AND operator, 139

&=, bitwise AND assign operator, 151

#
  preprocessor symbol, 34, 316
  stringizing operator, 328

##, token pasting operator, 329

#undef directive, 408

%
  conversion symbol in *printf( )* function, 31, 444
  remainder operator, 125, 126–135

%lf conversion character, example of, 80

%p print specifier. *See printf( )* function

%s format specifier, 183

+
  addition operator, 125
  unary plus operator, 124

++, increment operator, 96, 132
  applied to pointers, 185, 187
  applied to subscripts, 187
  postfix, use of, 309

−
  subtraction operator, 125
  unary minus operator, 124

—, decrement operator, 132

–>, structure member operator, 155, 247, 270

–D, macro defining option, 332

*
  dereference operator, 155
    See also dereference operator
  multiplication operator, 20, 125

*/, end comment, 26

/, division operator, 125

/*, begin comment, 26

^, bitwise exclusive OR operator, 143, 147

^=, bitwise exclusive OR assign operator, 151

|, bitwise inclusive OR operator, 143, 146

||, logical OR operator, 139

B

D

Cint Source Order Form

The source to the subset C interpreter from appendix F can be obtained on floppy disk. The sources consist of over 2500 lines of C code and come with a makefile compatible with Unix *make* or Microsoft C *nmake*. The sources have been compiled on a Sun 3/50 Unix workstation, HP/Apollo DN-50, and Microsoft C 5.1 on an IBM PC clone.

A test suite is included to verify the correctness of modifications to Cint. Users are welcome to send in bug fixes and improvements, where they will be integrated into periodic releases.

The disk includes the original code as published in the book as well as version 2 of the code which supports pointers, structures, unions, arrays, char, typedef, static, switch, and goto.

The price is $40. Please specify 5.25" or 3.5" disk. (Add $2 for 3.5" disk). Massachusetts residents add 5% state tax.

....

Format ❏ IBM 5.25 ($40)   ❏ IBM 3.5 ($42)

Shipping Information Name _____

Company _____

Address _____

City _____ State ___ Zip _____

Payment Options ❏ Check or money order   ❏ Cash   ❏ COD

Note ★★★ Free surface shipping for check, cash or money order ★★★

Mail To *Kangaroo Software*   *Tel   (508)692-5499*
PO Box 1414   *Fax   (512)692-3102*
Westford, MA 01886 USA

....

Note: This source code is intended to be used to introduce students of the C language to a body of C code containing a significant level of complexity. Certain aspects of the C language such as the preprocessor have been omitted from this code and left as an exercise for the student. No warranty is made as to the suitability of the code for purposes other than a teaching tool.